SPAIN
Trip Planner & Guide

La del alba seria cuarndo
Don Quijote salio de la a venta,
tan contento, tan gallardo, tan
alborozado por verse ya ar~
mado caballero que el gozo
le reventaba por las cinchas
del caballo.

(Don Quijote de la Mancha, cap IV)

Nivehica: Talavera:

SPAIN

Trip Planner & Guide

Second Edition

David Baird

PASSPORT BOOKS

NTC/Contemporary Publishing Group

This edition published in 2000 by
Passport Books,
A division of NTC/Contempory Publishing Group, Inc.
4255 West Touhy Avenue
Lincolnwood (Chicago), Illinois 60712-1975 U.S.A.

ISBN: 0-658-00992-3

Library of Congress Catalog Card Number: On file

Conceived, edited, designed and produced by
Duncan Petersen Publishing Ltd, 31 Ceylon Road, London W14 0PY
from a concept by Emma Stanford

Colour originated by Reprocolor International, Milan
DTP by Duncan Petersen Publishing Ltd; film output by SX Composing DTP

Printed by Delo-Tiskarna, Slovenia

Every reasonable care has been taken to ensure the information in this
guide is accurate, but the publishers and copyright holders can accept no
responsibility for the consequences of errors in the text or in the maps,
particularly those arising from changes taking place after the text was
finalized. The publishers are always pleased to hear from readers who wish
to suggest corrections and improvements.

Editorial director Andrew Duncan
Assistant editors Mary Devine and Nicola Davies
Revisions editor Tanja Boyle
Art director Mel Petersen
Design Beverley Stewart, Chris Foley
Maps by Chris Foley and Beverley Stewart
Illustrations by Beverley Stewart

Photographic credits
All photographs by David Baird
except page 215 Adam Hopkins and page 175 Neil Setchfield

David Baird was born in Oswestry, Shropshire, the year that Spain erupted into Civil War. He first learned to examine life with a critical eye at school, where he was told that he and his fellow pupils were destined to be 'leaders of men'. Unconvinced, he did National Service, which refused his requests for an overseas posting in Cyprus or Kenya, and instead sent him to the backwaters of North Wales.

More dangerous and demanding service followed in provincial journalism, after which he started his travels, working on newspapers and magazines in Canada, Australia, Hong Kong, London and Belgium.

For the past 20 years David and his Dutch wife have lived in a village in southern Spain, where his photographs of neighbours' children earn him, as payment in kind, a steady flow of fruit and vegetables. His reporting and photographs on Spain, Portugal and North Africa have appeared in leading British, Canadian and American publications. Over the past two decades he has travelled far and wide in his adopted country for pleasure, for work and, of course, to research this guide. He has had two other books published on Spanish subjects and his travel writing on Spain has twice won Spanish national awards.

The Madrid city section and sections on Central Spain (pages 240 and 250) are the work of **Fiona Duncan,** who travelled the region in depth for her research. She devised the *American Express Pocket Travel Guides* while working at Mitchell Beazley Publishers; and has written guide books on London, Paris, Venice, Manhattan, Amsterdam and France.

Master contents list

This list is for when you need to use the guide in the conventional way: to find out about where you are going, or where you happen to be. The index, pages 300–304, may be just as helpful.

HOWEVER...
There is much more to this guide than the region-by-region approach suggested by the contents list on this page. Turn to page 8; and see also pages 10-11.

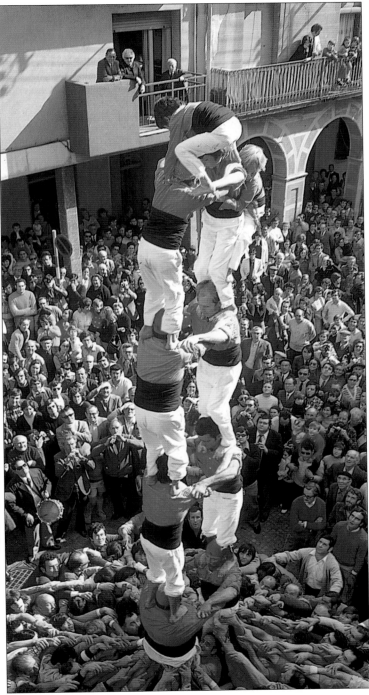

CONTENTS

Spain Overall
- master map

Spain Overall, pages 30-169, is a traveller's network for taking in the whole country, or large parts of it.

Each 'leg' of the network has a number (i.e., Spain Overall: 1); you will also find it described as a National Route, plus the number.

The term National Route does *not* simply mean a line on a map. Each route 'leg' features a whole region, and describes many places both on and off the marked route. Think of the National Routes not only as physical trails, but as imaginative ways of connecting all the main centres of Spain and of describing and making travel sense of the state as whole.

They are designed to be used in these different ways:

1 *Ignore the marked route entirely*: simply use the alphabetically arranged Gazetteer of Sights & Places of Interest, and the map at the start of each route, as a guide to what to see and do in the region, not forgetting the hotel and restaurant recommendations.

2 Follow the marked route by public transport (see the transport box), ferry, or by car. You can do sections of the route, or all of it; you can follow it in any direction. Link the routes to travel the length and breadth of Spain.

The routes are broken down into manageable 'legs'. Each leg has a section to itself, beginning with an introduction and a simplified map. The page number for each such section is shown on this master map.

Always use the simplified maps in conjunction with detailed maps (suggestions are given on the introductory pages).

On the simplified maps:

RED *marks key sights and centres, not to be missed.*

BLUE *marks important places, certainly worth a visit.*

GREEN *places are for those who aren't in a hurry and want to experience the region in some depth.*

Some practical hints on how to travel red, blue and green are given in the introductory pages and the simplified maps, including key roads and their numbers. Generally, though, there are no absolute rules for going red, blue or green and you are meant to link the places, using a detailed road map, in whatever way suits you best.

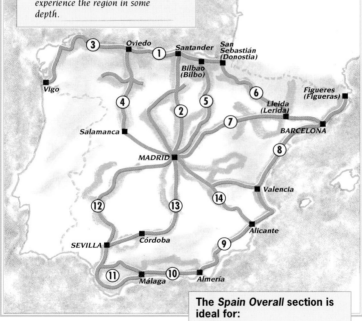

The Spain Overall section is ideal for:

■ Planning, and undertaking, tours of the whole country, or parts.

■ Making the journey to or from your eventual destination as interesting and as rewarding as possible.

■ Linking the in-depth explorations of localities provided by the Local Explorations section, pages 208-299.

Madrid, Barcelona and Seville have sections of their own, pages 170–192, 193–200 and 201–207.

CONTENTS

The Local Explorations
- *master map*

The Local Explorations – strategies for exploring all the interesting localities of Spain – complement the National Routes, pages 8-9. **They are designed to be used in these different ways**:

1 *Ignore the marked route entirely*: simply use the alphabetically arranged Gazetteer of Sights & Places of Interest, and the map at the start of each Local Exploration, as a guide to what to see and do in the area, not forgetting the hotel and restaurant recommendations.

2 Use the marked route to make a tour by public transport (see the transport box), ferry, or by car. You can do sections of the route, or all of it. (In the introduction it tells you how long you might take to cover everything the quickest way, by car.)

If you are driving, you can generally follow the tour in any direction; usually, the route as marked is an attractive and convenient way to link the places of interest; you may well find other ways to drive it. Always use our map in conjunction with a detailed road map (suggestions are given on each introductory page).

The Local Explorations, pages 208–299, generally follow each other in a north-south/west-east sequence.

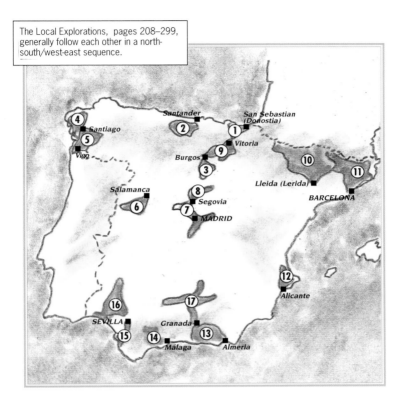

The *Local Explorations* are ideal for:

■ **Planning single-centre holidays**: each Local Exploration encapsulates an area which would make a great holiday. The introductory page to each section is designed to tell you whether the area will suit you: what you can expect; and something of its history, geography, people, customs and food.

■ **Entertaining yourself while you are there**: each section is packed with ideas

for things to see and do. The tour, followed in full, can fill several days, and will always make a memorable journey, but most of the sights and places of interest make fascinating day or part-day trips in their own right, not to mention the detours.

■ **Planning multi-centre holidays**: the map on this page shows you at a glance all the interesting parts of Spain. Combine them at will to experience the different faces of the state; or link them, by means of the national route network.

Madrid, Barcelona and Seville have sections of their own, pages 170–192, 193–200 and 201–207.

Conventions used in this guide

A single *peseta* sign – **P** – or several *peseta* signs, such as **PPP**, in a hotel or restaurant entry, denotes a price band. Its object is to give an indication of what you can expect to pay.

Bear in mind that accommodation or food offered at any one place may well span more than one price band.

Hotels
For a double (one night) at mid-season rate:

P   less than 6,000 pesetas
PP   6,000 – 14,000 pesetas
PPP   more than 14,000 pesetas

Restaurants
For a two-course mid-priced meal with wine for one, calculated on à la carte prices:

P   less than 1,500 pesetas
PP   1,500 – 5,000 pesetas
PPP   more than 5,000 pesetas

Restaurants usually offer a *menu del día*, a three-course set meal with bread and wine, at a special price – budget establishments charge around 700 to 800 pesetas.

Hotels and restaurants in this guide are a selection of personal recommendations – not exhaustive lists. They have been chosen to represent interest and quality, or to satisfy specific needs, at every price level.

Credit cards
The guide does not give credit card details for its recommended hotels because hotels almost always conform to the following rules:

Budget hotels, pensions, *hostals* and *ventas* (inns) don't accept cards.

Most medium-priced hotels, which includes some in our **P** band and most in the **PP** band, usually accept Mastercard and Visa, Visa being almost standard currency.

Hotels of three, four and five stars accept Mastercard and Visa, plus American Express and Diner's Club.

Access (or Mastercard) and Visa are accepted in many shops, but small businesses prefer cash and are more likely to give a discount for cash purchases.

Opening times of restaurants
Spain eats late. Breakfast can be any time up to 11 am, lunch is usually from 1.30 to 4 pm, dinner from 8.30 pm until midnight. However, in tourist areas, restaurants usually open earlier to cater for foreign visitors.

Opening times – museums and tourist attractions
Museums and national monuments are usually open from 10 am until 1 pm and from 4 pm to 6 or 7 pm. On Sundays they are only open in the mornings and they close on Mondays and on public holidays. These are guidelines only – to be certain, check opening times with the local tourist office.

Where the text mentions no opening/closing times, it is generally safe to assume that the sight or attraction follows the guidelines above. If it does not, times are given in the text.

However, local and seasonal variations are widespread, so if your enjoyment of a day is going to depend on gaining access, check opening times with the local Tourist Office before setting out.

Mileages for routes and tours are approximate. In the Spain Overall sections, they represent the shortest distances you could expect to travel, almost always the 'red' option.

In the case of Local Explorations, they also represent the shortest possible distance you could expect to cover, excluding detours.

Since the routes and tours are designed to be travelled in whole, in part, or indeed not at all, the mileages are given as much for passing interest as for their practical value.

Spelling of place names
In this guide, place names are spelled in the Spanish way, which is generally

↗ after a place name on a map means that the sight or place of interest is covered in detail in another part of the book. To find out exactly where, look up the place in the **Sights & Places of Interest** gazetteer which follows the map: a cross-reference is given in every case.

easily recognizable, Zaragoza for example instead of the anglicized Saragossa. Several regions prefer to spell place names in the local tongue, for example Lleida for Lerida, Donostia for San Sebastián, and also use these on road signs. Where there is a possibility of confusion, both Castilian and local spellings are given.

DEFINITIONS
Of cultural terms used frequently in this guide: see page 27.

🛏 after a heading in **Sights & Places of Interest** means that there is an accommodation suggestion (or suggestions) for that place in **Recommended Hotels**.

✕ after a heading in **Sights & Places of Interest** means that there is a suggestion (or suggestions) for that place in **Recommended Restaurants**.

Something for everyone
Getting the most from your guide

Here is a *small* selection of ideas for enjoying Spain, as opened up by this guide, aimed at a range of needs and tastes. The list is just a start: the guide offers many, many more ideas for what really matters: suiting *yourself*. You'll find that it takes into account not only your tastes, but how much time you have.

Living it up in Barcelona
Barcelona city section, pages 193–200.

Beaches, seafood and sherry
Spain Overall: 11; Local Explorations: 15.

Exploring the wilderness
Local Explorations: 2.

Castles of Castile
Local Explorations: 7.

The Pyrenees
Spain Overall: 6: Local Explorations: 10.

Glories of Ancient Rome – Mérida
Spain Overall: 12.

The Art of Spain
Madrid city section, pages 170-192.

Wild seas and green hills – Galicia
Local Explorations: 4.

Fiery fiestas – The Levant
Spain Overall: 8 and 9.

In the footsteps of Columbus – Huelva
Local Explorations: 16.

SPAIN:
an introduction

There may be somebody somewhere who, when asked their opinion of Spain replied: 'It's not a bad place'. But the chances are a million to one against. This is a land which can excite admiration, disbelief, exhilaration, or exasperation. But never indifference.

As Fernando Díaz-Plaja observed in his classic work, *The Spaniard and the Seven Capital Sins*: 'Spain is like strong liquor which can delight or repel, but can never be drunk with the indifference with which one swallows a glass of water.'

Spain's ability to provoke intense emotion and its limitless capacity for surprise make it one of Europe's most beguiling countries. Even now, after living here many years, I am still bowled over by new discoveries, whether a dramatic view, an unsuspected quirk of character, a beautiful building, a friend's opinion, or simply an encounter with an unknown wine. That is the magnetism of a land of astonishing diversity, of climatic, cultural and geographical extremes.

The millions of tourists who go no further than the beaches experience mere fragments of the pleasures in store. Those who know only Benidorm will sadly never enjoy the other Spain, one of infinite variety, as green as Ireland, as arid as Africa, as spacious as the Russian steppes (parts of *Dr Zhivago* were filmed here), as dramatic as the Dolomites.

The peninsula is inhabited by a people who speak Castilian, Gallego, Bable, Basque, Catalan, Valenciano, Aranés and a multitude of dialects. They do not only dance flamenco, but also the *jota*, the *bolero*, the *sardana*, the *muñeira*, the fandango, and ballet. They breed bullfighters and gigolos, but also top dress designers, world-renowned opera singers, and temperamental soccer idols.

The peninsula has been likened to a sun-dried ox-hide and to a battered shield, but the easiest way to picture Spain is as a castle. Inside the walls is a drought-scoured plateau, known as the *meseta*. The castle walls are formed by mountain ranges and outside them lies fertile, well-watered land extending to the coasts.

Twice the size of the British Isles, bigger than California, Spain is the third largest European country and the most mountainous after Switzerland. Nearly 40 million people inhabit the peninsula and the Balearic and Canary Islands. But the statistics tell little of the vivid life in and around the castle of Iberia.

Northern Spain, along the Bay of Biscay, is known as the Green Coast.

Most of Spain's rain falls here and on the Pyrenees, although often enough when you're visiting all of it seems to be falling on Galicia, in the north-western corner. There is a clear Celtic influence in those green valleys and granite villages, where the bagpipe is a favourite instrument.

In neighbouring Asturias, they drink cider, make fine cheese, and dig coal. You could be excused for thinking that you are in Wales, and indeed the heir to the Spanish throne bears the title Prince of Asturias.

In the steep valleys further east live the Basques, industrious, stubborn, enigmatic, addicted to such sports as rock-lifting. They are unrelated to other Spaniards and linguists are baffled as to the origins of their language. A small faction continues to fight for independence, but do not be put off from visiting this region for it boasts Spain's finest cuisine.

Skiers, climbers and hikers are attracted to the Pyrenees, as well as naturalists. One of the attractions of the Iberian peninsula is that fauna and flora wiped out in the rest of Europe survive here. In the remoter wildernesses, now mostly incorporated into protected park areas, live wolves, bears, lynxes and a rich variety of birds.

In many ways, Catalonia in north-eastern Spain is the closest region to Europe. Catalans pride themselves on their cultural progress and Barcelona, particularly after the colossal investment for the 1992 Olympics, dazzles visitors. It is a self-confident avant-garde metropolis, eternally fronting up to its rival, Madrid.

The Spanish capital, squatting four-square on the plains of Castile, challenges you not to like it. The *madrileños*, who scorn Barcelona folk as cold and mercenary, have a priority: to live life to the hilt. They love to enjoy themselves, to talk, to drink all night.

Around Madrid and across the great plains of Castile and La Mancha, you will find gems of medieval and Renaissance architecture. Although Spain has become a modern nation, whole villages and city centres have withstood time, their antiquity preserved as if just for your pleasure.

In the Levante, a network of irrigation channels and citrus orchards, the past lives on through annual re-enactments of battles between Moors and Christians. In Extremadura, little-changed in many cases since the time of the Conquistadores, Mérida stands as a monument to the grandeur of Ancient Rome.

To the south lie the eight provinces of Andalucía, where many of the stereotype images of Spain were born: the love of bullfighting, the fire of flamenco, sun-bleached villages, and arrogant aristocrats.

All stereotypes contain a grain of truth, but tell only part of the story. Modern Spain has up-to-the-minute fashions and fads, hi-tech industry, punks and rockers, but traditional charm endures.

A New York businessman gaped in disbelief at the office workers crowding a Madrid café at mid morning and demanded irritably: 'Why aren't these people working? What are they doing here?'

The answer – of course: living, as only the Spaniards know how.

Before you go

When to go, and to which parts

Spring is undoubtedly the pleasantest time of the year to visit almost anywhere in mainland Spain. The landscape is still green from winter rains and the temperatures are moderate. May is an ideal month because of the many interesting fiestas and other activities that take place.

Unless you are restricted by school holidays, avoid July and August. The coasts are inundated, prices and temperatures soar. And it is no time to travel through the interior, as cities such as Seville or Córdoba often register more than 40 degrees. Madrid is pleasantly empty of people, but very hot, and many businesses and restaurants are closed. The temperate north coast, from the Basque Country to Galicia, often rainy the rest of the year, does not suffer the same temperature extremes, but it too can get crowded.

Autumn is second best choice. The crowds have gone, the sea is warm, temperatures are not so extreme, and there is renewed cultural activity.

Inland Spain can be surprisingly cold in winter, thanks to its altitude. Snow and rainstorms are common. But the Mediterranean coast from Valencia south has a mild winter climate and frosts are virtually unknown. A spell of heavy rain is often followed by a week or more of brilliant sunshine and daytime temperatures of around 25 degrees.

Clothing

Take light, casual, easily washable clothing but include a sweater. In autumn or spring you will need it in the evenings. In summer you may need it in air-conditioned buildings.

A hat is recommended against summer heat. Fair-complexioned people should take extra measures to protect their skin from the powerful sun. Winter visitors to the interior need warm clothing and raincoats. Skiers in the Sierra Nevada should double their usual protection against the African-strength sun bouncing off the snow.

Comfortable walking shoes are essential if you are doing much sightseeing. Cobbles play hell with high heels.

Informal clothing is fine unless you are eating in expensive restaurants or attending social functions. Spaniards, particularly in provincial cities, tend to dress up more than Northern Europeans, who often seem scruffy by comparison.

On the Mediterranean tourist strip, anything goes. Topless sunbathing is common and there are a number of naturist campsites and beaches.

But visitors who parade around rural villages in skimpy beachwear are more likely to be objects of scorn than admiration. Nor are they welcome in religious buildings, where women should cover arms and shoulders.

Don't forget: first-aid kit, insect repellent, needle and thread, phrasebook, sun glasses, sun tan lotion, anti-diarrhoea tablets, a towel, a list of useful home phone numbers (bank, doctor, relatives and so on).

Documentation

Visitors from EC countries can enter and leave Spain as tourists freely with either a national identity document or passport. Agreements with other West European countries give their nationals similar rights. Though the rule is often ignored, visitors staying more than 90 days should apply for a *permanencia*, an extension. Anyone spending more than six months in Spain is required to seek a *residencia* (residence permit). U.S. citizens, Canadians and New Zealanders can stay for 90 days without visas; their passports should be valid for the entire period. Latin American visitors benefit from special arrangements. Other nationalities, including Australians, generally require visas. Check before travelling, as visa requirements change.

Medical and travel insurance

These are definitely advisable. EC members qualify for free medical treatment in Spain, provided they have obtained the form E-111 from their country's health authority. Austrian citizens qualify for free attention with form A/E3, Swedish nationals need form ES/1 and Finns SF/E7. However, the Spanish Social Security service is overloaded and you may get quicker and better attention if you go to a private doctor. Remember to keep all medical receipts and bills, including those for medicines and drugs, in order to qualify for repayment.

Any theft should be reported to the

nearest police station. The police may not recover the goods, but at least you will get the necessary report form to validate your insurance claim.

Money

Spain is no longer the bargain it once was, although careful travellers can still manage on a smaller budget than in many European countries. Peseta coins of 1, 5, 10, 25, 50, 100, 200, and 500 are in circulation. Check your change carefully as some coins are easy to confuse, particularly as newer, smaller coins are circulating alongside the older ones. The one-peseta coin is microscopic both in size and value so that change is often rounded up to the nearest *duro* (as the five-peseta coin is known).

Banknotes come in values of 1,000, 2,000, 5,000, and 10,000 pesetas. Try to keep some small change, as it can be difficult to change large-denomination notes.

Tourists, apart from those on package holidays, are officially required to have at least 5,000 pesetas per person per day or at least 50,000 pesetas, but this is rarely checked. Visitors bringing in or exporting cash worth more than 1,000,000 pesetas must declare it. These requirements are subject to change in accordance with EC legislation.

Import duty

There are no duties on importing or exporting goods between Spain and other EC countries. Non-Europeans can import personal effects, plus up to one litre of alcohol, 200 cigarettes and 0.75 litres of perfume, duty free. If the maximum quantity is exceeded, duty will be payable.

Non-EC residents can claim back value-added tax (IVA) on purchases made in Spain, but this time-consuming process is only worthwhile for expensive items.

Tourist information outside Spain

Turespaña, the national tourist promotion board, produces some excellent pamphlets on Spain's attractions in several languages, as well as abundant information on tourist facilities. In addition, individual Spanish regions publish information. Spain has tourist information offices in 28 cities around the world, including:

Brussels *Avenue des Arts* 21; *tel* 280 1926.
Frankfurt *Myliusstrasse* 14; *tel.* 72 50 33.
Geneva 15 *rue Ami-Lévrier*; *tel* 731 1133.
The Hague *Laan Van Meerdervoort* 8A; *tel.* 346 5900.
London 22-23 *Manchester Square*; *tel.* 020 7486 8077.
Los Angeles 8383 *Wilshire Blvd, Suite* 960, *Beverly Hills*; *tel.* 658 71 88.
Miami 1221 *Brickell Avenue*; *tel.* 358 82 23.
New York 666, *Fifth Avenue*; *tel.* 265 88 22.
Paris 43 *rue Decamps*; *tel.* 01 45 03 82 57.
Rome *Via del Mortaro* 19; *tel* 678 3106.
Toronto 2 *Bloor Street West, 34th floor*; *tel.* 961 31 31.

Local customs: what to expect, how to behave

When you greet or say goodbye, you shake hands. If you are already friends, it is normal to bestow a kiss on both of a woman's cheeks. Old male friends will embrace. Spaniards are not afraid of showing their emotions and expect you to show yours or they will suspect you are cold and unfeeling.

Those travellers who labour under the misconception that if you speak loudly enough the natives will understand should stay away from Spain. Despite more than 50 million foreign arrivals every year, Spaniards are amazingly tolerant of tourists and their ways, but they are proud people. Thus bluster and an air of superiority will quickly offend. By contrast, establishing good personal relations can work wonders.

Just a few words of Spanish will help immeasurably. If you travel with small children, you are already half way to Spanish hearts as they dote on them. And there is no nonsense about children not being allowed in bars or restaurants, at any hour.

Above all in Spain, be patient and flexible. Regulations, opening hours, and starting times are not carved in stone. Remember that appointments and plans can crumble in the face of the Spanish credo: 'Enjoy the moment'.

Getting there

• *Parque de los Descubrimientos, Seville.*

By air
Charter flights are the cheapest way to reach Spain from the rest of Europe. The drawback is that, once booked, you cannot change the date of departure or return, and the flights sometimes depart at very inconvenient hours. Also, they are more subject to delay as priority is given to scheduled flights, which are more expensive, more comfortable and more flexible. The big carriers run direct flights to Spain from Europe, North and South America, Africa and the Middle East. Iberia, the national airline, and Viva, also state-owned, both have numerous services.

As charter companies try to fill empty seats at the last moment, latecomers can often find bargain tickets from European capitals by studying local advertisements or contacting travel agents specializing in discount deals.

By rail
Comfortable international trains run from Paris to Madrid and Barcelona and from Milan and Zurich to Barcelona. The Paris-Madrid TALGO night express takes 13 hours, including a frontier stop to adjust the wheels to the wider Spanish rail gauge. You can take a car on a number of these trains.

By bus
Long-distance buses run from major European cities to Madrid and the Spanish Mediterranean coast. You may have to spend a night on the bus or in a wayside hotel. When you add meals *en route*, it may be just as cheap to fly by charter.

By ferry
Two companies offer regular overnight services in large, modern vessels from England to Northern Spain. It is a handy way to reach the peninsula, but somewhat expensive.

P&O European Ferries inaugurated a Portsmouth-Bilbao service in 1993. The voyage takes 28 to 30 hours. Contact: P&O office, Dover; tel. 0870 600 0600; The Continental Ferry Port, Mile End, Portsmouth PO2 8QW; tel. (reservations) 0870 242 4999; or Ferries Golfo de Vizcaya S.A., Cosme Echevarrieta n.1, 48009 Bilbao; tel. 94 423 44 77. Brittany Ferries sail between Plymouth and Santander. Average crossing time is 24 hours. For reservations and inquiries, call 0870 536 0360.

By car

Spanish roads have improved dramatically and four-lane highways now link most parts of the country. *Autovías* (motorways) are free, whereas *autopistas* are tollways – they have the sign *peaje* at the entrance and, over long distances, can prove expensive. Some of the pleasantest travelling is along minor roads; most are in good condition and have relatively little traffic.

The speed limit in urban areas has been reduced from 60 kph (37 mph) to 50 kph (31 mph). On main roads the limit is 100 kph (62 mph) and on *autovías* and *autopistas* 120 kph (75 mph). Seat belts should be worn at all times, although locals often flout the law. Driving in Spain – and Gibraltar – is on the right. Traffic from the right has priority unless otherwise signalled.

Petrol comes in four grades, normal (equivalent to two star), super (three star), Euro Super (95-octane leadless, *sin plomo*) and Super Plus 98 leadless. Diesel (*gasóleo*) is readily available. Prices differ little from those in the rest of Europe but will come as a nasty shock to U.S. visitors. Although many new petrol stations have opened, in country areas they are still few and far between and usually close at night. Leadless petrol – particularly the higher octane – is not always available in rural areas.

Car hire

The leading multinational car hire companies all have offices in the larger cities and at the major airports. Cheaper rates are usually available from local companies; however, the quality of their vehicles and their service varies and it is unlikely they will allow you to drop the vehicle off in another town. Some companies insist you are over 21, others over 19.

Ask if there are *tarifas promocionales* (special promotion rates) and you may get a cheaper deal. You will pay from 3,000 pesetas a day for unlimited mileage, plus insurance. Travellers' cheques and credit cards are accepted for payment.

Driving tips

Driving through Spain gives a visitor some useful insights into the national character. He will have abundant opportunity to appreciate the fatalistic atti-

• *Shadowplay at the aqueduct, Segovia.*

tude, the devil-may-care approach, and the in-built conviction that regulations are made for others, which help to give the country one of Europe's worst accident records. To avoid figuring in these dismal statistics, visitors should drive as though expecting a one-ton fighting bull to be lying in wait around every corner. Expect to meet vehicles hurtling towards you on your side of the road, particularly on country roads with dangerous bends. In other words, proceed with caution at all times.

Resist the temptation to beat red lights – Spaniards regularly get away with it, but you will probably be unlucky. In remoter areas, look out for mules, donkeys and goats. Motorbikes without lights are frequent night hazards; riders are supposed to wear crash helmets but often they don't. Be aware that Spain is only beginning to crack down on drunken drivers. Don't put too much trust in road signs – they do not always mark clearly the most dangerous spots and some are badly positioned. It may be unsafe to overtake, despite what the road signs indicate.

Main highways are patrolled by vigilant Civil Guards on motorcycles. Grin and bear it if stopped by these patrols, as they brook no nonsense. They can impose heavy, on-the-spot fines for everything from crossing a double white line to failing to turn on your lights in a tunnel. Radar speed traps are common.

When not behind the wheel, do not venture on to a pedestrian crossing without checking that the road is clear. Spanish drivers are reluctant to give way to anything and certainly not for recklessly presumptuous pedestrians.

When calculating journey times, remember that Spain is a very mountainous country and, particularly if you are straying off the beaten path, routes can be tortuous and time consuming.

If driving your own vehicle, bring all the car documents; international insurance and a bail bond in case of accident; an international driving licence (although for short stays by EC visitors your national licence should be sufficient); extra fanbelt; spare light bulbs and a red warning triangle. Carrying these last two items is obligatory.

Maps
Michelin's series of regional maps with a scale of 1:400,000 are among the best available. They have indexes of place names with map co-ordinates. Walkers will find useful the more detailed maps of the Instituto Geográfico Nacional.

Taxis
Taxi rides in cities are metered and fares are quite reasonable, with surcharges for baggage, travel after midnight, and for picking up or setting down at certain points. When seeking a taxi rank, ask for *la parada de taxis*. For longer unmetered trips, always establish the cost before making the journey. Airport fares to tourist resorts are fixed and usually posted in a prominent place so that you have no fear of being over-charged.

Domestic air travel
From Madrid, every corner of the peninsula can be reached within 55 minutes by air. Fares have fallen since Air Europa and other airlines have started competing with the traditional carriers, Iberia and Aviaco. If you book a return flight at least five days ahead and spend a Saturday night away before returning, a limited number of seats are available at a 40 per cent discount.

Buses
You can travel the length and breadth of Spain with the long-distance bus companies, which offer cheap and reasonably fast service. Tickets should be bought in advance to make sure of a place.

You can also hop between small towns using local buses, but you need plenty of time. Services are infrequent and villages may have only one bus a day. Comfort standards, however, have improved immeasurably in the past 20 years.

Trains
RENFE, the state-owned rail company, is upgrading its rail network to improve comfort and journey times. Fares are reasonable, although the train can often be slower than rival bus services. The most comfortable way to travel is on the Talgo, a smooth-running express for which you pay a hefty supplement. InterCity, Electrotren, and TER are also fast services. Don't be misled by the names of certain trains. Expresos are not express at all and Rápidos stop at virtually every wayside halt. Even slower, and harder on the backside, are other services, such as the Semidirecto or the Ferrobus.

Working out an exact fare can challenge a professor of calculus, because of the many supplements and discounts. Discounts offered by RENFE include reductions if you: travel on Días Azules (Blue Days), i.e., on off-peak days; are travelling with your family or in a group; are a senior citizen; or are between 12 and 26. A Tarjeta Turística allowing unlimited travel is available for non-residents. Visitors from outside Europe can use a Eurailpass, bought before leaving their home country. This permits unlimited travel in Western Europe for periods of 15 days and longer.

Special (costly) services include the AVE, a high-speed train that glides from Madrid to Seville in under three hours, the Al-Andalus, an Orient Express clone which makes a luxury trip through Andalucía, and the Transcantábrico, which does a similar run along the north coast.

Essential practical information

Accommodation

Details of 10,000 hotels and pensions, including prices, are listed in the Guía Oficial de Hoteles, published annually by Turespaña, a department of Spain's Tourism Ministry. This guide is well worth its 950 pesetas. Hotels are rated one to five stars. However, this does not tell the whole story as they are only judged by the amenities offered, not the quality of the service nor the atmosphere. Soulless package-tour establishments may have plenty of stars, but who wants to stay there?

Spain has its share of ultra-luxury establishments, but also an abundance of simpler, comfortable accommodation at very reasonable prices. If you want to spend the night in a medieval castle or a former convent, the state-run paradors will serve your purpose (information and reservations, Madrid 91 516 66 66). And there are an increasing number of private hotels located in fine old buildings, from Galician manor houses and monasteries to Andalucían farmhouses and hunting lodges.

Charming Small Hotel Guides – Spain published by Duncan Petersen in the U.K. and by Hunter in the U.S. is a useful guide to the best of such places.

A blue plaque at an establishment's door indicates its category. If it shows 'Hs', this signifies that it is a *hostal* – a small, simple hotel but which can provide perfectly adequate rooms if you do not require a built-in jacuzzi and room service. 'HsR' signifies *hostal residencial*, meaning it caters mainly to long-stay guests. Lower on the scale are the *pensión* (boarding house), the *fonda* (inn) and the *casa de huéspedes* (guesthouse): generally spartan but almost always clean – and the number of sagging beds has diminished. Spain also has 800 camping sites, most of them along the coasts.

Up-to-date hotel prices must be displayed in reception and in the rooms. Value added tax (IVA) is added at 15 per cent for five-star hotels and 6 per cent for the rest. Prices range from 3,000 pesetas or under for a double room in a rural one-star hostal to 15,000 pesetas upwards in a four-star hotel.

Note: an address written 'Real, 42 – 5°' indicates Number 42, fifth floor, on Real street. The letters 's/n' indicate *sin* *número* (no number). *Ctra* is short for *carretera* (highway); *Avda* for *Avenida* (Avenue).

Banks and currency exchange

Banking hours may vary slightly, but are usually from 9 am to 2 pm Monday to Friday, and 9 am to 12 pm Saturday. From June 1 to September 30, they close on Saturdays.

You can change currency and travellers' cheques at authorized money changers as well as banks. Savings banks (*cajas de ahorros*) tend to charge less commission than the big banks. Recognized European bank cards, Visa and Mastercards can be used in the extensive network of cashpoint machines (*cajeros automáticos*). Shopkeepers view personal cheques with suspicion, but will accept them when backed by a Eurocheque card.

Breakdowns

If you have a breakdown while driving a hire car, contact the hire company. Should any repairs be necessary, keep the bills so that you can be reimbursed. If driving your own car, take out insurance before leaving home to ensure cover in case of breakdown. Spain's national automobile association, RACE, has a free breakdown service for members and may be worth joining if you are in the country for any length of time. It also helps with legal advice and form-filling related to your car. Head office address: Real Automóvil Club de España, José Abascal, 10, 28003 Madrid; tel. 914 473 200.

Electricity

Spain is mainly 220V 50 AC. Sockets for hair dryers etc accept plugs with two round pins, so you may need an adaptor. In a few out-of-the-way spots, the power is still 110 or 125 volts. Even with voltage converters, American appliances may not work properly because of the difference in cycles.

Embassies

Embassies in Madrid (usually only open in the mornings):

Australia Plaza de Edescubidor, Diego Ordas 3; tel. 91 441 9300.
Canada Nuñez de Balboa, 35; tel. 91 431 43 00.

France *Salustiano Olózaga, 9;*
tel. 91 423 89 00.
Germany *Fortuny, 8; tel.* 91 559 90 00.
Italy *Lagasca, 98; tel.* 91 402 54 36.
Japan *Joaquin Costa, 29;* 91 562 55 46.
Netherlands *Paseo de la Castellana, 178-180; tel.* 91 359 09 14.
United Kingdom *Fernando el Santo, 16; tel.* 91 319 02 00.
U.S.A. *Serrano, 75; tel.* 91 577 40 00.

Emergencies

To contact the Municipal Police in towns and cities, dial 092. To call the National Police (for more serious matters), call 091. The emergency number for the fire brigade is 080. In towns under 20,000 population and in rural areas, call the Civil Guard on 062.

See also Medical matters, below.

Fiestas

There are more than you can imagine. Every town and village has an annual *feria* (fair), when several days are given over to dancing, bullfights, fireworks, sports and general carousing. But besides the *feria* there are innumerable other local festivities. Some are religious in origin – often with a colourful *romería* (pilgrimage) to a shrine to pay homage to a saint or the Virgin. Others are rooted in history – cacophonous battles between Christians and Moors are re-enacted. Some are of recent invention to pay homage to the sardine or to celebrate the harvest of sea urchins. In February, carnival madness seizes many communities bent on out-shining even Rio.

If you love exuberant crowds, heavy drinking, and dancing until dawn, you will love Spanish fiestas. However, if you have urgent business, they can be less enjoyable. When the next town to mine holds a fiesta, all mail services are cut off to my community. Fiestas are not the best time to do the sights. Many buildings will be closed, as well as shops and banks. Hotels may be full or charging higher rates. Sleep, in any case, will be difficult. Double check fiesta dates with local Tourist Offices since there can be variation.

Lost property

Town Halls usually have a lost property office. Passports as well as other items end up there.

Measurements

Spain operates on the metric system:

One litre =	1.7 pints
(1 imperial gallon =	4.54 litres;
1 U.S. gallon =	3.78 litres)
One kilogramme	
(1,000 grams) =	2.2 lbs
One kilometre	
(1,000 metres) =	0.62 miles

To convert kilometres to miles, multiply by five and divide by eight, and vice-versa.

Medical matters

Red Cross posts are located at strategic points on major highways and also on beaches. Social Security clinics known as 'Ambulatorios' are available for emergency cases in most towns. Most towns have private clinics. Hospital emergency entrances are marked 'Urgencias'.

If you have a condition that requires treatment or medication, take a descriptive letter in Spanish to help avoid misunderstandings.

Chemists, or *farmacias*, have a green cross outside. If closed, they will display a list of nearby late-opening chemists.

See also Emergencies, above, and Travel and medical insurance, page 16.

Opening hours

For banks, see page 21, under Banks and currency exchange.

Museums and tourist attractions: see Conventions used in this guide, page 12.

Most shops open from 9.30 or 10 am to 1.30 pm and from 5 to 8 pm, although times vary.

Bars traditionally stayed open until the last client went, but controls are tougher than they used to be and many close by midnight. At weekends and in resort areas, hours are often extended and night clubs and discos are open until 4 am or later.

Post and telephone

Letters to and from the rest of Europe go by air, but can take two days to a week to arrive. Mail to North America can take three days to three weeks.

Post offices are generally open 9 am-2 pm from Monday to Friday,

9 am-1 pm on Saturday. Those in larger cities may also open in the afternoon. Stamps can also be bought in *estancos*, shops which also sell cigarettes, hence the yellow and brown 'Tobacos' sign outside.

You can have mail sent to *Poste Restante* (*Lista de Correos* in Spanish). However, be careful in the use of names. Spaniards use two surnames, that of their father followed by their mother's, as in García Lorca. If a letter is addressed to William Grant Atkins, it may well be filed under Grant rather than Atkins.

Spain's highly profitable telephone service, part publicly, part privately owned, is often criticized, but it has modernized and expanded its network at a tremendous rate. You can make local, inter-city and international calls from a *cabina* (phone box). Use 5, 10, 25, 50, 100, 200 and 500 peseta coins. Calls can also be made from operator-manned exchanges in tourist areas and city central exchanges. Bars impose a surcharge for using their phones and only the rich – or the desperate – use hotel phones.

Area codes for each province start with a 9. Thus, when calling a number in Córdoba from another province, you use the prefix 957, but when calling from abroad, you drop the 9, dialling only 57 and the number. To call other countries from Spain, dial 07 and wait for a high-pitched tone before dialling the country code. For example, to call Britain, dial 00 44 followed by the area code and number. You can make reverse charge (collect) calls by dialling your home country operator (see list of numbers in phone booths)

Telex and fax facilities are available in larger post offices or in associated telegraph offices.

Public holidays
National holidays: January 1, New Year's Day; January 6, Twelfth Night (Día de los Reyes); Good Friday (Easter Monday is celebrated in all of Spain except Andalucía.); May 1, Labour Day; May/June, Corpus Christi (not observed in all towns); July 25, St. James's Day (Santiago); August 15, Assumption of the Virgin; October 12, Día del Pilar (Columbus Day); November 1, All Saints' Day; December 6, Day of the Constitution; December 8, Immaculate Conception; December 25, Christmas Day. Some regions take other days off in lieu of some of these holidays. Whenever a holiday falls on a Thursday or a Tuesday, Spaniards like to take a *puente* (a bridge), i.e., make a long weekend of it.

Rush hours
In the cities, peak hours are between 8.30 and 9.30 am as offices and shops open; between 1 and 2 pm as everybody heads for lunch; and between 7 and 8 pm as the time for the *paseo* (evening stroll) and *tapas* (snacks) approaches.

Security
Theft from cars is common in Spain, so when stopping overnight take all your baggage in with you. If possible, park your car in a garage or a guarded car park. Never leave anything of value, including your passport, when parking in city streets or on beaches. Spaniards often take their car radios with them. A useful ploy to avoid damage is to leave the boot interior exposed, indicating that it is empty. Bag snatching is a hazard in cities, particularly at night. Valuables and documents are best left in the hotel. Make photocopies if you want to carry identification (as required by the law though rarely asked for).

Spain has a confusing number of police forces. Several autonomous regions have their own. Apart from these, there are: the Civil Guard (olive-green uniforms, but no longer sporting the notorious tricorn) responsible for patrolling small towns and rural areas; the National Police, in dark blue uniforms, who attend to crime prevention and investigation; and the Municipal Police, also in dark blue, who control traffic and are concerned with minor infractions.

National Police stations (*comisarías*) in areas frequented by tourists often have report forms in several languages.

Time
Spain follows European Continental time, one hour ahead of Britain. Clocks go forward one hour in March and back in September. As a general guide, when it is noon in Madrid, it is 6 am in New York, 8 am in Buenos Aires, 8 pm in Tokyo, and 9 pm in Sydney.

SPAIN'S BEACHES

Spain's Mediterranean coastline has been seriously overbuilt and is very crowded in summer, but great efforts have been made to control new construction and to improve the beaches by pumping in thousands of tons of sand, building breakwaters and promenades, and gradually installing sewage treatment plants.

Sandy stretches tucked into intimate coves are a feature of the **Costa Brava**, while the **Costa Dorada** (Barcelona and Tarragona provinces) and **Costa del Azahar** (Castellón and Valencia) beaches are larger but less picturesque.

For dazzling white sand, you have to go to the **Costa Blanca**, which can boast some of Spain's finest expanses. Into Murcia beaches become grittier and parts of Almeria and Granada's coastlines are an unattractive slate-grey. **Costa del Sol** beaches vary from grit to coarse sand. Although far south, the water is no warmer, because it mixes with the cool Atlantic entering through the Straits of Gibraltar.

Some of the best sandy beaches are on the Atlantic coast. The pine-fringed **coast of Cádiz** north of Tarifa suffers strong winds, perfect for windsurfers, but not for sunbathers. It is less windy on the long stretches of the **Costa de la Luz** in Huelva province.

Northern Spain has magnificent beaches with less development, but chilly water. Sheltered beaches are found on **Galicia's rías** and in the many bays of **Asturias**. **Cantabria's** sand is good and the beaches extensive, while **Basque beaches** are generally confined to pretty bays, La Concha at San Sebastián being the most fashionable.

Tapas

One of the ironies of modern Spain is that fast food outlets have opened across the nation selling styrofoam hamburgers and other delicacies when the country already has its own – immeasurably superior – fast food. The *tapeo*, the habit of socializing while taking a drink with a snack, is one of the country's most civilized customs. The word *tapa* (lid) comes from the plate once placed on top of a glass to keep out the flies. Now it refers to the delicious morsels served at the counter with your drink. In the humbler establishments, they may be free. Generally, however, there is now a charge, but they are usually worth it. A *tapa* can be anything from mountain-cured ham to shrimps fried with garlic. In some towns, there may be no restaurant worthy of the name, but there will almost certainly be a bar where you can fill up on tasty *tapas*. If you want larger portions, ask for a *ración* (plateful), or a *media ración* (half a plateful). The favourite hours of *tapeo* are usually from 6 to 9 pm. After which, visitors may need no more sustenance before slipping into unconsciousness, but a true Spaniard will be ready for a three-course dinner.

Tipping

Ten per cent is the rule in taxis and restaurants, except budget establishments where it is enough to round up the bill to the nearest 100 pesetas.

Car park attendants, theatre ushers, and lavatory attendants expect a few coins. So do railway porters and hotel doormen who call your taxi. Petrol pump attendants hope for tips, but as the service is usually non-existent, most drivers resist the temptation.

Tourist information

Towns of interest have centrally-located information offices open Monday to Saturday, but – inexplicably – not always open on Sundays when their services are most in demand. Here you can get maps and details of local events. The staff are better trained than they used to be, are usually enthusiastic and may speak at least one language apart from Spanish.

For up-to-date tourist information, on everything from useful telephone numbers to hotels and sporting events, call 901 300 600 between 10 am and 2 pm, possibly later in summer, from Monday to Friday. You can call from anywhere in Spain at a special reduced rate. The service is in Spanish, French, and English.

A brief history of Spain

When Juan Carlos ascended the Spanish throne in 1975, he promised to be the king 'of all the Spains'. It was a worthy ambition, but a difficult one to achieve, for Spanish history has been characterized more by division than by cooperation. And never more so than this century when the Civil War tore the country apart, creating wounds that linger yet.

Conflict has pitted region against region, king against nobles, class against class. And the passionate, highly individualistic Spanish character has always made the task of controlling this volatile country a difficult one.

If it is a complex character, this is not surprising. Successive invaders have deposited rich seams of disparate cultures on this land which forms a bridge between two continents and two seas. Little wonder that history is only a spade deep in the Iberian earth. Builders digging house foundations stumble across Phoenician burial grounds; farmers' ploughs often turn up Roman coins; archaeological treasures foil the best-laid plans of city engineers.

Earliest settlers
The early inhabitants, the 'Iberians', were reportedly a quarrelsome bunch, stoical, devoted to bulls, and suspicious of organization, features that still ring a bell. An advanced culture existed along the fertile Guadalquivir Valley in south-western Spain some 3,000 years ago. Near the mouth of that river the city or kingdom of Tartessus is believed to have flourished, a place of fabled wealth yielding, according to a Biblical reference, 'gold and silver, ivory, apes and peacocks.'

Cádiz, on its narrow tongue of land, claims to be Europe's oldest city, since on this site around 1,000 BC Phoenician traders established the colony of Gadir. Greeks and Carthaginians came next, but the Romans left the most imposing evidence of their rule, which lasted 600 years. The Emperor Hadrian and Seneca the Younger were born on the peninsula and Rome planted linguistic roots and such architectural gems as the Segovia aqueduct and the theatre at Mérida.

In contrast, few traces remain of the Visigoths, whose speciality appears to have been regicide. Then came the Moors, a word used loosely to cover all Muslim invaders, Arab or Berber. They hopped across the Straits of Gibraltar in 711 and stayed long enough to leave a deep imprint. The centuries of Moorish rule and intermarriage gave Spain some unique traits, however much Spaniards now argue that they are not so different from the rest of Europe.

Moorish rule
A romantic haze covers Moorish rule, overlooking the atrocities committed by successive waves of religious fanatics from Africa. However, Al-Andalus, as the Moors called the peninsula, became renowned for its culture. Philosophy, the arts, crafts, commerce and agriculture flourished under the Caliph of Córdoba, who permitted Jews and Christians to practise their religions. Personal cleanliness was important to the Moors, who noted: 'Christians are sprinkled with water at birth and thus relieved from washing for the rest of their lives.'

The seeds of the Reconquest of Spain by Christian forces were sown shortly after the Moors arrived, when they failed to crush a small band led by Pelayo at Covadonga in Asturias. Pelayo's descendants became kings of Asturias and León and Covadonga became a symbol of Christian resistance. The campaign to oust the Moors went on for centuries, partly because of shifting alliances among the multitude of mini-kingdoms. Sometimes Moors and Christians fought together and even the legendary warrior El Cid was not always on the Christian side.

The Christian Reconquest
The beginning of the end for Muslim Spain came in 1212 when Christian forces inflicted a stunning victory at Las Navas de Tolosa (now in Jaén province). The Moors were pushed southwards until they only retained the Kingdom of Granada, which finally fell in 1492 to the army of Isabel of Castile and Ferdinand of Aragón; their marriage had led to the uniting of those two powerful kingdoms.

A stern Catholic regime took over, heralding a golden age for Spain or a plunge into bigotry and obscurantism, depending on your point of view.

The Moors left behind a rich her-

• *Monument to Columbus, Huelva.*

after that city fell, all Jews refusing baptism were ordered out of Spain. Some 200,000 people left: known as the Sephardic Jews, they were finally invited back to Spain in 1982. The crown enriched itself with the property of many of those expelled, but Spain lost the skills of a thriving merchant class. A similar ultimatum was forced on the Muslims in 1502, even though they had been previously guaranteed the right to continue their customs and their religion.

At the same time, Columbus's voyage to the New World opened up new opportunities for conquest and wealth. The Conquistadores slashed and shot their way through the Americas in search of gold and silver, followed by missionaries in search of souls. Spain ruled the seas and her navigators circumnavigated the globe.

The accession of Charles I, who also headed the Holy Roman Empire as Charles V, expanded national interests further. Much of the treasure brought home by Spanish galleons was squandered on wars waged by Charles and his son Philip II to defend or extend their possessions.

That depressing grey granite mass, El Escorial palace outside Madrid, was the work of Philip, virtually a stereotype of the dour, devout Castilian. While he endlessly shuffled papers, the Black Legend of the evil Spaniard was nurtured by his enemies. It was fed by horrendous tales, sometimes exaggerated, of cruelty to the Indians by the Conquistadores.

itage: the feather-light beauty of their architecture as seen in the Alhambra; efficient methods of irrigation; Arab numerals and paper manufacture. Many of their words have entered the Castilian language, such as *arroz* (rice), *naranja* (orange), *alcalde* (mayor). However, their love of plunder and intrigue was a less benevolent influence. A preference for show over substance and for poetic fancy over practicalities also left their mark.

Empire

While laying the foundations of an empire, Isabel and Ferdinand, the Catholic Monarchs, also fostered xenophobia and religious intolerance, contributing to the bad name which Spain enjoyed for centuries (known as the Black Legend). They rewarded their followers with vast estates, creating the enduring problem of *latifundios* and landless peasants. The monarchs used the Inquisition, founded in 1478, to consolidate their power. Initially, it was aimed at Jews who claimed to be Christians but were secretly carrying on their rites.

Although loans from Jewish bankers financed the war against Granada, soon

17th century decline

The 17thC was one of decline, thanks to feeble rulers, costly conflicts, and a medieval economy, but it also heralded an explosion of artistic creativity. This was the Siglo de Oro (golden century), when Murillo, Velázquez, and Zurbarán flourished and great writers such as Cervantes, Lope de Vega and Calderón de la Barca were at their zenith.

The Bourbons who took over from the degenerate Hapsburgs attempted to unify and liberalize Spain. Charles III, a shining exception among the sad parade of monarchs, launched an amazing number of public works. After him, however, came the bloated, tyrannical ruler Ferdinand VII and invasion by Napoleon's forces.

Although Ferdinand rejected the liberal constitution approved by the Cortes (parliament) in 1812, the urge for reform could not be crushed and liberals confronted traditionalists in the First Carlist War.

Battle lines were being drawn which would have their logical bloody outcome a century later. On the conservative side were the monarchists, the church, rural landowners, generals and high-ranking civil servants; on the other, those who supported change: the emerging middle classes, intellectuals and merchants.

Holding together a country of fierce regional loyalties, of Basques, Galicians, Catalans, Navarrese and others, was difficult enough. Added to this was the problem of the two Spains, the haves and the have-nots. While the élite played musical chairs in Madrid, frustration and anger grew among the landless and the dispossessed. Anarchism took root among poverty-stricken rural-dwellers and among the new working class of industrial Barcelona; hatred of the church simmered.

The Civil War, and after

In 1936 the pot boiled over. In the three-year Civil War the Republicans had right on their side, but little else. Increasingly, the Communists dominated their actions, making it easier for the Nationalist rebels to present their cause as a Christian crusade. Afterwards Spain endured decades of military dictatorship, the crushing of critical thought, and ostracism by the righteous nations which had not lifted a finger to stop General Franco's rise to power. The country slumbered in a sort of medieval limbo.

Foreign investment and mass tourism began to change things and, after Franco's death in 1975, came a virtual renaissance amid a surprisingly peaceful transition to democracy. King Juan Carlos was instrumental in that. He gained new respect after his baptism of fire, the 1981 coup attempt.

The new Spain has proved stable and progressive. Today it is one of Europe's most dynamic nations, with a youthful exuberance missing in some of its northern neighbours – and Juan Carlos can truly claim to be 'king of all the Spains'.

DEFINITIONS – SPANISH WORDS AND ARCHITECTURAL TERMS FOUND IN THIS GUIDE

alcazaba	Moorish fortress
alcázar	Moorish palace
Ayuntamiento	town hall
azulejo	patterned tiles
barrio	quarter
bodega	wine cellar, winery
chiringuito	beach restaurant
Churrigueresque	ornate Baroque decoration
corrida	bullfight
cortijo	farmhouse
encierro	bull-run
estanco	shop selling tobacco and stamps
feria	annual fair
fonda	inn
gitano	gypsy
mihrab	prayer niche in mosque wall facing Mecca
Morisco	Muslim converted to Christianity
Mudéjar	Islamic art in Christian-occupied territory after the Reconquest
Mozarabic	the work of Christians under Moorish rule
Plateresque	ornate Renaissance-style architecture
romería	religious pilgrimage
tablao	flamenco nightclub
vega	fertile plain
venta	inn

KEY DATES

40,000 BC	Cro-Magnon man begins invading the Iberian peninsula
3,000 BC	Neolithic culture arrives
1,100 BC	Phoenician traders establish settlements, including Gades (Cádiz)
1,000-500 BC	Legendary kingdom of Tartessus flourishes
900 BC	Celts move in
600 BC	Greeks found trading settlements
237 BC	Carthaginians begin conquest
218 BC - 409 AD	Roman rule
1C AD	Christianity arrives on the peninsula
409	Vandals, Alans, and Suevi over-run peninsula
5C-8C	Visigoths hold sway
711	Moors cross the Straits of Gibraltar and conquer most of the peninsula
713	Pelayo inflicts first Christian defeat on Moors at Covadonga
778	Charlemagne's retreating army attacked at Roncesvalles
785	Work begins on Córdoba's Great Mosque
928	Abd-ar-Rahman III declares Andalucía an independent caliphate
1085	Recapture of Toledo, first big victory in the Reconquest
1140	Spain's first great epic poem; *El Cantar del Mío Cid*
1212	Moorish forces annihilated at Las Navas de Tolosa
1469	Isabel and Fernando marry, leading to the uniting of Castile and Aragón
1478	Inquisition created to weed out 'false' Christians
1492	The Catholic Monarchs conquer Granada, the Moors' last stronghold
	Expulsion of Jews who refuse to be baptized
	Columbus lands in the New World
1502	Muslims ordered to convert or go into exile
1519	Magellan starts global voyage
1568-70	Morisco rising crushed in Andalucía
1587	Drake raids Cádiz
1588	Spanish Armada defeated
1609	Moriscos expelled from Spain
1702-13	War of Spanish Succession
1704	Britain seizes Gibraltar
1805	Nelson's fleet routs Spanish and French navies off Cape Trafalgar
1808-14	Peninsular War
1812	Liberal constitution declared in Cádiz
1833-39	First Carlist War
1835	Measures introduced to confiscate church property
1844	Civil Guard founded
1881	Pablo Picasso born
1898	Spanish-American War marks end of empire
1931	King Alfonso XIII abdicates, Second Republic begins
1936-39	Spanish Civil War
1960	Tourism boom begins along Mediterranean coast
1975	General Franco dies, monarchy restored
1977	First post-Franco democratic government elected
1978	Spain becomes a constitutional monarchy
1980-82	Autonomy granted to regions
1981	Coup attempt fails
1982	Spain elects a Socialist government
1986	Spain joins the European Community
1992	World Expo, Seville
	Olympic Games in Barcelona

The Spanish character

At a meeting of Spanish academics, an earnest professor of literature decried the image of their country peddled abroad, one of folk dances, matadors, and throbbing guitars. The others nodded agreement, until somebody pointed out that propaganda showing car factories and tower blocks, while presenting an accurate picture of Spain, was unlikely to lure visitors to the peninsula.

The meeting had been called, at considerable expense, to debate the question of what others thought of Spain and the Spaniards. When I asked why they should give a damn what others thought about them, the question clearly bemused these erudite gentlemen. Both the debate and their bemusement revealed something about the Spanish character.

Arrogance and self-doubt fight for supremacy in the national psyche. A Spaniard would not deny his arrogance: rather, he would claim it as a virtue, as an indication of his macho pride and his unassailable individualism.

At the same time, he needs constant reassurance that the rest of the world recognizes his stature and Spain's importance as a modern nation. One of the most thankless jobs for Spanish journalists falls to correspondents in London and New York, endlessly asked by Madrid to dredge up foreign reaction to Spanish events.

The academics could accept the point about not needing outside recognition; but they could not understand why I questioned the need for debate. A Spaniard needs no incentive to pontificate at any time, and to be invited especially to do so, with a captive audience to boot, was reason enough for the whole exercise.

Although the average Spaniard reads little, he is ready to give his opinion on any subject, as a visit to the country's debating chambers, the countless bars, confirms. There, where the general cacophony generates a very Spanish sense of activity and well-being, he can develop his monologue, regardless of the fact that each of his companions is also talking. In such company he may bitterly disparage his country, but do not take this as a signal to join in; criticism is not really welcome from foreigers. While dialogue is not a strong point, human contact is. A letter or phone call will get you nowhere in Spain, but a personal relationship will move mountains. Even today, in a democratic state, the average Spaniard knows that only a good *enchufe* (connection) will cut through the monstrous tangle of red tape that threatens to engulf the country.

The trust in personal relationships, as opposed to the cold semblance of efficiency worshipped in puritanical Anglo-Saxon countries, may be an Arab legacy. It is certainly rooted in the Spaniard's pampered childhood and in the concentric rings of constantly polished relationships that give him his enviable confidence. At the heart is the family, still the centrepiece of Spanish life, headed by La Madre, a revered figure. Women are still fighting for equal rights, but mothers have always ruled the home.

Perhaps it is because at heart the Spaniard still feels he is an *hidalgo* (literally, son of somebody, i.e., a noble) that he is capable of grand gestures and heartwarming generosity. The number of beggars in Spain is not just a sign of poverty – some of them are far from poor – but of Spaniards' readiness to give.

Family ties and the Catholic Church still play a major role (though comparatively few people actually attend services), but moral codes and popular culture imported from beyond the Pyrenees have markedly changed attitudes. While many scorn American influences, teenagers flock to hamburger joints and pop music is under the sway of British and American rock. Some Spanish husbands even do the washing up these days, despite the risk of being labelled a *maricón* (homosexual).

Yet the Spaniard will not quickly abandon his time-honoured customs. Eager young executives ape other societies, eat lunch at their desks, and chatter on cellular phones, while the man in the street talks proudly of being 'a part of Europe' at last. But improvization, rather than organization, remains a national art form and Spain has not yet abandoned the *mañana* philosophy. Taking a siesta still makes sense in the crucible of a Spanish summer. And, despite well-meaning protests, men still walk out to risk their lives before the bulls at five in the afternoon.

Between San Sebastián and Oviedo
The Cantabrian Coast

426 km; map Michelin 442, 1:400,000

They call it La Costa Verde, and with good reason. Lush and green year-round, Spain's northern coast edging the Bay of Biscay is a stark contrast to Castile and southern Spain. It offers the best of two worlds, fine beaches interspersed with rugged, wave-pounded headlands, and, just inland, forested hills, cow and sheep pastures, and magnificent wilderness where species extinct in other parts of Europe still roam. Often it is bathed in the sirimiri, a poetic name for light drizzle.

Strong regional differences gives one the sensation of visiting several different countries. Nearest to the French border is Euskadi (the Basque Country), formed by Guipúzcoa, Vizcaya, and Alava provinces and inhabited by an ancient people who rarely miss an opportunity to stress their uniqueness. Indeed, some Basques (not least the violent separatist movement, ETA) still dream of creating an independent state. Industrious and tenacious, the Basques speak a language unlike any other in Europe and practise their own sports such as jai-alai (or pelota). As a visitor, you will find the Basques helpful and friendly.

Basque appreciation of good food is equalled only by that of the French. 'New Basque cuisine' has swept the country and you can eat superbly, though not cheaply.

Cantabria, next door, one of the smallest autonomous regions, covering Santander province, offers a succession of fine beaches, fishing communities and meadows, with gentle hills swelling upwards towards the rugged Cordillera Cantábrica. Santander, the capital, is a focus for intense artistic and intellectual activity from June to September

Different again is the autonomous region and province of Asturias (traditionally the heir to the Spanish throne takes the title Prince of Asturias). Its people are proud that here, in the 8thC Battle of Covadonga, the onward advance of the Moors was stayed. Asturians, who drink cider rather than wine and prefer the bagpipe to the guitar, even have a dialect of their own, known as bable. Viewing the needle-sharp summits of the Picos de Europa which back the rocky coast, you will understand why the Visigoths declared the region 'walled in by the hand of God'.

Between the French border and Torrelavega, east of Santander, the fast route for drivers is the four-lane E70 and A67. If you want to take it more slowly, meander along the N634, taking in sights marked blue and/or green. Local Explorations: 1 and 2 complete the coverage of this area, both highly recommended.

TRANSPORT

This stretch of coast is well served by public transport. There are frequent bus services between the main cities and towns. FEVE, a narrow gauge railway, runs between Bilbao, Santander, Gijón, and Oviedo. Another line runs inland between Bilbao and León. Two narrow-gauge services run from San Sebastián, one through particularly splendid scenery to Bilbao and another – known as The Mole because it passes though so many tunnels – to Irún on the French frontier. RENFE has services between Bilbao and San Sebastián and Vitoria and between Santander and Reinosa. Holders of the Carnet Joven, restricted to people between 14 and 26 years, get a 20 per cent discount on longer journeys by RENFE and FEVE.

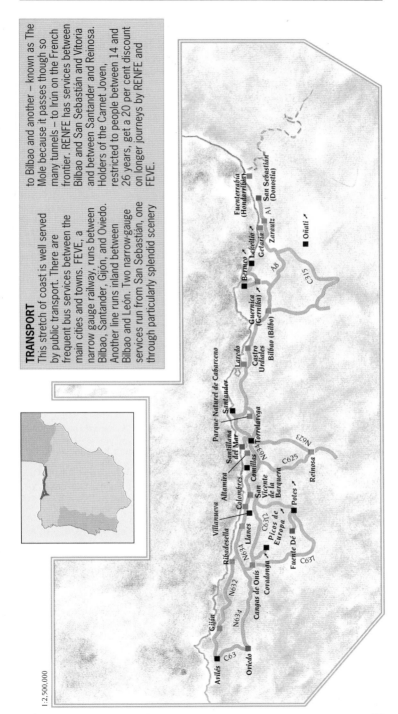

1:2,500,000

SIGHTS & PLACES OF INTEREST

ALTAMIRA, CUEVAS DE

Off the N634, 2 km SW of Santillana del Mar, 32 km from Santander. First, the good news. You will be able to see the famous prehistoric paintings in the Altamira Caves. Then, the bad news. What you will view will actually be a replica. Plans are under way to reproduce every ripple in the rock, every finger stroke of ochre, animal fat and blood that created the drawings possibly 15,000 years ago, and to put this reconstruction on show. Alternatively you can put your name on a waiting list (apply to Museo de Altamira, 39330 Santillana del Mar, Santander, tel. 942 81 80 05) and maybe a year later you will see the real thing. The number of visitors has been strictly controlled because of the damage done by human breath and body temperature.

News of the finding of the paintings back in 1879 was greeted with scepticism: they were the first such Paleolithic art ever discovered. The bulges and hollows in the rock were cleverly exploited by the artists to make representations of deer, bison, boar, horses and other animals seem remarkably lifelike. If you do gain access, look for the finest examples in a chamber that has been called 'the Sistine Chapel of Quaternary Art'. Open for viewing daily, except Mondays, is an adjacent cave of stalactites and a museum.

AVILES

On the N632, 28 km N of Oviedo. An industrial city, important for steel manufacturing. It has an old quarter of interest and several Romanesque churches, but little else to detain the traveller. One of its sons, Pedro Menéndez, is credited with founding the first American city, San Agustín de la Florida, in 1565. Another Menéndez, José, was dubbed King of Patagonia after he became the world's largest landowner, acquiring two million hectares in South America.

BERMEO

See *Local Explorations: 1*

BILBAO (BILBO) ⊨ ✕

On the A8 (E70), 92 km W of San Sebastián. Tourism Office, Paseo del Arenal 1; tel. 94 479 57 60. At first sight Bilbao is an unlovely industrial city, with grimy dwellings, factories, and docks squeezed into the narrow valley around the Nervión river. Yet, like Liverpool or Hamburg, it has dynamism, community spirit, and friendly natives. Soccer is a religion, centred around the Athletic de Bilbao Club. The name betrays Bilbao's close links with the British, who helped found it.

The outspoken philosopher, Miguel de Unamuno, was born in Bilbao. Perhaps it was just as well that he did not live to see the Nationalists take the city in 1936 by raining 20,000 shells on it. Bilbao's traditional shipbuilding and steel industries are declining. Fresh interest in the city has been created by Frank O. Gehry's spectacular sculptural design in limestone and titanium, which houses the Guggenheim Museum Bilbao (Tues to Sun, 11 a.m to 8 p.m.);. and there are ambitious plans for 'El Nuevo Bilbao', including a Metro, and new bridges across a cleaned-up river.

The *cascoviejo* (old quarter), across the river from the modern section known as the Ensanche, holds most interest for a visitor. It is presided over by the Gothic **Basílica de Begoña**, dedicated to the patron of the province. Feverish activity takes place in the evening, especially at weekends, in the **Siete Calles** quarter where the alleys are filled with *tapa* bars, restaurants, and drinkers. If you want an insight into Basque nationalist feeling, try the **Taberna Txomin Barullo**, on Barrencalle, where the walls bear pictures of Che Guevara and militants 'killed in the revolutionary struggle'. In the Ensanche, the area around Licenciado Poza Street is another happy hunting ground for *tapa* enthusiasts.

Carnival is a big fiesta in Bilbao, but the most riotous time is the **Semana Grande** in the third week of August.

CABARCENO, PARQUE NATUREL DE

Off the N634, 16 km S of Santander. Iron was mined from pre-Roman times until 1989 around the Cabarga mountain. Now the tortured landscape has been rehabilitated, planted with trees and grass and converted into an unusual nature park, around which you can drive or walk. Tigers, elephants, giraffes, bears and other animals roam in spacious surroundings. There are a restaurant and a café in the park and fine views can be enjoyed from **Peña Cabarga.**

CANGAS DE ONIS
On the N625, 63 km E of Oviedo. Tourism Office, Avda de Covadonga (jardines del Ayuntamiento); tel. 98 584 80 05. On the route to Covadonga and the Picos de Europa, Cangas is a pleasant little town on the Sella River, over which passes a famous Romanesque bridge. It was the first capital of Asturias. Nearby is the **Buxu Cave** with Paleolithic wall paintings; visitor numbers are limited.

The N625 runs south from Cangas through stirring scenery bordering the Picos de Europa. You pass **Los Beyos Gorge**; **Oseja de Sajambre** where there is a viewing point; the **Pontón Pass**; then swing east over the **Panderruedas Pass**, near which is the **Mirador de Piedrafitas.**

CASTRO URDIALES ✕
On the N634, 35 km NW of Bilbao. Castle walls enfolding a lighthouse and a remarkable **Gothic church** loom over the fishing port. Beautifully situated, surrounded by mountains, Castro Urdiales (Flavobriga to the Romans) has grown into a highly popular tourist resort.

COVADONGA
See Local Explorations: 2

COLOMBRES
Off the N634, 15 km W of San Vicente. Spain's north coast is dotted with splendid old mansions, constructed in the 19thC or early 20thC by wealthy *Indianos* (emigrants returned from the Americas). This sleepy village has one, a noble blue structure amid lawns and trees, built by the *Indiano* Manuel Ibáñez, the first Conde de Ribadeva, born here in 1838. He intended the building to accommodate the Mexican president on a visit to Spain, but he never came. Now it houses the Archivo de Indianos, a centre for study of emigration to America.

COMILLAS
On the C6316, 50 km W of Santander. A delightful old village with two excellent beaches and some unusual buildings. The latter include the neo-Gothic **Papal University**, the **Palace of the Marqués de Comillas**, and **El Capricho de Gaudí**, an entertaining example of

---

SOME BASQUE WORDS
aizkolari: axe-man who competes in log-chopping
bai: yes
bertsolari: singer who improvizes elaborate verses
egun on: good morning
ertzantza: police
eskerrik asko: thank you
ez: no
irteera: exit
itxita: closed
jai-alai: game in which a ball, the *pelota*, is hit against a wall with hand, bat, or racket. Basques have exported the game to many countries, including the United States, Mexico, and the Philippines.
mesedez: please
sarrera: entrance
zenbat da?: how much is it?

---

the Catalan architect's brilliant eccentricity. The Capricho houses a restaurant with some imaginative but somewhat pricey dishes.

FUENTERRABIA (HONDARRIBIA) ⊠
Off the A8, 20 km E of San Sebastián. Facing France across the Bidasoa River, the old fortress town of Fuenterrabía occupies a strategic spot and suffered many a siege. It is an important fishing port, with good seafood restaurants, with its **walls** and **medieval quarter** preserved. Stroll up the main street to examine the mansions with their wrought ironwork balconies, the 18thC **Ayuntamiento**, and the Gothic-Renaissance **Asunción Church**, where Louis XIV's proxy wedding to the Infanta María Teresa was celebrated in 1660.

Take the winding minor road to Monte Jaizkibel and San Sebastián for some inspiring views of the coast.

GETARIA ✕
On the N634, 26 km from San Sebastián. A cobbled street leads from the main road to the old church, with its altar set high above the heads of the congregation, and runs under it to the fishing port. Beyond is a small island, known as 'the mouse'. The village is famed for its seafood restaurants – outside you will see fish being grilled on braziers – and for the locally-produced *txacoli*, the dry, low-alcohol Basque white wine.

Whalers used to operate from here and there is a monument to Getaria-born Juan Sebastián Elcano, who in 1522 became the first navigator to sail around the world.

GIJON

On the A8, 28 km N of Oviedo. Gijón is a modern port, with more than a quarter of a million inhabitants, which ships out millions of tons of coal annually from the Asturias mines, although the future for many of these is bleak. Industry concentrates around the port area of El Musel. But Gijón also lays claim to be a seaside resort and indeed the golden sands of **San Lorenzo beach**, edged by apartment blocks, attract many visitors.

There is not much left of the **old town**, thanks to heavy damage in the Civil War. A desperate siege of the Nationalist-held Simancas barracks took place in August 1936, the miners hurling sticks of dynamite against the defenders. The fanatical commander, a Colonel Pinilla, sent a radio message to the Nationalist warships off-shore: 'The barracks are burning and the enemy are starting to enter. Fire on us!' So they did, and the defenders perished.

Gijón's old quarter is to be found on the Santa Catalina headland, site of the fishermen's quarter of **Cimadevilla**. There, in the narrow streets, you can enjoy an evening rolling from *chigre* (bar) to *chigre*, sampling the freshly-caught sardines and drinking the local cider. Nearby are the remains of **Roman baths** built in the time of Augustus.

GUERNICA (GERNIKA)

See Local Explorations: 1

LAREDO

On the N634, 50 km E of Santander. Tourism Office, Alameda de Miramar; tel. 942 61 10 96. Laredo's old town has been dwarfed by the extensive construction of high-rise apartments. Known as the capital of the Costa Esmeralda, it has a splendid long **beach**.

On the last Friday in August a spectacular **battle of flowers** is held.

LEKEITIO

See Local Explorations: 1

LLANES 🛏

Off the N634, 106 km east of Oviedo. Tourism Office, Alfonso IX (edificio La Torre); tel. 98 540 01 64.

An intimate little town with a fishing port and the remains of old fortifications, including a castle. For a pleasant stroll, walk along the Paseo de San Pedro, which runs atop the cliffs with pleasing views.

Llanes has some 30 beaches within its boundaries, spliced by headlands and odd-shaped rock formations. Torimbia beach is favoured by nudists. All along the Asturias coast are sandy coves and surf-battered cliffs. In the autumn, hundreds of carts head for the beaches to collect tons of seaweed washed ashore. This is a minor industry, the dried seaweed being sold to pharmaceutical and cosmetics manufacturers.

Llanes is a handy base for expeditions into the Picos de Europa, which rise behind the often-cloud-capped Sierra de Cuera. Enquire at the tourism office about the possibilities of trips in four-wheel-drives, canoeing and renting horses and mountain bikes. If you are interested in helping preserve Asturias wild life, contact FAPAS, a highly active ecological group based here (*tel.* 98 540 12 64).

Llanes has several campsites, usually open only in summer. If you are here between mid-July and September 8, you will have the opportunity to witness several fiestas with unusual traditional dances; the **Pericote** is believed to be of Celtic origin, the **Dance of the Pilgrims** commemorates those who follow the Road to Santiago, and the **Corri-Corri** is an old erotic rite in which six girls dance around a youth.

OÑATI

And other places in Basque country south of San Sebastián, see Local Explorations: 1.

OVIEDO 🛏 ×

At the junction of the A66 and N634, 168 km W of Santander. Tourism Office, Plaza Alfonso-II el Casto 6; tel. 98 521 33 85. It is a miracle that anything remains of old Oviedo after the horrendous events of the 1930s. Asturias miners staged a rebellion in 1934, mobilising workers into a 'Red Army'. Sent in to put down the revolt, Generals Franco and Goded employed the Foreign Legion and

• Santa María de Naranco, Oviedo.

Moroccan troops, who wreaked terrible revenge. In 1936-37, 3,000 Nationalists held the town during a prolonged siege.

Oviedo has a long history (it was founded in 757 and in 810 Alfonso II made it capital of the tiny Kingdom of Asturias). It endures today as the centre of the Asturias region's coal and iron industry, presenting a bustling, if unglamorous persona. The extensive **Parque de San Francisco**, once a monastery garden, brings welcome greenery to the modern section, but it is the **old quarter** which attracts the visitor's attention.

King Alfonso, reportedly 'kind to God and man' and known as 'The Chaste' because of his sobriety, was an energetic warrior who more or less stood alone against the all-conquering Moors. Thanks to his dream of recreating the splendour of the Visigoth capital, Toledo, Oviedo has some splendid buildings to offer the visitor.

In the 9thC the Oviedo region saw the flourishing of a highly innovatory art, which bore little resemblance to contemporary artistic trends and sharply contrasted with Mozarabic (Arab-influenced Christian) art. The pre-Romanesque architecture of Asturia, simple but elegant, is characterized by slender proportions, latticed windows, semi-circular arches, and flat outside buttresses. Two centuries before the style appeared elsewhere, buildings featured totally vaulted naves and aisles.

Somehow three of these remarkable 1,100-year-old structures in Oviedo have survived the pillaging of the past.

A 45-minute walk, or a No. 6 bus from the city centre, brings you to the wooded slopes of **Monte Naranco**, where Alfonso's successor, Ramiro I, established a pleasure estate. The rectangular, two-storeyed **Santa María de Naranco**, originally a palace, impresses mostly for its perfect harmony. Its features include spiral columns, shield-like medallions on the ceiling arches, and a mirador from where you can gaze out over Oviedo towards the Picos de Europa. Nearby is another piece of harmony in stone, the Chapel of San Miguel de Lillo, which is surprisingly lofty in relation to its width and has some Byzantine touches.

Within the city, you find **Santullano**, or San Julián de los Prados, largest of Spain's pre-Romanesque churches. It lies near the Gijón highway, construction of which damaged its frescoes. Apparently, the Vandals are alive and well.

Even dynamiting during the Asturias

35

uprising could not obliterate Oviedo's **cathedral**, a much-restored Gothic marvel dating from the 14th and 15thC. The west front has three porches, with richly-ornamented doors. Soaring 80 m, the south tower is regarded as one of the most beautiful in Spain. In a side chapel, a baroque shrine contains the remains of Santa Eulalia, patron saint of Asturias. Priceless relics, including a dazzling gold and agate casket dating from 910, are stored in the **Cámara Santa** (Holy Chamber). Part of the chamber was built by Alfonso the Chaste to house pieces of the true cross, fragments of the Holy Shroud, a lock of Mary Magdelene's hair, and a sandal of St Peter. The chamber was destroyed in 1934 but rebuilt. At the entrance, six pilasters depicting the Apostles are masterpieces of 12thC carving. Another remarkable piece of religious art in the cathedral is **El Salvador**, a 12thC polychrome stone carving, before which pilgrims to Santiago would prostrate themselves.

The Plaza del Fontán has a **market** on Thursdays and Sundays and at night the old quarter's *chigres* (bars serving cider) do steady business. As a local guidebook solemnly reminds you: 'The-life in Oviedo is serious and deep, although it is manifested with gaiety and rejoicing.' Two of the most popular *chigres* are El Cantábrico, Río San Pedro, 11, and El Ferroviario, Gascona, 5.

RECOMMENDED HOTELS

BILBAO
Igeretxe, PPP; *Playa Ereaga, s/n, Algorta; tel. 94 460 70 00.*
On the beach 12 km out of the city, an old spa hotel with modern comforts.

FUENTARRIBIA
Obispo, PP; *Plaza del Obispo; tel. 943 64 54 00.*
A bishop's palace dating from the 15thC has been transformed into a comfortable 14-room hotel, preserving the original stonework. It lies next to the town walls.

Parador El Emperador, PPP; *Plaza de Armas; tel. 943 64 21 40.*
If you fancy staying in a stately medieval castle, this is the place. Much of the present structure, on foundations going back 1,000 years, is credited to Charles V.

LLANES
La Posada de Babel, PP;
La Pereda; tel 98 540 25 25.
Surrounded by green lawns and trees with views of distant mountains, this eight-room hotel is an ideal spot to relax and enjoy country walks or cycle rides (bikes provided). The modern, two-storey building is furnished with restored antiques and has under-floor heating. A fire glows in the spacious living room on cool nights. The young owners, Lucas and Blanca, speak excellent English and are particularly proud of the fresh products used in their restaurant, which serves sophisticated dishes at reasonable prices (**PP**; *credit cards* AE, DC, MC, V). Try the venison with wild mushroom sauce. Buffet breakfast is served until 12.30 pm.

OVIEDO
La Gruta, PPP; *Alto de Buenavista, s/n; tel. 98 523 24 50.*
On the edge of the city with views of Mount Naranco. A modern hotel in a complex that includes one of the city's most famed restaurants.

RIBADESELLA
La Playa, PP; *La Playa, 42; tel. 98 586 01 00.*
Creaking polished floors in a 12-room house on the beach with an old world atmosphere.

SAN SEBASTIAN
María Cristina, PPP; *Paseo Republica Argentina, 4; tel. 943 42 49 00.*
For those who like a little style and are ready to pay for it. This stately five-star Belle Epoque hotel is rated one of the best in Europe. Exquisitely furnished and attentive service.

Niza, PP-PPP; *Zubieta, 56; tel. 943 42 66 63.*
Traditional, but renovated, hotel next to the Paseo de la Concha, with splendid views of the bay.

Asturias cider, it should be noted, is poured with the bottle at a great height above the glass. This creates effervescence, though in practice it means that half the cider ends up on the floor.

PICOS DE EUROPA
See Local Explorations: 2

POTES
And other places in the Picos de Auropa, see Local Explorations: 2.

REINOSA
On the N611, 72 km S of Santander. At 851 m, this is a handy centre for making excursions into the highlands on the border of Santander and Palencia

SANTANDER
Central, PP; *General Mola, 5; tel. 942 22 24 00.*
This turn-of-the century hotel with its handsome blue-and-white façade has been stylishly restored and offers value for money in the heart of the city.

Las Brisas, PP; *Travesía de los Castros, 14, El Sardinero; tel. 942 28 11 73.*
Tucked into a corner near El Sardinero beach, this distinctive white building with a square tower was built by an *Indiano* (an emigrant returned from the Americas) early this century. It has a cosy, family atmosphere, with plenty of woodwork and antique furnishing.

SANTILLANA DEL MAR
Altamira, PP; *Cantón, 1; tel. 942 84 01 36.*
This 32-room hotel is housed in a 15thC stone mansion. Simple but comfortable. The restaurant is recommended, in a town where the tourist influence is all too evident from some local eateries' steep prices and the proliferation of *hamburgueserías*.

TORRELAVEGA
Hostería de Quijas, PP; *Ctra Santander-Oviedo, Quijas, Reocín (5 km from Torrelavega, on N623, 26 SW of Santander); tel. 942 82 08 33.*
Ask for a room away from the highway in this beautifully restored 18thC house, set in large gardens. You can dine in style in the restaurant.

VILLANUEVA DE COLOMBRES
La Casona, PP; *off the N634, 22 km E of Llanes; tel. 98 541 25 90.*
Behind a high stone wall stands this fine 18thC mansion, offering bed-and-breakfast in a tranquil rustic village of balconied houses.

VILLAVICIOSA
La Casona de Amandi, PPP; *Amandi, just south of Villaviciosa; tel. 98 589 01 30.*
Roses and hydrangeas bloom around this peaceful country retreat, created with immaculate taste from an old colonial mansion by owners Rodrigo and his wife María.

provinces. Cattle from the parched south are brought here to graze on the upland meadows. Cervatos, just south, has an interesting Romanesque church. The C628 leads west to Tres Mares (Three Seas), a 2,275m peak which spawns three rivers, each flowing into a different sea. The Nansa flows to the Cantabrian Sea, the Pisuerga, tributary of the Duero, to the Atlantic, and the Híjar, joining the Ebro which gushes up from moss-covered rocks amid ash trees and poplars near Fontibre, to the Mediterranean.

At Braña Vieja is the **Alto Campóo** ski resort. If the chairlift is running, take it to the top of Tres Mares for stunning views. The bracing mountain air will give you an appetite for a favourite Santander dish, *cocido montañés*, a rich stew with a chickpea base.

RIBADESELLA 🚾

On the N632, 84 km E of Oviedo. Tourism Office, Marqueses de Argüelles; tel. 98 586 00 38. This small port has numerous establishments serving fresh seafood; also an adjacent villa-lined beach. Both attract many summer visitors.

The big event of the year is the **Descenso Internacional del Sella** on the first Saturday in August, when large quantities of Asturias cider flow. Hundreds of canoeists paddle down the Sella river to the finishing line at Ribadesella, watched by vast crowds including a number travelling by a special train which follows the river valley.

Just outside town, across the bridge, the **Tito Bustillo Cave** is worth visiting for its stalactites and prehistoric paintings. The original entrance was by a 120m-long chimney, but a new entrance has been cut by dynamiting tons of rock. Visitors pass through a series of doors on entering to prevent damaging air currents from rushing through the cave. Enquire at the tourism office as numbers are limted.

SAN SEBASTIAN (DONOSTIA) 🚾 ✕

On the A8, 92 km E of Bilbao. Tourism Offices, Reina Regente, 8; tel. 943 48 11 66 & Paseo Fueros, 1; tel. 943 42 62 82. Few Spanish – or European – cities can match the beauty of San Sebastián's setting, arrayed as it is around the perfect curve of La Concha (The Shell) beach and backed by green hills. It became a fashionable resort in the

19thC after Queen Isabella II visited for health reasons. Soon the royal family established a summer residence in the **Palacio Miramar**, on an outcrop between La Concha and Ondarreta beaches. It is now used for public functions. Europe's aristocracy followed; gracious boulevards and fine hotels and houses were constructed.

Stylish San Sebastián is more expensive than most Spanish resorts – reflecting its elegance and its facilities. You can indulge in everything from horseracing to golf, surfing to *pelota*. There are fine shops and restaurants and a succession of cultural events. The city has three beaches, but the **La Concha** is the one along which the *donostiarras* love to stroll, gossiping, taking the air, jogging, flirting. At one end is the imperious-looking city hall, originally built as a casino. Today's **casino** operates in the luxurious Hotel de Londres.

Eating is the favourite local pastime. Not for nothing has the city a disproportionately large number of top-class restaurants in relation to its population (175,000). Gastronomic clubs, usually all-male, meet regularly to cook and sample typical dishes. Leading restaurateurs insist on serving only fish that has been hooked rather than netted, as this allegedly guarantees fresher flavour.

Next to the fishing port, the dark, narrow streets of the **old quarter** with its peeling walls harbour some 120 *tapa* bars and numerous restaurants. On the bar counters are displayed a vast range of *banderillas* and *pinchitos*, tasty titbits on skewers. Favourite bars include **La Cepa**, on 31 de Agosto, **José Mari** on Fermín Calbetón, and **Tamboril**, Plaza de la Constitución. *Tapa* bar-crawling is about the cheapest way to eat in San Sebastián and in summer you can also order a cheap plate of grilled sardines served outside cafés near the port.

Take a **funicular** up to Monte Igueldo, which has an amusement park, to enjoy the finest views of the city. Looking across the bay, you see Monte Urgull on the other headland, with the remains of a castle and a giant figure of Christ. In summer boats ply to Santa Clara island.

July's **jazz festival** attracts international performers and in September

celebrities arrive for the annual film festival. Stay away in mid-August if you dislike crowds as that is when the monster fiesta **Semana Grande** is held. On the first two Sundays in September thousands flock to the Concha to watch races between *traineras*, rowing craft once used for fishing.

Hiking, rafting, canoeing, and horse-trekking can be enjoyed in the nearby mountains.

SANTANDER ⇌ ×

On the A8 and A67, 105 km W of Bilbao. Tourism Offices, Jardines de Pereda; tel. 942 21 61 20; Plaza de Velarde 5; tel 942 31 07 08. Spread over a peninsula protecting its harbour, this busy port and commercial centre is the capital of the Cantabria region. It is also a tourist resort, rivalling San Sebastián, and in summer has some claim to be Spain's cultural and intellectual capital. Much of Santander was rebuilt following a disastrous fire in 1941, and it has gracious boulevards and gardens. If it does not have the instant appeal and charisma of some Spanish towns, this no doubt reflects the character of the *santanderinos*, who are notoriously conservative.

Towards the end of the 19thC fashionable villas appeared along **El Sardinero**, a fine stretch of sand with three beaches, a trend which gained momentum when the city gave **La Magdalena**

• *Sand, sea and sky, El Sardinero.*

Peninsula, at one end of the Sardinero, to King Alfonso XIII and Queen Victoria Eugenia, a great-granddaughter of Queen Victoria. She had an English-style mansion built there. Every summer the **Magdalena Palace**, now the summer seat of the Menéndez Pelayo International University, welcomes students and distinguished academics from around the world.

The city is chock-a-block in season, when it hosts an international piano competition and a classical music and dance festival. Foreign and Spanish visitors are elbow to elbow on the city beaches. But there are 13 beaches at hand so you can escape to less crowded ones, such as **Somo** across the bay, by ferry or other transport.

After the 1941 fire the **cathedral** had to be largely rebuilt. Beneath it is a **12thC church**, under the floor of which have been found extensive Roman remains. The heads of the Roman soldiers Emeterio and Celedonio, martyred around 300 AD and the subject of much veneration and pilgrimages in the Middle Ages, are kept in silver caskets. The cathedral shelters the tomb of Marcelino Menéndez y Pelayo, the Spanish philosopher, whose library on Rubio is open mornings. He left nearly 45,000 books to the city.

By night Santander offers a vast range of *tapa* bars and restaurants. On Vargas, try the bars **La Solera** and **El Rey de la Raba**. A short distance from where the ferries from Plymouth dock are narrow streets throbbing with life. More than 30 establishments jostle for business in the Río de la Pila. At El Solórzano on Peña Herbosa you can swig vermouth from the barrel and enjoy a variety of shellfish. **La Conveniente** is an old wine cellar on Gómez Oreña where a piano tinkles away while you sample black pudding or cheese. For a more relaxed and elegant atmosphere amid polished brass and marble-topped tables, try the **Café de Pombo** on the Plaza José Antonio.

SANTILLANA DEL MAR ⌂

On the C3616, 30 km W of Santander. Tourists threaten to swamp this amaz-

ingly well-preserved medieval village. But it returns to its bucolic self in the evenings when most board buses and depart. If you stay overnight (a parador is located in the 15thC residence of the Barreda-Bracho family), you have time to absorb the atmosphere as you wander the cobbled streets, lined with noble, balconied stone houses, each with its coat-of-arms.

You may be disappointed when you penetrate the **Calle de las Lindas** (the Street of Beautiful Women), but not with the austere dignity of the dwellings. Castilian nobility built their mansions in Santillana (despite the name it is set well back from the sea) and a proud, swashbuckling lot they were. The Casa de Bustamentes bears the motto: 'The Bustamentes marry their daughters to kings' and a crest on a house in Santo Domingo Street declares: 'A glorious

RECOMMENDED RESTAURANTS

BILBAO

Bermeo, PPP; E*rcilla*, 37; *tel.* 94 470 57 00; AE, DC, MC, V; *closed Sat lunch and Sun eve.*

Located in the four-star Ercilla Hotel, the Bermeo is among the city's best, offering innovative dishes with an emphasis on game and on seasonal produce. A suggestion: veal stuffed with goose liver, with Biscay sauce.

Víctor, PP-PPP; P*laza* N*ueva*, 2; *tel.* 94 415 16 78; *credit cards* AE, DC, MC, V; *closed Sun and Jul 25-Sep12, except Semana Grande.*

You can take an aperitif at a table on the harmonious square with its wrought-iron balustrades before moving inside to try the traditional dishes which are the speciality of this long-established place.

CASTRO URDIALES

Mesón El Marinero, PP-PP; L*a* C*orrería*, 23; *tel.* 942 86 00 05; *credit cards* AE, DC, MC, V.

Three lifebelts hanging outside give an appropriately nautical air to this restaurant overlooking the port. Excellent seafood and an interesting range of wines. The bar offers a variety of *tapas* as does the Marisquería Alfredo next door.

GETARIA

Elkano, PP; H*errerieta*, 2; *tel.* 943 14 06 14; *credit cards* AE, DC, MC, V; *closed* N*ov.*

You are spoiled for choice in this fishing village. At the Elkano Pedro Arregui maintains a firm quality control on such excellent seafood dishes as grilled turbot and stuffed hake cheeks. In summer you can eat on the terrace.

OVIEDO

El Raitán y El Chigre, PP; P*laza* T*rascorrales*, 6; *tel.* 98 521 42 18; *credit cards* AE, MC, V; *closed* M*on.*

Just around the corner from the city hall, this restaurant is decorated in rustic style with heavy beams and drying corncobs. It specializes in regional dishes such as *fabada*, a mighty stew of beans, pork, and beef, and you could do worse than try the mighty set meal, the *menú asturiano.*

SAN SEBASTIAN

Akelarre, PPP; P*aseo del* P*adre* O*rcolaga*, 56; *tel.* 943 21 20 52; *credit cards* AE, DC, MC, V; *closed* S*un eve*, M*on, first fortnight* J*un*, D*ec.*

This restaurant, regarded as one of Spain's best, is located in a low, modern building outside the city on the Monte Igueldo coast road. Large picture windows in the wood-panelled dining room give beautiful sea views as you tuck into chef Pedro Subijana's death crowns life with honour.' Two giant knights bear the coat of arms of the Villas dynasty, explaining the popular name of their residence, Casa de los Hombrones (Big Men's House).

Traffic is banned within the village by day. The focal point is the **Colegiata**, the 12thC Romanesque church which holds the remains of Santa Juliana (from which the name Santillana derives). She suffered a sticky end in the 4thC. The cloister is supported by twin columns, topped by elaborately-carved capitals.

SAN VICENTE DE LA BARQUERA 🛏

On the N634, 58 km W of Santander. Tourism Office, Avenida Generalísimo, 20; tel. 942 71 07 97.
San Vicente is a pleasant fishing port and holiday resort on an estuary crossed by a 28-arch bridge. Clams, cockles and shrimps are harvested from the sand flats and many bars and restaurants serve fresh seafood.

TORRELAVEGA 🛏

See Recommended Hotels, page 37.

VILLANUEVA DE COLOMBRES 🛏

See Recommended Hotels, page 37.

VILLAVICIOSA 🛏

See Recommended Hotels, page 37.

ZARAUTZ ✕

On the N634, 21 km E of San Sebastián.
A fashionable and popular summer resort, the town of Zarautz has nothing special to recommend it except its long, sandy beach, which attracts surfers. The tourism office (Nafarroa, 26; tel. 943 83 09 90) has information about walks into the mountains and about the **Agorregi Park**, a short distance inland.

---

imaginative creations. Try the special menu to gain an idea of his *nueva coci-na* or maybe go for the *pato salvaje preparado en dos formas* (wild duck prepared in two styles) followed by one of his puff pastries.

Arzak, PPP; *Alto de Miracruz, 21; tel. 943 27 84 65; credit cards* AE, DC, MC, V; *closed Sun eve, Mon, two weeks in Jun, Nov.*

Awarded three stars by Michelin, this restaurant has a low-key exterior and is easy to miss on the busy road out of the city towards Rentería. However, it has been dubbed the Gourmets' Palace for the quality of the *nueva cocina vasca*, pioneered by its owner and chef Juan Mari Arzak who has influenced cooking all over Spain. Some of the dishes which may tempt your taste-buds are *chipirones de anzuelo en su tinta* (squid cooked in their own ink), *ragú de pato con fram-buesa, naranja y piñones* (duck ragout with raspberries, orange and pine nuts), and delicious desserts such as *higos frescos con crema de grosella y moras* (fresh figs with redcurrant and blackberry cream).

Alderdi Zahar, PP; *Fermín Calbetón, 9; credit cards* MC, V; *closed Sun, Mon.*

A typical good-value restaurant in the old quarter, with basic decoration and excellent local dishes such as fish soup and *merluza a la vasca* (hake Basque-style).

SANTANDER
Bodega Cigaleña, PP; *Daoíz y Velarde, 19; tel. 942 21 30 62; credit cards* AE, DC, MC, V; *closed Sun, Oct 20-Nov 20.*

Rare bottles of wine are on display in this typical *tapa* bar and restaurant, which has an excellent range of wines. Roast lamb, cured ham, and fresh fish.

Bodega del Riojano, PP; *Río de la Pila, 5; tel. 942 21 67 50; credit cards* AE, DC, MC, V; *closed Sun eve, Mon.*

Barrels painted by well-known artists adorn the walls in this old wine cellar. Specialities from the Rioja region. Recommended: stew of venison macerated in wine.

ZARAUTZ
Karlos Arguiñano, PPP; *Mendilauta, 13; tel. 943 13 00 00; credit cards* AE, DC, MC, V; *closed Wed & Sun eve.*

Karlos is a national figure thanks to his culinary programmes on television. Worth trying in his restaurant overlooking the beach are fish soup and *solomillo de buey relleno* (stuffed sirloin). He runs a luxury 12-room hotel in the same three-storey stone building, adorned with a crenellated tower.

North-Central Spain

Between Santander and Madrid
Old Castile, Burgos and Valladolid

480 km; map Michelin 442, 1:400,000

C astile is the land of knights and castles and groaning platters of roast lamb and suckling pig, the land of El Cid, of burning plains and Gothic splendours. As the Cantabrian mountains peter out, the plateau begins. Winters are harsh and the summers searingly hot, the anvil on which Spain hammered out its destiny in the Middle Ages.

The fusion of the kingdoms of Asturias, Galicia, and León with that of Castile formed a powerful new kingdom, known as Castile, which – linked with Aragón – would end up ejecting the Moors and creating the Spanish nation. Power was centred in Castile as wealth poured in from foreign conquests and trade. Fortunes were amassed during the period of the Mesta, a privileged sheep farmers' association, but the sheep ravaged the land and orderly agricultural development was stifled. Spain's decline came soon enough, as its unsoundly-based economy ran into trouble.

Today's autonomous region of Castilla-León embraces nine provinces but only 2.5 million people. Many of the old communities have been virtually abandoned as new industries attract youngsters to the towns, but nobody can fail to be impressed by the rich heritage of art and architectural treasures. Nor can one easily forget the gargantuan meals. Castile's food is strong stuff, consisting of belly-filling stews and roast meat, and a range of cheeses from the creamy to the chewily mature. Across the region flows the Duero river (the Douro when it enters Portugal), along whose banks are produced some of Spain's finest wines.

Four-lane highways link the main cities, the N620 running between Burgos and Valladolid, and the NV1 and A6 between Valladolid and Madrid. Once south of the green heights of Cantabria, there are few mountain ranges to slow your pace. Burgos and Valladolid offer some of the richest treasures (the glories of León, Salamanca, and Avila are described in Spain Overall: 4). You could pass through the region in a couple of days if you stopped just at the red centres. However, don't overlook the many villages, such as those on the Pilgrim's Way to Santiago, with surprisingly well-preserved splendours. And to wander around the scores of castles (Castile, after all, means 'land of castles') could take you weeks rather than days.

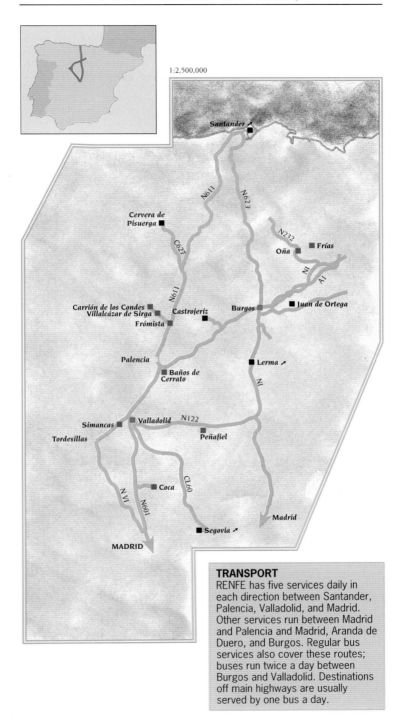

1:2,500,000

TRANSPORT

RENFE has five services daily in each direction between Santander, Palencia, Valladolid, and Madrid. Other services run between Madrid and Palencia and Madrid, Aranda de Duero, and Burgos. Regular bus services also cover these routes; buses run twice a day between Burgos and Valladolid. Destinations off main highways are usually served by one bus a day.

SIGHTS & PLACES OF INTEREST

BAÑOS DE CERRATO
See *Palencia, page 46.*

BURGOS ⋈ ×
On the N1, 151 km S of Santander, 240 km N of Madrid. Tourism Office, Plaza Alonso Martínez, 7; tel. 947 20 31 25. As you approach Burgos across the Castilian plain, the soaring twin spires of the cathedral, a Gothic wonder ranking among Europe's most remarkable religious structures, present a stirring sight.

Seven hundred metres above sea level, commanding the northern plains, just south of the mountains of the Cordillera Cantábrica, Burgos has occupied a strategic position in Spanish history since early times. A defensive bastion was established in the shallow Arlanzón River valley in 884 and eventually, under Ferdinand I, Burgos became capital of a kingdom uniting Castile, Asturias and León.

Rodrigo Diaz, known as **El Cid**, the Champion of Castile, was born in Vivar, just outside the city, in the 11thC. These were tumultuous times: Moorish and Christian warlords struggled for supremacy over pieces of the peninsula. By all accounts, El Cid was a ruthless soldier of fortune who fought on whichever side appeared to offer the greatest return at a particular moment. But legend, the centuries, and Hollywood have transformed him into a heroic figure, enshrined in Spain's first epic poem, *El Cantar del Mío Cid* and – more recently – personified by Charlton Heston in the film *El Cid*.

From 1492 Valladolid took over from Burgos as capital, but Burgos's richness in monuments reflects its flourishing economy as trade with northern Europe increased. The huge flocks of the Mesta (the sheep farmers' league) grazed on the plains of Castile and

---

RECOMMENDED HOTELS

BURGOS
España, PP; *Paseo del Espolón, 32; tel.* 947 20 63 40.

A two-star hotel in the centre, on the Espolón promenade.

Mesón del Cid, PPP; *Plaza Santa María, 8; tel.* 947 20 59 71.

Modern, comfortable rooms, whimsically named after historic characters, right opposite the cathedral.

Landa Palace, PPP; *Ctra Madrid-Irún, km 235; tel.* 947 20 63 43.

If you are in the mood for something really over-the-top and you have cash to burn, this is the place. Gothic fantasy rules in a luxury hotel in a reconstructed medieval tower outside Burgos. Antiques, attention to detail, and attentive service set it apart.

CERVERA DE PISUERGA
Parador Fuentes Carrionas, PP; *Cervera is on the C627, 117 km N of Palencia; the parador is at Crta Resoba, km 2.5; tel.* 979 87 00 75.

In the far north of Palencia province, *en route* to the Picos de Europa, this modern parador is in a beautiful mountain region, great for hunters or hikers. Some of the few remaining bears inhabit the woods. The restaurant serves fresh trout and game in season.

PALENCIA
Los Jardinillos, PP; *Eduardo Dato, 2; tel.* 979 75 00 22.

Near the Post Office and railway station, this modern hotel offers comfort and value.

TORDESILLAS
Parador, PP; *Ctra Salamanca, Suroeste: 2 km; tel.* 983 77 00 51.

A one-storey building in a peaceful pine grove; swimming-pool.

VALLADOLID
Felipe IV, PPP; *Gamazo, 16; tel.* 983 30 70 00.

Behind the glass-and-marble façade lies a recently-renovated four-star hotel with appropriate amenities.

Feria, PP; *Avda Ramón Pradera; tel.* 983 33 32 44.

Across the Pisuerga River near the exhibition grounds, but handy enough for the centre. Adequate facilities, including parking.

León, their wool so valued that no Merino sheep could be taken out of Spain under pain of death. Accorded special privileges, members of the Mesta ran their sheep where they pleased, dealing out their own justice to anybody opposing them. As Spanish wool went north, architects and magnificent talents such as Flemish sculptor Gil de Siloé came south to fulfil commissions from Spaniards enriched by the wool-wealth.

The cosmopolitan dynamism of those years is most evident in the **cathedral**, flamboyantly melding Spanish and northern styles. It was founded in 1221, but work continued for 300 years. El Cid lies buried under a marble slab below the ornate, 54m-high cupola in the transept. It is not diplomatic, by the way, to remind your Burgos guide that some historians question whether he really existed. He or she will surely point out the actual letter in which El Cid promised to bestow certain treasures on his wife-to-be, Ximena. Other curiosities include **Papamoscas**, a clock which features a mouth opening and closing as though catching a fly on the striking of the hours, and in a side chapel an **image of Christ** said to have been brought from the Holy Land where it was modelled directly from the dead Saviour. This grotesque creation of animal hide and human hair is highly venerated. A magnificent golden **Renaissance double staircase**, designed by Diego de Siloé, leads to the **Puerta Alta de la Coronería**, but most striking of all is the **Capilla del Condestable** (Constable's Chapel). Hans of Cologne and his son Simon designed this sumptuous chamber, dating from 1482, and leading sculptors decorated it. In the centre, beneath an octagonal dome, repose the marble figures of the Constable Hernández de Velasco and his wife Doña Mencia on their tombs. In the little sacristy off the chapel, a guardian dramatically swings open a door to reveal a painting attributed to Da Vinci.

On the edge of the city stands the **Monasterio de Las Huelgas**, a mixture of Romanesque and Gothic architecture with Mudéjar flourishes – not at all your everyday monastic retreat. Originally a royal summer residence (*huelgas*: leisures, recreations), it was converted into a Cistercian convent to house nuns of noble birth. Among the tombs of royalty and their scions in the church are those of the founders Alfonso VIII of Castile and his wife, Eleanor of England. A revolving pulpit is an unusual feature. In the chapterhouse, where hang portraits of monarchs and abbesses, General Franco's government met for the first time. A **museum** opened by King Juan Carlos in 1988 displays a unique collection of 13thC high fashion, the clothes of the Infante Fernando de la Cerda.

There are more royal bodies in the **Cartuja** (Carthusian monastery) **de Miraflores**, 4 km east of Burgos. The **church,** divided into separate sections for public, lay brethren and monks, was designed by Hans of Cologne and his son Simon. Gil de Siloé was responsible for the elaborate, star-shaped **mausoleum of Juan II and Isabel of Portugal**, and he and Diego de la Cruz devoted several years of their lives to creating the dazzling **altarpiece** in polychrome wood. Some of the first gold brought from America is said to have been employed in the gilding.

The church's colour and splendour contrast with the sombre lives of the 35 resident monks, who wear hair shirts, are allowed to hold conversation only once a week, and must endure the bitter Castilian winters without any heating.

Ugly new buildings have sprung up in tranquil Burgos among the fine old ones, but it is pleasant to stroll the streets and the riverside **Paseo del Espolón**. Cassocked priests flit along alleyways and, as throughout its history, the military are in evidence. On the military headquarters a plaque commemorates **General Mola**, who lived there during the Civil War when leading the 'glorious Nationalist movement' (considered a rival to Franco, he died in a mysterious air crash).

A good *tapa* bar in the old quarter, just around the corner from the **Ayuntamiento** (City Hall) at Calle Sombrería, 8, is the **Mesón Burgos**, with typical Castilian decoration of tiles and beams. Cider, *patatas bravas* (peppery baked potatoes), and shrimps are on offer. Puebla and Calzadas streets, with pubs and music bars, become animated in the evening. More traditional is the **Café España** on Lain Calvo. This 70-year-old café has a marble-topped bar with a brass footrail, old photos on the walls, papers to read, and occasional jazz entertainment.

CARRION DE LOS CONDES

On the C615, 40 km N of Palencia. Set among the monotonous cereal-growing plains known as Tierra de Campos, Carrión, a way-station for pilgrims on the Camino (Pilgrim's Way) de Santiago, has two **churches** of note and the 11thC (later rebuilt) Benedictine **Monasterio de San Zoilo**. Note the detailed carvings of figures at work on the Santiago Church portal. El Cid sent his knights to wreak vengeance on the counts of Carrión after they married his daughters for their dowries, then beat and abandoned them. In good Christian style, the treacherous nobles were put to the sword.

CASTROJERIZ ✕

See Recommended Restaurants, page 49.

CERVERA DE PISUERGA ⊨

See Recommended Hotels, page 44.

COCA

On the SG351, 22 km W of the N601, 54 km NE of Segovia. As you approach Coca, the sight of delicate, pinkish turrets above the pinewoods may convince you that you have strayed into Disneyland. Coca's **castle** is just too pretty for words. The influential Fonseca family had it built by Moorish craftsmen in the 15thC and its Mudéjar battlements and towers are a breathtaking sight, but you have the feeling El Cid could have conquered it before breakfast.

FRIAS

See Oña, this page.

FROMISTA ✕

On the N611, 32 km N of Palencia. Four refuges used to offer shelter to pilgrims here, one of which is now a restaurant. A considerable Jewish community once resided here, and traces remain of a **synagogue**. But *the* sight is the **Church of San Martín**, all that remains of a Benedictine monastery. Built in 1066, it is hailed as the perfect culmination of Romanesque architecture. The harmonious lines, the proportions and the delicately carved stone-work of the three-nave edifice delight the eye.

LERMA

And other places south and south-east of Burgos — see Local Explorations: 3.

OÑA

On the BU510, 73 km NE of Burgos. A three-decked main square is the focal point of this old town amid the rocky grandeur of the Oca river gorge. Eight counts and kings are buried in the **church of San Salvador**, which has a memorable cloister. The Black Prince, with Pedro the Cruel, sacked Oña in 1367.

Frías, to the north-east, reached via La Aldea del Portillo de Busto, is dramatically sited on a rocky spur surmounted by a castle, with a restored Roman bridge crossing the Ebro below.

PALENCIA ⊨ ✕

Off the N620, 86 km SW of Burgos. Palencia is a pleasant, unhurried market town which would be an ideal location for somebody bent on studying provincial life or those just eager to escape from fellow tourists. Others may just find it dull. Palencia's elongated province embraces peaks rising higher than 2,000 m in the north, the cereal plains of Tierra de Campos, and the irrigated lands of the south.

Alfonso VIII established Spain's first **university** in Palencia in the early 13thC. The **cathedral**, dubbed La Bella Desconocida (the unknown beauty), stands over a **Romanesque chapel**, which was erected on top of a 7thC Visigoth chapel. The ruined chapel is said to have been discovered by a king of Navarre while out hunting wild boar.

Outstanding 16thC features of the cathedral include an altarpiece carved by Philippe de Vigarni and sculptures by Gil de Siloé and Simon of Cologne. Four Flemish tapestries and an El Greco can be seen in the cathedral museum.

You will be lucky to find much night-life in Palencia, but it does have an outstanding *tapa* bar. **La Tia Piedad**, Antonio Maura, 11, has an agreeable atmosphere, wine from the barrel, and some very tasty snacks. Try a plateful of sizzling mushrooms and shrimps.

Fourteen kilometres to the south of Palencia stands the **Basilica de San Juan Bautista**, reputedly Spain's oldest church in use. Turn off the N620 to Venta de Baños, then look for signs to **Baños de Cerrato**. The small church may be locked, but Patricio, the keeper, will appear with a key. Apparently the Visigoth king Recesvinto built the sanctuary after visiting the baths (long disappeared) in 661. Eight arches supported by marble and jasper columns (some of Roman origin) divide the church into three aisles. Note the windows, delicately carved from single pieces of stone. Many weddings are celebrated here and a mass is held on June 24, when St John the Baptist's image is carried in procession from the parish church.

PEÑAFIEL

On *the* N122, 56 *km* E *of* Valladolid. Like a white ship breasting the blue heavens, **Peñafiel Castle** sails arrogantly above the Duero. One of the most impressive in Spain, it was built in the 15thC on ruins of an earlier fortification. The narrow, 210m-long structure commands seven valleys. You can climb to the top of its keep to enjoy the view, but the castle itself is empty. On the hillside below notice the strange chimneys protruding from the earth. These are ventilation shafts for wine cellars, burrowed below.

The enormous main plaza, with its wooden-balconied houses, is the scene of bullfights. During the **Sant Roque fiesta**, August 14-17, a bull-run takes place ending in the plaza.

SAN JUAN DE ORTEGA

N *of the* N120, 20 *km* E *of* Burgos. In undulating fields of cereals, this Romanesque church has an unusual feature known as the Miracle of the Light. Twice a year, at the March 21 and September 22 equinoxes, the sun angles through a high window to strike the carving on one of the columns' capitals. Briefly and dramatically, it illumines the carvings, first illuminating the Annunciation scene, then Christ's birth, then the arrival of the Three Kings.

Look out for Calixto, a white, black-spotted dog, which welcomes pilgrims to the adjacent hospice and likes to see them safely on their way as far as the outskirts of Burgos.

On the way to Burgos lies the hamlet of **Atapuerca,** the scene of a battle in 1057 in which Fernando I of Castile killed his brother, García of Navarre.

Spanish archaeologists, aided by British academics, have been examining the remains of more than 20 humans, found in a deep shaft in the Sierra de Atapuerca. They believe that they date back 350,000 years, making this the oldest graveyard known to man.

SANTANDER
See Spain Overall: 1.

SEGOVIA
See Local Explorations: 8.

SIMANCAS

On *the* N620, 11 *km* SW *of* Valladolid. Simancas's **castle** is the sort of place which either makes you groan in despair or tremble with anticipation, depending on your interests. Emperor Charles V established the national archives here and paper and parchment have been accumulating ever since. Never has so much red tape been stored in one place. More than eight million – it says here, but who is actually counting? – state documents are available for researchers to delve into (closed November to February).

TORDESILLAS 🏨

On *the* NVI, 28 *km* SW *of* Valladolid. This historic town on the banks of the Duero was where in 1494 Spain and Portugal carved up the New World. With Pope Alexander VI, one of the Borgias of Valencia, arbitrating, it was agreed that all territory west of a line 370 leagues west of the Cape Verde Islands should belong to Spain, thus granting Spain all Latin America except Brazil.

If you can't get to Seville or Granada, Tordesilla's **Convento de Santa Clara** will indicate a little of what you are missing. A Mudéjar-style palace was built by Alfonso XI in the 14thC. His son Peter the Cruel (a title for which there seems to have been abundant competition, although Pedro did eliminate a surprising number of friends, relations, and rivals) converted it into a convent, where he installed daughters by his mistress María de Padilla. Visitors are taken on guided tours (free on Wednesdays for EC citizens). You won't see the 13 *monjas de clausura* (nuns of an enclosed order), but the monastery has several gems, including a small Moorish patio, the **Capilla Dorada**, and the church cupola's magnificent gilded coffered ceiling. In 1991 further examples of Arab-style architecture were discovered during restoration work.

The clavichord of tragic Juana la Loca (the Mad) is on view. Juana, daughter of Isabel the Catholic, inherited the Spanish throne but was incapable of ruling. Besotted with her unfaithful husband, the Hapsburg Philip (the Fair), she could not accept his death in 1506. When a Carthusian monk advised her that he could be resuscitated by sufficient prayer, she wandered the country with Philip's body, allegedly opening the coffin several times to check on progress. He was finally buried at Tordesillas, though later transferred to the royal chapel in Granada. Juana stayed on at Tordesillas, passing 46 years in seclusion. Even now it is not clear if the queen really was insane, but her son, the Emperor Charles V (Charles I of Spain), ordered her to be kept under house-arrest. Juana was not exactly alone, however, being attended by more than 150 persons, among them a clutch of nobles, 6 butlers, 14 chaplains, and a partridge-hunter.

Animal-lovers should steer clear of Tordesilla in September when a barbaric medieval ritual known as **El Toro de la Vega** takes place. A bull is released for sporting types armed with lances to chase it over the countryside.

VALLADOLID 🛏 ✕

On the N601 & N620, 193 km NW of Madrid. Tourism Office, Plaza Zorilla, 3; tel. 983 35 18 01. Capital of the Castilla-León region, Valladolid is a solid, conservative industrial city of more than 300,000 inhabitants. The unsightly approaches and the mind-spinning traffic congestion in the centre may persuade you to keep driving, out of town. If you arrive by bus or train and are whisked straight to your hotel by taxi, however, you may take a more positive view of the place. Certainly, Valladolid is bulging with artistic treasures and has some impressive architecture, the fruit of its years as the residence of kings and as the capital of Spain. Ferdinand was crowned king of Castile and married Isabel here; Columbus died here (a museum stands on the spot where he breathed his last in 1506); and Philip II was born here, which did not deter him from transferring the court to Madrid in 1560.

If you have little time to spend in Valladolid (known less than affectionately by leftwingers as Fachadolid, referring to its past allegiance to the Fascist cause), there is one building you should not miss. The San Gregorio College houses the **Museo Nacional de Escultur Religiosa**, a remarkable collection of religious carvings. Founded by Alonso of

Burgos, confessor to Queen Isabel, the college is one of the finest examples of the exuberant Isabeline architecture which preceded the Plateresque style. As you will see from the overpowering entrance, this embodies delicate traceries, heraldic motifs, and all sorts of fantasy elements. The two-level patio uses decoration laid on top of decoration to create a woven effect on its columns, balustrades and arches.

Complete sets of choir stalls, altar pieces, and processional floats are among the exhibits. Outstanding works include a realistic depiction of St. Paul's decapitated head, Alonso Berruguete's *Magdalene*, Gregorio Fernández's *Recumbent Christ*, and *Christ's Burial*, a masterpiece by the French-born sculptor Juan de Juni.

Juni was also responsible for the lifelike figures in the retable in Valladolid **cathedral**. Philip II commissioned Juan de Herrera to start designing this sober structure as soon as he had completed another little task entrusted to him, the construction of the monstrous Escorial palace-monastery. The cathedral was never completed as Herrera envisaged and Churriguera added some Baroque flourishes which would surely have scandalized the original architect.

Other architectural splendours worthy of attention include the Plateresque façade of **Collegio de Santa Cruz**, founded in 1479, the **church of San Pablo**, with its façade by Simon de Cologne, where Philip II was baptized, and the **University**, founded in 1346. **Casa de Cervantes** (a house where Cervantes lived) is open to the public and the **Museo Arqueológico** has interesting Iron Age relics.

Several centuries back, Pinheiro da Vega, a Portuguese visitor to Valladolid, reported: 'The lamb is quite simply the best in the world... Of everything I ate there, I cannot remember ever having anything better or cheaper.' It is a recommendation still worth following up in the many restaurants serving typical Castilian roasts, which go well with the Duero red and *rosado* wines. If you are bent on a *tapa* crawl, there is plenty to choose from in the area near the Plaza Mayor, particularly along Correo.

VILLALCAZAR DE SIRGA

On the P980, 13 km W of Frómista on N611. Amid the hedgeless fields of cereals, this hamlet is almost crushed by the massive grandeur of the **church of Santa María la Blanca**. It has a fine southern façade and contains the ornately-carved tombs of a brother of Alfonso X and his wife.

Villalcázar sheltered a hospital and hostel for Santiago pilgrims and it continues to offer pilgrims free lodging in a dormitory.

This is a favourite spot for *excursion-istas*, who love to eat and be entertained in the Mesón de Villasirga, a rustic restaurant (**PP**; *Plaza Mayor; tel. 979 88 80 22; only open weekends in winter*). It is run by Pablo Payo and family, usually attired in pilgrim gear and likely to burst into appropriate song; the food, typically roast suckling pig, is pretty good too. But weekends can be very crowded. A special menu is offered to threadbare pilgrims.

RECOMMENDED RESTAURANTS

BURGOS
Mesón del Cid, PP; *Plaza Santa María, 8; tel. 947 20 59 71; credit cards* AE, DC, MC, V; *closed Sun eve.*

This 15thC house breathes Castilian tradition and the dishes are appropriately traditional too, with an interesting selection of Rioja and Duero wines. Ask to try the *Tropiezas de Don Diego*, a delicious mixture of such dishes as stuffed peppers. (Don Diego was the son of El Cid).

Casa Ojeda, PP; *Vitoria, 5; tel. 947 20 90 52; credit cards* AE, DC, MC, V; *closed Sun eve.*

A wood oven, wood-panelled ceiling, and professional service are features of this restaurant, founded in 1912. Traditional and modern dishes. Try venison cooked in wine, or *Pichón estofado al estilo de la abuela* (pigeon stew the way grandmother cooked it).

CASTROJERIZ
El Mesón, P; *Cordón, 1; tel. 947 37 74 00; credit cards* AE, V.

Home cooking in an old mill. Ask if they have *olla podrida* (literally rotten pot), a rich stew of beans, pork sausages, and chicken. Seven simply-furnished bedrooms are available if you wish to stay the night in this key village on the Camino de Santiago, with its castle and collegiate church.

FROMISTA
Hostería de Los Palmeros, PP; *Plaza San Telmo, 4; tel. 979 81 00 67; credit cards* MC, V; *closed Tues except in summer.*

Old beams, antique furniture and paintings help create a pleasant atmosphere in this restored pilgrims'

hospice. Creaking stairs lead up to the first-floor dining room. Traditional Castilian dishes.

PALENCIA
Casa Lucio, PP; *Don Sancho, 2; tel. 979 74 81 90; credit cards* AE, MC, V; *closed Sun & Sept 15-Oct 1.*

A wood oven catches the eye in the brickwork bar where business types linger over morning coffee. A low curved ceiling and chintzy curtains lend an intimate atmosphere to the restaurant. Roast suckling pig and other traditional dishes are the speciality.

VALLADOLID
La Parrilla de San Lorenzo, PP; *Pedro Niño, 1; tel. 983 33 50 88; credit cards* AE, DC, MC, V.

You pass through the bar and the wood-fired oven to reach the restaurant, which is actually within the medieval Real Monasterio de Monjas Recoletas. The monastery has existed here since 1596. Vaulted stone ceilings, oil paintings and polychrome sculptures reinforce ambience. As good a place as any to try *cordero asado* (roast lamb).

Santi, PP; *Correo, 1; tel. 983 33 93 55; credit cards* AE, DC, MC, V; *closed Sun & Aug.*

Housed in a 16thC mansion which was previously an inn, this restaurant reeks of Old Castile. At the rear is the Taberna Caballo de Troya tavern, with a large stone fireplace and massive beams, a pleasant spot to enjoy *tapas*. Sara prepares a special example of home cooking according to the day of the week. On Thursday it is bull's tail with potatoes, on Friday *potaje*, a hearty stew.

Between Oviedo and Vigo
Galicia

480 km; map Michelin 441, 1:400,000

With its green hills, ancient myths, tormented coastline and poetic, melancholy people, Galicia, in the north-western corner of Spain, was for long a land apart, isolated by mountain ranges and poor communications (the last now being rectified). And so it remains in some ways, more like Brittany or indeed Wales than the rest of Spain. Celtic, rather than Latin, influences prevail; history and legend interweave. *Meigas* (witches) are part of rural folklore.

Everything, from fences to weathered churches, even the features of women scything hay or guarding their cows on country lanes, seems to be carved from granite. Wooden-wheeled carts lumber along narrow lanes. Everywhere you will see *hórreos*, grain stores raised on stilts.

Galicians, or *gallegos*, speak their own tongue, similar to Portuguese. They have a reputation for conservatism and shrewdness: if you meet one on a staircase, goes the old joke, you can never tell whether he is going up or coming down. Certainly, there is a tendency to give nothing away. If you ask a question, the reply is often another question. Franco was born in Galicia and its contemporary political leader, Manuel Fraga Iribarne, also fits the stereotype.

Galician women, renowned for their independence, have traditionally worked the land while the men were away, earning money abroad or crewing fishing boats. Poverty has forced many to emigrate, to the point where Buenos Aires has been called Galicia's fifth province.

Romerias, pilgrimages to shrines, are important fiestas, where you will surely hear the wail of the *gaita* (the Galician bagpipe) and taste octopus, consumed in vast quantities, or *caldo gallego*, a nourishing soup. Seafood is a speciality and so are *empanadas* (meat- or fish-filled pastries). Galicia produces two excellent white wines, Albariño and Ribeiro.

My route (diversions apart) follows the Asturias coast before entering Galicia. Allow at least three days if you're covering it in full. It has been designed to dovetail neatly with Local Explorations: 4 and 5, which complete the guide's coverage of Galicia.

Two Spanish words crop up repeatedly in this section: *rías* are drowned river valleys, similar to the firths of Scotland or fjords of Norway; and *pazo* meaning a palace or mansion.

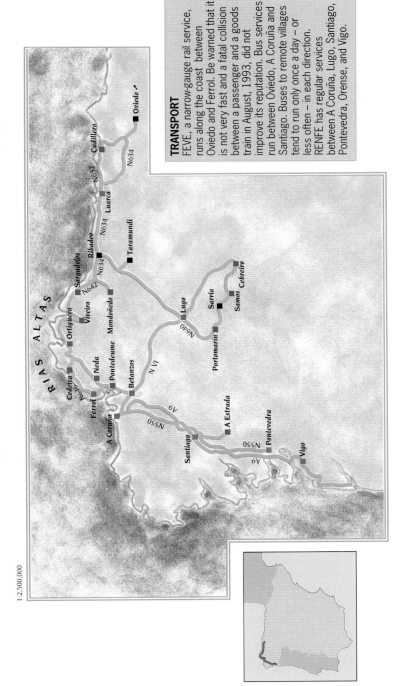

TRANSPORT

FEVE, a narrow-gauge rail service, runs along the coast between Oviedo and Ferrol. Be warned that it is not very fast and a fatal collision between a passenger and a goods train in August, 1993, did not improve its reputation. Bus services run between Oviedo, A Coruña and Santiago. Buses to remote villages tend to run only once a day – or less often – in each direction. RENFE has regular services between A Coruña, Lugo, Santiago, Pontevedra, Orense, and Vigo.

1:2,500,000

SIGHTS & PLACES OF INTEREST

BETANZOS

On NVI, 23 km SW of A Coruña. Betanzos is an attractive old town overlooking a curve in its ría, where sea-going vessels used to tie up until silt closed the port. The Romans had a settlement here called Brigantium Flavium; a number of buildings testify to Betanzos's prosperity in the Middle Ages. Narrow streets, lined by houses with enclosed balconies, lead to the top of the town, where you can inspect the twin-steepled Gothic **church of Santa María**. Dedicated to St James, this is a 'Santiago church', with carvings of Saint-Iago himself on horseback dealing out death to the Moors. It was financed by the tailors' guild. Also at the top of the town is the **Ayuntamiento**, built by Ventura Rodríguez, an 18thC architect with a remarkable workload to judge by the number of edifices all over Spain bearing his stamp.

Just north of Betanzos, on the N651, is **Pontedeume**, another picturesque town, with porticoed streets wandering up a hillside, a square keep near the river, and a long, long bridge across the Eume river. The Counts of Andrade once held sway here and the marble tomb of Fernando de Andrade, hero of the 16thC Italian wars, can be seen in Santiago church.

CEBREIRO

Also Samos, Portomarrín and Sarría, see Detour – Lugo, page 56.

CORUÑA, A (LA CORUÑA) ⌘ ✕

On the NVI and A9, 95 km from Lugo, 69 km from Santiago. Tourist Office, Dársena de la Marina, s/n; tel. 981 22 18 22. In marked contrast to rural Galicia, A Coruña is a bustling commercial centre, with petrol refineries and a canning industry. The modern port of 250,000 inhabitants occupies a peninsula, on the ría side of which are the quays and on the ocean side the beaches of Orzán and Riazor.

Few traces remain of the city's long history. Perhaps the most striking one is the so-called **Torre de Hercules**, standing on a headland facing the Atlantic rollers. The 104m-high tower is the only Roman lighthouse still functioning. It has been beaming out its warning

to mariners since the time of Trajan. But I find it difficult to get too excited about the stumpy structure. It has been restored several times, most recently in the early 1990s, so one wonders how much of the original remains. When open to the public, you can climb 242 steps for a formidable view of city

RECOMMENDED HOTELS

CORUÑA, A

María Pita, PPP; Avda Pedro Barrié de la Maza; tel. 981 20 50 00.

A crimson-cloaked doorman greets guests at the entrance to this gleaming glass-and-marble block overlooking the Orzán beach, opened in 1993. One of the Tryp chain, the 188-room hotel offers the amenities you would expect from a four-star establishment, including – they couldn't resist it – the Sir John Moore piano bar.

Atlantico, PPP; Jardines de Méndez Núñez; tel. 981 22 65 00.

Overlooking gardens and the port, this is a modern, functional, four-star hotel. Guests get free admission to the casino, in the same building.

LUGO

Méndez Nuñez, PP; Raiña, 1; tel. 982 23 07 11.

Close to the Town Hall and Plaza de España. An old-established hotel with large public rooms and an old-fashioned atmosphere. (see also Villalba.)

NEDA

Pazo da Merced, PP; 15510 Neda – off the NVI, 10 km E of Coruña tel. 981 38 22 00.

A fine old pazo (mansion) tastefully converted by architect Alfredo Alcalá, aided by decorator Marinela Medina. In the past it housed a tannery and a convent. It has its own chapel, a swimming-pool and sauna, and just six vast bedrooms furnished with antique reproductions. A lawn sweeps down to the ría.

PONTEVEDRA

Parador Casa del Barón, PP-PPP;

and Atlantic (including a rusting ship-wreck below testifying to the treachery of these waters).

The not-so-invincible Armada sailed from Coruña in 1588 after being delayed by gales. The fleet of 130 ships, carrying 29,000 sailors and soldiers, planned to pick up reinforce-

Maceda, s/n; tel. 986 85 58 00.

This noble stone palace, former home of the Condes de Maceda, is belived to stand on the site of a Roman villa and is in the heart of the old town. A massive carved granite staircase, antique furnishings, tapestries and chandeliers lend a distinguished atmosphere. The restaurant looks out on the garden and a tinkling fountain.

PORTOMARIN
Pousada de Portomarín, PP; A*vda de Sarria; tel.* 982 54 52 00.

Formerly a parador, this hotel was enlarged and renovated in 1992. Now under private management, it offers modern comfort and attentive service. The restaurant is recommended.

SANTIAGO DE COMPOSTELA
Los Reyes Católicos, PPP; P*laza Obradoiro,* 1; *tel.* 981 58 22 00.

One of Spain's most splendid five-star hotels. Built by the Catholic Monarchs in 1499 to house pilgrims, it claims to be the world's oldest hotel. Few pilgrims can afford to stay now, but – following ancient tradition – every day up to ten genuine footsore arrivals can eat lunch free, if only in the staff canteen. A sign in the lobby quotes the *Book of Proverbs*: 'The generous man is blessed because he gives his bread to the poor.' The rooms are somewhat cavernous (oppressive, dare I say), but the general effect of the Gothic architecture, the patios, the hundreds of oil paintings and vast public rooms is overwhelming.

Hogar San Francisco, PP; C*ampillo San Francisco,* 3; *tel.* 981 58 16 00.

Clean, but austere rooms in a converted convent, dating from the 13thC and founded by St Francis, whose statue stands outside. The dining hall is monumental, with stained glass and a

---

---

vaulted ceiling, and there are two cloisters, one neo-classical, the other Renaissance. The convent library has 80,000 books, if you care to browse. And the cathedral is a step away.

TARAMUNDI
La Rectoral, PPP; 65 *km* NE *of Lugo, off the* N 640; *tel.* 98 564 67 67.

If you are looking for rural tranquillity, this is the place, an 18thC house in the hills of Asturias close to Galicia. Rooms are well equipped and facilities include a sauna and gymnasium. Often booked up at weekends. The village of Taramundi is famed for its hand-made knives.

VILLALBA (Lugo)
Parador Condes de Villalba, PP; V*aleriano Valdesuso,* 34 *km* NW *of Lugo, on the* N634; *tel.* 982 51 00 11; *closed Dec.*

Book early as there are only six rooms – in a medieval octagonal tower with walls 2m thick. It has a baronial feel, with a vast fireplace, wrought-iron chandeliers, and a view from the roof over town and country.

• *Galician fishing village.*

ments from the Low Countries before attacking England, but bad weather and harassment from the British, under Hawkins and Drake, ruined the strategy and only half the vessels made it back. A year later, Drake's men further damaged Spain by storming ashore at A Coruña, setting fire to the town.

Drake figures large as a hero in English history books, but it is María Pita who touches Spanish hearts. A true Galician woman, courageous and independent, she seized the English standard and gave the alarm, saving the city from destruction. Her heroism is commemorated by a plaque on her house at 24, Herrerias. This is one of the narrow streets of the old town (La Ciudad), which has pleasant little squares and one or two interesting churches.

A short distance away is the tree-shaded **Jardín de San Carlos**, where the English general Sir John Moore lies in a granite tomb. He was fatally wounded in battle against Napoleon's forces under Marshal Soult in 1809. On a wall overlooking the harbour is inscribed the well-known poem of Charles Wolfe: 'Not a drum was heard, nor a funeral note/As his corse to the ramparts was hurried...' Also inscribed here are verses in *gallego* by poet and novelist Rosalía de Castro, who reflected her people's melancholy character and championed their land and culture.

Bordering the wide boulevard by the port, Avenida de la Marina, are many examples of the houses with glassed-in balconies, typical of local architecture. Coruña has a lively night-life and crowds of all ages flock to the bars of Juán Florez and the old town's many *tapa* establishments near Plaza Azcárraga and Plaza María Pita (dominated by the grandiose triple-domed city hall).

CUDILLERO

Off the N632, 56 km from Oviedo. This is a typical Asturias fishing community, the red-tiled houses tumbling down a cleft to the harbour where you can sample the fresh catch in bars and restaurants. From **Cabo Vidio**, west of the town, you can admire the waves crashing against the rocky indented coast, particularly impressive when a storm is whipping across the Bay of Biscay.

Here and there are sandy inlets, but access is not alway easy, usually along wooded valleys between ridges running north to the sea.

ESTRADA, A

On the C541, 25 km S of Santiago. Wild horses still roam the hills of Galicia and each year there is a series of round-ups known as **A Rapa das Bestas**. One such round-up occurs on the first weekend of July at San Lorenzo de Sabucedo, near A Estrada. The horses are herded into a stone-walled corral next to the church. A spectacular scene ensues as men separate the animals, brand them and cut their manes. Other round-ups take place between May and August in Coruña, Lugo, and Pontevedra provinces.

FERROL

On NVI, 60 km from A Coruña. Perhaps the most remarkable sight in Ferrol is the massive equestrian statue of General Franco around which the traffic swirls in the Plaza de España. Monuments to the implacable dictator have toppled across Spain, but here in his birthplace he remains firmly on his plinth despite one or two attempts to blow him up.

However, there is little else to remind you of the glories of his long rule, during which the town was known as El Ferrol del Caudillo. Shortly after his death, the Caudillo was dropped and only a discreet plaque behind a balustrade on the first floor of 136, Calle María, reminds you that Franco was born there on December 4, 1892. He does not even have a street named after him (since the coming of democracy thousands of Spanish street names have changed, making life somewhat confusing for the visitor, particularly as some of the old names are still used by locals). Pablo Iglesias, founder of the country's Socialist party, was also born here and he too has a monument, though somewhat smaller.

Ferrol's deep *ría* has made it an important naval base since the 18thC, although it is currently in decline due to the lack of new orders for its dockyards. For a truly nautical flavour, stay at the Parador (tel. 981 35 34 00), next to the naval base and overlooking the harbour.

LOS ANCARES

This mountainous area straddles the borders of Asturias, León and Lugo provinces. It is noted for its wildlife and surviving prehistoric dwellings.

LUARCA ×

On N632, 101 km NW of Oviedo. Lobster pots line the quayside at this small Asturias fishing port hugging the banks of the sinuous Río Negro below sheer cliffs. It is a pleasant place to try the seafood after bathing on one of the nearby beaches. My first visit was enlivened by a brass band contest and the booming notes of the lighthouse as a fog rolled in from the Bay of Biscay.

In the mountains behind the coast live the descendants of the *vaqueiros de alzada* (literally, cowboys of the high ground). They were cattle farmers, who lived in remote farmhouses and refused to pay taxes and tithes. This bought them persecution by church and state: they were segregated from other worshippers at church services and buried in segregated parts of the cemeteries. Although their origins are obscure, their singing appears to have had Celtic and Druidic connections. Ancient traditions with pagan links surface in 'cowboy' fiestas and weddings in the highlands behind Cudillero, Luarca, and Navia.

Tortuous roads lead high up into the Cordillera Cantábrica and some of the peninsula's wildest country. Take the N634 from Luarca, then the AS14 at La Espina to Cangas del Narcea. The AS15 leads over the Leitariegos Pass, 1,525 m up into León province. In these mountains roam deer, boar, wolves, and – hiding in the woods – even a few of Spain's last brown bears.

MONDOÑEDO

On the N634, 78 km N of Lugo, 44 km SW of Ribadeo. Whitewashed houses graced by wrought-iron balconies and noble crests testify to the long history of this town, once the capital of Galicia. The imposing **cathedral**, dating from the 12thC, contains a curiosity, La Virgen Inglesa. The polychrome wood image was brought from St Paul's Cathedral in London 400 years ago.

NEDA 🛏

See Recommended Hotels.

• Ancient palloza, Cebreiro.

DETOUR – LUGO 🖂 ✕

On the NVI, 100 km SE of A Coruña. Tourism Office, Plaza Maior, 27; tel. 982 23 13 61. Interested in walls? Lugo has them, more than 2 kilometres of the most perfect Roman walls of their kind, girdling the whole town. Although the town stands above the Miño River, from where the Romans loved to fish lampreys for their feasts, the presence of the walls is not immediately obvious because of the many buildings that have sprouted about them. Averaging 10 m high and 6 m thick, they are topped by a gravel path. It makes a pleasant walkway, from which you can peer into people's back windows and view the cathedral.

As the capital of an agricultural province, Lugo is peaceful today after a history which includes sackings by the Suevi, the Moors, and the French.

Within the walls, the Plaza de España is a pleasing spot in which to linger, with open air cafés, trees and lawns. From there you can plunge into the medieval town of narrow stone-paved streets, lined by old houses with iron grillwork. Some of it has a down-at heel air and in a crumbling back-street I was surprised to come across a red light district. A friendly lady, sporting heavy make-up and a multi-coloured tracksuit, directed me back to the spiritual delights of the cathedral, a French-influenced Romanesque building modelled on that of Santiago.

From Lugo, you can make a day trip to survey part of the Camino de Santiago – the Pilgrim's Way. Drive 70 km south-east on the NVI to the 1,100m pass of Pedrafita do Cebreiro on the León border. In 1809, during the retreat of Sir John Moore's army in the Napoleonic Wars, hundreds of English soldiers succumbed to the cold as they struggled up the Valcarce Valley to the pass. Moore's treasure chests were tossed into a chasm. Today, as for centuries past, pilgrims trudge over the pass *en route* for Santiago.

Turn south on the LU634 to **Cebreiro**. Wayside signs indicate that you are following the Camino. The hamlet of Cebreiro rides a windy ridge some 1,000 m above sea level – a remote and bleak spot, but as the first stop in Galicia it has always represented a beacon of hospitality for pilgrims. After weeks on the road, hikers, horsemen and cyclists know that their goal is in sight. The hamlet has several *pallozas*, thatched stone dwellings of prehistoric origin, one of which has been converted into a pilgrims' refuge.

The 1,000-year-old church contains a miraculous chalice. According to legend, a peasant struggled up to the church to hear Mass despite a terrible storm. The priest muttered to himself:'This man's a fool, coming so far on a day like this, just for a bit of bread and some wine.' But then, when he blessed the bread and wine, they turned to flesh and blood. When the Catholic Monarchs (Ferdinand and Isabel) came in 1486, they donated silver caskets to shelter the precious relics of the miracle.

Continue west on the LU634, through a land of rounded, misty hills, ablaze in spring with yellow-flaming broom. Oaks and chestnuts populate the valleys. In one such valley, of the Ouribio river, nestles the great bulk of the **Benedictine Monastery** at Samos. The valley is so narrow that the illustrious 18thC scholar and moralist Fray Jerónimo Feijóo noted that the monks' only horizon was heaven. The building has been restored after a disastrous fire in 1951. One of the 16 monks in residence will show you the two vast cloisters and a series of murals, one of which depicts 'friends of the monastery', recognizable as leading figures of the Franco regime. If you are in the mood for a meditation, you can stay in one of the monastery's austere bedrooms. The meals are frugal but the cost low.

Beyond **Sarria**, a small town with a Renaissance convent and the vestiges of a feudal castle, the C535 leads to **Portomarín**, crossing the reservoir formed by damming the Miño river. Beneath the waters lies the old village, but several of the most historic buildings have been transferred stone by stone to the new hill-top community. These include a 16thC palace and two Romanesque churches, San Pedro and the fortress-like San Nicolás. Walking Portomarín's arcaded main street, I found it difficult to believe that the place was constructed only in the 1960s.

OVIEDO
See Spain Overall: 1.

PADRON
On the N650, 20 km S of Santiago. Padrón, Iria Flavia to the Romans, figures large in the legend woven around St James and his association with Galicia (see also Santiago de Compostela, page 58). According to tradition, he visited Spain twice. On the first visit, he toured the peninsula to spread the Gospel, visiting among other places Zaragoza, where he saw a vision of the Virgin (see Spain Overall: 7), before returning to Judaea.

After his execution, two disciples, Atanasio and Teodoro, carried off his body to a boat, which miraculously transported them from the Holy Land to Padrón. Local legend declares that as the craft moved up the Ulla River, salmon provided a fishy escort. James thereupon emerged from his marble coffin to deliver a sermon, in which he exhorted the salmon to rejoice because they had been called to satisfy the hunger of Christians. Doubters should ask to see the stone kept under the altar in Padrón's **church of Santiago**: it is said to be the post to which was moored the saint's funeral boat.

Padrón also has literary associations. The revered writer Rosalía de Castro spent the last two years of her life at Padrón, dying in 1885. Her house is open to the public (La Matanza, Carretera de Herbón, closed Mon). A more recent literary association is that of Nobel Prize-winning novelist Camilo José Cela, born here in 1916.

PONTEDEUME
See Betanzos, page 52.

PONTEVEDRA 🛏 ✕
On the N 550, 57 km S of Santiago Tourism Office, General Mola 1; tel. 986 85 08 14. Wandering the streets in the centre of Pontevedra is a charming introduction to the Galicia of old. As a port at the head of the Ría de Pontevedra, it thrived in the Middle Ages, but slipped into slow decline as the Lérez river silted up. Signs of the prosperous past abound in the tranquil little squares and narrow streets with their fine granite houses. Weather-beaten crosses dot the plazas of the town. Look for one in the fishermen's quarter, which has two

nude female sculptures at the base, modestly covering their lower portions with fig-leaves.

A few steps away is another Calvary, which stands outside **Santa María Church**, built by the mariners' guild in the 16thC and decorated with some suitably menacing gargoyles. Cornelius of Holland and Juan Nobre executed the Plateresque western façade; inside there is a mixture of Isabeline, Gothic and Renaissance styles. The **Museo Provincial** occupies two Baroque mansions on Calle de Sarmiento, named after Pedro Sarmiento de Gamboa, the 16thC navigator and cosmographer who lived in Pontevedra. In it you can find items from naval history, Sargadelos pottery, Celtic artefacts, and one of Galicia's best libraries, with 55,000 volumes on all aspects of Galician life and culture. Besides Galician art, also on show are works by Brueghel, Murillo, El Greco, Caravaggio and Tiepolo.

A tall, unusual-looking church, with a floor in the shape of a scallop, stands just off the Plaza de la Herrería. This is **La Peregrina**, a stopping place for pilgrims on the way from Portugal to Santiago. A visit to the food market reveals an astonishing variety of fish, also typical Galician cheeses shaped like women's breasts. Bland and creamy, these are known as *tetillas*.

PORTOMARIN
See Recommended Hotels.

RIAS ALTAS
This area covers Galicia's northern coast from Ribadeo on the Asturias border to Ferrol. Travelling along this coast, pierced by *rías*, is slow going, whether you drive along the weaving N642 or take the FEVE. The hilly country is interspersed with meadows, woodland of eucalypt and pine, and crops of maize. Traditionally, the communities along the coast made their living from whaling and tuna fishing and trading in hemp and linen with the Baltic countries.

Spain's first blast furnaces were installed at **Burela** in the 18thC and a little further west, near Cervo, are the **ceramics works of Sargadelos**, famed for their quality products (open to the public on weekdays).

Viveiro, at the head of a deep *ría* 92 kilometres from Ferrol, retains a medieval air, with its Charles V gate and galleried houses. Its beaches and seafood attract many summer visitors. A typical Galician pilgrimage, the Romería de Naseiro, takes place here on the fourth Sunday in August. Northwest of Viveiro, the granite headland Estaca de Bares juts out into the Atlantic. It is Spain's northernmost point and also one of the wettest, a detail which does not deter ornithologists eager to check the birds of passage. More than 100,000 sea-birds are estimated to fly past between August and November. There are plenty of beaches as you proceed west and the coast grows more abrupt, with gorse and oak trees taking over from cultivated fields. One of the region's oldest pilgrimages takes place on September 8 at the lonely seaside hamlet of **San Andrés de Teixido**, 10 km from Cedeira. According to a popular saying, 'He who does not go to San Andrés in his lifetime will go there when he is dead.' People invite a relative recently deceased to accompany them to the shrine, reserving a seat at the table or on the bus for the dear departed.

RIAS BAIXAS
See Local Explorations.

RIBADEO ×
See Recommended Restaurants.

SANTIAGO DE COMPOSTELA ⌘ ×
On the A9, 69 km S of A Coruña, 37 km N of Pontevedra. Tourism Office: Rúa del Villar, 43; tel. 981 58 40 81. A leading Santiago citizen told me: 'You are in a magic city, where even the stones understand one another. They are all different styles, but they are in harmony. Everybody who comes here comes as a pilgrim in one sense or another.' With that sort of build-up, you prepare yourself for disappointment. In fact, Santiago *is* one of Europe's most remarkable cities, a magnificently preserved medieval city but also a lively modern one with a university, regional government headquarters and constant flow of visitors of all nationalities.

With Rome and Jerusalem, Santiago was one of the great medieval centres of Christian pilgrimage. According to legend, the Apostle James preached in Spain and later his disciples brought back his body to Galicia in a marble coffin. In the 9thC, a star shining on a wood led a hermit to his grave at the present site of Santiago's cathedral. (The name Compostela derives from Campus Stellae or field of stars, according to one theory.)

About the same time as the discovery of St James's grave, another amazing phenomenon occurred: a phantom knight on a white charger appeared during a battle and helped the Christians to trounce the Moors. From that moment, St James (Sant-Iago) became known as *Matamoros* (Slayer of the Moors) and began appearing in all sorts of unlikely places, including the Americas where he is credited with helping the Spaniards crush the Indians, who after all have dusky skins just like the Moors. Without any apparent irony, the blood-lusting, sword-wielding Apostle was made Spain's patron saint.

News of miracles and promises of indulgences encouraged thousands of pilgrims to make the perilous journey to the Santiago shrine. Most came via France, aided by the Benedictines and Cistercians of Cluny and Citeaux. They took months, even years, over the journey, and they bore the traditional uniform of cape, stave with water gourd attached, and felt hat bearing scallop shells (the scallop became a symbol after a knight crossed a *ría* and emerged covered with shells).

Up to two million pilgrims a year followed the Camino de Santiago, inspiring Aymeric Picaud, a French monk, to write a guide for their benefit. This early travel guide – perhaps *the* earliest travel guide – forms part of the *Codex Calixtinus* finished around 1139. He told pilgrims: '(Galicia) is agreeable because of its rivers, its meadows and rich apple orchards, its good fruit and clear springs...The Galicians adapt themselves to our people, but are irascible and very contentious.'

The pilgrim route created an economy all its own: hospitals and refuges were set up, churches constructed, craftsmen, pedlars, clerics, beggars, brigands and con-men were attracted. After several centuries the pilgrimage fell into abeyance, but today there is renewed enthusiasm for it.

Even the cynical can find a visit to Santiago fascinating: ruck-sacked pilgrims, cassocked priests, gaping sight-

THE CULT OF SANTIAGO – FACT AND FICTION

It is highly unlikely that St James was buried in Spain: he was beheaded by Herod Agrippa in Jerusalem and his body probably buried in the Nile Delta.

But, so the tale goes, his body was brought back to Spain by his followers, coming ashore at Padrón (see page 57): a miraculous voyage that took seven days to complete. Then the body was forgotten for 750 years – until its 'rediscovery' at Compostela in 813. This was a time of great significance for the Spanish Christian Church. For the past century, the Moors had swept across the peninsula. The invaders were motivated by passionate belief in the prophet Mohammed.

Historians see the Cult of Santiago as the early Spanish Church's answer to this potent motivating force. If the Moors could focus on belief in a prophet, then so could Christians, in a saint. And indeed, the saint was adopted as the champion of the Christians against the Moors in the subsequent wars of Reconquest. Conveniently enough, within decades of the discovery of St James's remains, the saint was 'appearing' alongside Christians in battle to slaughter (on one occasion) tens of thousands of Moors. When people have a reason to believe, they will.

seers and boisterous students all mingle in the centre of old Santiago, a labyrinth of arcaded streets, monasteries and churches, more often than not seen through a gauze of drizzle, for this is one of Spain's wettest places.

The focal point is the **Plaza del Obradoiro**, edged with majestic buildings. On the west is the **Ayuntamiento**, originally built as a seminary in 1772; on the south **Colegio de San Jerónimo**; on the north the Plateresque pomp of the **Hostal de los Reyes Católicos**, once a pilgrims' hostel, now a luxury hotel.

Dominating all is the **cathedral**, rebuilt over James's supposed tomb from the 11th to the 13thC after the

Moor Al Mansur destroyed an earlier building. The **Obradoiro façade** is an amazing piece of Baroque imagination, but even that hardly prepares you for the **Pórtico de la Gloria**, just inside. This Romanesque masterpiece shows, carved in marble, the Jewish people and Old Testament scenes on the left; on the right, gentiles and pagans; and in the centre Christ and the Evangelists. It is said that a prudish bishop ordered the ample curves of one figure reduced because Daniel appeared to be smiling at her in roguish fashion.

To signal their safe arrival, pilgrims queue up to place their hands on the centre column, which represents the tree of Jesse, and – hoping, perhaps, to absorb his talent – bump their heads on the image of Mateo, the maestro responsible for the Pórtico 800 years ago. So many fingers have touched the granite that they have created five distinct hollows. Within the cathedral, the faithful climb the steps behind the richly adorned high altar to embrace St James's image and descend to the crypt, which contains relics of the saint. Hidden when the 'pirate Drake' attacked Galicia, they were lost for 300 years until turning up again in 1879.

On special occasions (and when a group wants to make an offering, paying 30,000 pesetas), worshippers can see one of those crowd-pleasing pieces of theatre at which the Catholic Church is so adept. Eight hefty red-robed acolytes, known as the *tiraboleiros*, carry out the *botafumeiro*, an 80-kilo censer of silver-plated brass. They heave on a rope linked to pulleys, causing the censer to swing until it is soaring across the transept and up to the cathedral roof, leaving a trail of smoke, sparks, and incense. The performance is greeted with applause, perhaps at relief that the *botafumeiro* has not broken loose, as it reaches a speed of nearly 70 kph. The display takes place every day in Holy Years, when July 25 (St James's Day) falls on a Sunday. Only in those years is the Puerta Santa, on the east façade, opened. Nearby is the **Oficina del Peregrino**, where genuine pilgrims receive the Compostela, a document confirming that they followed the Camino.

Thirsty pilgrims assure good business for Santiago's bars and restaurants. In and around Calle Franco, on the approaches to the cathedral, many bars serve scallops baked in the shell. In El 42, a typical establishment popular with business types, you can have half a dozen oysters accompanied by Ribeiro wine served in porcelain cups.

A worthwhile excursion from Santiago is to the **Pazo de Oca**, 25 km south-west on the N525. This is a splendid Baroque mansion, open to the public. The beautiful gardens with avenues of chestnut and lime trees are a dreamy oasis of water and greenery.

SARGADELOS
Also Viveiro and Cedeira, see Rias Altas, page 58.

TARAMUNDI ⊨
See Recommended Hotels, page 52.

VIGO ✕
On the A9, 27 km S of Pontevedra. Commanding the south shore of the *ría* of the same name, Vigo is a busy port and Galicia's major industrial city, with more than 270,000 inhabitants. Shipbuilding, car-making and canning are important. In the 15th and 16thC English buccaneers, hungry for the treasure of the New World, raided the town. In 1702 a British and Dutch fleet attacked French and Spanish ships in the estuary, sinking many. The ships and the treasure remain at the bottom of the *ría*.

Vigo's setting is impressive, but sights are few. Down near the harbour is the old fishing quarter of **Berbés**, where night life surges and ebbs about its bars, but most of the city is of recent construction. For views over city and estuary, head up the broad boulevard of the Gran Vía, turn off on the Plaza de España, where water cascades over an amazing, 15m-high metal sculpture of wild horses, and you reach the **Castro**, a hill-top park with a castle. There are a number of beaches near the city: **Samil** accounts for much of the summer action – but it would seem wiser to head for less frequented waters if you intend to bathe.

Ferries leave from Vigo for the resort of **Cangas** on the north side of the *ría*, passing a fleet of rafts below which millions of mussels are reared.

VILLALBA ⊨
See Recommended Hotels.

RECOMMENDED RESTAURANTS

CORUNA, A

Asador Castellano, PP; *Gómez Zamallos*, 5; *tel.* 981 25 07 70.

Medieval armour, swords and beams provide the atmosphere. Roast lamb is the speciality. Near the Parque Santa Margarita.

Coral, PPP; *Callejón de la Estacada 9; tel.* 981 20 05 69; *credit cards* AE, D, M, V; *closed Sun, except Jul and Aug.*

An established favourite in the heart of the city, presided over by César Gallego. Dark panelling, chandeliers and pink tablecloths lend elegance. Try the steamed sea bass in sea-urchin sauce.

La lebolina, PP-PPP; *Troncoso*, 18; *tel.* 981 20 50 44; *credit cards* DC, V; *closed Sun.*

There is no doubt that the speciality, seafood, is fresh here: shellfish were waving a puny protest on the counter when I lunched. It is an intimate wood-panelled place, off Plaza María Pita.

LUARCA

Casa Consuelo, PP; *Ctra.* N 634, *km* 317 (*in Otur, 6 km from Luarca*); *tel.* 985 47 07 67; *credit cards* AE, DC, M, V; *closed Mon, except Aug.*

A roadside restaurant with a reputation for solid Asturias food, such as *fabada* (stew), hake cooked in cider, and *entrecôte* with Cabrales cheese.

LUGO

Alberto, PP; *Cruz*, 4; *tel.* 982 22 83 10; *credit cards* AE, DC, M, V; *closed Sun.*

An austere but noble stone building with iron balconeis in the heart of the old quarter. The window full of crustaceans and shellfish indicates the specialities of the house. *Revuelta de grelos con gambas* (turnip greens cooked with shrimps) and *empanada de vieiras* (scallop pie) are both delicious.

Verruga, PP-PPP; *Cruz*, 12; *tel.* 982 22 98 55; *cards* AE, DC, M, V; *closed Mon.*

If you want traditional dishes, this restaurant will satisfy you. Start with fresh oysters and continue with roast kid from the wood-fired oven or the paprika-flavoured octopus.

PONTEVEDRA

Doña Antonia, PP; *Soportales de la Herrería, 4-1°; tel.* 986 84 72 74; *credit cards* AE, MC, V; *closed Sun and first three weeks Jun.*

Pleasantly situated on a first floor with views of the colonnaded Herrería square and church of San Francisco. Try the sea urchin vol-au-vent and, for dessert, 'grandmother's cake'.

SANTIAGO DE COMPOSTELA

Alameda, PP; *Porta Faxeira*, 15; *tel.* 981 58 47 96; *credit cards* AE, DC, MC, V; *closed Sun.*

Green shrubs and white ironwork on the terrace, plus lobsters in a window tank, welcome you to this popular meeting place. The restaurant has two floors or you can sit outside and check on the passers-by. Attentive service. Try the *vieira al horno* (scallops baked in the shell) or the *cabrito* (roast kid).

Don Gaiferos, PPP; *Rúa Nova*, 23; *tel.* 981 58 38 94; *credit cards* AE, DC, MC, V; *closed Sun.*

One of Santiago's best restaurants, serving both local and international dishes, this establishment on a street leading to the cathedral takes you back: there is medieval stonework, in fact it was once a stable. Choose the menu of the day if you want to hold the price down.

VIGO

El Castillo, PPP; *Paseo de Rosalia de Castro; tel.* 986 42 11 11; *credit cards* AE, MC, V; *closed Sun eve, Mon.*

Unequalled position in a park commanding splendid views. Proprietor Manuel Gómez Carpintero and his wife María worked 20 years in Britain, Germany and Switzerland. Recommended: grilled salmon and *Filloas a la crema*, cream-filled Galician pancakes, served cold.

North-Central Spain

Between Oviedo and Madrid
Castilla-León: León, Salamanca and Avila

530 km; maps maps 441 & 444, 1:400,000

A traveller might well have second thoughts about visiting Castilla-León if he were to read the words of Miguel de Unamuno, the Spanish humanist, in full flight in *The Essence of Spain:* 'Here are arid stretches, bare and vast, without leaf or stream, great spaces where torrents of light outline sharp thick shadows, drowning middle tones. The farming lands present themselves like immense slabs of mosaic of extremely little variety, over which spreads the intense blue of the sky.'

But there is more variety in Castilla-León than those words suggest. The region's western provinces (see Spain Overall: 2 for details of the rest of the region including Burgos, Soria, and Valladolid) embrace fine mountain scenery as well as the endless plains of the *meseta* (plateau). This was the scene of epic struggle in the Middle Ages, between Christian and Moor, warlord against warlord, and its historic cities with their majestic architecture are testimony to the glorious past.

The west of León province, where you will find some of Spain's wildest landscapes and most primitive communities in the Ancares zone, borders rainy Galicia. In the north, next to Asturias, there are green pastures, bristling peaks, and tumbling rivers (León has 3,000 km of trout streams). In the south, forming a formidable barrier with Toledo and Extremadura, are the wild Gredos mountains. In the region's south-west lies the Peña de Francia range, barring the approach to Las Hurdes, still a land apart decades after Luís Buñuel made his shocking film about it, *Land Without Bread* – see Local Explorations: 6.

Between these ranges are the plains of León, Zamora, Salamanca, and Avila provinces: wide, often monotonous, lands. Flowing through them, west to the Portuguese frontier, is the Douro.

In the north lies León, once the capital of its own kingdom and still highly aware of its uniqueness within the Castilla-León region. León's Gothic cathedral rivals anything you will see in the rest of Europe.

To the south is Salamanca, famed since the Middle Ages as a centre of learning. In the south-east is Avila, 'the town of stones and saints' as it has been described, recalling the knights and clerics who dominated life there. Strolling about the old town with its medieval walls intact is akin to visiting a living museum. Apart from Castile's famous roast lamb and suckling pig, some of the dishes you will enjoy are frogs' legs, grilled trout, *chanfaina* (a spicy stew with varying contents but usually including sausage, liver, and tripe), and *yemas* (egg-yolk candies).

TRANSPORT

Regular train and bus services run between Madrid, Avila, León, Salamanca, and Zamora. FEVE, a narrow-gauge railway, serves the northern part of León province, connecting León with Bilbao. There is usually at least one bus a day between the provincial capitals and smaller towns. Times are carried in the region's daily papers. A night train runs from Salamanca to Lisbon and Oporto (Portugal) via Ciudad Rodrigo.

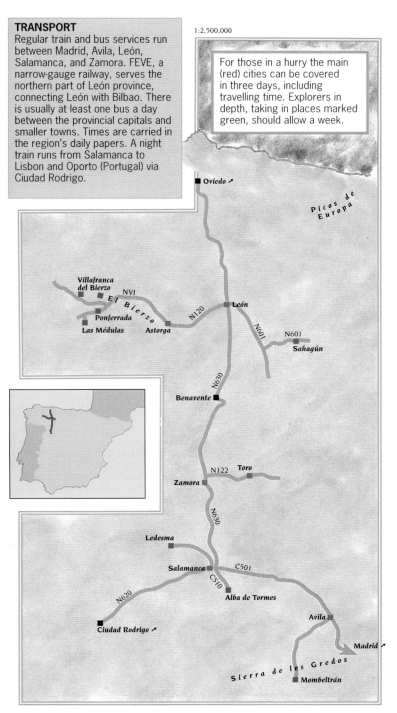

1:2,500,000

For those in a hurry the main (red) cities can be covered in three days, including travelling time. Explorers in depth, taking in places marked green, should allow a week.

Oviedo

Picos de Europa

Villafranca del Bierzo

NVI

El Bierzo

Ponferrada

Las Médulas   Astorga

N120

León

N601

N601

Sahagún

N630

Benavente

N122   Toro

Zamora

N630

Ledesma

Salamanca   C501

N620   C510

Alba de Tormes

Ciudad Rodrigo

Avila

Madrid

Sierra de los Gredos

Mombeltrán

SIGHTS & PLACES OF INTEREST

ALBA DE TORMES

On the C510, 23 km SE of Salamanca. Santa Teresa de Avila's body lies in the Convento de las Carmelitas, attracting a large number of pilgrims. An arm and her heart are preserved separately as objects of veneration (General Franco kept her right arm on his desk).

Among Alba's old ecclesiastical buildings are the **church of San Juan**, with a Churrigueresque reredos (decorative screen covering wall at back of altar) and Romanesque sculptures of the Apostles; also the Romanesque-Mudéjar **church of San Miguel** with tombs dating from the 13thC.

Traditionally, Alba has been a centre for potters. Although the number has diminished, you will still find their attractively decorated work on sale.

All that remains of a castle, which belonged to the Duques de Alba, is the keep, the **Torre de la Armería**. The third duke achieved notoriety for his bloody repression of the Low Countries and is regarded by the Dutch as one of the great villains of history, while the present Duchess of Alba holds more titles than any other Spaniard, around 50 at the last count.

ASTORGA ✕

On the NV1, 45 km W of León. In Roman times, Asturica Augusta was a key communications point, lying on the Vía de la Plata which ran south to Seville. **Roman mosaics** may be viewed in a square beyond the Plaza Mayor. In the Middle Ages, it welcomed pilgrims on their way to Santiago.

Today, Astorga is known as the capital of the Land of the Maragatos. The **Maragatos**, a people of unclear origin (but they could be descendants of Berbers), inhabit the area around Astorga. Until phased out by modern transport, they were muleteers, transporting goods in long mule trains across Spain. They lived as a tribe apart, following their own customs, and still retain some independence. The men wore black breeches and embroidered shirts and the women black skirts with colourful embroidered aprons and shawls. These clothes, as well as traditional dances, may still be seen at Corpus Christi and at fiestas – and when the Astorga town hall clock chimes the hour: two figures in Maragato costume strike the bells.

Flying buttresses and a pink sandstone façade in Plateresque style distinguish the **cathedral**, begun in 1471. The Baroque portal is embellished with scenes from the New Testament.

RECOMMENDED HOTELS

AVILA
Parador Raimundo de Borgoña, PPP; Marqués de Canales y Chozas, 16; tel. 920 21 13 40.

If you are stirred by tales of knights, crusades, and chivalry, this medieval palace, right against the ancient walls, is where to indulge your fantasies.

BENAVENTE
Parador Rey Fernando II de León, PP; off the N630, 66 km N of Zamora – Paseo Ramón y Cajal; tel. 980 63 03 00.

Handily situated at the junction of roads leading to León and Galicia, the parador is housed in modern wings added to the Torre del Caracol (tower of the snail), all that remains of an ancient castle burned by Napoleon's troops. Tapestries, ironwork, and the main salon's coffered ceiling add to

the atmosphere.

LEON
Parador Hostal San Marcos, PPP; Plaza San Marcos, 7; tel. 987 23 73 00.

More a national monument than a hotel, this former monastery offers sumptuous surroundings. Along with the Reyes Católicos in Santiago de Compostela, it is the pride of the state-owned Parador chain. Enormous public rooms decorated with antiques and tapestries, beautiful cloisters and gardens, and 256 spacious bedrooms. The restaurant is of similar standard.

SALAMANCA
Don Juan, PP; Quintana, 6; tel. 923 26 14 73.

Close to the Plaza Mayor, this small two-star hotel has all the modern amenities, including satellite television in the rooms.

Inside, the reredos (screen on wall behind altar) by Gaspar Becerra is worthy of note and the cathedral treasure includes Islamic art and San Toribio's crystal chalice.

For something completely different, walk around the corner to a neo-Gothic fantasy, designed in the 19thC by Catalan architect Gaudí, master of Modernism, as a **Palacio Episcopal.** Soaring ribs of stone and swelling arches continue the fantasy in the interior, which houses an exhibition of art related to the Camino de Santiago – Pilgrim's Way to Santiago – (closed Sun).

Astorga is known for its *mantecadas* (a type of sweet) and pastries.

Seventeen km east, near Hospital de Orbigo, a bridge crosses the Orbigo River. This is not just any old bridge but the one where a knight of León entered into legend. Suero de Quiñones could almost have served as a model for Don Quixote. Besotted with a beautiful lady named Doña Leonor, he decided in 1434 to demonstrate his love by throwing down a challenge to other knights travelling the Camino de Santiago. No knight could cross the bridge until he acknowledged that Doña Leonor was the fairest maid of all: excuse enough for a fight. Joined by nine other local knights, Suero swore to maintain the challenge until they had broken 300 lances. The jousts against knights of various nationalities went on for 30 days and then, undefeated, Suero rode off to Santiago to give thanks.

AVILA ⌨ ×

On the N501, 115 *km* W *of Madrid.* Avila reflects the medieval mixture of war and religion that once had the plains of Castile in its grip. The **granite walls**, possibly the best-preserved medieval walls in all Europe, are a reminder that this was an important frontier town. After Alfonso VI of Castile ousted the Moors in the 11thC, he ordered his son-in-law, Raymond of Burgundy, to fortify it against further attacks. He built the walls, 2,500 m long and of daunting solidity and thickness, and there they still stand, with their 88 round towers and nine entrance gates. One of the best views is from a ridge outside town on the Salamanca road at a point called the Cuatro Postes.

Today Avila is a small provincial capital whose youngsters yearn for the bright lights of Madrid, a sentiment I can understand having once spent a Saturday night of memorable dullness here. Although it was May, snowflakes were drifting down, for Avila's altitude,

Palacio de Castellanos, PPP; *San Pablo, 58-64; tel.* 923 26 18 18.

The former palace of the Marqués de Castellanos has been expensively restored to create a four-star hotel. Parts of the building, including the delightful glassed-in, colonnaded patio, date from the 15thC.

VILLAFRANCA DEL BIERZO
Villafranca del Bierzo, PP; *Avda Calvo Sotelo, s/n; tel.* 987 54 01 75.

Modern rather than historic, this parador is a pleasant stop-over with attentive service and a recommended restaurant.

ZAMORA
Hostería Real de Zamora, PP; *Cuesta de Pizarro, 7; tel.* 980 53 45 22.

The patio with a balustrade is a focal point of this historic building, recently converted into a small hotel with careful attention to detail. Televi-sion and 'antique' telephones in the rooms. The restaurant is good and serves Castilian and Basque food.

BUDGET ACCOMMODATION

AVILA
El Rastro, P; *Plaza del Rastro, 1; tel.* 920 21 12 18.

LEON
Paris, P-PP; *Ancha, 18; tel.* 987 23 86 00.

SALAMANCA
Laguna, P; *Consuelo, 13; tel.* 923 21 87 06.

1,130 m (it is Spain's highest provincial capital), and its exposed position on a bleak, rocky plateau make it one of the country's coldest towns. It is an appropriate place to scourge the body and to dwell on spiritual matters, and indeed one of the great Catholic mystics, Santa Teresa, was born here.

The knights of Avila – thus the old title 'Avila de los Caballeros' – gained renown in the wars of the Reconquest and in the New World. The town flourished, but the expulsion of the Moriscos in 1609, with the attendant loss of traders and craftsmen, started a sharp decline.

Wandering about Avila's streets is like a stroll through a museum of medieval art and architecture. It abounds with churches and convents. Several styles are evident in the fortress-like **cathedral** which was constructed between the 12th and 14thC. Cornelius, a Dutchman, carved the figures of saints on the choir stalls and Pedro Berruguete, Jean of Burgundy, and Santos Cruz painted the beautiful altarpiece. The alabaster tomb of Alfonso de Madrigal, a 15thC bishop, was sculpted by Vasco de Zarza. The bishop has been nicknamed El Tostado (The Toasted One), but I have been unable to pin down whether this refers to his dark complexion or the colour of the image.

Lying outside the walls, **San Vicente** is a magnificent Romanesque church with some Gothic touches. The three naves and the portal were designed by Fruchel, a pioneer in introducing French Gothic art into the peninsula in the 12thC. A fine tomb contains the remains of San Vicente and his two sisters, the reliefs relating their martyrdom which is said to have taken place in the 4thC on this spot.

A painting hailed as a masterpiece adorns the high altar of the **Convento de San Tomás**, some distance outside the walls. The work of Berruguete, it illustrates the life St Thomas Aquinas. The Dominican monastery was used as a summer residence by the Catholic Monarchs Ferdinand and Isabel and their beloved only son Juan is entombed in white marble here.

Another celebrity lies under a slab in the church sacristy: Tomás de Torquemada, who sent thousands to be burned at the stake during his control

of the Inquisition. The convent's cloisters are particularly impressive.

Avila is a place of pilgrimage, thanks to Teresa de Cepeda y Ahumada, otherwise known as Santa Teresa de Avila, or de Jesús. Born in 1515, she was as much a crusader as the armoured knights of the time. Imbued with piety and reforming zeal, she travelled across Spain to preach her belief in austerity, penance, and contemplation, often meeting with hostility from clerics and civic leaders. However, she won the admiration of the most influential man in the kingdom, Philip II and altogether founded 17 convents of the reformed Carmelites.

Her letters to the poet and mystic Juan de Yepes, later San Juan of the Cross, and her other spiritual writings have had profound influence. Manuscripts and other relics are on view in the **Convento de la Encarnación**, where she took the veil in 1533 and lived for 27 years. The convents of **Las Madres**, the first the saint founded, and **Santa Teresa**, built over her birthplace, can also be visited.

From Avila it is possible to visit the Sierra de Gredos (see Spain Overall: 12 for more information on this mountain range). Daily buses run to Arenas de San Pedro, 69 km away in the Gredos mountains.

BENAVENTE 🛏

See Recommended Hotels, page 64.

BIERZO, EL

For the thousands of pilgrims who have trudged across northern Spain over the centuries on the way to Santiago, the last stretch before entering Galicia has always been one of the most testing. To surmount the mountain barrier in the far west of León province, they had to make the long, slow ascent up the Valcarce Valley (today threaded by highway NV1). Slate-grey villages are dotted about a landscape of rounded, treeless hills covered in gorse and split by wooded valleys. In the remotest part, the wild heathland of the Sierra de Ancares, which spreads into Lugo province, roam deer, wolves, boar, and a few bears. Some inhabitants still live in *pallozas*, semi-circular stone structures with thatched roofs.

This is the region of El Bierzo. In the lower zone (Bierzo Bajo) lies the shel-

• *Astorga Cathedral - see page* 64.

tered Sil Valley, where crops flourish and the excellent Bierzo wines are produced. While Ponferrada is the largest town in the area, a pleasanter base from which to explore it is **Villafranca del Bierzo**. The French founded a settlement here in the 11thC and the monks of Cluny built a church. Among the many fine old buildings is the **Hospital de Santiago**, now a school, one of a number of hospitals that once existed for pilgrims. Rounded towers mark the corners of the castle built in the 16thC. The Romanesque **church of Santiago** has a Puerta del Perdón (Entrance of Pardon), recalling that pilgrims who reached here, but were too feeble to continue to Santiago, were granted all the indulgences they would have enjoyed had they completed their pilgrimage. Next door is a **refuge** where present-day pilgrims can eat cheaply and rest their limbs free of charge. It is run by the Jato family, famed along the Santiago trail.

CIUDAD RODRIGO
See Local Explorations: 6.

GREDOS, SIERRA DE LOS
This mountain range marks the boundary between Avila province and the provinces of Toledo and Cáceres. See Spain Overall: 12 for details.

LEDESMA
On the SA300, 34 km NW of Salamanca.
Well-preserved medieval walls surround

67

this pleasant town on a bend of the Tormes river, reached from Salamanca along a picturesque valley. The **church of Santa María** has sumptuous 400-year-old tombs. The Tormes wends its way north-west to its junction with the Duero on the Portuguese frontier.

LEON ⌖ ×

On the N630, 115 km S of Oviedo. When I entered **León Cathedral**, my first inclination was to lie on my back. Not to rest, but better to study what surely are among the most dazzling stained glass windows in Christendom. Slanting sunrays spread a rainbow of light in the cathedral gloom. Only the glass of the Sainte-Chapelle in Paris has impressed me to such an extent. The oldest of León's windows, some 1,800 square metres in area, date from the 13thC; particularly outstanding is the rose window on the façade.

While that glass alone is justification, there are a number of other good reasons to dally awhile in León, a pleasant city of 130,000 inhabitants. Its name derives from Legio Septima, the seventh legion which the Emperor Augustus quartered here. Ordoño II of Asturias established his court here in the 10thC, making it the most important city in Christian Spain. Al-Mansur, feared leader of the Moors, burned the town in 996, but it was soon recovered and for two centuries played a leading part in the campaigns of the Reconquest. Finally, it came under the domination of the Kingdom of Castile, based in Burgos, during the reign of Ferdinand III. Yet, even today, some inhabitants yearn for León to have its own autonomous government, instead of being lumped in with the Castile region.

A flourishing modern city now surrounds the **old quarter**, with its vestiges of fortified walls. Within them are two remarkable structures, the **cathedral** and the **Real Colegiata de San Isidoro**. With a marked French influence, the cathedral is an outstanding example of classic Gothic construction. It was begun in 1258 on the site of three earlier churches. The three-nave cathedral is 91 m long, 40 m wide, and reaches a height of 39 m. The stalls of the choir are Flemish-influenced while the *trascoro* (retrochoir) is carved in alabaster in Renaissance style. You

pass through the cloister to reach the museum, where the exhibits include a crucifixion carved by Juan de Juni and a Bible dating from 920.

Among the striking sculptures adorning the main façade is one of Santiago (St James). León has always been an important staging post for pilgrims travelling to Galicia along the Pilgrim's Way or Camino de Santiago. Reflecting this long tradition, many León women are baptized with the name Camino and villages carry the tag 'del Camino' (of the Way). In the cathedral, you may well encounter some pilgrims, carrying the traditional staff and gourd. Not all are Catholics or even believers. One woman, a 50-year-old psychoanalyst, told me: 'I decided to celebrate my half century with something special. It has been an important experience, even though I am not at all religious. Walking the Way has helped me differentiate between the essential in my life and the superfluous.'

Weaving your way through the old quarter's narrow streets, you reach **San Isidoro**, founded in the 11thC. It contains the pantheon of the early Spanish kings, one of the earliest examples of the Romanesque style in the peninsula. It was badly damaged by French troops under General Soult in 1808. The carvings on the capitals, depicting such themes as Daniel in the lions' den, are the earliest in Spain relating scenes from the Gospels. The remarkable 12thC **frescoes** on the vaulted ceiling, colours still vivid, have inspired elegies, including the rather far-fetched claim that this is the 'Sistine Chapel of Romanesque art'.

Away from the old quarter, on the banks of the Bernesga river, stands a third building of renown, the **Convento de San Marcos**. Originally a hospital stood here to attend to the needs of the Santiago de Compostela pilgrims. Ferdinand the Catholic, grand master of the Order of Santiago, planned a new building on which work began in 1513. The present edifice is as flamboyant a piece of Renaissance self-confidence as you could imagine, with the 100 m-long Plateresque façade representing a roll-call in stone of historic figures. On it, amid cornices and friezes, you will find likenesses of Hercules, Isabel the Catholic, Julius Caesar, the Emperor Trajan, El Cid, and others. A Baroque addition relates incidents from the life of Santiago (St James), including his slaying of the Moors. Scallop shells adorn the façade of the church, which has magnificent choir stalls. A 16thC cloister, coffered ceilings, a grand staircase, and tapestries delight the eye of guests with enough cash to book rooms in the luxury hotel that now occupies the building.

As a complete contrast, in the centre of the city stands a dignified, many-windowed building with spiked corner turrets, designed by Gaudí, the Catalan genius. The **Casa de Botines** is not, however, open for visits, being occupied by a savings bank. It stands on the Plaza San Marcelo, close to an imposing 16thC palace, the **Palacio de los Guzmanes**, occupied by the provincial government.

Just around the corner, at 25, Generalísimo Franco, is the **Café Victoria**, a traditional spot for consuming delicious pastries while studying the passers-by through the large windows. For *tapas* and animation, particularly at weekends, a tour of the **Barrio Húmedo** (humid quarter), the zone around the Plaza Martín, is recommended.

MEDULAS, LAS
See Ponferrado, below.

MOMBELTRAN
On the N502, 58 km SW of Avila. A well-preserved medieval **castle** crowns a ridge in this village in the Sierra de Gredos. It was given by King Henry IV to one of his favourites in 1461 and is owned by a descendant, the Duque de Alburquerque. For more information about the Gredos, see Spain Overall: 12.

OVIEDO
See Spain Overall: 1.

PICOS DE EUROPA
This range of mountains forms part of León province's border with Asturias and Santander. For details, see Local Explorations: 2.

PONFERRADA
On the NVI, 105 km W of León. First impressions of the slate-roofed capital of the Bierzo region in its rainy valley are not encouraging, owing to the gloomy influence of coal and iron min-

---

SALAMANCA AND THE PICARESQUE
The Renaissance spirit flourished in Salamanca: the intricate, carved style known as Plateresque offers a stunning display on many buildings (José Churriguera, the architect who gave his name to the flamboyant style known as Churrigueresque, was born in Salamanca).

Lazarillo de Tormes, a trend-setting novel published anonymously in the 16thC, was set in Salamanca. The account of the adventures of a *pícaro* (rogue) set the tone for a whole new genre, the picaresque novel. Visiting Salamanca in the 19thC, the English traveller Richard Ford observed that its students were 'amongst the boldest and most impertinent of the human race, full of tags, and rags, fun, frolic, licence, and guitars'. They sound suspiciously like *pícaros* in the making.

---

ing. But seek out the **old quarter**, with its arcaded streets, and especially the **castle** (closed Mon), a vision of (heavily restored) medieval turrets and battlements. The Knights Templar extended and embellished this fort in the 13thC to protect the Pilgrim's Way or Camino de Santiago. To ease the way for the pilgrims, a bridge was built across the Sil River in the 11thC. It was reinforced with iron, from which the town's name derives, Pons Ferrata being Latin for iron bridge.

If you travel 25 km west of Ponferrada on the N536, you encounter near Carucedo an area of strangely-eroded red hills at **Las Médulas**. Here the Romans mined gold between the 2nd and 4thC. Thousands of slaves toiled, and died, cutting galleries through which were released torrents of water. The current washed out ore-bearing soil and rock, carrying it to a point where the gold could be filtered out. A thousand tons or more of the precious metal are estimated to have been extracted.

SAHAGUN
On the N120, 65 km SE of León. A rising

• *Bell tower, León.*

here in 1110 against the domination of the Benedictine monastery was an early demonstration of people power. After Alfonso III ordered a sanctuary built on the Pilgrim's Way or Camino de Santiago, a flood of French clerics arrived. The monastery grew in importance until in 1085 Alfonso VI granted a *fuero* (privilege), giving the abbot virtually total control over the surrounding area. This finally provoked a series of rebellions by the downtrodden populace. After the burghers, aided by the king of Aragón, refused to give money or services to the monastery, the abbot had to leave Sahagún and the *fuero* was abolished. Little remains of the great **monastery** as fires and other disasters destroyed it, but the main front is

preserved. The convent of the Benedictine nuns shelters royal tombs and a museum with a prized 16thC monstrance (vessel for the bread or host in holy communion) by Enrique de Arfe.

San Tirso is a Romanesque church dating from the 12thC, with a Mudéjar-style tower, while Morisco stucco can be seen in a chapel of the Santuario de la Peregrina, the church of a former Franciscan convent. Five km away at Grajal de Campos is a square, 16thC **fort.**

SALAMANCA ☒ ×
On the N501 & N630, 97 km NW of Avila, 212 km NW of Madrid. The golden

stones of Salamanca have attracted scholars, kings, and clerics for centuries, and they continue to do so. Hannibal, Franco, Charles V, Unamuno, Fray Luis de León, and Columbus are some of the famous whose feet have trod these narrow streets and noble squares. Despite the onslaughts of armies and developers, the splendidly harmonious architecture of the old quarter haş survived and its university, founded in 1220, continues to fill its classrooms with students. In summer large numbers of foreign students of all ages arrive to study Spain, its language and culture, and there could not be a more appropriate setting.

The Iberian settlement here was conquered by Hannibal in 217 BC. Next came the Romans, who made it a station on their highway, the Vía de la Plata. Visigoths and Moors followed, until Alfonso VI gave it to his son-in-law Raymond of Burgundy, the builder of Avila's walls, who set about repopulating the area. During the Middle Ages the university was famed throughout Europe. In a significant battle near Salamanca in 1812, the Duke of Wellington trounced Napoleon's troops, who did considerable damage to the town. During the early part of the Civil War, Franco made the city his headquarters.

The best way to appreciate the city is to enter it via the Roman footbridge across the Río Tormes. On the ridge above stand two cathedrals, the **Nueva** and the **Vieja**. Construction of the 'new' structure began a mere four centuries ago, by Juan Gil de Hontañón and his son Rodrigo. The west front is notable for the richness of its carving and inside you will find several works by the Churriguera family. While the mixture of Gothic, Renaissance, and Baroque styles is impressive, I find the Romanesque magnificence of the Catedral Vieja (its exterior is masked by the newer building) more appealing. Consecrated in 1160, it has a beautiful dome and at the main altar a remarkable 15thC reredos (decorative screen behind altar). Fifty-three **paintings by Nicolás Florentino** depict the life of Christ, with a fresco above showing the Last Judgment.

A short walk takes you to the **Patio de Las Escuelas**, a courtyard wall-to-wall with Plateresque carving. The entrance to the university, in the courtyard, is particularly brilliant. Among the sculpted figures are the Catholic Monarchs, Ferdinand and Isabel, whose gift this masterpiece was. In the Middle Ages Salamanca University was one of the great European centres of learning, ranked by Pope Alexander IV alongside Bologna, Oxford, and Paris. It was a spearhead of intellectual thought and had more than 10,000 students and 25 colleges. The teachings of Copernicus were permitted here when they were regarded as heretical elsewhere and Columbus consulted the astronomy professors when planning his voyage. Only later would the heavy weight of the Inquisition crush all intellectual inquiry. Salamanca today is a marvellous place to study, but it has yet to retrieve its ancient prestige.

In the university (closed Sunday and holiday afternoons), you can visit two shrines to the principle of free thought. The first is the gloomy hall where students listened to the teachings of the eminent theologian Fray Luís de León. You can sit on the same uncomfortable benches on which they sat. In 1572 he was jailed on charges of heresy. Set free after five years of interrogation, spirit unquenched, he returned to Salamanca and, before an expectant audience, began his lecture with the words: 'As we were saying yesterday...' Another significant event occurred in the Paraninfo, an assembly hall where in 1936, as Fascism enveloped the country, the one-armed, one-eyed General Millán Astray, founder of the Spanish Legion, publicly clashed with the Rector of the university, Miguel de Unamuno, Spain's greatest thinker of the time. Courageously, Unamuno attacked the general's Neanderthal views and especially his mindless slogan *Long live death!* 'No!' said Unamuno, to an audience that included Franco's wife.'Long live intelligence!'.

Salamanca has numerous other buildings of note, including the **Convento de Las Dueñas** with its magnificent 16thC cloister and **Colegio de Fonseca**, with its Berruguete altarpiece and Renaissance patio, also known as Colegio de los Irlandeses because it was founded in 1592 to train Irish priests. The Gothic-Renaissance **Casa de las Conchas**, so-called because of the scallop shells, symbol of Santiago, carved on its walls, was closed for more than 20 years. But in 1993, after costly renovation, it was re-opened as a public library with 44,000 volumes.

The focus of the old city is the **Plaza Mayor**, perhaps the finest square in Spain (though there is serious competition). Philip V built it between 1729 and 1733 in thanks for Salamanca's loyalty in the War of Succession; the Churriguera brothers and Andrés García Quiñones were responsible for the harmonious design, with its arcades and three storeys of balconies. There's no better place to dally over a cool drink, watching the strollers endlessly circling the plaza as they gossip, debate, negotiate, flirt.

TORO

On the N122, 33 km E of Zamora. Toro breaks the skyline dramatically as you approach, silhouetted on its eroded red ridge, still looking as the English writer Laurie Lee described it: 'like dried blood on a rusty sword'. The town is less dramatic when you reach it. It has a burned-out air, a has-been of a place where historic events took place but which is now just a small market town. Ferdinand III of Castile was crowned King of León in Toro in 1230, uniting the two kingdoms, and Peter the Cruel kept his wife María of Portugal prisoner here. The Spanish government met in 1505 in the Palacio de Las Leyes (you can see the façade). And, in 1645, the once all-powerful Duque de Olivares

RECOMMENDED RESTAURANTS

ASTORGA
La Peseta, PP; Plaza San Bartolomé, 3; *tel.* 987 61 72 75; *credit cards* MC, V; *closed* Sun eve, mid-Oct to mid-Nov.

Once upon a time, long ago, no doubt you could eat for not much more than a peseta in this popular establishment. Then along came James Michener and heaped praise on its chick peas and marinated pork in his book *Iberia*. Instant fame. Large helpings of local dishes are guaranteed, although the locals murmur that it is no longer a bargain.

AVILA
El Molino de la Losa, PPP; Bajada de la Losa, 12; *tel.* 920 21 11 01; *credit cards* MC, V; *closed* Mon in winter.

The restaurant is located in a 15thC water-mill which has been tastefully restored. A beautiful setting in which to enjoy such dishes as suckling pig and *Alubias del Barco* (beans of El Barco).

Mesón El Rastro, PP; Plaza del Rastro, 1; *tel.* 920 21 12 18; *credit cards* AE, DC, MC, V.

In an old house against the walls, this is a handy spot to sample traditional cooking, including kid stew, lamb chops, and sweetbreads.

LEON
Bodega Regia, PP; General Mola, 5;

tel. 987 21 31 73; *credit cards* AE, MC, V; *closed* Sun.

In a cul-de-sac just off Mola Street, Bodega Regia offers traditional dishes in its beamed dining-room. Oven-baked trout and frogs' legs León-style are recommended. An interesting range of Duero wines.

Mesón Leonés del Racimo de Oro, P-PP; *tel.* 987 25 75 75; *credit cards* AE, DC, MC, V; *closed* Sun eve, Tue.

Right against the city walls, with a decaying, yellowed exterior, this former inn for pilgrims looks old enough to have welcomed Cervantes as a diner. Excellent traditional dishes at reasonable prices.

SALAMANCA
Río de la Plata, PP; Plaza Peso, 1; *tel.* 923 21 90 05; *credit cards*, none; *closed* Mon & Jul.

You may need to reserve as it is a popular, fairly-priced restaurant. Regional dishes such as stuffed partridge and rabbit stew are recommended.

ZAMORA
Casa Mariano, PP-PPP; Avda Portugal, 28; *tel.* 980 53 44 87; *credit cards* AE, DC, MC, V; *closed* Sun & Mon eve.
A reliable standby.

died here in exile and disgrace.

Old houses line the arcaded Plaza Mayor, where there are a number of bars and restaurants. The most striking sight is the finely-carved, polychromed *Last Judgment* of the **Pórtico de la Gloria**, the western entrance of the Romanesque **collegiate church of Santa María la Mayor**. From the esplanade nearby you have a fine view of the Duero River and its plain. A modern three-star hotel, the **Juan II** (**PP**; *tel.* 980 69 03 00), with a reasonably-priced restaurant, commands the same view.

The bull-ring, dating from 1828, is one of the oldest in Spain. Toro, long known for its wine, has made a big effort to upgrade the quality. Several *bodegas* can be visited.

VILLAFRANCA DEL BIERZO 🛏

See Bierzo, El, page 66.

ZAMORA 🛏 ✕

On the N630, 98 km W of Valladolid. When the wars to push back Moorish dominance of the peninsula were in full fury and warlords struggled for control of Castile, walled Zamora standing proudly on its bluff above the Duero River was a key strategic point. Some of the most dramatic events in the career of El Cid took place in or near Zamora. The long cobbled streets of the elongated old town bring you to the **cathedral**, a transitional Romanesque-Gothic structure. The pointed vaulting in the interior is said to represent a turning point in early Gothic.

Zamora has several charmingly simple and uncluttered Romanesque churches, among which the small **church of Santiago del Burgos** is beautifully proportioned, and breathes a serenity not always found in the more elaborate architectural styles. The **Doña Urraca** gateway is named after the daughter of Ferdinand I. Given power over the Zamora fiefdom, she was forced to defend it against her brother Sancho, who was murdered near this gate.

Zamora's Holy Week processions are solemn and spectacular.

Between Bilbao and Madrid
Vitoria, Logroño and Soria

490 km; map Michelin 442, 1:400,000

Sharp changes in scenery, climate and culture in this slice of the peninsula between Madrid and the Bay of Biscay will shake any stereotyped ideas you may have about Spain. Whether travelling the whole route or visiting places of interest at random, you have the chance to see places well away from the tourist track.

From Bilbao the road weaves its way up green, wooded valleys to scale the Cantabrian range before descending to the *meseta*, the central plateau. You will immediately notice a change in atmosphere in Vitoria, which though capital of the Basque Country lies in a transition area, on the threshold of Castile.

A little south of Vitoria is the famed wine region of La Rioja, covered in detail in Local Explorations: 9. The vines grow along the valley of upper Ebro River, which rises in Cantabria and flows across northern Spain to debouch in the Mediterranean.

South of La Rioja stretches the least populated of the peninsula's provinces, Soria, which forms the eastern boundary of the Castilla-León region. Perhaps because it has few outstanding monuments, Soria receives little attention from visitors. It has a slow, relaxed pace and you will certainly feel as if you are breaking new ground if you explore its old towns with crumbling castles, its bleak moorlands and the wild mountains of the Sierra de Urbión. The same can be said of Guadalajara province, so close to Madrid but in many ways locked in the past, with medieval townships such as Atienza to remind you of feuds and crusades.

Pork dishes and snails in sauce are favourites in the Basque province of Alava, while the Rioja area is an ideal place to enjoy roast lamb accompanied by the outstanding wines. Roast suckling pig and lamb, game dishes and smoked trout are some of the specialities of Soria.

Two days are enough to see the main sights if you stick to the red route, using the fast four-lane A68 between Bilbao and Logroño. Allow an extra day if you want to linger around the wineries of Rioja and one or two days more (the green route) if you have time to clamber the battlements of Berlanga and Gormaz castles or roam the heights of the wilderness areas. If you want to explore a particular area from a base, Vitoria, Logroño, and Soria are the obvious overnight spots.

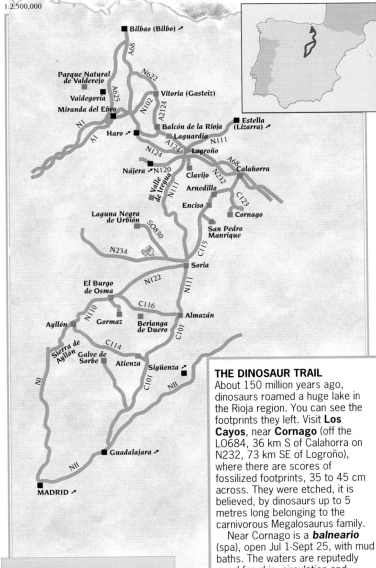

1:2,500,000

THE DINOSAUR TRAIL

About 150 million years ago, dinosaurs roamed a huge lake in the Rioja region. You can see the footprints they left. Visit **Los Cayos**, near **Cornago** (off the LO684, 36 km S of Calahorra on N232, 73 km SE of Logroño), where there are scores of fossilized footprints, 35 to 45 cm across. They were etched, it is believed, by dinosaurs up to 5 metres long belonging to the carnivorous Megalosaurus family.

Near Cornago is a *balneario* (spa), open Jul 1-Sept 25, with mud baths. The waters are reputedly good for skin, circulation and breathing problems.

More fossilized footprints are visible at **Enciso** (on the C115 near **Arnedillo**, south-east of Logroño). Arnedillo too has a spa, open mid-June to mid-October, with a hotel (**Balneario de Arnedillo, PP**; *tel.* 941 39 40 00). Spain is particularly rich in dinosaur traces (see also Galve in Spain Overall: 14).

TRANSPORT

Regular bus services link the main cities; rail services are not so comprehensive. Vitoria has five trains a day to San Sebastián and to Madrid via Burgos. Passengers between Vitoria and Logroño have to change at Miranda de Ebro. Soria is poorly connected by train: there are four trains a day to Madrid and others to Pamplona and Zaragoza.

SIGHTS & PLACES OF INTEREST

ALMAZAN
On the N111, 35 km S of Soria. Ancient walls and three original entrance gateways bear witness to this small town's troubled past. It was on the frontier of Aragón and played an important role in the Reconquest. The Order of St John of Acre was founded here in the 13thC. Almazán has a number of Romanesque churches and Renaissance palaces. The beautiful façade of the **Palacio de Hurtado de Mendoza** faces the Plaza Mayor, where you also find the **church of San Miguel** which has a remarkable cupola showing Muslim influence. A carving in the north transept depicts the murder of St Thomas Becket in Canterbury Cathedral.

Yemas, sweets made from sugar and egg yolks, are a local speciality.

ARNEDILLO
Also Enciso and Cornago, see The Dinosaur Trail, page 75.

ATIENZA ✕
On the C114, 85 km NE of Guadalajara. Approaching Atienza across bleak, empty uplands, with here and there a lone shepherd guarding his flock, a visitor can easily imagine that El Cid still rides these ranges. Atienza Castle thrusts upwards from a 1,250 m rock above a medieval village of tiled roofs and church towers.

Besieged many times, Atienza now has barely 400 inhabitants and welcomes the latest invaders with open arms. Several bars and restaurants cater to their needs. A colourful fiesta, **La Caballada**, is held at Pentecost to mark a heroic 12thC ride by local horsemen to rescue the infant Alfonso VIII from Ferdinand II of León.

AYLLON
On the N110, 36 km SW of El Burgo de Osma. In the north-west of Segovia province, close to the Soria border, Ayllón is a quaint medieval village, complete with old walls and arcaded plaza. Thirty kilometres to the south is the **Sierra de Ayllón**, an extension of the Guadarrama range. This zone of upland meadows, mountains, and forests includes the **Hayedo de Tejera Negra Nature Park** with a vast stand of beech

trees. Far removed from the rest of the world, it is a great area for hiking and observing birds of prey. The best access is from Cantalojas, via the village of **Galve de Sorbe**, on the GU160, 95 km north of Guadalajara – buses run there from Guadalajara.

Villages in the Galve area, known as the *pueblos negros* because of their black slate roofs, preserve a number of medieval fiestas. Often the *botarga* , a masked, vividly-garbed figure representing the devil or Judas, takes part. He appears in an ancient dance performed on the Sunday after Corpus Christi in the remote hamlet of **Valverde de los Arroyos**, south of Galve. Eight men, with elaborate flowery head-dresses and embroidered shawls around their waists, perform ritual steps to the music of drum and whistle.

BALCON DE LA RIOJA
Off the A2124, 35 km S of Vitoria. As you cross the 1,100 m Herrera Pass, this look-out offers magnificent views of the mountains, villages and vineyards of the Ebro Valley.

BERLANGA DE DUERO
Off the C116, 24 km SE of El Burgo de Osma. The 15thC castle dominating the skyline behind Berlanga breathes military arrogance with its double walls and circular towers. Entering the town through an ancient gateway, you wander along pillared streets to the **Plaza Mayor** and to the **Colegiata**, a Renaissance church with impressive reredos (decorative screen behind altar) and tombs.

Eight kilometres south-east of Berlanga off the Sigüenza road is the well-preserved **Ermita de San Baudelio**, a curious 11thC Mozarabic sanctuary. Only fragments remain of its frescoes, most of which were removed to New York in 1922 and are in the Metropolitan Museum, an example of the pillaging that deprived Spain of many valuable art works.

BILBAO
See Spain Overall: 1.

BURGO DE OSMA, EL 🍴 ✕

On the N122, 56 km SW of Soria. Traffic thunders past El Burgo intent on reaching Madrid and ignoring this gem of a town, with its crumbling medieval walls, delightful main square and colonnaded streets. 'Osma' derives from Uxama Argelae, a Roman settlement nearby where mosaics are still preserved.

The bishopric of El Burgo is one of Spain's oldest, dating back to Visigothic times, and the splendid local architecture is the result of long-standing church patronage. Bishop Alvarez de Acosta founded the **Universidad de Santa Catalina** (now a school) in the 16thC; it has a fine Plateresque façade. A century later, Bishop Arévalo y Torres built the Baroque **Hospital de San Agustín**. In the 17thC, Bishop Calderón constructed the Town Hall and the **Plaza Mayor**, one of Castile's pleasantest squares.

However, none could match the grandeur of the Gothic **cathedral**, founded by Bishop Pedro de Osma in the 12thC. He is El Burgo's patron saint and his elaborate **carved tomb** is inside the temple, which has an outstanding reredos (decorative screen behind altar) created by Juan de Juni. Other points of interest include the **Capilla de Palafox** designed by Juan de Villanueva, regarded as the pioneer of neo-classical architecture in Spain, and the cathedral **museum** with a priceless collection of codices (manuscript books).

A number of bars serve *tapas* around the Plaza Mayor, but particularly recommended is the convivial **Taberna El Machote** on Plaza Santo Domingo. Its excellent *tapas* – you can gracefully decline the beans with pig ears – go down well with the traditional accompaniment here, *un claro* (a glass of rosé

RECOMMENDED HOTELS

(EL) BURGO DE OSMA
Virrey 11, PP; Mayor, 4; *tel.* 975 34 13 11.

A Baroque, kitsch marble palace, guaranteed to blow your mind. This modern three-star hotel incorporates coats of arms, carved and polished walnut, stained glass, and in the lobby an 8 m-high 5,000-piece chandelier. It is a dream come true for proprietor Gil Martínez. And it offers pretty good value for money.

BUDGET ACCOMMODATION
(EL) BURGO DE OSMA
Virrey Palafox, P; Universidad, 7; *tel.* 975 34 02 22.

Basic accommodation in the same building as the restaurant recommended on page 81.

SORIA
Las Heras, P; Plaza Ramón y Cajal, 5; *tel.* 975 21 33 46.

Close to the Tourism Office.

VITORIA
Dato 28, P; Eduardo Dato, 28; *tel.* 945 14 72 30.

Small, cosy, near the station.

LOGROÑO
Herencia Rioja, PPP; Marqués de Murrieta, 14; *tel.* 941 21 02 22.

A modern, well-appointed, four-star hotel in downtown Logroño.

SORIA
Leonor, PP; Paseo del Mirón, s/n; *tel.* 975 22 02 50.

This three-star hotel on a hilltop overlooks city and countryside. It is a pleasant, three-storey stone building. The basement banquet hall is often occupied at weekends by wedding parties after ceremonies at the neighbouring 16thC Baroque church, Ermita del Mirón.

Parador Antonio Machado, PPP; Parque del Castillo; 975 21 34 45.

A modern, comfortable hotel on the hill where Soria's castle once stood. Beautiful views. The restaurant, serving traditional Castilian fare (roasts, trout, game), is recommended.

VITORIA
Parador de Argómaniz, PP; Ctra Madrid-San Sebastián, Argómaniz (off the N1, 15 km E of Vitoria); *tel.* 945 29 32 00.

Converted from a 17thC palace, the stone-built parador is in a peaceful spot; fine views. Excellent Basque dishes are served in the restaurant, which occupies the former granary.

wine). El Burgo also has a famed restaurant and one of Spain's more unusual hotels (see pages 77 and 81).

CALAHORRA

On the N322 and A68, 48 km SE of Logroño. Once the Celtiberian stronghold of Calagurris Nassica, which fell to the Romans after an horrendous siege, Calahorra today is an undistinguished town, living from fruit and vegetable preserves. In 1236 Henry of Trastamara was proclaimed king of Castile here. The cathedral, rebuilt in the 15thC, has a Plateresque reredos (decorative screen behind altar) and a north portal with Renaissance embellishments. The **Parador Marco Quintiliano (PPP**; *tel.* 941 13 03 58) is a useful stop.

CLAVIJO

See Logroño, this page.

ESTELLA (LIZARRA)

See Spain Overall: 6.

GALVE DE SORBE

See Ayllon, page 76.

GORMAZ

Off the SO160, 15 km SE of El Burgo de Osma. Dominating the plain around it, the walls and turrets of the **castle** are deceptive. It is just a shell, but it grabs your attention from afar due to its immense size: locals claim it is Europe's largest castle. Built by the Moors in the 10thC, it was later conquered by Christian forces and modified. Do not confuse Gormaz with **San Esteban de Gormaz**. This is a walled town on the N122, 13 km west of El Burgo, near an ancient bridge over the Duero river. It has two examples of Romanesque architectural harmony, the churches of **San Miguel** and **Del Rivero.**

GUADALAJARA

See Spain Overall: 7.

HARO

See Local Explorations: 9.

IREGUA, VALLE DE

Travelling south from Logroño towards Soria on the N111, you follow the Iregua River valley, soon encountering towering rock faces at Islallana. Scenery is spectacular as you ziz-zag into the **Sierra de Cameros**, passing picturesque

Villanueva, towards the 1,700 m **Piqueras Pass**. Even in May, I have been blocked by snow on this road.

LAGUARDIA

On the A124, 18 km NW of Logroño. Tourism Office, Sancho Abarca; tel. 941 60 08 45. Medieval gateways pierce the 13thC walls of this charming hill-top town in the Alava section of the Rioja wine district. The **church of San Juan Bautista** and the naves of **Santa María** date from the 12thC. Coats of arms grace medieval mansions. The streets are too narrow to allow cars to park, so you really feels as if you are stepping back into the past, an illusion shattered at weekends and on holidays when crowds arrive to sample the local wine, stored in cellars below the houses. The many signs declaring: 'Se vende vino en garrafones' indicate that you can buy it in demijohns.

There are a number of dolmens in the area and on the outskirts of town the remains of **La Hoya**, a primitive settlement where you can see a replica of an Iron Age home (from November to April, only open mornings); enquire at the helpful Tourism Office.

LAGUNA NEGRA DE URBION

On the SO830, off the N234, 54 km NW of Soria. Vast pine forests clothe the slopes of the wild Sierra de Urbión, rising to more than 2,000 m. The road deteriorates as it climbs upwards to a parking spot below the Laguna Negra (black lagoon). Walk up through the pines to the dark lake bounded by high cliffs. At one end a spectacular waterfall cascades down. It is an ideal picnic spot on a fine day. Another Laguna Negra (de Neila) lies to the west in Burgos province (see Spain Overall: 2).

LOGROÑO 🛏 ✕

Off the A68 and on the N111, 86 km SE of Vitoria. Tourism Office, Paseo del Principe de Vergara; tel. 941 26 06 65. A busy industrial city of 130,000 inhabitants, occupying a strategic spot on the Ebro, Logroño prospers from a fertile region producing crops of peppers, asparagus and artichokes, and the Rioja wines.

An unusual feature of the **church of Santa María del Palacio** is its 13thC pyramid-shaped lantern tower; originally the church was part of the **Palacio de Alfonso VII**. Logroño's **cathedral** was built in the 15thC but a later addition was the Baroque façade with an ornate portal recessed between the building's twin towers.

The area around Calle Laurel has numerous bars serving *tapas*.

Fifteen km south of Logroño, ruins of a **castle** stand at Clavijo where in 844 St James miraculously appeared on a white charger to help the Christians rout the Moors. From this grew the legend of St James the Moor-slayer (Santiago Matamoros) (see Spain Overall: 3).

MADRID

See pages 170-192.

NAJERA

See Local Explorations: 9.

SAN PEDRO MANRIQUE

Off the C115, 35 km NE of Soria. This village in a remote corner of Soria province attracts crowds every June when an unusual rite takes place in front of the parish church. On June 23, the eve of San Juan, villagers walk barefoot over red-hot ashes, sometimes carrying another person on their back, emerging unscathed. It is said that the rite symbolizes the crossing of the equinox. During the same fiestas, another clearly pagan ceremony takes place when young girls known as the Las Móndidas, crowned with fanciful head-dresses, perform a series of rites. They are believed to represent the priestesses of Celtiberian tribes.

SIGUENZA

See Spain Overall: 7.

SORIA 🛏 ✕

On the N111, 226 km NE of Madrid. Tourism Office, Plaza Ramón y Cajal, 2; tel. 975 21 20 52. Serene, serious Soria (population 30,000) is one of Spain's smallest provincial capitals. Industry has had little impact and poor communications have meant that the province has been largely forgotten – and undeveloped. Antonio Machado, one of Spain's greatest 20thC poets, lived here for many years and praised its 'martial, mystical' spirit, far removed from that of Machado's birthplace, Seville.

Strategically positioned on the Duero river, Soria was heavily involved in the wars to oust the Moors. It prospered during the heyday of the Mesta, the

• *Laguna Negra de Urbión - see page 78.*

sheep farmers' league, which moved its vast flocks between Soria's pastures and those of the rest of Castile and Extremadura.

Featureless modern structures have not enhanced the city, but it retains enough of past splendour and easy-going atmosphere to make a visit pleasant and worthwhile. The unhurried pedestrians have that in-from-the-country look, as you stroll from the Plaza Ramón y Cajal to the Plaza Mayor where two lions sternly face the City Hall. Byzantine influences are evident in the 12thC century Romanesque **church of San Juan de Rabanera**, the portico of which, depicting the life of San Nicolás, was transferred early this century from another church. The Gothic **church of San Pedro** has a magnificent 12thC cloister, while across the river are the remains of the **Monasterio de San Juan de Duero**, built by the Templars. It has a remarkable cloister, combining

79

Muslim and Romanesque features, with interwoven arches.

Continuing south along the river bank, one of Machado's favourite walks, you pass the former Templars' **Capilla de San Polo** and reach the **Ermita de San Satuario**, a chapel perched on a rock. Dedicated to Soria's patron saint, it has 13thC frescoes.

Sheep tycoons constructed some fine residences, several of them on Calle de Caballeros (Gentlemen's Street) and Aduana Vieja, but these are outshone by the **Palacio de los Condes de Gómara**, with its vast Renaissance façade.

Eight km north of Soria on a hill overlooking the junction of the Duero and Tera rivers are the **ruins of Numancia**, once the centre of Celtiberian resistance to Roman invaders. The Romans, commanded by Scipio Aemilianus, sealed off the town by building 10 km of ramparts around it. After eight months of siege, the people destroyed their houses and themselves rather than surrender: the word *numantino* has entered the Spanish language to describe a hopeless cause. The remains are largely of the city rebuilt by the Romans. Tool, ceramics, and statuary from Numantia and prehistoric relics can be seen in Soria's Museo Numantino on Paseo Espolón.

Soria is at its liveliest during the **San Juan fiestas** at the end of June, which last nearly a week. But in winter this is one of the coldest places in Spain.

VALDEREJO, PARQUE NATURAL DE
Off the N625, 80 km S of Bilbao. This sparsely inhabited mountainous zone lies in the extreme west of Alava province, virtually surrounded by Burgos province. Access is via the L622 to Valdegovía (full name Villanueva de Valdegovía) and up the valley of the Omecillo River.

Sheer limestone cliffs, lush meadows, and beech, pine and oak woods haunted by deer and boar make it an attractive area for outdoor types. Information on walks in the park area is available from the Basque government Tourism Office in Vitoria.

VITORIA (GASTEIZ) ⊯ ✕
On the N240, 66 km SE of Bilbao. Tourism Office, Parque de la Florida; tel. 945 13 13 21. Vitoria's well-preserved **old town** is

an island of solid grey stone monuments and Renaissance palaces rising above the modern industrial city which spreads over a fertile plain. As capital of the Basque country and the province of Alava, Vitoria (population 200,000) has grown fast. The regional parliament meets here and it is the seat of various official institutions. Even so, Alava is less fervently Basque than the two other Basque provinces and only a small minority speak the Basque tongue.

The name Gasteiz has been revived by the regional government, recalling Visigothic origins. A hill settlement existed here when, in 1181, King Sancho the Wise of Navarra fortified the site; remains of the walls endure.

Vitoria prospered as a commercial centre trading in wool, iron and cereals between Castile and the coast. A famous battle was fought in 1813 west of the city on the road to Nanclares. Anglo-Portuguese and Spanish forces, commanded by the Duke of Wellington, defeated the French under Joseph Bonaparte and Marshal Jourdan. The French, who lost 8,000 men and large amounts of booty, were forced to retreat to Pamplona and then abandon Spain.

A sensible spot from which to start a walk through the old quarter is the Plaza de Santo Domingo. From there you climb up the hill via Correría (Tanners) Street – the names of the narrow streets indicate the trades of those who worked there, for example Herrería (blacksmiths') Cuchillería (knife-makers'), and Zapatería (shoe-makers'). At number 151 on Correría is a particularly imposing brick and timber medieval house with a massive studded door. Inside is a lofty beamed lobby, with tree trunks forming part of the structure. The building, an inn in the 15thC, houses the El Portalón restaurant (see Recommended Restaurants).

Further up the hill stands the 14thC **Catedral de Santa María**, which has a magnificent portal featuring a polychrome Virgin and Child and a highly ornate tympanum. A capital of one of the pillars inside is most unusual, as the carving depicts a bullfight scene.

Magnificent palaces, such as that of **Escoriaza-Esquibel**, and old churches dot the quarter. The **church of San Miguel** shelters the highly-venerated jasper image of the city's patron saint, the **Virgen Blanca**. She gazes out from an alcove outside the church.

Just below San Miguel is the **Plaza de la Virgen Blanca**, lined with balconied houses, where a large monument to the Battle of Vitoria erupts from the flower beds. Vitoria's annual fiesta in honour of the Virgin has those odd features that always pop up to surprise you in Spain. As bells chime the start of the fiesta at 6 pm on August 4, El Celedón, an image symbolizing the typical peasant landing in the capital, descends by cable from San Miguel's tower to the plaza while everybody lights cigars. He wings back up to the tower in the early hours of August 9 to mark the fiesta's end.

The **Cafeteria Virgen Blanca**, in one corner of the plaza, is handy for refreshment. With its stone walls and marble-topped tables, it looks like an age-old meeting place, but until recently a shoe-shop occupied the premises.

Adjoining this square is the **Plaza de España**, a harmonious arrangement of porticoes and iron balconies. Vitoria claims to be Europe's 'greenest city per inhabitant' and one of its numerous parks, La Florida, graced by a bandstand and statuary, is a block or so to the south-west of the Plaza de España. The **Basque government building** stands in the park and the Tourism Office is on the far side.

Prehistoric axes and suits of armour are on display in the **Museo de Armería** (Arms and Armour Museum) on Fray Francisco de Vitoria, next to the **Palacio de Ajuria-Enea**, residence of the *Lehendakari*, the Basque chief minister. A large student body helps to enliven the nights in Vitoria. The streets of the old town harbour a multitude of taverns, while more polished surroundings are to be found in the area of the Plaza de la Virgen Blanca and towards the modern Avenida de Gasteiz.

RECOMMENDED RESTAURANTS

ATIENZA
Mesón de la Villa, PP; *Plaza Trigo, s/n; tel. 949 39 90 08; credit cards V; closed last two weeks Oct.*

Off the main square in an old house, this restaurant offers a greater level of sophistication than you might expect in a little village. Try the venison steak in mushroom sauce.

(EL) BURGO DE OSMA
Virrey Palafox, PP; *Universidad, 7; tel. 975 34 02 22; cards AE, DC, MC, V; closed Sun eve in winter, Dec 15-Jan 15.*

Classic Castilian cuisine in a restaurant famed in the region for its huge fixed-price banquets in February and March, celebrating the annual pig-killing. The Hotel Virrey (page 77) is run by the same family.

LOGROÑO
Avenida 21, PP; *Avda Portugal, 21; tel. 941 22 86 02; credit cards AE, DC, MC, V; closed Sun & Aug.*

Wine cellar ambience where you can enjoy Rioja dishes such as fennel-flavoured venison.

Cachetero, PP-PPP; *Laurel, 3; tel. 941 22 84 63; credit cards AE, DC, MC, V;*

closed Sun, Wed eve, Jul 15-Aug 15.

An old-established restaurant with national and international dishes.

SORIA
Mesón Castellano, PP; *Plaza Mayor, 2; tel. 975 21 30 45; credit cards AE, DC, MC, V; closed Sun, except summer, and last fortnight Jan.*

Roast suckling pig and an extensive wine list (including the renowned Vega Sicilia at 12,000 pesetas a bottle) are among the attractions of this restaurant just opposite the City Hall.

VITORIA
Casa Felipe, PP; *Fueros, 28; tel. 945 13 45 54; credit cards MC, V; closed Mon, Jun 20-Jul 20.*

A friendly, unpretentious spot with a popular bar. Simple local dishes and their own Rioja wine.

El Portalón, PPP; *Correría, 151; tel. 945 14 27 55; credit cards AE, DC, MC, V; closed Sun, Aug 10-Sept 5, Christmas, Holy Week.*

There's no sign outside to indicate one of Vitoria's finest restaurants, located in a medieval building of character. Go up to the first floor to enjoy Persian caviar or traditional regional dishes.

North-Eastern Spain

Between San Sebastián and Lleida
Navarra and Upper Aragón

400 km; maps Michelin 442 & 443, 1:400,000

Virtually a country on its own, the 10,400-square-kilometre Navarra region has just about everything but a coastline. Once an independent kingdom, it extends from the Ribera, the fertile but monotonous Ebro Plain, to the wooded valleys and peaks of the Pyrenees. You will find vineyards and cow pastures, medieval villages and an enduring sense of tradition, visible in such fiestas as that of San Fermín, the week-long carousing which envelops Navarra's capital, Pamplona, every July. Navarra has an autonomous government and has firmly resisted the embrace of the Basque Country, although many inhabitants in the north are Basques.

This section also covers the approaches to the Pyrenees in Huesca province, part of the Aragón region. For details of Huesca's Pyrenean valleys, and of the valley of Arán, further east, see Local Explorations: 10. This section and Local Explorations: 10 are highly complementary, and there are many interesting extra details on the map and in the text for Local Explorations: 10 which can be used in conjunction with this section.

Relatively few passes and tunnels traverse the Pyrenees. Roads are narrow and winding once you are north of the Ebro Valley, which offers the only fast route between the Bay of Biscay and the Mediterranean. East-west travel is slow because of the series of valleys running north to south. If you want to explore the different valleys, it makes sense to base yourself in a centre such as Pamplona or Jaca.

Navarra produces some excellent wines in vineyards of the Ebro Valley, bordering La Rioja, and *pacharán*, a strong anise-flavoured liqueur made from sloes, which is popular all over Spain. It also has some renowned cheeses, particularly that of the Roncal Valley. A local dish served all over Spain is *Trucha a la Navarra* (trout cooked with cured ham). *Bacalao al ajo arriero* (cod with peppers and tomatoes), *chistorra* (a type of sausage), and white asparagus served with mayonnaise are also typical.

My suggested red route between San Sebastián and Lleida can take under two days along the N240. Allow three to four days if you want to visit the blue sights as well. If you have abundant time to explore, take in the green sights, and Local Explorations: 10. Remember that from October to May roads in the Pyrenees may be blocked by snow.

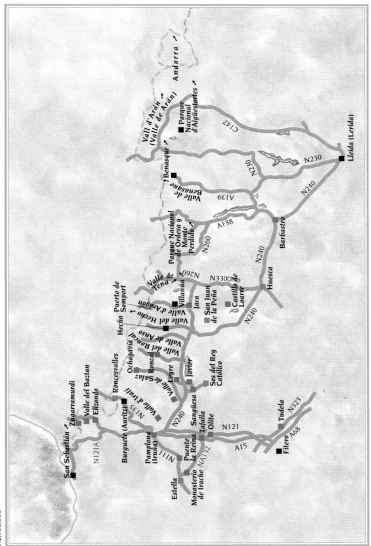

1:2,500,000

Map labels: Andorra, Vall d'Arán (Valle de Arán), Parque Nacional d'Aiguestortes, CI47, Benasque, N230, Lleida (Lerida), N230, Valle de Benasque, N230, A139, N240, A138, Parque Nacional de Ordesa y Monte Perdido, Barbastro, N260, N240, Valle de Tena, N260, Villanua, N330, Huesca, Puerto de Somport, Valle d'Aragón, Jaca, San Juan de la Peña, Castillo de Loarre, N240, Hecho, Valle del Hecho, Roncesvalles, Valle de Ansó, Ochagavía, Valle del Roncal, Roncal, Javier, Sos del Rey Católico, San Sebastián, Zugarramurdi, Valle del Baztan, Elizondo, Burguete (Auritz), Valle d'Irati, Legre, N135, N240, Sangüesa, Tafalla, Olite, Tudela, N323, Pamplona (Iruña), Puente la Reina, N111, NA132, N121, A15, Fitero, A68, Estella, Monasterio de Irache

TRANSPORT

Regular bus and train services link Lleida, Huesca, Pamplona, and San Sebastián. North of this route you have to rely on buses or minibuses from the main towns, which usually run once a day along the valleys, connecting the villages. A car is almost essential to reach the remote spots.

SIGHTS & PLACES OF INTEREST

AIGUESTORTES, PARQUE NACIONAL DE (AIGUESTORTES NATIONAL PARK)

And Pyrenean valleys nearby, see Local Explorations: 10.

ANDORRA

See Local Explorations: 11.

ANSO, BENASQUE, HECHO, TENA VALLEYS

See Local Explorations: 10.

ARAN, VALL D' (VALLE DE ARAN)

See Local Explorations: 10.

BARBASTRO ✕

On the N240, 52 km E of Huesca. A crossroads since Roman times when it was destroyed by Pompey, Barbastro has a 16thC Gothic cathedral with a separate, six-sided tower. It is the centre of the Somontano wine district.

BAZTAN, VALLE DEL

In the north of Navarra, midway between Pamplona and Biarritz, the River Bidasoa flows south from the Pyrenees, then does a U-turn 50 km north of Pamplona to flow north to the Bay of Biscay. **Elizondo** (on the N121B, 58 km N of Pamplona) is the capital of this area of charming Basque villages, fertile pastures, salmon streams and witches – close to the French border visit the **Cueva de Zugarramurdi**, a witches' meeting place.

BURGUETE (AURITZ) ⊨

See Recommended Hotels, page 85.

ELIZONDO

See Baztan Valley, above.

ESTELLA

On the N111, 43 km SW of Pamplona. Called Estella la Bella (the beautiful) for the splendour of its many historic buildings, Estella was repopulated by French settlers in 1090. Perhaps for this reason Aymeric Picaud, the French chronicler of the Camino (Pilgrim's Way) de Santiago, who had little good to say of Navarra, praised Estella as 'fertile with good bread, the best wine, meat and fish, and full of every type of delight'.

Estella is a friendly little town on the River Ega, with a bustling market on Thursdays. At one time it was capital of the Kingdom of Navarra. Sancho the Wise built the **Palacio de los Reyes** (Royal Palace), a rare example of secular Romanesque, in the 12thC. Up some steps from the palace is the most impressive building in town, the **church of San Pedro de la Rúa**, of the same era as the Royal Palace. It has a dazzling Romanesque **cloister**, with biblical and other scenes carved on its capitals.

The **church of San Miguel**, on the other side of the river, is notable for its Romanesque façade with magnificent sculptured tympanum.

Pilgrims on the way to Santiago found shelter in the **Monasterio de Irache**, 3 km south of Estella on the NA132. The Benedictine abbots once had the right to vote in Navarra's parliament and for several centuries Irache's university was held in esteem.

FITERO ⊨

See Recommended Hotels, page 85.

HUESCA

On the N240, 72 km N of Zaragoza. Tourism Office, General Lasheras, 5; tel. 974 22 57 78. Modern Huesca, capital of the northern province of the Aragón region, is not over-stimulating, but its past addiction to decapitation has a certain bloody appeal. Four heads on the town coat of arms are those of Berber leaders killed when Pedro I of Aragón ousted the Moors in 1096.

Next door to the **Provincial Museo**, where there are several works by Goya, is a 12thC hall known as the **Bell Chamber**. Ramiro II, who against his will gave up his life as a monk to become king of Aragón, found his rule was made impossible by the intrigues and manipulations of his nobles. So one day he called them to this chamber to see 'a bell that would resound throughout Aragón'; as they entered, they were killed and their heads neatly arranged in a circle to represent a bell, with one hanging above to represent the clapper. Ramiro's bell did indeed resound throughout the land and its message was clear.

As a monk, Ramiro lived in the Benedictine monastery of San Pedro el Viejo and, along with Alfonso The Battler, is buried in the Romanesque San Pedro Church. Huesca's Gothic **cathedral** is

RECOMMENDED HOTELS

FITERO
Virrey Palafox, PP; *off the* N113, 104 *km* S *of Pamplona at Extramuros, s/n; tel.* 948 77 61 00; *closed* Dec 13 *to* Mar 15.

A spa hotel with thermal baths. Fitero, at Navarra's south-western corner, has an impressive 12thC monastery.

LEYRE
Hospedería, PP; *Yesa; tel.* 948 88 41 00; *closed* Dec 8–Mar 1.

Next door to the monastery in a beautiful mountain area.

OLITE
Parador Príncipe de Viana, PPP; *Plaza Teobaldos,* 2; *tel.* 948 74 00 00.

Four-posters and regal splendour await you in this parador in Olite Castle, a haughty structure with multiple square towers, once the residence of the kings of Navarra.

PAMPLONA
La Perla, PP; *Plaza del Castillo,* 1; *tel.* 948 22 77 06.

Pamplona's oldest hotel and it

shows, but it has atmosphere.

Maisonnave, PPP; N*ueva,* 20; *tel.* 948 22 26 00.

Comfortable, central.

SOS DEL REY CATOLICO
Parador Fernando de Aragón, PP; *Arquitecto Sainz de Vicuña,* 1; *tel.* 948 88 80 11.

A solid stone building blending with the medieval surroundings. An excellent restaurant.

BUDGET ACCOMMODATION
Consult Aragón and Navarra's *Turismo Rural* guides for bargain-priced stays in farms and village houses.

BURGUETE
Hostal Burguete, P; U*nica,* 51; *tel.* 948 76 00 05.

This simple inn has changed little since Hemingway occupied room number eight in the 1920s, as described in *The Sun Also Rises*.

JACA
Ciudad de Jaca, P; 7 *de* Fe*brero,* 8; *tel.* 974 36 43 11.

Central, one-star hotel.

PAMPLONA
Bearán, P; *San Nicolás,* 25; *tel.* 948 22 34 28.

Located over a restaurant of the same name.

also worth a visit, if only to view the exceptional alabaster reredos (decorative screen behind altar) by Forment.

Colourful processions, bullfights and concerts of jazz, rock, *salsa* and *zarzuela* feature in the annual homage on August 10 to Huesca's patron saint, San Lorenzo. On August 15 offerings are made to the saint, attended by folk dancers in regional dress – a chance to see the *jota*, Aragón's lively dance.

IRACHE, MONASTERIO DE
See *Estella, page* 84.

IRATI, VALLE DEL
See *Roncesvalles, page* 88.

JACA 🛏 ✕
On *the* N240, 68 *km* N *of Huesca. Tourism Office, A*vda Regimiento de Galicia,* 2; *tel.* 974 36 00 98. The main town in the Aragón Pyrenees, Jaca is a small but important communications centre. It was one of the first towns to drive out the Moors, around 810, and its *fueros*

(rights) were confirmed in 1063, making them among the oldest in Spain.

The star-shaped, 16thC **Ciudadela** (citadel) impresses for the sheer massiveness of its ramparts.

Hemmed in by other buildings, the 11thC **cathedral** is one of Spain's oldest in Romanesque style, showing the classic architectural features imported from France, which served as a model for other churches along the Camino (Pilgrim's Way) de Santiago. The **Diocesan Museum**, well-lit and arranged, partly in the cathedral cloister, should not be missed. It has some magnificent medieval art, particularly the Romanesque frescoes rescued from various churches. On the first Friday in May, young Jaca women take part in a mock Christians v Moors battle to commemo-

DETOUR – **LA OLIVA**
The ancient Cistercian **Monasterio de La Oliva,** 34 km SE of Olite, is worth a detour. Take the N121, turn left on the NA124, and right at Carcastillo. La Oliva's austere 12thC church is said to be the oldest in Gothic style in Spain. A Gothic cloister was added three centuries later. Continuing southeast on the NA124 towards Sádaba, you can branch off southwards to view **Las Bárdenas Reales**, a large desert area of spectacular eroded hills. You can also view this from the **shrine of Nuestra Señora del Yugo,** 18 km from Tudela: turn right off the NA134 at Arguedas.

rate a victory 1,200 years ago.

JAVIER
Off the N240, 45 km E of Pamplona. This picture-postcard castle dates from the 10th and 11thC, but much has been rebuilt. It is the birthplace of Francis Xavier, who helped Ignatius Loyola found the Jesuit movement and did missionary work in the Orient, particularly in Japan where he converted 200,000. He was canonized in 1622. Jesuit guardians now organize guided visits.

LEYRE, MONASTERIO DE 🏠
Off the N240, 52 km E of Pamplona. Amid the mountains above the turquoise Yesa reservoir, the monastery of San Salvador de Leyre was once the Navarra kings' burial place. Their bones are stored in a lead-lined, iron-clad chest in the Romanesque-Gothic **church**. The oldest part of the building is the primitive Romanesque **crypt**, with its squat columns of varying height. Benedictine monks occupy the rebuilt monastery.

Near the Hospedería (see Hotels, page 85), you will see an iron grill covering a hole in the ground. The monks used this as a primitive refrigerator, packing snow around their food.

LLEIDA (LERIDA)
See Spain Overall: 7.

LOARRE, CASTILLO DE
Off the N240, via Ayerbe, 40 km NW of Huesca. Few military structures can match the sheer drama of this mighty 11thC fortress, built by Sancho Ramírez, King of Navarra and Aragón, for the use – although he was not to know it – of modern film-makers. It bestrides a rocky outcrop, commanding panoramic views. Within the walls is a beautiful Romanesque **church**.

North-west of the castle, near the village of Riglos, are **Los Mallos**, first sight of which may well have you rubbing your eyes. They are pinkish hills of conglomerate eroded into pillars and popular with climbers.

OCHAGAVIA
See Roncal, Vall de, page 87.

OLITE 🏠
On the N121, 36 km S of Pamplona. A 13thC **castle** dominates Olite. A palatial addition was made to the old fortress early in the 15thC by Charles III, The Noble, who had lived in France and incorporated many elaborate French features to please his queen, Leonor.

ORDESA Y MONTE PERDIDO, PARQUE NACIONAL DE
And the Pyrenean valleys nearby, including Ara, Vellos, Cinca and Yaga, see Local Explorations: 10.

PAMPLONA (IRUÑEA) 🏠 ✕
On the N111, 92 km SE of San Sebastián. Tourism Office, Duque de Ahumada, 3; tel. 948 22 07 41. Capital of the old Kingdom of Navarra, Pamplona has an international image of reckless revelry thanks to its annual **San Fermín fiesta**, made famous by the American writer Ernest Hemingway. (See box, page 87.) In fact, for most of the year it is sedately provincial.

The city, said to have been founded by Pompey, was occupied by the Moors but they were soon expelled by Charlemagne and the Kingdom of Navarra came into being. It extended north of the Pyrenees, until in 1512 it was forced to join Castile, although retaining some independence until 1841.

On the **Plaza del Castillo**, with its bandstand, trees and arcades, you can follow Hemingway's example by enjoying a drink at the century-old Café Iruña. A step away are the Tourism Office and the **Palacio de Navarra**, housing the regional government. Next door are Navarra's **archives**, which include the *fueros* (ancient rights).

Head north from the square to the **Ayuntamiento** with its Baroque façade; from its balcony a rocket launched on July 6 opens the fiesta of San Fermín, Pamplona's first bishop and the city's patron saint.

Narrow streets lead to the recently restored **cathedral**. Behind the imposing neo-classical façade by Ventura Rodríguez you find five Gothic naves, the grandiose alabaster tomb of Navarra's Charles III and his wife Leonor of Trastamara, carved by French sculptor Jean de Lomme; also a fine cloister.

Stroll to the park and ramparts of **La Ciudadela**, a huge fortress built at Philip II's command.

Hotel prices double and triple during the fiesta week and many rooms are booked up to a year in advance. If you only plan to spend 24 hours in Pamplona and cannot be bothered searching for a bed, dump your baggage at a special deposit near the bus station and join the revellers.

PUENTE LA REINA

On the N111, 24 *km SW of Pamplona.* This is where the two main pilgrim routes to Santiago, coming from Roncesvalles and Aragón's Puerto de Somport (Somport Pass), converged. Doña Mayor, a queen of Navarra, gave her name to this town by ordering a bridge built across the Arga River to aid the pilgrims; nearly a thousand years later, they still tramp across it. They pay their respects at the **Iglesia del Crucifijo**, which houses a carving of Christ said to have been brought from Germany, before walking along the town's main street, with its balconies and coats of arms, to the **church of Santiago.**

RONCAL & SALAZAR, VALLES DE

Visiting these two valleys (60 *km E of Pamplona, via the* N240 *and* NA178) makes a handy round trip. *En route* are pastoral landscapes and villages such

---

PARTY TIME AT PAMPLONA

Only one thing is in short supply during the good-humoured Las Sanfermines fiesta: sleep. Bleary-eyed, I was finally dozing off one morning when a brass band came blasting past my *pension* – at 4 am. Five million litres of wine and beer are consumed during Europe's biggest, wildest party. Hundreds of thousands of visitors of all nationalities dance, drink, sing and philander around the clock for eight days, July 6-14. Some return again and again, to run with the bulls, or just for the party. Sensitive local residents leave town for the duration.

Hemingway started it all when he wrote *The Sun Also Rises*, based on his experiences in 1925. He recorded buying a goatskin containing seven litres of wine for four pesetas. Americans, in particular, fell for Pamplona; as writer Allen Josephs, a bullfighting and Hemingway *aficionado*, explained it to me: 'Running with those bulls is a way of dealing with your own fear and heightening the sense of being alive.' Since the *encierros* (bull-runs) began in the 19thC, 12 people have been killed, some crushed by fellow-runners. Many more have died owing to accidents, mostly related to over-indulgence.

The *encierro* takes place every morning at 8 am, on the dot, and usually lasts only a minute or two as the bulls for each day's *corrida* charge 825 m through narrow, barricaded streets to the bull-ring, the Plaza de Toros. It is not easy to get a clear view, so arrive early. So many runners pack the streets that the biggest hazard is from tripping over others. Some have been drinking all night, but others have been in serious training. The challenge is to run as close to those tossing horns as possible, then peel off without harm.

If you do run, stay sober and carry a folded newspaper, which serves to distract a bull's attention if it starts hooking at a vulnerable part. A bull is most dangerous when it is parted from its fellows.

Following the bull-run, young bulls are released into the ring to allow runners to show their daring and collect a few bruises. If you miss the Pamplona *encierros*, don't worry – there are many more in other Spanish towns.

as **Ochagavía** and **Roncal**, with their wooden-balconied houses. Off the N240, north-west of Sangüesa, are two spectacular gorges, the **Hoz de Lumbier** and the **Hoz de Arbayún**.

Roncal, the more Alpine of the two valleys, produces excellent cheese and its traditions include the **Tributo de las Tres Vacas** (the Three Cows' Tribute). Every July 13 dignitaries in period costume meet French counterparts from the Barétous valley up at the frontier. The French hand over three cows, confirming a peace treaty dating from 1375. Salazar holds a similar ceremony on September 29, when the *junta* (valley council) of 14 villages meets French authorities to review boundaries.

RONCAL
See *Roncal Valley, page 87.*

RONCESVALLES
On *the* N135, 47 *km* NE *of Pamplona*. Below the 1,000 m **Ibaneta Pass**, gateway for pilgrims heading for Santiago de la Compostela, stands the grim, grey

RONCESVALLES AND THE *CHANSON DE ROLAND*

Events at the Roncesvalles Pass more than 1,200 years ago are celebrated in a famous epic poem, *Le Chanson de Roland* (*The Song of Roland*). In 778, after a foray into Spain, the Emperor Charlemagne retreated into France over the pass above Roncesvalles. However, he had antagonised the Navarra people and they wreaked bloody revenge on the rearguard, rolling rocks down on them. Among those who perished was the knight-errant Roland, according to the *Chanson*, written about 1100, possibly by a Norman.

The poem somehow converted the Navarra fighters into dastardly 'Saracens' and soon it became a Christian rallying call. The grief-stricken Charlemagne is supposed to have buried Roland (some historians doubt his existence) at the **Sancti Spiritus Chapel** of Roncesvalles, where the bones of dead pilgrims were later placed.

bulk of the monastery that gave succour to footsore travellers. On stormy nights a bell would ring out to help guide them down the mountain, although not a few succumbed by the side of the track or in the monastery hospital.

The huge, fortress-like building looks about as cosy and welcoming as San Quentin, but pilgrims still sleep there (two-tier bunk beds, maximum stay one night, lights out 11 pm, free but donation requested).

Roncesvalles **Collegiate Church** was built by Sancho The Strong, who helped conquer the Moors at the battle of Las Navas de Tolosa in 1212. In a chapter house stands the mausoleum of Sancho and his wife Clemence, daughter of a count of Toulouse.

Hop over to the Irati Valley to stroll through the **Bosque del Irati**, one of Europe's largest beech and oak forests.

SANGUESA
On *the* NA127, *off the* N240, 43 *km* SE *of Pamplona*. The little town of Sangüesa, on the main Santiago pilgrim route, has numerous buildings in the Romanesque style. Thousands of pilgrims crossed the Aragón river here and strode along the Rúa Mayor. Well-heeled merchants and nobles constructed fine mansions: note the Baroque **Palacio de Vallesantoro** , with carvings of human and animal heads outside.

The fortified residence of the Prince of Viana is now the **Ayuntamiento**.

A dazzling sculpted portal dating from the 12thC is the outstanding feature of **Santa María la Real**, a triple-apsed former royal chapel.

SAN JUAN DE LA PEÑA
Off the N240, 21 *km* SW *of* Jaca. This is the sort of place to inspire anybody with the fear of God. Indeed, legend affirms that a deer hunter who found the spot was so overcome that he became a hermit here, to be followed by Benedictine monks. An awesome cliff appears about to crush their 9thC monastery at any moment. A Romanesque **church**, with three Moorish-style arches on sculptured capitals, is partly underground, and the rock forms a roof over a 12thC cloister. The former sacristy contains the pantheon of the first kings of Aragón. For several centuries an agate chalice, claimed to be the Holy Grail (now in Valencia Cathedral, see Spain

Overall: 8), was kept here.

On the summit of a nearby mountain known as Pano is a second, Baroque monastery, restored after being destroyed by French troops in 1809.

SAN SEBASTIAN
See Spain Overall: 1.

SOS DEL REY CATOLICO ⛌
On the C137, off the N240, 56 km SE of Pamplona. Sos is a superb, recently restored, medieval village. Within its walls are many distinguished buildings. You can visit the **Palacio de Sada**, where in a first-floor room Ferdinand, later King of Aragón and husband of Isabel the Catholic of Castile, was born in 1452.

TAFALLA ✕
On the N12, 32 km S of Pamplona. A prosperous market town, Tafalla is dominated by its medieval castle. Note the Renaissance altarpiece in the **church of Santa María**. More impressive than Tafalla is **Artajona**, 11 km north-west on the NA603. The local people live in a modern section below the **Cerco**, as it is known, a fortified enclave occupied in the 12thC by the Templar Knights.

TUDELA ✕
On the N121 and N232, 84 km S of Pamplona. If you missed the bull-runs in Pamplona, you can catch them here at the time of the July 26 **fiesta of Santa Ana**. In the 18th and 19thC bullfights were held in Tudela's central square, the Plaza de los Fueros, and you will see related scenes on the façades of some of the houses.

Midway between Pamplona and Zaragoza, on the Ebro River, Tudela is the capital of the Ribera, the fertile, southern part of Navarra, and is important for its excellent wine, fruit and vegetables. Founded in 802 by the Córdoba emirate, it has inherited from that epoch a Moorish quarter known as the **Morería**, along with traces of Mudéjar architecture. Several eminent Jews were born here, including Judah Ha-Levi, 11thC poet, and Benjamín de Tudela, 12thC rabbi and traveller.

For a moral lesson carved in stone, do not miss *The Last Judgment* on the portico of Tudela's **cathedral**, where no pains have been spared to frighten the devil out of sinners.

VILLANUA
And Pyrenean valleys nearby, see Local Explorations: 10.

ZUGARRAMURDI
See Baztan, Vall de, page 84.

RECOMMENDED RESTAURANTS

BARBASTRO
Flor, PP; *Goya*, 3; *tel*. 974 31 10 56; *credit cards* AE, DC, MC, V.

Try the lamb stew with prunes in this spacious restaurant; interesting wine list.

JACA
La Cocina Aragonesa, PP; *Cervantes*, 5; *tel*. 974 36 10 50; *credit cards* AE, MC, V; *closed* Wed.

Friendly service, Basque-Aragón dishes, in a tiled and timbered dining room. Try the *hojaldre de cebolla* (onion in pastry) and the *jabalí* (boar).

PAMPLONA
Tapa bars in the old quarter, along such streets as Estafeta and San Nicolás, offer sound value. Restaurant eating tends to be expensive. An old favourite is **Las Pocholas, PPP**; *Paseo Sarasate*, 8; *tel*. 948 22 22 14; *credit cards* AE, DC, MC, V; *closed* Sun & Aug. Run by sisters, this serves traditional Navarra dishes in an agreeable setting.

TAFALLA
Tubal, PPP; *Plaza de Navarra*, 2; *tel*. 948 70 08 52; *credit cards* AE, DC, MC, V; *closed* Sun eve, Mon, end Aug.

First-class service and attention to detail in one of Navarra's top-rated restaurants. Delicious desserts.

TUDELA
Hostal Tudela, PP; *Avda Zaragoza*, 56; *tel*. 948 41 08 02; *cards* AE DC, MC, V; *closed* Sun eve.

Value for money, and located in a comfortable hotel (**PP**).

North-Eastern Spain

Between Barcelona and Madrid
Zaragoza and Guadalajara

620 km; maps Michelin 442 & 443, 1:400,000

S plendid medieval towns and scenery of bleak grandeur await travellers between Barcelona and Madrid. Ascending from the shores of the Mediterranean, you enter the heartland of Spain, passing out of Catalunya into the former kingdoms of Aragón and Castile. Through the centuries the Aragonese fought stubbornly to retain their *fueros* (privileges and liberties wrung from the kings) and have a name for being down-to-earth, reflecting the character of their home territory.

While the Pyrenean valleys of northern Aragón are well-watered (see Local Explorations: 10) and there is fertile land along the Ebro, much of Zaragoza province is arid and harsh. A toughness of spirit is needed to survive. The same can be said of the neighbouring, sparsely populated Guadalajara province, where the 20th century is slow to arrive.

Between Lleida and Zaragoza the monotonous, desert-like area known as Los Monegros may encourage you to speed past Zaragoza itself. A mistake, as Spain's fifth largest city is a handsome, thriving metropolis with considerable artistic and architectural attractions. Between the 11th and 15th centuries, Zaragoza was capital of the Kingdom of Aragón which, linked with Catalunya, became a major European power. King Ferdinand of Aragón's marriage in 1469 to Isabel of Castile forged a united Spain. By marrying their daughter, Catherine of Aragón, to the heir to the English throne they hoped for another powerful alliance; too bad about her husband, the monstrous Henry VIII.

During the Civil War, the Ebro Valley was the scene of fierce fighting. You can gain a vivid idea of that era by visiting shattered Belchite (see page 92) and reading *Homage to Catalonia* by George Orwell, who fought in the Sierra de Alcubierre, north-west of Zaragoza.

A popular Aragón dish is chicken or lamb *al chilindrón* (stewed with red peppers), while kid, roast or stewed, is a Guadalajara favourite. Aragón produces some highly drinkable wines, particularly those from the Campo de Borja and Cariñena. You can purchase hearty Cariñena reds direct from the wineries (50 km south-west of Zaragoza on the N330).

The excellent, four-lane A2 and N11 highways allow fast movers to cover the distance between Barcelona and Madrid comfortably in a day, with a quick look at Zaragoza. Those with another day to spare should take in some blue sights as well. A more leisurely approach will allow you to detour to such 'green' locations as Alcañiz, Daroca and the little-visited Alcarria.

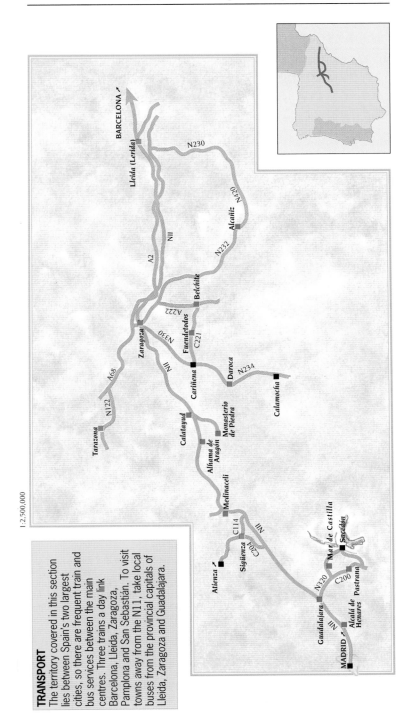

1:2,500,000

TRANSPORT

The territory covered in this section lies between Spain's two largest cities, so there are frequent train and bus services between the main centres. Three trains a day link Barcelona, Lleida, Zaragoza, Pamplona and San Sebastián. To visit towns away from the N11, take local buses from the provincial capitals of Lleida, Zaragoza and Guadalajara.

SIGHTS & PLACES OF INTEREST

ALCALA DE HENARES

On the N11, 30 km E of Madrid. Tourism Office, Callejón de Santa María, 1; tel. 91 889 26 94. Alcalá was renowned as a seat of learning in the Middle Ages. Today it is an unprepossessing industrial city and dormitory for Madrid. Cardinal Cisneros founded a university here in 1498, which published a polyglot Bible, in Greek, Hebrew, Latin, and Chaldean in 1517. It was named the *Biblia Computensis*, harking back to the name of the Roman colony here, Complutum.

Alcalá declined when its Complutense University transferred to Madrid in 1837, also as a result of confiscation of monastic wealth.

Miguel de Cervantes was born in Alcalá in 1547. A replica of a 16thC house stands where he supposedly lived, at 48, Calle Mayor and there is a Plaza de Cervantes in the town centre. East of it stands the splendid Renaissance building of **San Ildefonso College**, formerly the university. The beautiful Plateresque façade, by Rodrigo Gil de Hontañón, bears the arms of Cisneros, whose marble tomb is in an adjoining chapel. Inside the college is the fine Patio Mayor and El Trilingüe, the patio where Latin, Greek and Hebrew were taught.

ALCAÑIZ ⌂

On the N232, 103 km SE of Zaragoza. Above the town sits the castle, once a headquarters of the knights of Calatrava, now – considerably rebuilt – a state-owned hotel. Most of the structure dates from the 18thC, as does the town's **Collegiate Church of Santa Maria**, which has a sumptuous Baroque façade. You can use Alcañiz as a gateway to the Maestrazgo region (see Spain Overall: 8).

ALHAMA DE ARAGON

See Recommended Hotels, page 93.

ATIENZA

See Spain Overall: 5.

BARCELONA

See pages 193-200.

BELCHITE

On the C221, 52 km S of Zaragoza. The devastated town of Belchite stands like a mirage on the Ebro plain, a monument to Civil War horrors. Before the entrance gate a sign warns of the danger from collapsing buildings. Inside you find crumbling walls, debris-strewn streets and the shells of churches. A desperate siege by Republican forces took place here in 1937. The next year the Nationalists retook it; last to retreat from the ruins was the XVth International Brigade. A new town was built next door.

GOYA COUNTRY

One of the great figures of European art, Francisco de Goya, was born in the tiny village of **Fuendetodos**, south of Zaragoza, in 1746 (see also page 95). He achieved fame as a court painter, but also for his satirical works and the dramatic realism of his depiction of the horrors of war.

A number of his works can be seen in and around Zaragoza. His first important commission was to paint frescoes on the cupolas of the **Pilar Basilica** (see page 95). **Zaragoza Museum** (Bellas Artes) has some fine portraits, including one of the tyrant Ferdinand VII. His etchings, including *Los Caprichos* (The Caprices) and *Los Desastres de la Guerra* (The Disasters of War), can be seen here and also in the **Camón Aznar Museum**.

In 1774 Goya painted a series of murals at the **Aula Dei Carthusian Monastery**, 10 km north-east of Zaragoza on the A123. Seven remain in the Renaissance-style monastery, founded in 1564. It can only be visited by males, on Wednesdays and Thursdays. Behind the scenes, the monks busily run a computer supply service. More early Goya works can be found in **La Fuente Sanctuary** at Muel (on the N330, 28 km south-west of Zaragoza); at **Remolinos Church** (on the A126, 35 km north-west of Zaragoza), and in **Huesca Provincial Museum** (see Spain Overall: 6.)

CALAMOCHA
See Recommended Hotels, below.

CALATAYUD
On the N11, 86 km SW of Zaragoza. Wedged against an eroded hillside, Calatayud's dusty old quarter, with its tiled roofs and ancient towers, suggests a scene out of Africa or Arabia. The unusual name probably derives from Kalat Ayub, and in turn from Ayub, the Moor who built a castle here in the 8thC. Several Mudéjar belfries dot the town, including that of Santa María la Mayor.

Some 13 km north-east of Calatayud are traces of Ancient Bilbilis, an Iberian then a Roman settlement, where the satirical poet Martial was born and returned from Rome to die.

DAROCA
On the N234, 86 km SW of Zaragoza. More than 100 towers dot the 3 km of walls that girdle Daroca, graced by noble entrance gates and old houses. The **church of Santa María** has a Mudéjar tower dating from 1441 and a chapel recalling an incident in 1239, when a Moorish attack interrupted Mass. Consecrated bread was hidden in two altarcloths, on which bloodstains were later found. These are preserved in the chapel and the miracle is celebrated every year at Corpus Christi.

FUENTETODOS
On the C221, 48 km S of Zaragoza. Dirt-poor Fuentetodos was Goya's birthplace (see also page 92). You can visit the humble two-storey house, with stone-flagged floors and a large fireplace; it was bought in 1916 by the painter Ignacio Zuloaga, who helped found a Goya museum. The present **museum**, a short distance away, displays Goya engravings and a video explaining his technique. The amiable museum staff have the key to the birthplace.

GUADALAJARA ✕
On the N11, 55 km E of Madrid. Tourism Office, Plaza Mayor, 7; tel. 949 22 06 98.

RECOMMENDED HOTELS

ALCAÑIZ
Parador La Concordia, PPP; *Castillo de los Calatravos; tel. 978 83 04 00; closed Dec 12-Feb 1.*

Perched magnificently above town and country, in a former castle of the Knights of Calatrava. Local specialities in the restaurant.

ALHAMA DE ARAGON
Termas, PP; *(off the N11, 114 km SW of Zaragoza), Constitucion, 20; tel. 976 84 00 11.*

In gardens near a spa famed for its curative powers.

CALAMOCHA
Calamocha, P-PP; *(on the N330, 111 km SW of Zaragoza), Ctra Sagunto-Burgos, km 192; tel. 978 73 14 12.*

Immaculate modern hotel making a useful overnight stop between Zaragoza and Teruel.

PIEDRA MONASTERY
Monasterio de Piedra, PP; *Afueras, s/n, Nuevalos; tel. 976 84 90 11.*

Monastery buildings have been adapted to make a comfortable hotel in beautiful surroundings of water and woods.

SIGUENZA
Parador Castillo de Sigüenza, PPP; *Subida al Castillo; tel. 949 39 01 00.*

Once the fortified residence of the influential Bishops of Sigüenza, this parador offers baronial-style tranquillity.

ZARAGOZA
Gran Hotel, PPP; *Joaquín Costa, 5; tel. 976 22 19 01.*

Opened in 1929 by King Alfonso XIII, this recently renovated hotel breathes old-world style and elegance. Meet in the domed and pillared lounge before dining in the chandeliered restaurant.

Santiago, P; *Santiago, 3; tel. 976 23 42 72.* Two-star *hostal* close to Plaza del Pilar.

Tibur, PP; *Plaza de la Seo, 2; tel. 976 20 20 02.*

A modern, three-star hotel, ideally located near the two cathedrals.

The main highway sweeps around Guadalajara and there is little reason why you should not do the same. The capital of one of Spain's poorest and least-populated provinces, Guadalajara had its heyday in the Middle Ages when the Mendoza family, the Duques del Infantado, were powers in the land. Many buildings were destroyed in the Civil War. The main point of interest in the modern industrial city is the **Palacio del Infantado**, on Plaza Caidos. Built by the second Duque del Infantado in the 15thC, it has a dazzling Plateresque façade, with delicate Mudéjar windows, and a beautiful patio. Philip II married his third wife, Isabel de Valois, in the chapel.

LLEIDA (LERIDA) ×

On the N11, 156 km W of Barcelona. Tourism Office, Arc del Pont s/n. Lleida province (one of the four making up Catalunya, the others being Barcelona, Girona and Tarragona) extends north to the spectacular scenery of the Pyrenees and the French border. It is more attractive than the capital, an industrial city, commanding fertile farmland and orchards along the Segre river.

Romans, Moors, French, and Spaniards have assailed Lleida's fortress, **La Zuda**, the remains of which stand next to the city's outstanding sight, **La Seu Vella**, the old cathedral, worth an hour or so's exploration. You climb steeply from the city to La Seu, bounded by gardens and mighty ramparts. Since the occupying garrison left in 1947, a huge task of restoration has been carried out, recreating at least some of the magnificence of this transitional Romanesque-Gothic structure. Following the ousting of the Moors from Lleida, the cathedral was constructed between 1203 and 1278. Houses once hemmed in the cathedral but, when Lleida fell to Philip V's Bourbon army in 1707, they were demolished and the cathedral was converted into a fortress. Horses were stabled inside during a long, disastrous military occupation.

La Seu Vella (entry fee) has interesting **carving** on the capitals along the aisles and on the portals. The beautifully-proportioned **cloister**, which once housed soldiers' kitchens and canteen, has an unusual feature: the southern side is open, giving views over the city.

At one corner is an octagonal, 60 m **bell-tower**, a style which was copied in Valencia Cathedral's Micalet tower (see Spain Overall: 8).

Unimaginative by comparison, the 'New' Cathedral, an 18thC Corinthian structure in the lower city, was gutted in the Civil War and later restored.

Lleida has several respectable eating places and the usual busy *tapa* bars. For entertainment, you could head for Big Ben (on the N11, 25 km east at Golmés), a macro-disco with seven dance floors and 14 bars. If you are over 25, you'll need to be a masochist: at weekends the place is thronged by up to 5,000 youngsters.

Giant figures and bigheads announce the start of the annual **fiesta** on May 11. There are *sardana* dances, processions, fireworks and an offering of flowers to the patron saint, San Anastasio, by children in regional costume.

MADRID

See pages 170-192.

MAR DE CASTILLA

This is the name given to two huge reservoirs, Entrepeñas and Buendía, 60 km south-east of Guadalajara in the Alcarria region. They attract summer visitors eager to indulge in watersports. The main village is **Sacedón**, near which at Córcoles is the 12thC Cistercian **Monasterio de Monsalud**.

MEDINACELI ×

Off the N11, 150 km NE of Madrid. From the highway Medinaceli's ancient monuments on a hilltop have a majestic appeal. Climb up and you find a slumbering medieval village, with a Roman three-span triumphal arch and some proud, decaying mansions, including the 17thC **Palacio de los Duques de Medinaceli**. On the nearest Saturday to November 13, the *toro de jubilo* is released in the bull-ring. Balls of fire are fixed to the bull's horns, mud being smeared over its head and back for protection. It careers madly about while the local bloods show their daring.

Near Medinaceli (24 km north-east) is the beautiful Cistercian **Monasterio de Santa María de Huerta**, whose features include a huge vaulted Gothic refectory and a Renaissance upper cloister.

PIEDRA, MONASTERIO DE ✕

On the C202, 30 km SW of Calatayud.
This oasis of waterfalls, caves, lakes
and woods comes as a delightful surprise in the arid surrounding country.
Marked paths show you the way. The
monastery, established by the Cistercians in 1194, is now a hotel.

PASTRANA

On the N320, 47 km SE of Guadalajara.
Pastrana, with just over 1,000 inhabitants, is a typical stone-built village of
La Alcarria, a primitive region south-
east of Guadalajara, where rivers have
carved deep valleys through a 1,000
m-high plateau.

Built on a former Roman settlement,
the village once belonged to the Order
of Calatrava and was later the seat of
a dukedom. One member of the ducal
family was the tragic one-eyed Ana,
Princess of Éboli, a favourite of Philip
II. Married at 13, mother of ten, briefly
a nun, she became involved with the
king's secretary, incurring royal wrath,
and was imprisoned in the ducal palace
from 1581 until her death in 1592. The
palace has been restored and the
tombs of the princess and Pastrana
nobles are in the collegiate church,
which conserves 15thC tapestries.

Near Almonacid de Zorita, on the
C200, 15 km south-east of Pastrana,
stands Spain's oldest nuclear power
station. You may want to steer clear:
in 1994 scores of cracks were discovered in the reactor, leading to calls for
its closure.

SIGUENZA ✕

On the C114, 83 km NE of Guadalajara.
Sigüenza makes a pleasantly tranquil
stopover away from the busy Madrid-
Zaragoza highway. Dominating the
small medieval town above the Henares
river is the reconstructed **castle**, now a
parador. The Catholic Monarchs (Ferdinand and Isabel), Cardinal Mendoza and
King Juan Carlos are among those who
passed the night here.

Sigüenza has been the seat of a bishopric since the 6thC and a fortified
emplacement much longer. Napoleon's
troops sacked the castle and in the
Spanish Civil War it was reduced to
ruins again.

Old houses with wrought-iron balconies, cobbled streets and the noble,
porticoed Plaza Mayor, built by Men-

doza in the 16thC, are worth noting, but
the big sight is the fortress-like **cathedral**, begun 800 years ago and clearly
French-influenced. A lugubrious guide
introduces you to the building's secrets
(payment required). He snaps on a light
to reveal the highlight, an alabaster
masterpiece sculpted by Juan de Toledo between 1491 and 1497. It depicts
El Doncel, a young man with a serene
expression reclining gracefully while
reading a book. El Doncel was Martín
Vázquez de Arce, killed in 1486 when
fighting the Moors at Granada. He was
a favourite of Queen Isabel, who
ordered the tomb constructed.

The cathedral archives are hung with
large Flemish tapestries and in a chapel
stand two standards taken from the
English in the battle of Lisbon in 1589.
Other features include the doorway to
the Anunciación chapel which mixes
Gothic, Renaissance and Mudéjar elements and the remarkable **sacristy
ceiling** with more than 300 carved
heads by Covarrubias.

TARAZONA

On the N122, 89 km NW of Zaragoza. Four
centuries of Moorish domination and
the residence here of Aragón's kings
left its mark on this small town. In the
old quarter, you find the **Palacio Episcopal**, once a royal palace, the church
of **La Magdalena** with a Mudéjar
tower, and an octagonal, four-storey
bull-ring converted into dwellings. Moorish influence is plain in the **cathedral**,
rebuilt in the 15th and 16thC.

ZARAGOZA

*On the N11, 300 km W of Barcelona.
Tourism Office, Torreón de la Zuda; tel. 976
39 35 37.* Approaching Zaragoza along
the fertile Ebro Valley, you see the towers of its great cathedral thrusting up
from the plain. Zaragoza is a thriving
city of 600,000 inhabitants with textile
and car manufacture among its industries. Slower moving than Barcelona
and Madrid, it is a pleasant city to
explore and, as the most important
Marian sanctuary in Spain, a major pilgrimage centre.

The Iberians called their settlement
Salduba and the present name derives
from Caesar Augustus, the colony
established here by the Romans.

The obvious place to start is in the
vast **Plaza del Pilar**, where pigeons

THE SIEGES OF 1808 AND 1809

A lofty monument on Zaragoza's Plaza de los Sitios is dedicated to 'The fatherland and the heroes of 1808 and 1809'. It commemorates two sieges by French forces in the Napoleonic Wars. During the first unsuccessful siege, a woman named Agustina de Aragón became a symbol of heroic resistance. When her lover was killed, she took over his gun and stopped the attackers from forcing an entrance. Byron immortalized her in his poem *Maid of Saragossa*. But the French returned, with 30,000 men. For two months the defenders of Zaragoza under General Palafox held out. Finally, after 54,000 people had died from disease, famine and wounds, the city surrendered.'The devils certainly knew how to fight,' declared the French General Lannes.

swirl about the **Ayuntamiento**, the 16thC **Lonja** or commercial exchange (note the Plateresque adornment), two tourist information offices and two – yes, two – cathedrals.

Pilgrims head for the **Nuestra Señora del Pilar**, with its ten distinctive tiled cupolas around a central dome. It is built on the spot where, it is said, Saint James (Santiago) was preaching in AD 40 when he saw a vision of the Virgin (see Spain Overall: 3). Descending from heaven on a marble pillar borne by angels, she ordered him to build a chapel in her honour. The Virgin of the Pillar (Virgen del Pilar) is Spain's patron saint and Pilar is a popular girl's name.

The cathedral, designed by Francisco Herrera the Younger, was remodelled by Ventura Rodríguez and José Ramírez in 1754. Giant pillars divide the interior into three aisles. Entering, you will see worshippers filing into the first chapel on the right, dedicated to St John the Baptist, to kiss the feet of a 17thC **carving of Christ**.

The **Virgin** is in the domed **Santa Capilla**, richly adorned in silver, copper and marble. She is so small that at first you may have difficulty in locating her; the tiny image, on the right of an elaborate altarpiece, wears a mantle that looks remarkably like a lampshade. She is enshrined atop the fabled pillar, which is sheathed in embossed silver. Behind the altar, part of the pillar is exposed for the kisses of the faithful. An alabaster carving by Damián Forment adorns the cathedral's high altar. The museum displays precious jewellery and many of the 400 gem-studded robes in the Virgin's wardrobe. They include a silk robe bordered with gold which was adapted from a bullfighter's cape, given by the matador Pepe Luis Vázquez in 1946. Her clothing is changed daily, except on the 2nd and 12th of each month, dates revered as anniversaries of her apparition.

Zaragoza's other cathedral, a few steps to the east, is the **Seo**, which has been undergoing heavy restoration and may not be open. Its exterior lacks unity, because of the jumble of styles from Mudéjar to Churrigueresque. Parts of the huge structure date from the 12thC. The octagonal tower was designed by the Italian Contini in 1685 and the Greco-Roman façade was added in the 18thC. The Seo's museum has some immensely valuable religious objects, outstanding medieval tapestries and works by Goya and Zurbarán. A brisk ten-minute walk west of the Plaza del Pilar brings you to a majestic moated fortress with six towers, flying the flags of Aragon, Spain and Zaragoza. This is the **Aljafería**, where the Aragón parliament meets. Built by the Benihud dynasty in the 9thC, it is the setting for part of Verdi's opera *Il Trovatore*. It was once occupied by kings of Aragon, then by the Inquisition and later used as a hospital, prison and barracks. The heavily restored inner patio, with multi-lobed arches and delicate plasterwork, is a delightful example of the airy beauty of Moorish palaces. A grand staircase leads up to first-floor chambers sumptuously decorated in Gothic style, with ornate coffered ceilings in the throne room and the room in which Isabel, future queen of Portugal, was born in 1271.

In the centre of the city, on Plaza Paraiso, penetrate the soulless glass bulk of Ibercaja, a savings bank, to visit the delightful **Patio de la Infanta**, a two-storey Renaissance structure transported here and used for exhibitions (open during office hours).

Other Zaragoza sights include: the **Museo Provincial**, on the Plaza de los Sitios, with archaeological finds and Goya works; the **Museo Camón Aznar**, at Espoz y Mina, 23, with a valuable art collection; the Modernist central market, **Mercado de Lanuza**; and the **Museo Pablo Gargallo**, Plaza San Felipe, 3, with more than 100 works by this outstanding sculptor.

A cheap way to get around, once you have mastered the bus routes, is to buy a Bonobus, a book of ten tickets obtainable from savings banks.

Scores of bars are to be found in **El Tubo**, the narrow streets between Alfonso 1, Jaime 1, Coso and Espoz y Mina streets. Scots may need a stiff drink after checking out the **Taberna Harry McNamara**, at Méndez Núñez, 36, all tartan and tankards. Beyond Magdalena Church, with its Mudéjar tower, is the cavernous **Bodega Tío Faustino** at Don Teobaldo, 14. The wine barrels and a vast hearth for grills are impressive, less so the service – my waiter was apparently in training for the national don't-give-a-damn championship. For excellent *tapas* and a wide range of wines in a bar which attracts better-heeled *zaragozanos*, try the **Cervecería Marpy**, at Plaza Santa Marta, 8. Bullfight pictures cover the walls; particularly recommended are the *Patatas asadas al ajillo* (roast potatoes with garlic).

Among the live music hangouts is **El Monaguillo**, Refugio, 8, through a steel door and down steps into an atmospheric vaulted cellar where a blues guitarist may be plonking away or Gregorian chant echoing while clients make use of two bars. Jazz groups and other entertainers perform at **La Ruelle** at Espoz y Mina, 7.

The day Columbus sighted land in 1492, October 12, is also celebrated as the **Día del Pilar** and the **Día de la Hispanidad** (day of the Hispanic race). It is a national holiday and Zaragoza celebrates the event with a week of impressive religious processions, bullfights, and merrymaking. Look out for the spirited regional dance, the *jota*.

RECOMMENDED RESTAURANTS

ALCALA DE LOS HENARES
Hostería del Estudiante, PP; *Colegios, 3; tel. 91 888 03 30; credit cards AE, DC, MC, V; closed Mon, midday Jul and Aug.*

Located in a 16thC building with plenty of Old Castile atmosphere. Filling local and national dishes.

GUADALAJARA
Horche, PP; (*off the N320, 10 km SE of Guadalajara), Cañada de Alcohete, s/n, Horche; tel. 949 29 02 11; credit cards AE, DC, MC, V.*

Advisable to book before seeking out this country restaurant serving such Basque dishes as peppers stuffed with crabmeat, flavoured with garlic and parsley. Open-air dining on the terrace in summer.

MEDINACELI
Las Llaves, PP; *Plaza Mayor, 13; tel. 975 32 63 51; credit cards AE, V; closed Sun eve, Mon.*

Cosy dining room in a century-old house. Delicious home-made dishes.

ZARAGOZA
Alberto, PP; *Pedro María Ric, 35; tel. 976 23 65 03; credit cards AE, DC, MC, V; closed Sun in summer.*

Amiable, excellent service and value for money characterize this popular no-nonsense restaurant. The bean casserole and grilled rabbit are recommended.

Gurrea, PPP: *San Ignacio de Loyola, 14; tel. 976 23 31 61; credit cards AE, DC, MC, V; closed Sun in summer.*

Polished brass and woodwork give a classy air to this restaurant next to the Corte Inglés store. First-rate fish dishes and desserts.

Eastern Spain
Between Figueres and Valencia
Mediterranean Coast:
Catalunya, Castellón and Valencia

450 km; maps Michelin 443 & 445, 1:400,000

This stretch of Spain's Mediterranean coast is a history lesson, a cultural adventure and an invitation to sheer indulgence. Between the French border and Valencia you will find some of Spain's most exciting cities, best restaurants, finest beaches and richest artistic treasures. The culture of successive invaders has helped make the Catalunya and Valencia regions among the most prosperous, progressive and sophisticated in Spain.

Catalan and *Valenciano,* a variation, are the languages of the two regions, but everybody speaks Castilian too. If you know any Castilian, French or Latin, you will find Catalan not too difficult to read. Mastering a few spoken phrases will certainly please the native residents. In any case, English is widely spoken.

Many visitors find Catalunya remarkably similar to southern France in its customs and its language. Catalans, who enjoyed independence for nearly six centuries, regard themselves as special and Barcelona has a well-founded reputation for being among Europe's most dynamic and avant-garde cities.

Further south you come to El Levante, a traditional name for the Mediterranean coast between Catalunya and Andalucía (see also Spain Overall: 9). The term stems from *levantar* (to rise), referring to the sun which rises first over this part of the peninsula. The Levante includes the three provinces, Castellón, Valencia and Alicante, forming the autonomous region of Valencia. In Moorish times an independent Valencia dominated the coast from Almería to the Ebro. Today it is known for its industrious people and for its valuable citrus fruit exports.

While Valencia offers you the chance to try a whole range of rice dishes, including the ubiquitous *paella* (see Recommended Restaurants, page 108), Catalunya can rightly claim to be a leader in Spanish *cuisine*. One of the first European cookbooks, *El Llibre del Cuiner*, was published in Catalan in 1520. Regional specialities include *Butifarra* (sausage), *Escudella* (vegetables in a meat broth), *Llagosta amb pollastre* (lobster with chicken), and *Sarsuela* (seafood stew). Wines from the Penedès areas enjoy a growing reputation.

The A7 *autopista* allows you to drive between Figueres and Valencia in a few hours. Those travelling 'red' can drop in at the major cities and do it in two days. If you take in the blue sights as well, allow four days. Going 'green' – dropping in on ancient monasteries, exploring the *bodegas* of San Sadurniú and stopping to swim – could double that time. To explore Catalunya in depth, consult Local Explorations: 11 and the Barcelona section, pages 193-200.

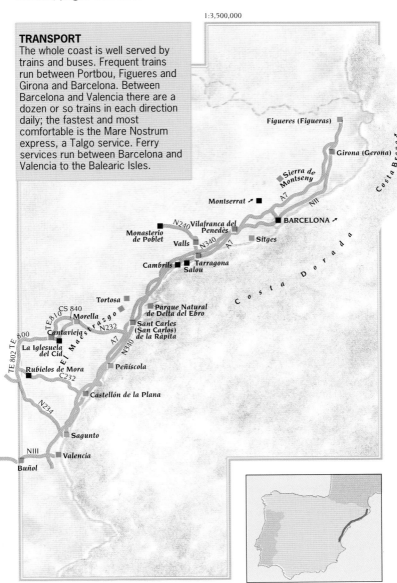

1:3,500,000

TRANSPORT
The whole coast is well served by trains and buses. Frequent trains run between Portbou, Figueres and Girona and Barcelona. Between Barcelona and Valencia there are a dozen or so trains in each direction daily; the fastest and most comfortable is the Mare Nostrum express, a Talgo service. Ferry services run between Barcelona and Valencia to the Balearic Isles.

Figueres (Figueras)

Girona (Gerona)

Costa Brava

Sierra de Montseny

Montserrat

A7

NII

Vilafranca del Penedès

N240

BARCELONA

Monasterio de Poblet

Valls

N340

A7

Sitges

Cambrils

Tarragona

Salou

Costa Dorada

Tortosa

CS 840

Morella

El Maestrazgo

N232

Parque Natural de Delta del Ebro

TE 810

Cantavieja

Sant Carles (San Carlos) de la Rápita

A7

N340

TE 800

La Iglesuela del Cid

Rubielos de Mora

C232

Peñíscola

N234

Castellón de la Plana

TE 802

Sagunto

NIII

Valencia

Buñol

SIGHTS & PLACES OF INTEREST

BARCELONA
See pages 193-200.

BUÑOL
On the N111, 40 km E *of Valencia.* If you are anywhere near this small town on the last Wednesday in August, wear your oldest clothes. It is the occasion of Spain's loopiest fiesta: the **Tomatina**. In 1945 some youngsters began hurling tomatoes at one another during an argument. Every year the battle was renewed. Now more than 100,000 kilos of ripe tomatoes are shipped in to provide ammunition for the thousands who participate in the annual tomato-slinging orgy.

CAMBRILS ✕
See Recommended Restaurants, page 108.

CANTAVIEJA ✕
See Maestrazgo, El, page 101 *and Recommended Restaurants, page* 108.

CASTELLON DE LA PLANA
On the N340, 65 km N *of Valencia.* Mostly modern and undistinguished, industrial Castellón stands in a large fertile plain. The **Provincial Museum** on Caballeros contains paintings by Ribalta and Ribera. Between the port of El Grau, at 4 km, and Benicásim, to the north, a vast beach of fine sand attracts holidaymakers.

COSTA BRAVA
See Local Explorations: 11.

COSTA DORADA
The sandy beaches of the Costa Dorada stretch from Barcelona province's border with Girona province as far as the Ebro Delta. North-east of Barcelona is the coastal plain of La Maresme, important for its market gardens; heavy traffic and ugly construction blight much of the coast here. South-west of Barcelona, **Sitges** (see page103) is the most attractive stopover.

Salou (off the N340, 10 km south-west of Tarragona) is a package holiday resort. There is a wide variety of entertainment (try the *kamikaze* in the Aquapark), but summers are crowded and what would you do here in winter?

DELTA DEL EBRO, PARQUE NATURAL DE
Off the N340, 28 km E *of Tortosa,* 85 km SW *of Tarragona.* Information, Uldecona s/n, *Deltebre (formerly La Cava); tel.* 977 48 96 79. You can see ducks, herons, flamingos and other bird species among the dunes, marshes and lagoons of the Ebro Delta, a 7,700-hectare Nature Park. Rice is grown on the flat farmland, ideal for exploration by bicycle. Hire bikes in Deltebre (tel. 977 48 40 49), from where you can also make boat trips. Baby eels fried with garlic and hot peppers are a local speciality.

FIGUERES (FIGUERAS) ⇔ ✕
On the N11, 37 km N *of Girona. Tourism Office, Plaza del Sol; tel.* 972 50 31 55. This unassuming provincial town attracts connoisseurs of the outrageous by the thousand, thanks to its most famous son, the well-known prankster Salvador Dalí (1904-1989).

He converted its old theatre into a **museum** (on Plaça Gala i Dalí, open every day) and his body lies inside. Was he a fraud or a genius, a technical wizard or a clumsy exhibitionist? You have ample opportunity to decide as you view a bizarre representation of Mae West and other surreal images.

Just down the hill is the pleasant main square, the Rambla, lined with plane trees and cafés such as the Royal, with its tiled walls and old-fashioned atmosphere. Snails and sausage are local specialities.

In the square is the **Museu de Joguets** (closed Tuesday in winter), a toy museum. Above the town stands the 18thC **Castillo San Fernando**, occupied by the military. The Republican parliament held its last meeting in the dungeons here on February 1, 1939. More recently, Lt-Col Tejero, the Civil Guard who held the Spanish parliament at gunpoint during the 1981 attempted coup, spent part of his jail sentence in comfortable confinement within the massive ramparts.

GIRONA (GERONA) ⇖ ✕

On the N11, 100 km N of Barcelona. Tourism Office, Rambla de la Llibertat, 1; tel. 972 22 65 75. Capital of the province of the same name in Spain's north-eastern corner, Girona has one of Catalunya's finest old quarters. Because of its strategic position, on the route south from France, it became known as 'the city of a thousand sieges'. In 1809 the city held out for nine months against a French army.

Start your visit at the helpful Tourist Office on the busy arcaded Rambla Llibertat, on the north bank of the Onyar River, and thread your way through the narrow streets uphill towards the cathedral. You reach Carrer de la Força, part of the Via Augusta when this was a Roman settlement. It has some classy boutiques, antique shops and cafés, tastefully blended into the medieval stonework.

This is the heart of El Call, the old Jewish quarter. More than 300 Jews once lived in the darkened web of streets and made it a renowned religious centre. Its most illustrious figure was Bonastruc de Porta, Grand Rabbi of Catalunya, doctor and philospher. Enjoying the protection of the King of Catalunya and Aragón in return for financial tribute, the Call was virtually independent, a source of conflict with the city fathers. After ever-increasing persecution, the Jews were expelled from Spain in 1492.

Look for a narrow alley climbing up from Força to the **Museo Isaac El Sec**, a labyrinth of old restored buildings where Jewish-related exhibitions are held.

At the top of Força, 90 wide steps lead up to Girona's **cathedral**. Of the original Romanesque structure, there remain only the cloister, with elaborate friezes of Biblical scenes, and part of the tower. The façade is Baroque, while a single nave, at 22 m the widest Gothic nave known, lends the interior a feeling of limitless space. A Coca Cola machine strikes an incongruous note at the entrance to the **museum**, which shelters the priceless 10thC Beatus manuscript and the *Tapestry of the Creation*, a unique, 900-year-old work depicting Christ presiding over the different stages of creation.

Just outside the city walls is the Romanesque-Gothic **church of Sant Feliu,** with eight ancient sarcophagi. Walk down the hill to the 13thC **Arab Baths**, noting the horseshoe-shaped arches. (It was not, in fact, built by Arabs.)

Across a bridge stands the **Museo Arqueològic**, housed in buildings of Sant Pere de Galligants Benedictine Abbey. Exhibits include Roman remains from Empúries (see Local Explorations: 11).

Reflected in the River Onyar are lofty houses dating back to the Middle Ages, when they were attached to the city walls. Just across the river, in the newer part of the city, lies the Plaça de la Independencia with bars and cafés. The **Café Royal**, brick-vaulted, with stone walls and large windows, is a pleasant spot for people-watching while consuming delicious cakes.

IGLESUELA DEL CID, LA

See Maestrazgo, El, below.

MAESTRAZGO, EL

On the border of Castellón and Teruel provinces. An area of splendid, forbidding mountain scenery, with harshly eroded terrain and a distinctive, timeless feel. In the Middle Ages it was dominated by military orders, the Templars and then the Montesa, which fortified the villages to protect them against the Moors.

You can approach the area from Teruel (see Spain Overall: 14) or via Morella (see page 102).

Among the interesting, well-preserved villages are **Cantavieja** (on the TE800, 49 km south-west of Morella), a stronghold in the 19thC of a Carlist general known as 'the Tiger of the Maestrazgo'. There is a porticoed square and Romanesque town hall, poised on the edge of a ravine. Walled and cobbled **Mirambel** (15 km N of Cantavieja) is worth a visit, as is **La Iglesuela del Cid** (13 km SE of Cantavieja), with a shrine to the Virgin where El Cid is said to have prayed. **Rubielos de Mora** (on the C232, 93 km north-west of Castel-lón) conserves ancient walls and entry gates, mansions with escutcheons and a 16thC town hall. On Saturdays in July and August a bull with flaming torches on its horns charges through the streets.

MONTSENY, SIERRA DE
Off the A7, 60 km N of Barcelona. Granite peaks thrust 1,700 m high above pine and beech woods. The most attractive route through it is between Sant Celoni and Santa Fe de Montseny. Part of the range is a Nature Park.

MONTSERRAT
see Barcelona, page 193.

MORELLA ⚐
On the N232, 106 km N of Castellón. Tourism Office, Torre de San Miguel; tel. 964 17 30 32. Detour inland to this delightful old hilltop town. It looks par-ticularly dramatic approached at night, when the **castle** and well-preserved 14thC **walls** are floodlit.

Climb up to the castle, passing by the **Monasterio de San Francisco**, under restoration, for magnificent views over the Maestrazgo (see page 101). Two handsome portals distin-guish **Santa María la Mayor**, the Gothic church at the top of town. It has a raised Renaissance choir on four pil-lars, with a beautifully carved spiral staircase. Unlike some medieval show-places, which can be eerily deserted, Morella is a living community. Craft shops dot the arcaded main street, bustling during the Sunday morning market, held since the 13thC. Truffles (a local speciality), cheese, sausage, honey and ceramics are on sale.

PEÑISCOLA
Off the N340, 72 km NE of Castellón. Offensive modern blocks have sprouted around the sandy bay, which gets crowded in the holiday season. But the old fortress of Peñíscola (pronounced 'payNYEEscola'), crowning a peninsula, is as impressive as ever. Wander through the ramparts and the narrow streets of the **old town** to the **castle**, built by the Templars in the 13thC. The coat of arms of **Papa Luna**, with its crescent moon, can be seen on a wall.

Papa Luna was an anti-pope, elect-ed by French cardinals in 1394. Styling himself Benedict XIII, he insisted on his right to the title, but as support with-ered away he took refuge in Peñíscola. On his voyage here, a violent storm is said to have blown up and Benedict called on heaven to save him if he were the true pope. Suddenly the storm abat-ed and he declared: 'I *am* the Pope.'

Peñíscola also has a more recent claim to attention: a famous moment in Spanish history, supposed to have occurred at Valencia, was re-enacted here in the film *El Cid.* Strapped to his mount, the dead El Cid galloped out from the castle to do battle, terrifying the besieging Moors.

The fishing town-cum-beach resort of **Benicarló** (on the N340, 8 km to the north; Tourism Office, Plaza San Andrés; tel. 964 47 31 80) holds its **San Bartolomé fiesta** the last week of August: boat races, bullfights and folk dancing. Bulls, let loose along the quay-side, chase cheeky youths, bull and run-ner often ending up in the water. Beni-carló's Parador Costa del Azahar, named for the local stretch of coastline, is a relaxing stopover by the sea (**PP**; *tel.* 964 47 01 00).

POBLET MONASTERY ⚐
Off the N240, 50 km N of Tarragona. For a thought-provoking insight into clerical pomp and power, visit **Santa María de Poblet**. Ramón Berenguer IV, Count of Barcelona, gave the land to 12 Cister-cian monks from the French abbey of Fontfroide in 1153. When the kings of Aragón endowed it (and made it their burial place) it became one of the rich-est monasteries in the land.

In the Middle Ages, however, as Poblet grew in influence, its monks became notorious for their dissipated life style. Finally, in 1835, they were ejected and the monastery plundered. In 1940, Cistercian monks returned; now the immense complex of buildings has been restored.

At the entrance, the **Puerta Dora-da**, monarchs dismounted and knelt to kiss the cross offered them by the abbot. The **main cloister** is a magnifi-cent example of Romanesque-Gothic architecture, with a hexagonal pavilion and fountain. Off it are the enormous kitchens, the 87-m-long dormitory, the library and the refectory. An outstand-ing feature of the church, built in the 12thC by Aragón's Alfonso II, is the the

altar-piece sculpted by Damián Forment. The statues of the Aragón-Catalan monarchs on the royal pantheon were reconstructed by the sculptor Frederic Marés from fragments left after the mob raged through in 1835.

RUBIELOS DE MORA
See Maestrazgo, El, page 101.

SAGUNTO ✕
On the N340, 25 km N of Valencia. Tourism Office, Plaza Cronista Chabret; tel. 96 266 22 13. Sagunto, an industrial town, figures in Spanish history books because of a battle in 218 BC at the start of the Second Punic War. As Hannibal's besieging army entered the seaport, which was allied with Rome, the defenders started a fire and threw themselves into the flames. Scipio Africanus the Elder later rebuilt the settlement.

Among the Roman ruins, the **theatre** is outstanding. It dates from the 2ndC AD, seats 8,000 and hosts an annual choral festival and a season of classical drama. An adjacent **archeological museum**, undergoing major renovation, contains valuable relics. The **Acropolis**, the fortified site of the original settlement, offers fine views. Sagunto also has an interesting old

• *Morella and its castle - see page* 102.

Jewish quarter.

SALOU
See Costa Dorada, page 100.

SANT CARLES (SAN CARLOS) DE LA RAPITA
On the N340, 98 km SW of Tarragona. Two hundred years ago, Charles III planned to establish a major port here, but it did not work out. Instead you have a fishing community famed for its *langostinos* (prawns) – they serve them at restaurants on the Paseo Marítimo.

SITGES 🛌
On the C246, 35 km SW of Barcelona. Tourism Office, Sìnìa Morera, 1; *tel.* 93 894 42 51. Well-heeled Barcelona *bourgeoisie,* artists and intellectuals have been coming to Sitges since the 19thC; many built elegant residences. Now they are joined by tourists of all nations and this picturesque but somewhat pricey resort gets crowded and noisy in summer. Bars, restaurants and night spots abound. Exuberant night-life centres on **Primero de Mayo**, also known as Calle del Pecado (Sin Street). If you prefer a drink in tranquil old-world surroundings, the Café Roy, at Parellades,

9, is for you.

Sitges has become a meeting point for Europe's gays. They are in particularly flamboyant evidence during Carnival in February.

From the 17thC church on the waterfront the Passeig Maritim runs west, bounding **La Ribera**, a long sandy beach. East of the church, on Calle Fonollar, facing the sea, is **Cau Ferrat**, where a famous Catalan painter, Santiago Rusinyol (see Els Quatre Gats in the Barcelona city section, page 193), organized Modernist art festivals. It has been converted into a museum, containing paintings by Picasso, El Greco and Catalan artists plus a collection of ironwork (Cau Ferrat means Den of Iron).

Next door is the **Museo Maricel del Mar** Museum, which houses the medieval and modern collections of Dr Pérez Rosales. The **Palacio de Maricel**, in front, previously owned by an American, Charles Deering, is used for congresses and conventions. Giant figures take part in the **Corpus Christi processions** which pass over thousands of flowers arranged in intricate patterns on the streets. Sitges also hosts an antique car rally; a wine harvest festival; an international theatre festival and a fantastic film festival.

TARRAGONA 🚉 ✕

On the N340, 98 km SW of Barcelona. Tourism Office, Fortuny, 4; tel. 977 23 34 15. Stroll along Tarragona's broad, tree-lined avenue, the Rambla Nova, to reach the **Balcó del Mediterráni**, overlooking the sea. The port lies to the right and to the left are remains of a

---

RECOMMENDED HOTELS

FIGUERES
Mas Pau, PPP; *(4 km SW of Figueres), Avinyonet de Puigventós; tel. 972 54 61 54; closed Jan, Feb.*
Rustic charm is the main selling point of this creeper-covered, converted 17thC farmhouse, with spacious, comfortable rooms and a recommended, expensive restaurant *(credit cards* AE, DC, MC, V).

POBLET
Masía del Cadet, PP; *Les Masies de Poblet, Espluga de Francolí; tel. 977 87 08 69.*
A tranquil old country house 2 km from Poblet Monastery. Excellent meals are available in the restaurant *(PP; credit cards* AE, DC, MC, V).

SITGES
Romàntic y la Renaixença, PP; *Sant Isidre, 33; tel. 938 94 83 75; closed Nov-Mar.*
Exuding colonial charm, this reasonably priced one-star hotel is housed in villas built by rum barons returned from Cuba.

TARRAGONA
Imperial Tarraco, PPP; *Paseo Palmeras, s/n; tel. 977 23 30 40.*
A four-star luxury hotel in a modern, curved building with magnificent views

of the Mediterranean. Close to all the main sights.

Lauria, PP; *Rambla Nova, 20; tel. 977 23 67 12.*
A slightly cheaper three-star alternative to the Tarraco, on the lively main avenue.

TORTOSA
Parador Castillo de la Zuda, PPP; *(on the C230, 83 km SW of Tarragona), Castillo de la Zuda, s/n; tel. 977 44 44 50.*
Vestiges of Roman and Moorish structures have been incorporated into the parador, on the lofty site of a 10thC fort. If you cannot be bothered trekking down to town, the restaurant offers specialities from the Ebro, including eels and frogs' legs.

VALENCIA
Parador Luis Vives, PPP; *Ctra El Saler (km 16 S of Valencia); tel. 961 61 11 86.*
Set among pine trees and on a golf course, close to the Mediterranean and the fresh water lagoon La Albufera. A perfect place to relax but within handy distance of Valencia. Tennis courts, swimming- pool and sauna.

Inglés, PPP; *Marqués de Dos Aguas, 6; tel. 96 351 64 26.*
Traditional style in a converted palace. A three-star hotel close to the main sights.

Roman **amphitheatre**, partly cut into the rock.

Conquered by the Romans in 218 BC, Tarragona abounds with relics of the era when, as Tarraco, it was capital of their northern province in Spain. Straddling a 70-m-high escarpment, Tarragona is today a breezy Mediterranean city, mixing spacious modern commercial areas with rich vestiges of antiquity. The only dissonant note comes from the ugly petro-chemical plants south of the city.

Just up from the Roman amphitheatre is the **Museo Arqueológic** (on the Plaça del Rei), a feast of Roman art, including coins, ceramics, friezes and mosaics. Tradition has it that Pontius Pilate was born in the adjoining building, the **Praetorium**, which formed part of the forum; and that Emperors Augustus and Hadrian lived there. Considerably modified later, the building now houses the **Museo d'Historia**.

Tarragona's impressive kilometre-long Roman **walls** were built on older foundations and embellished in the Middle Ages. Pass through the **Portella Gate** and follow first San Antoni Avenue northwards, then the Passeig Arqueológic, which runs between ramparts erected by the English in 1707 during the War of Succession and 2,200-year-old walls.

Within the walls are the narrow streets of the medieval city, including the **cathedral**, the largest in Catalunya, built on the site of a Temple of Jupiter and a mosque. Begun in 1171, the building mixes architectural styles, with some Moorish influence in the cloister (note on one capital the unusual carving of rats attending a cat's funeral). Among the many treasures in the cathedral is the high altar's intricate 15thC reredos (decorative screen behind altar), an alabaster masterpiece by Pere Johan showing scenes from the lives of the Virgin Mary and Santa Tecla. The saint, patron of the city, is said to have been converted by St Paul when he preached on the spot where the Sant Pau chapel stands, north of the cathedral.

More remains of interest include: pagan and Christian sarcophagi in the **Museo Paleocristià**, off Avenida Ramón y Cajal; **Acueducto de les Ferreres**, a two-tier, 217 m-long Roman aqueduct, 4 km to the north, off the N340; and the **Arco de Barà**, a triumphal arch built astride the Via Maxima in the 2ndC, 20 km north-west on the N340.

In and around the Rambla Nova you will find numerous *tapa* bars and restaurants. Fish features in many dishes, often with a local speciality, *romesco*, a sauce made of peppers, hazelnuts, breadcrumbs and wine. Tarragona has long been famed for its wines, particularly Priorato, a full-bodied red. If you enjoy wine, head for the **Sumpta**, a café at Prat de la Riba, 34, where you can sample a vast selection of wines with snacks.

TORTOSA ⊨

See Recommended Hotels, page 104.

VALENCIA ⊨ ✕

On the N340 and A7, 349 km SW of Barcelona, 352 km E of Madrid. At first sight, Valencia is short of romantic charm. Spain's third largest city, with 800,000 inhabitants, plus 600,000 in the surrounding area, is beset by the usual urban problems: pollution. Many of the finest buildings have been demolished.

Thousands of citrus trees blossom on the fertile, well-irrigated Valencia plain, the *huerta* (*horta* in *Valenciano*),

---

BUDGET ACCOMMODATION

FIGUERES
Travé; P; *Ctra de Olot; tel.* 972 50 05 91.
First-class value for money in a modern hotel on the edge of town.

GERONA
Condal, P; *Joan Maragall,* 10; *tel.* 972 20 44 62.
A clean, reliable stopover.

MORELLA
Elías, P; *Colomer,* 7; *tel.* 964 16 00 92.
The necessary comforts. Some rooms suffer noise from the restaurant ventilator.

VALENCIA
Venecia, PP; *En Llop,* 5; *tel.* 96 352 44 21. Central two-star, with all facilities, recently renovated.

• *House front, Valencian style.*

and the region produces more than three million tons of fruit annually – a major export. But around the city industry has blotched the landscape.

Although not beautiful, Valencia is dynamic, culturally and commercially. An indication of local mercantile acumen is the yellowed document stored in the Municipal Museum, a bill of exchange dated February 19, 1376, believed to be the oldest in the world. And Valencia is active in music, art, and design. *Valencianos* have dubbed the huge, glass-capped concert hall, the **Palau de la Música**, inaugurated in 1987, the *microondas* (microwave), but it attracts world-class orchestras and is an indication of the city's interest in music.

Art, too, is important. The **Museo de Bellas Artes**, on San Pio V Street, contains work by Goya, Ribera, Velázquez and Bosch, also by such important Valencia artists as Reixach the Elder, Espinosa and Sorolla, the last famed for his ability to imbue his canvases with the luminosity of the Mediterranean. Avant-garde artists have their showplace at **IVAM**, the Instituto Valenciano de Arte Moderno, opened in 1989.

El Cid, Champion of Castile, (see Spain Overall: 2) besieged Valencia for nine months in 1094, finally releasing it from Moorish rule, although his own army largely consisted of Moors too. Following his death, the Moors recov-

ered the city, and remained in control until in 1238 James I 'The Conqueror of Aragón' wrenched it from their grasp and made it capital of a kingdom whose influence extended around the Mediterranean.

Valencia's finest buildings, often lurking behind modern assaults on good taste, date from its golden era in the Middle Ages. Decline started in the 16thC.

You will find most of interest in the **old quarter**, cupped in a bend of the Turia river bed (dry because the river has been diverted). Near the Turia are the **Torres de Serranos**, built in the late 14thC to defend one of the entrances to the old walled city; a **maritime museum** (open mornings) has been installed in a lower floor.

The animated **Plaza del Mercado**, where executions and bullfights once took place, is the sensible place to start your explorations. Two remarkable buildings stand here. First, there is the **Lonja de la Seda**, built in 1483 as a silk exchange, and one of Europe's finest examples of civic Gothic architecture: 24 twisted pillars support ogival arches in the lofty former trading hall. Then, for stark contrast, stroll through the Modernist-style **Central Market**, all iron and stained glass, where more than 1,000 stalls display a dazzling array of fish, meat and vegetables, plus everything from herbal remedies to exotic spices.

A short walk through labyrinthine streets brings you to Valencia's **cathedral**, on which work began in 1262. Embracing Romanesque, Gothic and Baroque styles, it stands on the site of a Roman temple to Diana and a mosque which El Cid converted into a church. While not Spain's most outstanding ecclesiastical building, it does have something that others cannot match. Take the first right turn on entering to visit the **Sala Capitular**, the superbly Gothic-vaulted chapter house, and examine the **chalice** enshrined there. It is carved out of emerald-green oriental agate, which shifts in colour according to the light. This, we are assured, is the legendary Holy Grail, the cup used by Christ at the Last Supper. Brought to Spain in the 4thC, it was kept at San Juan de la Peña Monastery in Huesca province (see Spain Overall: 6) until King Alfonso The Magnanimous of Aragón donated it in 1428.

It is worth the effort to climb the 207 steps up the 51 m-high **Torre del Micalet**, the octagonal bell tower, to enjoy the view.

Outside the richly ornamented Gothic Puerta de los Apóstoles, facing the Plaza de la Virgen, an institution that dates back more than 1,000 years meets every Thursday midday. The **Tribunal de las Aguas**, the water court, settles problems associated with water use in the *huerta*. This ingenious irrigation system, started by the Romans, but vastly improved by the Moors, made the fertile plain of the Turia flourish. The court was set up during the Caliphate of Córdoba and continues to dispense instant justice, an example that Spaniards wish their other (notoriously tardy) courts would follow.

Nearby is the **Palacio de la Generalitat**, a Gothic monument and official seat of regional government. Once representatives of the Kingdom of Valencia met here in the Salón de Cortes. Note especially the coffered ceiling. Baroque mansions dot Valencia, but surely the most remarkable is the **Palacio de Marqués de Dos Aguas**, on Rinconada de García Sanchiz. Two huge figures bearing amphoras guard the entrance. Inside is the **National Ceramics**

HUMAN CASTLES

Television has boosted the popularity of the *castells* (human castles) cult, an astonishing display of strength and fearlessness, which originated in Valls (page 108) 200 years or so ago. A *colla* (team) of barefoot *castellers* climb on to one another's shoulders, eight or nine men high, and then a young boy claws his way to the top to crown the castle. If the *castellers* lose their balance, serious injury may result. The castles vary in structure, and teams dream of re-creating a legendary monster called the *cinc de nou amb folre* (nine storeys, five persons per level).

It is said that when Spain besieged a Moroccan town in the 19thC, General Prim called on the Valls *castellers* to scale the walls and run up the Spanish flag.

The best place to see the human castles is in the main plaza of Valls during the **Santa Ursula fiesta** in October. However, they also appear in many Catalan fiestas.

Museum, containing 5,000 exhibits from down the ages. Valencia has long been renowned for its ceramics: at **Manises** (8 km north-west of the city) there are many potteries (which can be visited) producing pots and tiles in traditional and modern styles.

Outside the city next to the motorway to El Saler is the **Ciudad de las Artes y las Ciencias**, opened in stages from April 1998. This 'city within a city' offers wide spaces for relaxation together with cultural antidotes to sun-and-beach tourism: among them art galleries, a science museum and an ocean park.

Valencia has numerous *horchaterías*, ice-cream parlours where you can drink *horchata*, a chilled, highly-refreshing drink with a nutty taste. It looks like milk but in fact is made from a root called *chufa*.

Finding *tapa* bars is no problem in the centre: stroll into the Bar Pilar, an old-fashioned place with ceiling fans, at Moro Zeit, 13, off Caballeros, and try the mussels. El Palacio de la Bellota, at Mosén Femades, 7, specializes in cured ham, but has many other snacks from which to choose.

Once a year Valencia comes close to burning down, when the week-long **fiesta of Las Fallas** is held. Huge, elaborate *papiermaché* effigies are set up in public places, each district trying to outdo its neighbours. Satirizing well-known personalities and events, the grotesque figures are finally put to the torch on March 19, the day of San José, in what ranks as possibly Spain's noisiest fiesta (quite a claim).

The custom originated with medieval carpenters burning their wood shavings in bonfires known as *fallas*.

VALLS

On the N240, 20 km N of Tarragona. Tourism Office, Plaça Blat, 1; tel. 977 60 10 50. This small industrial and agricultural centre is renowned as the birthplace of 'human castles' (page 107).

The Cistercian abbey of Santa Creus (16 km NE of Valls, off the A2) was founded in 1168 by a Cistercian community from Languedoc, France, which benefited from royal protection. The tombs of Peter the Great, James II and his wife Blanche of Anjou lie in the austere church, begun in 1174, which has a beautiful rose window and a notable Gothic cloister.

VILAFRANCA DEL PENEDES

On the N340, 48 km SW of Barcelona. Vilafranca is the main town of the Penedès wine district, which produces some of Spain's finest wines. It has a number of fine Gothic and Modernist buildings and the **Museu dei Vi** (wine museum) in an old palace on Plaça Jaume displays methods of wine production down the ages.

RECOMMENDED RESTAURANTS

Paella is Spain's most famous dish, but many sins are committed in its name. Warmed-up, mushy, highly coloured rice with meat and fish tossed on top bears no resemblance to the real thing. Short-grained, low-starch rice, which absorbs the flavour of the food with which it is cooked, is essential. This type, grown in the Valencia region, forms the basis of many delicious dishes typical of the coast from Castellón to Murcia. Cooked in a special shallow, two-handled pan, true *paella* requires fresh ingredients, fine olive oil and precise timing to avoid overcooking.

Genuine *paella a la valenciana* comes with rabbit, snails, and broad beans. A *paella a la marinera* is served with seafood, while a *paella mixta* includes seafood, chicken, sausage and vegetables. Variations are found in other parts of Spain.

Other rice dishes you will come across in the region include *arroz a banda* (rice cooked in fish broth and served separately) and *arroz negro* (rice cooked with cuttlefish ink to turn it black).

While a *Valenciano* is likely to tell you that nobody can make *paella* as good as his mother's, he will probably recommend a visit to one of the beach-side restaurants near the port (see below). *Paella* is best cooked and eaten in the open air.

CAMBRILS

On the N340, 18 km SW of Tarragona.

Three restaurants highly rated for seafood belong to the same family: the **Can Gatell** (*Paseo Miramar*, 27); the **Eugenia** (*Consolat del Mar*, 80); and the select **Joan Gatell-Casa Gatell, PPP** (*Paseo Miramar*, 26; *tel.* 977 36 00 57; *credit cards* AE, DC, MC, V; *closed Sun eve, Mon, Jan.*) This last is expensive, but after tasting *Rodaballo con setas* (turbot with mushrooms) or *Lubina al hinojo silvestre* (bass with wild fennel) you can pay up with a smile.

CANTAVIEJA

Buj, PP; (*on the E800, 49 km SW of Morella*), *Avda del Maestrazgo*, 6; *tel.* 964 18 50 33; *no credit cards; closed eve and Feb.*

Run by Doña Francisca and her two daughters, this little restaurant is a dazzling surprise in the heart of the Maestrazgo district. There is no written menu, but non-Spanish speakers can peek into the kitchen to see what's available. Impeccably served, the dishes are tasty and imaginative, using local ingredients; the *Pavo trufado* (truffled turkey) and almond tart are fond memories. Definitely worth a detour.

The year's big **fiesta**, August 29-September 2, coincides with the end of the grape harvest and usually presents an opportunity to see the *castellers* performing – see page 107.

Just up the road (12 km north-east on the C243) is **Sant Sadurní d'Anoia**, floating on a sea of bubbles. Spain exports around 50 million bottles of sparkling wine every year, the United States being a key market, and some of the most important **bodegas** are in this small town. Among those you can visit are the two giants, Codorniú and Freixenet. Spain's equivalent of champagne is called *cava* (French producers stopped the use of their name). A cheaper bubbly is *granvás*: the second fermentation takes place in large vats. Cheapest of all is *vino gasificado*: avoid it unless you want a splitting headache.

VALENCIA NIGHTLIFE

Nights are lively in Valencia. Join the young crowd at the pubs along Eugenia Viñes at the Malvarrosa Beach, around the Plaza de Cánovas and in the Carmen quarter, or at discos in the university area. On Reloj Viejo, a 16thC mansion houses the lively Calcutta pub.

To see Saturday night fever at its craziest, head out of town to the Spook Factory ('maximum concentration of irresponsible youth' in the words of a local guide), on the Nazaret-Oliva road.

Gamblers can make for the Casino Monte Picayo (admission charge), at Puzol, 14 km from the city centre, off the Autopista del Mediterráneo.

FIGUERES
Cal Sagrista; PP; (*at Peralada 6 km NE of Figueres off the N260*), *Rodona*, 2; *credit cards* AE, MC, V; *closed Tues, mid-Jan, Feb.*

An agreeable restaurant in part of a convent. Home cooking.

GIRONA
Edelweiss, PP; *Santa Eugenia*, 7; *tel.* 972 20 18 97; *credit cards* AE, MC, V; *closed Sun, last fortnight Aug.*

Careful use of stone, tiles and brickwork give this restaurant (Swiss overtones) a friendly atmosphere. Try the fondue or the *Filet de porc al Cabrales* (pork with Cabrales cheese).

SAGUNTO
L'Armeler, PP; *Castillo*, 44; *tel.* 96 266 43 82; *credit cards* AE, DC, MC, V; *closed Sun eve, Mon (except summer).*

Amparo learned her cooking in France. In what was her grandparents' house in the Jewish quarter, she has created a small restaurant serving excellent French *cuisine*. Home-made patés and delicious onion tart.

TARRAGONA
Les Fonts de Can Sala, PP; (*2 km N of Tarragona, just off the A7*), *Ctra de Valls*, 62; *tel.* 977 22 85 75; *credit cards* AE, DC, MC, V; *closed Tues, last two weeks Oct.*

Catalan dishes in a rural atmosphere, with open-air dining on the terrace.

VALENCIA
El Gourmet, PP; *Taquígrafo Martí*, 3; *tel.* 96 395 25 09; *credit cards* AE, MC, V; *closed Sun & Aug.*

Belle Epoque decoration, carefully prepared dishes, and reasonable prices. Reservations essential. Try the casserole of monkfish, prawns, and sole.

Taberna Alkazar, PP; *Mosén Femades*, 9; *tel.* 96 352 95 75; *credit cards* AE, DC, V; *closed Mon, Aug, Easter Week.*

Old-established seafood restaurant with a wide choice of wines; decoration on the bullfighting theme.

Restaurants (all on Las Arenas beach) specializing in *paella* include :

L'Estimat, PP; *Avda Neptuno*, 16; *tel.* 96 371 10 18; *credit cards* MC, V; *closed Sun and Mon eve, Tues.*

The seafood *paella* is renowned.

La Marcelina, PP; *Avda de Neptuno*, 8; *tel.* 96 371 20 25; *credit cards* AE, DC, MC, V; *closed Sun in summer, eve in winter, part of Jan.*

Boasts it's the oldest.

La Pepica, PP; *Avda Neptuno*, 6; *tel.* 96 371 03 66 *or* 371 41 11; *credit cards* AE, DC, MC, V; *closed Sun eve except Jul and Aug, and Nov.*

Hemingway ate here.

Between Valencia and Almería
Costa Blanca and Murcia

469 km; maps Michelin 445 & 446

Travelling the Spanish coast south of Valencia in February, you could be understood for thinking that you have run into a snowfall. Thousands of almond trees are bursting into bloom over the hillsides, a breath-taking sight, part of the magic of the Costa Blanca – the White Coast – along with beaches of white sand, secluded bays, and a dry, sunny climate. Not surprisingly, the region attracts vast numbers of tourists as well as thousands of sun-starved North European retirees, who make their home here.

Rice fields and citrus orchards on Valencia province's intensely culti-vated plain fill the view at first on the road south. From Denia, in Alicante province, where the Costa Blanca begins, the landscape changes to one of eroded ochre hills and azure seas. In summer the coast is always crowded and the traffic is overpowering, particularly around the package-holiday capital of Benidorm. Road signs are often in the local language, *valenciano*, a form of Catalan, as well as in Castilian. But so many expatriates vacation or live here that you are just as likely to hear English, French, German, or a Scandinavian tongue.

It is easy to escape the Costa Blanca and its cosmopolitan crowds by going just a few miles inland: if that is what you need, see any of the detours marked on the map and described in the text; see also Local Explorations: 12.

Invaders are nothing new to the Mediterranean coast between Cat-alonia and Andalucía, known traditionally as El Levante because it is in the east (Spanish, *levantar,* to rise). Three thousand years ago the Phoenician traders sailed in. Later, the Greeks gave the name Akra Leuka (White Headland) to a colony they set up near modern Alicante. The Carthagini-ans established a naval base on the site of present-day Cartagena, before giving way to the Romans. The Moors ruled the region as part of al-Andalus (Andalucía), leaving behind an ingenious irrigation system, which converted the arid coastal plain into lush *huertas* (irrigated plain, typically supporting orchards and vegetable farms). You will stillcome across *norias*, the giant water-raising wheels introduced by the Moors.

South of Alicante, the beaches are backed by salt flats and palm groves and then the tomato and pepper fields of Murcia. The heat grows more intense as you enter the arid moonscapes and badlands of Almería, featured in many a spaghetti Western. This desert-like terrain is the gate-way to Andalucía.

If you're driving, the quickest way south (or north), the red route, is the A7 (E15) *autopista*. Hopping on and off the A7, you can see the major sights in two days. But it is more rewarding to wander along the N332, making forays inland (the blue route). Those with time to spare can travel green by following the numerous detours (such as the N301 to Jumilla) and taking the N340 inland between Alicante and Valencia, which doubles as the trail followed by Local Explorations: 12.

Valencia

La Albufera

Cullera

N340

N332

Xátiva

A7

Gandía

Denia

Jávea (Xabia)

Cabo de la Nabo

Guadalest

C3313

Calpe

Altea

Benidorm

A7

N332

Villajoysa

Jumilla

Alicante

Elche (Elx)

N340

N301

Caravaca de la Cruz

C415

Orihuela

Isla de Tabarca

Mula

Murcia

Sierra Española

N340

N301

Aledo

Mar Menor

Vélez Blanco

Vélez Rubio

N342

Los Alacazares

La Manga

Lorca

Puerto Lumbreras

Puerto de Mazarrón

Cartagena

Costa Cálida

Aguilas

Sorbas

Mojacar

rnas

N344

Almería

1:2,500,000

TRANSPORT

Long-distance buses run between the major cities, Valencia, Alicante, Murcia and Almería, with connecting local services to smaller towns. Rail services tend to be slower and more expensive. A small-gauge railway (the FEVE) hugs the coast between Denia and Alicante, offering a pleasant change from the highways.

SIGHTS & PLACES OF INTEREST

AGUILAS
See Costa Calida, page 114.

ALBUFERA, LA
Off the N332 15 km S of Valencia. La Albufera is Spain's largest lagoon, a glittering sheet of fresh water famed for its thousands of migratory birds and for its fish. A pine-dotted sand bar holds back the sea.

All-i-pebre de anguilas (eels fried in garlic and paprika) are a speciality at the rustic restaurants at **El Palmar**, on the lakeside. You can hire a boat here or at El Saler for a trip over the lagoon, which will give you the oppportunity to sight ducks, egrets, terns and others of the 250 bird species recorded. Ecologists are fighting to save the lagoon from pollution and encroaching development.

ALEDO
Off N340, 9 km NW of Totana. This little town rides a spur, commanding beautiful views of the *huerta* (irrigated plain) and the pine-covered slopes of the **Parque Natural de Sierra Espuña**, the haunt of a number of protected species including the black vulture, tawny owl and golden eagle.

The **castle** with its square tower was once commanded by the Knights of Calatrava. Pigeons perch about the statues adorning the golden-stone façade of the 15thC **church of Santa María La Real** with its twin towers. Nearby **Totana** is a centre for ceramics, particularly giant *tinajas* (water jars).

ALICANTE (ALACANT) ⇔ ✕
On the N332, 166 km S of Valencia. Tourism Office, Esplanada de España, 2; tel: 96 520 00 00. With its back-drop of arid hills, date palms and dusky street pedlars, Alicante has an African air. It is a pleasant port city, which was a favourite winter resort long before the Costa Blanca had been heard of. It is a city for strolling, with wide boulevards and interesting shops. Beaches are within easy reach. Enjoy the sea breezes along the palm-lined **Esplanada**, sinuously patterned in marble.

A lift whisks you up to the **Castillo de Santa Barbara** from whose glow-ering battlements there are stupendous views over the city and Mediterranean. Back in town, Miró, Picasso, and Tápies are among the masters with works in the **Museo de Arte Siglo**, while the **Ayuntamiento** is also worth a visit. It is a Churrigueresque 18thC palace with an ornate façade. Note the brass plaque on a pillar of the main stairway. This indicates sea level and is the benchmark from which Spain calculates all its altitudes.

Alicante was under Republican control during the Civil War when José Antonio de Rivera, founder of the fascist Falange, was imprisoned here. His execution made him into a martyr for the Nationalist cause. Another martyr was created in Alicante after the war, this time a Republican one, when in 1942 the life of the poet Miguel Hernández ebbed away in an Alicante jail. See also Orihuela, page 119.

The city is at its liveliest in the week that includes June 24, when the **Hogueras de San Juan Fiesta** takes place. Apart from the usual round of processions and bullfights, huge images are set up in public places and burned. This legacy of pagan rites sometimes goes tragically wrong when the leaping flames engulf more than they ought. Another fiesta celebrated here and in scores of towns in the province is that of the Moors and Christians. Communities work and save all year around to prepare the sumptuous costumes for these extravagant re-enactments of the battles of the Reconquest.

A worthwhile local excursion, especially for snorkellers, is to the **Isla de Tabarca**, a tiny island which was once a den of pirates. The 150 inhabitants, reduced to 15 in winter, have Italian surnames, revealing their descent from Genovese migrants. There are no motor vehicles and, apart from a 14-room hotel, there is no accommodation, but there are several eating places, where lobster is a speciality. You can reach Tabarca by ferry from the harbour or, a shorter sea journey, from Santa Pola, the fishing port 17 km south of Alicante.

Ferries run from Alicante to the Balearic Isles and to Oran in Algeria. Join the narrow-gauge FEVE line (see Transport, page 111) at the Estación de la Marina.

ALMERIA
See Spain Overall: 10.

ALTEA ✕
On the 332, 50 km NE of Alicante. Tourism Office, San Pedro, 9; tel 96 584 4114. By some miracle, urban blight has spared Altea's old quarter. Its narrow streets straggle up the hill to the blue-domed church. The adjacent plaza is a pleasant spot to sip a limon granizado (lemon juice served over crushed ice) while watching the swifts dive-bombing the church tower. In nearby streets men play an odd ball game called pilota de carrer on Sunday afternoons. A cosmopolitan bunch of artists have settled in Altea (the Moorish name Altaya means health for all), certainly the prettiest town on the coast.

BENIDORM ⇌ ✕
Off the N332, 42 km NE of Alicante. Tourism Office, Avenida Martinez Alejos, 16; tel. 96 585 32 24. The very name sends a chill down the spines of discerning hispanophiles, synonymous as it is with cheap, chips-with-everything package tours. Yes, it is a high-rise horror. But enter into the spirit of the place, toss aside snobbish pretensions, and – with the help of generous doses of sangria – you may even enjoy it.

Back in 1960, Benidorm was a poverty-stricken fishing village with two fine beaches. The beaches are still there, but all else has changed. Hundreds of hotels and apartment blocks crowd the shoreline, hundreds of thousands of holidaymakers pack the beaches in high season. 'Beni' has scores of bars and restaurants; all-night discos; jousting tournaments; lager unlimited; Nordic beauties, lusting Don Juans, wet T-shirt contests… it's not Spain, but it can be fun.

Among the most popular after-dark haunts are discos such as Black Sunset, Penelope, Star Garden and the Benidorm Palace night club.

In an attempt to repair some of the damage caused by lack of planning control, the local authority has robbed the bank to create parks, plant palm trees on the beach, clean the streets, provide courtesy patrols, and create the so-called Green Beret patrol, whose job is to jump very hard on trouble-makers. In fact, Benidorm is immaculately maintained. You will be lucky to find a room in summer, while in winter pensioners of all nationalities take over, attending keep-fit classes on the beach and tea dances in the afternoons and evenings (who said Ramona would never be top of the hit parade again?).

The crush has been intensified with the recent opening of **Terra Mitica**, (from Benidorm, take the Finestrat road; well signposted in 4 km on the right). The biggest theme park on the Mediterranean coast comes in five mythologically-themed zones - Egypt, Greece, Rome, Iberia and the Islands.

CABO DE LA NAO
See Jávea, page 116.

CALPE ⇌
Off the N332, 63 km NE of Alicante. Massive apartment blocks despoil the front, but fortunately – just one step ahead of the cement mixers – the **Peñón de Ifach** was made a Nature Park. This impressive thumb of rock juts 330 m out of the sea: you can climb it in about one hour. Tottery tourists occasionally fall off.

CARAVACA DE LA CRUZ
On the C415, 73 km from Murcia. This is a worthwhile detour: rising above the countryside, Caravaca is an imposing sight. The ramparts with their 14 towers were once manned by the Templars and the Order of Santiago. A steep walk takes you up through narrow streets to the 15thC **castle**, within which is the **church of Santa Cruz** with its impressive Baroque façade.

Colourful fiestas held every year in the first week of May are rooted in events of Moorish times. In 1231 the symbol of the town, a double-armed cross believed to be part of the True Cross, made a miraculous appearance – express-delivered from heaven by a posse of angels – when a Moorish chieftain ordered a captured priest to say Mass. The Moor was immediately converted. Honouring the cross is a focal point during the May fiestas; another (on May 2) is the **Caballos del Vino**, when finely caparisoned horses race through the streets. This marks the occasion when, in a desperate search for water, some Knights Templar broke out of the besieged castle. Finding none, they filled their skins with wine before dashing back.

Largely-uninhabited, pine-clad sierras, home of vultures and wild boar, cover the arid, north-western corner of the province beyond Caravaca. *En route* from Murcia, on the C415, you pass by **Mula**, with the remains of its castle standing high above town and orange orchards.

CARTAGENA

On N301, 48 km from Murcia. Tourism Office, Plaza Bastarreche; tel. 968 50 64 83. Spain's most important naval base, situated in a usefully sheltered harbour. This was Carthago Nova of Ancient times, founded by the Carthaginians, sacked by the Goths, pillaged by Francis Drake, bombed in the Civil War. In 1931, King Alfonso XIII, rejected by his people, sailed into exile from here. The best view is from the Castillo de la Concepción, in a park where an Arab-built lighthouse stands. Cartagena is a workaday place and few of its sights are remarkable.

By the port, close to a monument to sailors who died in the Cuban war against the United States in 1898, is poised an over-size brown and grey cigar. This 75-ton object is a **pioneer submarine**, constructed by local inventor Isaac Peral in 1888. Close by is the Plaza del Ayuntamiento, with the pedestrian mall, Calle Mayor, leading out of it, pleasant for a stroll and a drink.

The **National Museum of Maritime Archeology** lies outside town at the Dique de Navidad, and is definitely worth a visit. Amphoras, anchors, jewellery, and other items rescued from the depths are on show, as well as a full-size model of a Roman galley.

If you are in the area during **Holy Week**, don't miss Cartagena's solemn and sumptuous processions.

COSTA CALIDA

This is the name under which Murcia promotes its 250 km of relatively undeveloped coast. With the exception of Mar Menor, this is mostly unspoilt rocky inlets, small islands, and shallow coves suitable for swimming and snorkelling. However, the scenery is generally bleak and charmless.

Puerto de Mazarrón and **Aguilas** are the only two towns of any note, both of which are striving to become tourist centres.

CULLERA ✕

Off the N332, 40 km S of Valencia. This is the sort of place to which town planners should be taken for a lesson in how to crush the intimate appeal of a small fishing port with high-rise madness. In summer about 100,000 people crowd the endless apartment blocks; in winter the place is an echoing ghost town. But up on the rock that towers over it all are the ruins of a **castle**, with fine views, and a restaurant that is worth a detour.

DENIA ✕

Off the N332, 98 km SE of Valencia. Tourism Office, Plaza de Oculista Büigues, 9; tel. 96 642 23 67. The Greeks had a name for this site, Hemeroskopeion, but fortunately the Romans gave it a more pronounceable one, Dianium (after a temple of Diana). A thousand years or so ago, Denia enjoyed a period of cultural splendour when its mini-kingdom or *taifa* exerted influence as far as the Balearic Islands and Sardinia. Modern Denia is an attractive town, with battered ramparts testifying to its strategic value – French troops were besieged here for five months during the Napoleonic Wars. Scale the castle hill to visit the **Museo Arqueológico** and enjoy the view over town and fishing port. Ferry services run to Ibiza, and Denia is a terminus of the FEVE line to Alicante. The trip takes 2 hours 20 minutes and is a relatively painless way to see the Costa Blanca.

ELCHE (ELX) 🛏 ✕

On the N340, 23 km SW of Alicante. Tourism Office, Paseig de l'Estació; tel: 96 545 38 31. Hundreds of thousands of date palms, originally planted by the Phoenicians, grow in the irrigated flatlands around Elche. They are valuable both for their dates, which only grow on female trees and are harvested from December to March, and for their leaves, used in Easter Week processions. Many palms are shrouded in black plastic to bleach the leaves, which are woven into decorations.

The garden known as the **Huerto del Cura** has a large collection of cactus and tropical flowers as well as the unusual 'priest's palm' – with seven branches sprouting from the same trunk. Dates from trees dedicated to King Juan Carlos and Queen Sophia are

• *Altea harbour – see page 113.*

supplied to the royal household.

A replica of the **Dame de Elche** stands in the Huerto. This bust, apparently of a noblewoman, may have been sculpted around 500 BC and was found at La Alcudia, 2 km south of town where there is a museum of Iberian and Roman relics. The original is in Madrid's National Archeological Museum.

Elche is important for shoe manufacture, but it has an additional claim to fame. Every August a local amateur cast performs the world's longest-running play, ***Misteri d'Elx*** (Mystery of Elche) in the Santa María Church. The play, celebrating the Assumption of the Virgin Mary, has been in production for some 600 years. As the songs are in ancient Catalan, not only the title spells mystery. However, special effects – including the descent of angels from the dome of the church are guaranteed to produce gasps from the audience. The first part of the play is staged on the evening of August 14 and the sec-ond part on August 15. In addition, condensed, one-day performances are performed on several other days. If you wish to attend, contact the Tourism Office for seating information well in advance.

GANDIA

On the N332, 65km S of Valencia. Tourism Office, Marqués de Campo; tel. 96 287 77 88. Set among orange groves, some of Gandía is a characterless modern development. But it retains interesting traces of the notorious Borgia family (Borja in Spanish) who were given a duchy here by Ferdinand the Catholic. The first Duke of Gandía, Rodrigo Borgia, born in nearby Játiva, became the notorious Pope Alexander VI. Immensely wealthy, he lived like a Renaissance prince and fathered numerous children, among them Cesare (Machiavelli's model for *The Prince*) and Lucrezia,

115

coldly used by her father and brother to further their interests.

In contrast, Alexander's grandson, Francisco, the Fourth Duke, became a leader of the Jesuits, was instrumental in spreading their word throughout Europe, and was canonized for his good works.

The Gothic and Renaissance **Palacio de los Duques**, where San Francisco was born in 1510, features an impressive patio and magnificent tilework. A Jesuit school is now housed there. Francisco founded a Jesuit college in Gandía, which was made a university by papal bull in 1547. Known as the Escuelas Pías, it has an 18thC façade.

Another local boy who did not do too badly was Joanot Martorell, the medieval knight and author of the outstanding novel of chivalry, *Tirant lo Blanc*.

These days, Gandía is known less for its historic associations than for the long, sandy beach, a few minutes away from the old centre. It is lined with apartment blocks and frequented by thousands of Spanish families in July and August. To cater for them, it does have some good seafood restaurants.

GUADALEST
Off the N332, 26 km from Benidorm on the Alcoy road. Constructed by the Moors at least 1,000 years ago, this is a spectacularly-sited fortress accessible only via a 16 m tunnel through solid rock. Inside, old ladies knit woollen shawls and ponchos, on sale at reasonable prices. Worth a visit, especially in the evening. During the day it is often overrun by tour groups from the coast. When returning to the coast, look for the **Algar Waterfalls**, just north of Callosa, where you can cool off in a 15 m cascade or in swimming-pools.

ISLA DE TABARCA
See Alicante, page 112.

JAVEA (XABIA) ⌨
Off the N332, 10 km SE of Denia. Tourism Office, Plaza Almirante Bastarreche, 11, Jávea port; tel. 96 579 07 36. Sheltering under the great bulk of 751 m-high Montgó, old Jávea is set back from the sea on a hilltop.

It has narrow streets and stone houses, plus Roman and Punic remains in a municipal museum in a noble 17thC

mansion built for Antonio Bañuls by Philip III. Apparently the king was playing *pelota* with the Marquis of Denia when a dispute arose. The king asked the watching Jávea townsfolk their opinion and Bañuls spoke up: 'The fault was not yours, your Majesty, but that of the ball.' Philip later constructed the house for Bañuls, demonstrating that a little sycophancy can go a long way.

Hundreds of whitewashed villas housing expatriates, mostly retirees, have sprouted amid the surrounding vineyards and almond-treed hillsides and around the bay. At the southernmost end are the rocky headlands **Cabo de Sant Martín** and **Cabo de la Nao**, with the tiny island of Porticho just offshore. The caves in the cliffs are known as *pesqueras de la muerte* (fishing grounds of death), because of their dangerous state.

JUMILLA
On the C344, 74 km N of Murcia. The landscape looks like something out of Arizona as you leave the fertile *huertas* (irrigated plains) and head north through eroded hills, dotted with conifers, to reach broad, steppe-like plains. Jumilla, in the northern corner of Murcia province, has several fine old buildings, including the **Salvador** and **Santiago** churches and the **Lonja** (market or exchange). However, the town, with neighbouring Yecla, is best known for its wines. Traditionally, these have been treacly brews, highly alcoholic and heavy-bodied. In fact, large quantities are still exported to Northern Europe for blending with the thinner local products (not that Jumilla ever gets any credit on the bottle). But some *bodegas* are now picking the grapes earlier and introducing modern fermentation methods to produce lighter, more palatable wines. They will be glad to show you the process at Viña Umbria, if you call beforehand on 968 78 11 12.

LORCA ⌨
Off the N340, 62 km from Murcia. Tourism Office, López Gisbert, 12; tel. 968 46 61 57. A by-pass now sweeps traffic past this market town, which is a centre for craftwork (Murcia province has more than 500 artisans). A squat tower looks down from the castle. Don't be put off by the undistinguished modern out-

RECOMMENDED HOTELS

BENIDORM
Gran Hotel Delfin, PPP; *Playa de Poniente, la Cala; tel. 96 585 34 00; closed Oct to Easter.*

Benidorm has scores of hotels worth a detour to avoid. This one, *not* built for package holidays, offers subdued comfort on the quieter southern side of town, near the beach. Pool, tennis courts. First time I stayed there, bullfighter El Cordobés was showing off his scars to assembled press in an adjacent room.

ELCHE
Huerto del Cura, PPP; *Porta de la Morera, 14; tel. 96 545 80 40.*

This uniquely-located hotel, in beautiful gardens with a grove of palm trees, is an ideal spot to relax in after a day's hard driving. Swimming-pool, air-conditioned rooms.

JAVEA
Parador de Jávea, PPP; *Avda Mediterráneo, 7; tel. 96 579 02 00.*

This is a useful base from which to explore the area or for just lazing about by the pool amid pleasant gardens. A modern building, it lies on a beautiful bay, with an adjacent boat dock.

Miramar, PP; *Plaza Almirante Bastarreche, 12; tel. 96 579 01 00.*

Small hotel on the sea front.

MOJACAR
El Moresco, PP; *Avda Horizonte, s/n; tel. 950 47 80 25.*

At the entrance to the village, with fine views, particularly from the rooftop pool.

MURCIA
Casa Emilio, PP; *Alameda Colón, 9; tel. 968 22 06 31.*

Just across the river from the town centre. Friendly service. Small but comfortable rooms.

Hispano-2, PPP; *Radio Murcia, 3; tel. 968 21 61 52.*

Right in the heart of town. Value for money.

VILLAJOYOSA
Montiboli, PPP; *Carretera N332, km 108; tel. 96 589 02 50.*

Away from resort hubbub, this hotel on a headland has fine sea views, two swimming pools, and beaches nearby. The Casino Costa Blanca is not far away for those in need of thrills.

BUDGET ACCOMMODATION

ALICANTE
Portugal, P; *Portugal, 26; tel. 96 592 92 44.*

Handy for bus and rail stations.

BENIDORM
Canfali, PP; *Plaza San Jaime, 1; tel. 96 585 08 18; closed Nov-Mar.*

Overlooks the sea.

CALPE
Venta la Chata, P; *Carretera Valencia, km 150; tel. 96 583 03 08.*

Handy roadside stop, pleasant garden, views of Peñon de Ifach.

LORCA
Alameda, PP; *Musso Valiente, 8; tel. 968 40 66 00.*

Three-star hotel in a useful central location.

LOS ALCAZARES
La Encarnación, P; *Condesa, 1; tel. 968 57 50 07; closed Oct-May.*

Spartan but characterful small hotel on the edge of the Mar Menor. A welcoming atmosphere and traditional cooking.

MURCIA
Hispano 1, PP; *Trapería, 8; tel. 968 21 61 52.*

Older and cheaper version of the Hispano-2.

skirts, as in the centre there are some fine old buildings, notably the **Casa de los Guevara,** with its magnificent spiral-columned façade and porticoed patio. The Plaza de España is graced by noble stonework of the **Ayuntamiento** (17-18thC) and the Baroque façade of the collegiate **church of San Patricio.**

Make a point of visiting the **Centro para la Artesanía**, near the Tourist Office. This imaginatively designed centre where an unusually large range of hand-made local products are exhibited, includes ceramics, embroidery and *jarapas* (rugs). The richness of the embroidery can be seen in Lorca's Easter processions, famous for their elaborate costumes.

LOS ALCAZARES
See Recommended Hotels, page 117.

MAR MENOR
Off N332, 20 km NW of Cartagena. This shallow salt water lagoon extending over 170 square km could be the centre of an attractive tourist area. It provides shelter for water-sports and the water itself, warmer than the Mediterranean, is said to have health-giving properties. Rheumatism sufferers seek relief by burying themselves in iodine-rich mud. But greed and lack of foresight have polluted the lagoon (a costly clean-up campaign is planned) and defaced the shores with nondescript construction. The worst crimes have been committed on **La Manga**, a narrow sandspit separating the lagoon from the Mediterranean, where a mini-Manhattan forms a concrete wall. This is not to be confused with the luxury resort of La Manga Club nearby, an oasis of golfing greensward, tennis courts, and expensive accommodation.

MINI HOLLYWOOD
See Sorbas, page 120.

MOJACAR 🛌
Off the N340, 92 km from Almeria. Tourism Office, Plaza Nueva; tel. 950 61 50 25. A white cubist vision crowning a hill top 2 km from the sea, Mojácar was virtually abandoned until, in the 1950s, the major had the initiative to persuade diplomats and artists to establish second homes here. They converted it into a trendy colony, which has given way to

package tourists with the corresponding eruption of car parks, souvenir shops and tea rooms. It looks more attractive from a distance. A local legend has it that Walt Disney was born here, something of which the Disney family appears oddly unaware. If you are into nude sunbathing, the naturist hotel **Vera Playa Club**, is 15 km away, near Vera (tel. 951 46 74 75).

MULA
See Caravaca de la Cruz, page 113.

MURCIA 🛌 ✕
On the N340, 75 km SW of Alicante; Tourism Office, San Cristóbal, 6; tel. 968 36 61 00. Pleasantly provincial, Murcia has spruced itself up lately. With 300,000 inhabitants, it is the capital of the autonomous region and province of the same name. At one time Murcia was a kingdom, which mediated between Moors and Christians, until it finally came under Castile in 1243. Valencia was conquered by Aragon in 1238, but Murcia continued for two more centuries as a separately administered kingdom.

Murcianos are generally regarded as a crafty lot by their fellow Spaniards, but this may be envy of a region which, although regarded as a backwater, has long prospered from its agriculture and mining. Murcia's fertile *huerta* (irrigated plain) watered by the Segura has always been a rich farming area.

Fire and pillage destroyed many buildings in the Civil War, but the **cathedral** endured, with its dazzling Baroque façade, which is particularly impressive under floodlights. Climb the tower for fine views. Although no *aficionado* of religious art, I was bowled over by the detailed realism of the cathedral's wooden images carved by 18thC sculptor Francisco Salzillo. There is a **Museo de Salzillo** on San Andrés. Several of his images are carried in procession in **Holy Week**, celebrated with great pomp. On Holy Wednesday, 3,000 people take part in one procession, among them musicians blowing horns so large they have to be trundled along on wheels.

In the Traperia district, visit the **Casino**, a private club for the local élite, which has a distinctly palatial air with its crystal chandeliers, elegant mouldings and carved wood. Visitors

are welcome, but should tip the porter.

On the Plaza Julián Romea, the century-old **Teatro Romea** holds a music and drama season from February to April.

Old ways linger in Murcia and in a side street, at number 26, Cartagena, I came across Antonio Rueda, an 80-year-old maker of *botas* (wine skins), the last of 30 following this craft. Traditional crafts, as well as costumes and implements, are on show at the **Museo Huerta**, 8 km out of town at Alcantarilla. You will spot the museum easily enough by its *noria* (waterwheel), 11 m in diameter. This is an iron replica of the wooden *norias* used by the Moors to raise water.

ORIHUELA

Off the N340, 22 km NE of Murcia. Tourism Office, Francisco Diez, 25; tel. 96 530 27 47. Approached through palm groves, Orihuela has a dusty, shabby aspect, but its monuments from more illustrious days lend it some interest. The fertility of the land, irrigated by the Segura River, justifies an old saying:

• Mini Hollywood.

'Rain or no rain, corn in Orihuela.'

The Gothic **cathedral**, with its unusual twisted columns, guards a Velázquez painting, *The Temptation of St Thomas Aquinas*, on view during museum opening hours. Velázquez executed the work at the request of Dominican friars. Their convent, **Santo Domingo**, which was a university in the 17thC, features fine Baroque cloisters and a beautifully tiled refectory.

Miguel Hernández, the goatherd who became a respected lyric poet but incurred the wrath of the Franco regime, was born in Orihuela. A map provided by the Tourism Office shows his family home and the place where he was arrested in 1939. After being shifted from one insanitary jail to another and contracting first tuberculosis and then typhus, he finally died in Alicante.

PUERTO LUMBRERAS

On the N340, 83 km from Murcia. This town is worth a mention for two reasons: one, that sooner or later every traveller finds himself either passing through it or stuck here for the night; two, that if there were a prize for the Spain's Most Undistinguished Municipality, hot and dusty Puerto Lumbreras would walk away with it. Do not be fooled by the 'Puerto', it lies nowhere near the sea but in an arid, desert zone on the Murcia frontier with Andalucía. If you *are* stuck here, apart from restaurants and pensions catering to truckers, there is also a comfortable modern parador (Avda Juan Carlos 1, 77; tel. 968 40 20 25) with air-conditioning and swimming-pool.

PUERTO DE MAZARRON
See Costa Calida, page 114.

SIERRA ESPUÑA
See Aledo, page 112.

SORBAS
On the N340, 57 km NE of Almería. The fast way south to Almería is via the newly-improved N344. But if you stay with the old N340, which branches off a few kilometres south of Vera, you reach Sorbas, an archetypal Andalucían village, where whitewashed houses huddle together above a precipice formed by a curve in the Río de Aguas.

Continue along the N340 to Tabernas. A by-pass swings around the slumbering town with its ruined castle far above. Nearby is the **Plataforma Solar de Almería,** where research is being carried out into exploiting solar energy: an ideal location since Almería province averages 3,100 hours of sunshine a year.

The parched landscape with its harshly-eroded hills and dusty, cactus-dotted river-beds has a bleak grandeur. You may well have seen it previously, for scores of films have been made in this area. Some of the film sets used in spaghetti Westerns – their heyday was in the 1960s – remain, most falling

---

RECOMMENDED RESTAURANTS

Since rice is grown in abundance, it is also the basis of many regional dishes, not only *paella*. Mediterranean seafood – such as squid, octopus and shellfish – also plays a large part. As for desserts, such sticky delicacies as *turrón* (nougat) and glazed walnuts have been handed down from the sweet-toothed Moors.

Horchata de chufa is a favourite summer drink, a chilled mixture of *chufas* (earth almonds), cinnamon, sugar, almonds and water. There are some drinkable local wines, both in Alicante and Murcia. *Arroz con costra* (pork and sausages with an egg crust on top) and *pescado de rustidera* (baked with onions, peppers, tomatoes and white wine) are specialities.

ALICANTE
Nou Manolín, PP; Villegas, 3; tel. 96 520 03 68; credit cards AE, DC, MC, V.

A beamed, tiled restaurant with good seafood, excellent desserts and a fine store of reserve wines. Try 'grandmother's stew' at the renowned downstairs bar.

Dársena, PP; Muelle del Puerto; tel. 96 520 75 89; credit cards AE, DC, MC, V; closed Sun eve, Mon.

More than 30 rice dishes feature on the menu. A suggestion: *Arroz a banda*, rice cooked in the juice of the fish it is served with. Pleasant views over the harbour, but lunchtime can be crowded.

ALTEA
La Costera, PP; Costera del Mestre de Música, 8; tel. 96 584 02 30; AE, DC, MC, V; eve only, closed Wed, Nov-Feb.

Albert Kramer, the Swiss proprietor, and his wife, serve up Swiss specialities and uninhibited entertainment in the old town. Reservations necessary.

BENIDORM
La Pergola, PP-PPP; Edificio Coblanca 10, Calle 25; tel. 96 585 38 00; credit cards AE, DC, MC; closed Mon.

Splendid view of the Benidorm bay from the terrace of this cliff-side establishment. International dishes and delicious desserts. Value-for-money fixed price menu.

into ruin but others now adapted as tourist attractions.

On the left a few kilometres along the Almería road from Tabernas is **Mini Hollywood**, a replica Western township where Clint Eastwood and Lee Van Cleef battled it out. You can have yourself pictured on a scaffold, tread the creaking sidewalks, and watch a shootout among a bunch of desperadoes – at a price, of course.

TABERNAS
See Sorbas, page 120.

VALENCIA
See Spain Overall: 8.

VELEZ BLANCO
On the C321, 6 *km* N *of Vélez Rubio,* 50 *km from Lorca.* Branch off from the N340 at Puerto Lumbreras joining the N340 in the direction of Vélez Rubio and you'll reach this spectacular medieval fortress. The 16thC **castle** jutting

above the small town was built by Italians and decorated in magnificent Renaissance style. But don't look for this decoration inside. In 1903 – a familiar story the interior was stripped out and shipped off to New York where you may it view it in the Metropolitan Museum.

Nearby is the **Cueva de Los Letreros,** which has prehistoric wall paintings, including a stick figure known as the Indalo. Believed to be an ancient deity, the Indalo is credited with the ability to fend off disease and natural disasters. You will see it around Almería province, painted on walls and lorries and worn as an item of jewellery.

VILLAJOYOSA 🛏
See Recommended Hotels, page 117.

XATIVA
And other places on the N340, see Local Explorations: 12.

I Fratelli, PPP; *Orts Llorca,* 21; *tel.* 96 585 39 79; *credit cards* AE, DC, MC, V; *closed Nov.*

More sophisticated than you may expect in Benidorm. Candle-lit dining, an outdoor patio, home-made pasta. Try the veal in Marsala sauce with *tagliatelli* or the duck *á l'orange.*

CULLERA
Les Mouettes, PPP; *Subida del Castillo, s/n; tel.* 96 172 00 10; *credit cards* AE, DC, MC, V; *open Sun lunch, Tues-Sat dinner only; closed mid-Dec to mid-Feb.*

This excellent small restaurant on the hillside above the town is a welcome surprise for the traveller. It offers authentic French cuisine. The menu is not large but the dishes are meticulously prepared. The extensive cellar includes Bordeaux and Loire wines. Try sole with cream and mushroom sauce or oyster *ragout.*

DENIA
El Pegoli, PP; *Playa de Les Rotes; tel.* 96 578 10 35; *no credit cards; closed Sun eve, Mon, mid-Dec to mid-Jan.*

The immaculate dining-room and terrace are on the rocky edge of the Mediterranean. First-rate seafood is the speciality.

ELCHE
Els Capellans, PP; *Porta de la Morera,* 14; *tel.* 965 45 80 40; *credit cards* AE, DC, MC, V.

Part of the Hotel Huerto del Cura, it has a marvellous setting. Dine out on the swimming-pool terrace and enjoy local rice and fish dishes or international cuisine.

MURCIA
Rincón de Pepe, PPP; *Apóstoles,* 34; *tel.* 968 21 22 39; *credit cards* AE, DC, MC, V; *closed mid-Jul to mid-Aug.*

Presided over by Raimundo González, this is the most elegant and prestigious dining spot between Alicante and Granada. Success has made it somewhat pretentious, not to say pricey, but it does offer traditional Murcia dishes, such as roast lamb cooked with apples, pine nuts and wine, or partridge in Jumilla wine. There is an extensive wine list. If you select one of the local wines, take the advice of your waiter. Underneath the restaurant and hotel (comfortable, **PPP**) you can view part of the city's ancient walls.

Between Almería and Málaga
Andalucía: Costa del Sol, Málaga and Granada

297 km; map Michelin 446, 1:400,000

From the delicate, dreamy halls of the Alhambra to the crowded beaches of the Costa del Sol... from the sublime to the ridiculous, some might say. Both are to be found in this area of southern Spain, which embraces desert vistas, fertile plains, majestically craggy mountains, and glorious architecture.

Granada, with its remarkable history and unparalleled setting below the snows of the Sierra Nevada, is justifiably on every visitor's list. Only the most jaded sightseer would not to be impressed by the delightful palace built by the Moors. The *granadinos* are regarded as serious, hardworking types while the people of Málaga (the *malagueños*) have a reputation for living for the moment. Fittingly, Málaga is the capital of one of Spain's most popular tourist zones. Almería is their poor relation, capital of an arid province, akin to Africa or Arizona.

While the cities are important, some of the best experiences in Andalucía lurk off the beaten track. Turn any corner and you will encounter a whitewashed village spilling down a ridge. Stop for a picnic and you may meet a farmer eager for you to sample his wine. Get into a conversation in a bar and, when you leave, you may find there is nothing to pay.

Local produce features exotic fruits – this is a sub-tropical zone; local specialities include *pollo granadina* (chicken cooked with wine and ham) and *tortilla Sacromonte* (the authentic version of this omelette is made with lamb's brains and testicles). The Málaga coast specializes in *fritura malagueña* (an assortment of fried fish) and sardines grilled on open fires on the beaches. Everywhere there are variations on the theme of

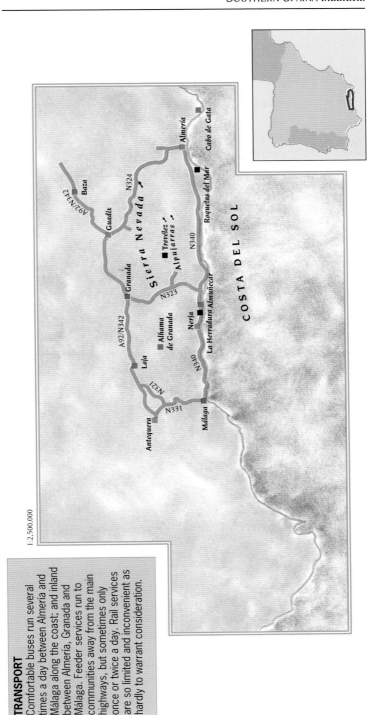

1:2,500,000

TRANSPORT
Comfortable buses run several times a day between Almería and Málaga along the coast; and inland between Almería, Granada and Málaga. Feeder services run to communities away from the main highways, but sometimes only once or twice a day. Rail services are so limited and inconvenient as hardly to warrant consideration.

• *Almería's Alcazaba - see page* 125.

gazpacho, the delicious liquid salad of tomatoes, cucumber, garlic and olive oil.

Perhaps most people explore this region piecemeal from a base on the coast, rather than journey through it. Plentiful and cheap air flights from northern Europe to Málaga make it a perennially popular short break; you can rely on sunshine most days in February and March. Think of three days as a minimum time for exploration. If you're driving, you can take the N324 north-west from Almería to Guadix, known for its cave-dwellings, then head west to Granada, skirting the Sierra Nevada. From the *vega* (fertile plain) of Granada, fast four-lane highways, the A92 and the N331, lead to Málaga and the Costa del Sol. This is a red route.

Or you can choose a green detour, meandering the by-ways of the Alpujarras and Sierra Nevada (see Local Explorations: 13). Or you can leave Granada for another time (but there would have to be a very good reason), travelling green on the N340 between Almería and Málaga. The section between Almería and Motril is unattractive, but there are fine vistas of sea and mountains between Motril and Málaga, and beaches where you can stop for a swim.

SIGHTS & PLACES OF INTEREST

ALHAMA DE GRANADA

On *the* C340, 35 *km* S *of Loja on the* A92. Alhama is a delightful little town, 860 m above sea-level and teetering on the edge of a chasm. The fine stonework of the 16thC **church of Carmen** has been restored recently. You can walk down the *tajo* (gorge). Just out of town are hot springs with Moorish baths, recommended for rheumatism and kidney problems. The hotel there, the Balneario (**P-PP**; *tel.* 958 35 00 11, *open during the summer*) is well placed for those visiting the baths.

ALMERIA 🏨 ✕

On *the* N340, 171 *km* E *of Granada*, 219 *km* SW *of Murcia. Tourism Office, Corner Parque Nicholás Salmerón & Martinez Campos; tel.* 950 27 43 55. Frowning down on city and port, Almería's **Alcazaba** (fortress) is an impressive introduction to this provincial capital. In the shadow of the fortress is a **rescue centre for Sahara animals**, where they breed endangered species including hyenas and beautiful gazelles. On a neighbouring hillside is the gypsy quarter of La Chanca, with some cave dwellings.

There are pleasant gardens within the much-restored **castle**, part of which was built 1,000 years ago by Abd-ar-Rahman III, the Caliph of Córdoba. (Note that the area near the castle has a bad reputation for bag snatching.) One opening is known as the **Ventana de la Odalisca** (the Concubine's Window). The story goes that the Moorish chieftain's favourite fell in love with a Christian prisoner. They were caught trying to flee and the prisoner was hurled from the window. His despairing lover then jumped to her death from the same spot.

Portus Magnus to the Romans, Almería was the Moors' most important city in the 11thC, when it was known as the Mirror of the Sea and noted for its culture and fine silk. An earthquake destroyed the mosque in 1522 and on its site rose the **cathedral**, a dauntingly solid mass with a Corinthian façade. In the Spanish Civil War, Almería suffered from the 1937 bombardment by German warships, retaliating for a Republican attack on a German vessel. After the war, it suffered for its support for the

• *Sahara animals rescue centre.*

Republican cause and was seriously neglected. The province was one of Spain's poorest, but tourism and agriculture have revived fortunes.

The city can be hot and dusty in summer, but it is pleasant to stroll along the broad main boulevard, the **Paseo**, with its pavement cafés. Ferries ply to **Melilla**, Spain's outpost on the African coast.

Countless spaghetti Westerns and parts of *Lawrence of Arabia* were filmed in the province, with its desert landscapes of eroded, cactus-dotted hills and occasional clusters of flat-roofed dwellings.

In the past 20 years plastic greenhouses have spread across some 12,000 hectares of barren Almerían desert. Drip irrigation and large quantities of fertilizer plus more than 3,000 hours of sunshine annually produce colossal crops of vegetables and flowers, mostly for export. Drive west of the capital on the N340 towards the unlovely boom-town of El Ejido for striking views of the glittering plastic sea.

Remains of houses, tombs and walls have been uncovered at **Los Millares**, a Bronze Age settlement 20 km north of Almería. To visit, take the N340, branching left on the Guadix road, N324, at Benahadux.

ALMUÑECAR ✕

On *the* N340, 70 *km* E *of Málaga*, 73 *km* S *of Granada. Tourism Office, Avda Europa-Palacete La Najarra; tel.* 958 63 11 25. The Phoenicians called their settlement here Sexi, not the word that springs to mind when you sight the high-rise apartments along the waterfront. Beaches tend to be gritty and grey. However,

125

the labyrinthine streets of the old town, crowned by the castle of **San Miguel**, retain their charm. A Roman aqueduct runs to the edge of town.

Behind Almuñecar the river bed and terraced hillsides are lush with irrigated orchards of custard apples and avocadoes. Because of its mild climate and sheltered position, this stretch of coast has been dubbed the Costa Tropical – confusing, since it is also known as the Costa de Granada.

A truly dizzying mountain road wriggles north from Almuñecar to Otivar, which has several *ventas* (inns) offering substantial rural fare, and to Granada, at one point etching its way across

• *Granada's City Hall: annual ceremony to mark the 1492 ousting of the Moors.*

a cliff face. Heading west from Almuñecar to Nerja, you encounter the southern coast's most spectacular section, stark limestone ranges tumbling straight into the sea. Here and there are secluded beaches, mostly of difficult access.

ALPUJARRAS
See Local Explorations: 13.

ANTEQUERA
Off A92, 57 km N of Málaga. Tourism Office, Plaza de San Sebastian, 7; tel. 952 70 25 05.

The most direct routes between Granada, Málaga and Seville all pass by Antequera, which sits where mountains meet plain, an important crossroads since early times. Three remarkable dolmen (prehistoric stone structures) indicate that an ingenious people lived here around 2,000 BC. The largest, known as Menga, is on the edge of town and consists of 31 slabs of rock weighing up to 180 tons each. How these were transported here remains a mystery. The chamber they form is believed to have contained the bodies of chieftains and warriors with their most precious possessions. This and the other two dolmen, Viera (nearby) and Romeral (3 km distant), can be visited every day except Monday.

The town (market) is notable for its number of churches and convents, seven of which are occupied by closed orders. The 17thC **Church of Los Remedios** is a national monument, as is **Santa María la Mayor**, which has a Renaissance façade and stands high up near the old Moorish fort.

To the east of the town is an oddly-shaped peak, the **Peña de los Enamorados**. It gets its name from a Moorish damsel's love for a Christian governor's son. The families frowned on the relationship and forbade them to meet. Embracing, the desperate couple leaped together to their deaths from the Peña.

Twelve kilometres south of Antequera, off the C3310, weirdly weathered rocks nudge the skyline. Three clearly marked paths thread this area, a nature park known as **El Torcal**. There is an information centre at the entrance.

BAZA

On the A92 (N342), 107 *km E of Granada.* This is a detour east from Guadix, across a steppe-like landscape sliced by ravines. Where there is water, fruit and vegetables flourish in oases of green. Baza is a small, intimate town with important cattle markets. In 1971, a painted stone sculpture of a seated goddess, weighing 800 kg, was found in an Iberian necropolis nearby. Estimated to be 2,400 years old, the remarkable statue is now in Madrid's Archeological Museum.

On September 6 each year one of Andalucía's more remarkable **fiestas** takes place. Guadix sends a volunteer to Baza to try to seize a Virgin, which it claims rightfully belongs to Guadix. To succeed, he must be spotless when he reaches the Virgin's image in the Franciscan Convent of La Merced. A welcome committee of hundreds of highly excited, oil-drenched Baza youngsters awaits the envoy, known as El Cascamorras, on a hilltop. They pour dirty oil over him too, and then the whole blackened tribe races through the streets of Baza. Later the Cascamorras, cleaned up, has an honoured place in a procession.

CABO DE GATA

31 *km* SE *of* Almería. Flamingos and griffon vultures are among the species to be seen in the **Cabo de Gata Nature Park**. You travel past salt flats (sometimes more than 2,000 flamingos gather here) to the lighthouse on the cape, but the park's soaring cliffs and secluded coves are only accessible on foot. To reach the growing resort of San José, it is necessary to double back. There is good snorkelling in the clear waters along the coast.

Inland from San José lies **Níjar**, noted for its pottery and blanket manufacture, also as the setting for one of García Lorca's most famous plays, *Blood Wedding*, based on a real-life peasant drama of passion and violence that occurred in 1928.

GRANADA ⌨ ✕

At the intersection of the A92 *and* N323, 250 *km E of Seville. Tourism Office, Plaza de Mariana Pineda,* 10; *tel.* 958 22 66 88. Like a delicate piece of oriental treasure, the **Alhambra** (literally 'The Red') palace stands majestically on its hilltop amid elms and cypresses, with the snowy bulk of the Sierra Nevada forming an unforgettable backdrop. Across the Darra River valley, the houses of the **Albaicín** (the Falconers' Quarter) balance on one another's shoulders to gain a better view of the great palace of the Nasrid dynasty that dominated the kingdom of Granada for 250 years. One of the best viewing points is the esplanade next to the church of San Nícolás.

Guitar maestro Andrés Segovia studied in Granada and described it as a 'place of dreams, where Our Lord put the seed of music in my soul.' And Federico García Lorca eulogized his native city thus: 'The hours are longer and sweeter there than in any other Spanish town.' Maybe, but Granada is still trying to live down the fact that it killed its gifted son. At the start of the Civil War, right wingers executed the poet and playwright near the city.

Critics allege that Granada remains introverted and narrow-minded. Certainly the people are less exuberant than the fun-loving inhabitants of Málaga. But 35,000 university students add zest to local life and democracy has broadened horizons.

Your first sight of Granada may disappoint. Modern blocks ring the city and traffic fumes smudge the clear mountain air. But, after recent refurbishments, the old quarter looks better than ever.

After visiting the Alhambra (see

RECOMMENDED HOTELS

ALMERIA
Torreluz, PPP; *Plaza Flores 1, 3 and 5; tel. 950 23 49 99*.

Three modern hotels, graded two three and four stars, around a small central square, offering reliable standards of comfort. The most luxurious has a sun terrace and a pool.

GRANADA
America, PP; *Real de la Alhambra, 53; tel. 958 22 74 71; closed early Nov-Feb*.

A small, friendly hotel right by the Alhambra. The bedrooms look on to the Alhambra gardens or the vine-covered patio. It is advisable to book.

Parador San Francisco, PPP; *Alhambra; tel. 958 22 14 40*.

So great is the demand to stay here that you should book several months in advance. This converted 15thC convent has an unequalled setting, in the gardens of the Alhambra. Antiques and traditional furniture add to the appeal.

HERRADURA, LA
Los Fenicios, PPP; *village on the N340, 65 kilometres E of Málaga; hotel at Paseo Andres Segovia, s/n; tel. 958 82 79 00*.

A low-rise, imaginatively-designed hotel on the horseshoe-shaped bay which gives the village its name.

LOJA
Finca La Bobadilla, PPP; *Ctra Loja-Sevilla, desvio Las Salinas; tel. 958 32 18 61*.

Luxury amid the olive groves. Riding, mountain-biking, swimming and tennis are among the many attractions (at no extra cost) of this masterpiece: nothing flash here, just unerring good taste. Worth a visit just to marvel over the architecture: it is not one building but several, built in the style of a Moorish village, sprawling over a hillock. The aim is to create the ambience of a private farming estate hidden away in the countryside, and under the intelligent direction of Antonio Arquelladas and Frank Pfaller, it succeeds.

You don't always get what you pay for in luxury hotels, but no question of that here. To reach the Bobadilla, turn right off the A92 Seville highway 16 km west of Loja at Las Salinas, following the C334 north towards Iznájar.

MALAGA
Parador del Golf, PPP; *Ctra de Málaga; tel. 952 38 12 55*.

Handily located on a golf course near the sea and close to the airport.

Los Naranjos, PPP; *Paseo de Sancha, 35; tel. 952 22 43 19*.

Pleasant three-star hotel not far from the bull-ring and seafront.

NERJA
Parador, PPP; *Almuñecar, 8; tel. 952 52 00 50*.

Beautifully situated with a cliff-top pool and gardens; Mediterranean views.

ROQUETAS DE MAR
Playasol, PP; *20 km SE of Almería – Urbanizacón Playa Serena; tel. 950 33 38 02*.

Modern beach hotel with full sporting facilities.

page130) you may find Granada's **cathedral** shockingly heavy and cumbersome in contrast.

A series of architects, Enrique de Egas, Diego de Siloé and Juan de Maeda, worked on this Gothic-Renaissance block, but only succeeded in emphasizing the tragedy of the fall of Granada to the Christian Monarchs, namely Ferdinand and Isabel, who rest in lead coffins in a vault below the **Capilla Real**. In the chapel, behind an elaborate wrought-iron grill, lie white marble sculptures of the monarchs and of Philip the Fair and Juana the Mad (her corpse was brought from Tordesillas in Castile where she had died after 46 years shut away from the world).

The sacristy contains banners used in the conquest of Granada and Isabel's crown and Ferdinand's sword. These last are carried in procession on January 2 every year amid the pomp celebrating the 1492 victory, although there are some protests from those who think the conquest is no cause for rejoicing.

Granada has a number of historic treasures, including the Baroque **Monasterio de la Cartuja** and the **Corral del Carbón**, once an Arab caravanserai. But one of its more intimate sights is the **Museo de Manuel de Falla**, at number 11, Antequeruela Baja. The composer (*Nights in the Gardens of Spain*) lived and worked in this beautiful *carmen*, a Moorish-style house, designed as a sort of private paradise, with fountains tinkling in flower-filled gardens, blocked from public gaze by high walls.

On the edge of town is the **Huerta de San Vicente**, the old farmhouse where de Falla's friend, García Lorca, wrote some of his most famous works. It is due to open to the public. The house where Lorca was born, in Fuentevaqueros, a village on the fertile plain 20 km west of Granada, off the A90, is a museum (closed Mon).

If you are desperate to see flamenco, you can visit one of the gypsy caves of **Sacromonte,** on the hill opposite the Generalife, but be prepared to pay dearly.

Several authentic old *tapa* bars with abundant atmosphere are to be found near the Plaza Nueva. Try Castañeda, at Elvira, 6; or La Trastienda, Placeta Cuchilleros. Another area for *tapa* bars

is the Campo del Príncipe. A handy restaurant for local dishes is **Los Manueles** (very traditional) at Zaragoza, 2, close to the **Ayuntamiento**.

GUADIX

On the N324, 55 km E of Granada. Two thousand years ago this area was noted for its silver, iron and copper and a wealthy local princess, Imilce, was swept off her feet by Hannibal. These days, buried in the interior of Granada province, in the shadow of the Sierra Nevada, Guadix has an unchanging air. There is a notable Gothic-Baroque **cathedral** where Diego de Siloé, the outstanding Renaissance architect, left his mark. It shelters relics of San Torcuato, who estabished here the peninsula's first Christian bishopric. Torcuato was martyred, as was the Guadix bishop during the Civil War.

A local *conquistador*, Pedro de Mendoza, established a fort in 1536 on the banks of the Río de la Plata in South America, and thus founded Buenos Aires. He died from syphilis on the voyage home.

The most remarkable sight in Guadix is the **Barrio de Santiago**. Here the strangely-eroded hills of compacted

---

BUDGET ACCOMMODATION

GRANADA
Niza, P; N*avas,* 16; *tel.* 958 22 54 30.
Centrally located one-star hotel.

California, P; *Cuesta de Gomérez,* 37; *tel.* 958 22 40 56.
On the road to the Alhambra.

GUADIX
Comercio, P; *Mira de Amezcua,* 3; *tel.* 958 66 05 00.
A basic one-star hotel.

MALAGA
Derby, P: *San Juan de Dios,* 1; *tel.* 952 22 13 02.
A *hostal* overlooking the port.

THE ALHAMBRA

According to an old Granada tradition, the palace raised by the Moors on a spur above the city has survived all vicissitudes thanks to magical protection. And indeed there is something magical about the Alhambra, the unique survivor of a sophisticated culture ejected from Europe five centuries ago.

Unlike many other grand structures, the Alhambra (from *al-Qalat al-Hamra*: Arabic for red fort, so-name for its red-brown walls) was not built to endure and impress later generations but for the pleasure of its privileged occupants, members of the Nasrid dynasty who ruled the Kingdom of Granada, formed by the present-day Málaga, Granada and Almería provinces, from 1238 to 1492. As Christian forces steadily squeezed the Moors out of other parts of the peninsula, traders, craftsmen and scientists poured into Granada and the kingdom prospered. Agriculture flourished thanks to ingenious irrigation systems. Granada's textiles, particularly silk, and its arms, were exported all around the Mediterranean.

However, internal feuding and the crusading enthusiasm of the Catholic Monarchs, Ferdinand and Isabel, led to Granada's fall to Christian forces in 1492. Legend has it that Boabdil, the banished ruler, burst into tears when he took one last look at Granada at a point on the road south known as El Suspiro del Moro (the Moor's Sigh), at which his mother jeered:'Do not weep like a woman for what you could not defend as a man.'

The palace, which al-Basid, a 15thC visitor to Granada declared was 'among the grandest and most beautiful sights in Islam', was largely the work of three Nasrid rulers, Yusuf I, Mohammed V and Mohammed VII in the 14thC. The Emperor Charles V knocked part of it down to build a Renaissance palace, **Palacio de Carlos V**, with a vast circular patio; it is no mean work, but next to the delicate Moorish architecture it has all the grace of an elephant.

The Alhambra had been neglected and pillaged by the time the American diplomat Washington Irving lived briefly in some of its rooms during 1829. He noted its abandoned state in his *Tales of the Alhambra*, which awakened widespread interest in the site. Since then the palace has been magnificently restored, although we can only guess at the rich furnishings it once contained.

The complex is split into three: the **Alcazaba**; the **Casa Real** and the **Generalife Gardens**, best visited in that order. Signposting makes it easy to find your way around in this recommended order: don't worry if on entry from the car park you feel bewildered by its geography and size.

The **Alcazaba**, a stern fortress, dates mostly from the 13thC and includes the **Torre de la Vela**, on which the flag of the conquering Christians was raised in 1492. Within the **Casa Real** or Royal Palace the ear is lulled by the tranquillizing sound of running water and the eye is dazzled by the succession of richly decorated patios and chambers, in which tiles, plaster, marble and alabaster are transformed into feathery stalactites and slender pilasters, ethereal arches and icing-sugar cupolas.

Off the **Patio de los Arrayanes** (Court of Myrtles), with its long pool edged by myrtles and graceful galleries at each end, is the sumptuous throne room or audience hall, the **Salón de Embajadores.** Built by Yusuf I, the square, two-storey chamber offers beautiful views over the Darra Valley. Below the intricate larchwood dome the walls are ornamented with scrolls, flowers and flourishes of calligraphy which include verses from the *Koran* and the reminder again and again that 'Allah alone is victorious.'

Passing to the Harem (i.e., the private quarters, to use the term correctly) you encounter the delightful **Patio de los Leones.** Twelve lions support the central fountain; the surrounding arches rest on 128 slender marble columns. French writer Théophile Gautier, who thought Granada a 'true paradise on earth', camped in this patio, cooling his wine in the fountain; no chance now, as more than a million tourists pass through each year. To one side is a chamber

• In *the gardens of the Alhambra.*

named after the Abencerraje clan, whose conspiring leaders were allegedly massacred there.

To get closer to nature, the sultans retired to their country estate, the **Generalife**, a name derived from the Arabic for the 'garden of high paradise'. Oleanders and cypresses, patios, pools and pavilions, form this magical setting, where every year in June and early July an international music and dance festival is held.

So great is the demand to visit the Alhambra that a computerized ticket system has been introduced to limit the number of people inside to not more than 400 at one time. You are given an entry time when buying your ticket.

Arrive early (open daily 8.30 am to 8 pm) or you will be behind all the bus tours. Advance tickets can be booked by calling 958 22 09 12. If you drive up, ignore touts who try to divert you to 'guarded' parking places and continue to the (free) official car park. A new road avoids the city centre and leads directly to the Alhambra.

clay have been honeycombed with cave dwellings. Television aerials sprouting from whitewashed chimney pots indicate that there is life down below. Southern Spain has some 30,000 troglodytes, many of them farmers who would have nowhere to park mules and goats if they lived in apartments. Cave living carries no social stigma, for many dwellings have modern facilities including flushable W.Cs.

There are more troglodytes in **Purullena**, on the road to Granada, where a discothèque occupies a two-storey cave, formerly an inn. Vast arrays of pottery line the road through Purullena, but virtually all of it is imported from other areas of Spain.

Eighteen kilometres south of Guadix, off the Almería road, the N324, stands the castle of **Lacalahorra**, atop a hillock. The stern walls conceal a unique palace with remains of Italian Renaissance splendour. The Marquis of Zenete, bastard son of Cardinal Mendoza, ordered it built between 1509 and 1512. You can gain access on Wednesdays, or by contacting Lacalahorra Town Hall (958 67 31 22).

RECOMMENDED RESTAURANTS

ALMERIA
A pleasant *tapa* bar with traditional decoration is **Bodega Las Botas**, on Fructuoso Pérez, which runs parallel to the Paseo de Almería. Nearby are several *marisquerías* (seafood restaurants) in Tenor Iribarne street. **Club de Mar** has good views of the port plus a variety of seafood (**PP**, *Playa de las Almadrabillas; tel. 950 23 50 48; credit cards* AE, MC, V).

ALMUÑECAR EL
Jacquy Cotobro, PP; *Hidden on a small bay west of Almuñecar; Paseo de Cotobro, 11; tel. 958 63 18 02; credit cards* MC, V; *closed Mon, and mid-Nov to early Dec.*
Beautifully-prepared French cuisine, extremely good value.

GRANADA
Mirador de Morayma, PP; *Callejón de las Vacas, 2; tel. 958 22 82 90; credit cards* AE, MC, V; *closed Sun eve and (in summer)* Mon.
You can enjoy magnificent views of the city from this restaurant in the Albaicín quarter, while trying local specialities such as breaded lamb chops with fried peppers and onion *tortilla* (omelette).
Mesón Antonio, PP; *Ecce Homo, 6; 958 22 95 99; closed Sun, Jul and Aug.*
You need to ring for admittance to this intimate restaurant in a typical old house off the Campo del Príncipe. It serves hearty home cooking baked in a wood oven.

MALAGA
Good *tapas* are available in small, atmospheric bars in the narrow streets of the centre, such as **La Tasca** and **Lo Güeno**, both on Marín García. For the traditional *fritura malagueña* (selection of fried fish), try the many beach-front restaurants in Pedregalejo or El Palo, the old fishermen's quarter to the east.

La Villa, PP; *Avda Juan Sebastián Elcano, 130; tel. 952 20 01 94; credit cards* AE, MC, V; *closed Sun.*
On the main road into Málaga from Almería, this restaurant is located in a fine old house. Green-panelled walls and stonework give a pleasant feel to the dining room. Try the delicious garlic soup, and *Medallones de rape americana* (monkfish in a rich sauce).

Antonio, PP; *Fernando de Lesseps, 7; tel. 952 22 33 97; credit cards* AE, DC, MC, V; *closed Sun.*
In a cul-de-sac off the pedestrian street Calle Nueva. Genuine Andalucían atmosphere, with wine bottles lining one wall and a lively *tapa* bar. Recommended: lamb in almond sauce and *Tarta de la casa* (house dessert).

HERRADURA, LA 🛏

See Recommended Hotel, page 129.

LOJA 🛏

Off the A92, 53 km W of Granada. Built on the banks of the Genil river, Loja is a typical Andalucían town of narrow streets, tiled roofs and old churches, such as San Gabriel and La Encarnación, with ruins of a **Moorish fort**. East of the town are **Los Infiernos**, where the river threads through a gorge. The easiest approach is from south of the river.

MALAGA 🛏 ✕

On the N340, 126 km from Granada, 207 km from Seville. Tourism Office, Pasaje de Chinitas, 4; tel. 952 21 34 45. Málaga is a lively, colourful Mediterranean port, dating back to Phoenician times, when it bore the name Malaca. Although claiming to be capital of the Costa del Sol, you are not too aware of tourism in this very Spanish city, proud of its liberal traditions.

From the lofty by-pass pinned to the surrounding hills, Málaga (population, 500,000) has a modern, high-rise aspect. But in the narrow streets around fashionable Calle Larios and the market there is an air of the past. Many of the customers crowding into bars have faces lifted from a medieval painting. They savour seafood *tapas* and swig wine in such atmospheric haunts as the barrel-lined **Casa Guardia**, on the Alameda, founded in 1840. A favourite drink is a *secopedro* (sweet Pedro Ximénez wine mixed with a dry wine).

Until phylloxera wiped out the vineyards in the 19thC, and fashions changed, Málaga's sweet wine was a major export. Today the surrounding hills grow pines rather than grapes and Málaga depends on service industries while trying to create its own Silicon Valley.

For a view of the city, climb to the much-restored **Gibralfaro Castle** (be alert: as muggers prey on the unwary). The hilltop also has space for a parador, pleasant for refreshment far above the city hubbub. The fortifications run down the hill to the Alcazaba, which houses the interesting **Museo Arqueológico**. Next door is a Roman theatre, on part of which Franco's vandals constructed – hard to credit – a cultural centre.

The Renaissance-style **cathedral** has an odd feature. It is nicknamed La Manquita (the cripple) because the second tower was never completed. The carved choir stalls are a highlight of the interior. Less uplifting but worth seeing is the **Museo de Artes Populares**, Pasillo de Santa Isabel, 7, where ancient crafts and life-styles are on display in a 17thC inn.

The **Casa de Picasso where the artist was born,** on the Plaza de la Merced, is open to visitors. Cultural events relating to the painter are held there.

On a tree-shaded hillside east of the city centre is the **English Cemetery**, last resting place for consuls, remittance men, poets, and sailors of various nationalities. Before the cemetery was created in the 19thC, non Catholics were simply buried on the beach, to make gruesome reappearances when the sand was washed away.

NERJA 🛏

On the N340, 53 km E of Málaga. Tourism Office, Puerta del Mar; tel. 952 52 15 31. Although heavily developed, this small town retains a certain intimate charm. The focal point of the old centre is the palm tree-lined **Balcón de Europa**, a promenade jutting out over the sea, which offers impressive views eastwards along the rocky coast.

Near the hamlet of Maro, 3 km to the east, is the **Cueva de Nerja**, discovered in 1959 by five boys out bat-catching. Wall paintings, skeletons, tools and pottery testify that Paleolithic man once dwelled there. It is now a major tourist attraction. In the Cave of the Cataclysms you are confronted with the world's largest stalactite, a monster measuring 60 m high and 18 m in diameter. An international music and dance festival is held every summer in one of the huge chambers.

ROQUETAS DE MAR 🛏

See Recommended Hotels, page 129.

SIERRA NEVADA

See Local Explorations: 13.

TREVELEZ

And other places of interest south of Granada and Guadix, see Local Explorations: 13.

<u>South-Western Spain</u>

Between Málaga and Seville
Costa del Sol and Cádiz Province

376 km; Michelin map 446 1:400,000

You could hardly ask for a greater contrast than that between the two coasts encountered in this corner of Spain. On the Mediterranean lies the Costa del Sol, one of Spain's most popular tourist zones, which attracts several million visitors every year. If you are interested in acquiring a tan, playing golf, eating at fine restaurants, or disco-dancing the night away, it is the place for you.

When you turn the corner at Tarifa, guarding the westernmost end of the Straits of Gibraltar, fresh breezes tell you that you have reached the Costa de la Luz (Coast of Light) and the Atlantic. The water is cleaner and colder and the beaches, often fringed by pines, magnificent. And there is much less development.

Lying between the two coasts is the Bay of Algeciras. From Algeciras you can hop on a boat to Africa, while across the bay that strange anachronism, a British colony in Europe, dominates the skyline. The Rock of Gibraltar, a recurrent bone of contention between Britain and Spain, is worth visiting, if only to savour its cosmopolitan atmosphere and the traces of past glories.

Cádiz retains the aura of the old port which once grew rich from trade with the Americas. Just north lies the Sherry Triangle, where you can sample every variety of sherry and visit the *bodegas* (see Local Explorations: 15).

Behind the Costa del Sol rises the Serranía de Ronda, wild mountainous ranges dotted with remote *pueblos blancos* (white villages). See Local Explorations: 14.

Southern Spain once had a bad name for food, but tourism has changed that: in this area you can probably eat as well as anywhere in the country. The Costa del Sol caters to all tastes, from the fish and chip brigade to those devoted to *nouvelle cuisine*. French, German, Italian, Chinese, Moroccan, and other restaurants all offer their specialities.

In the province of Cádiz, seafood really comes into its own: enjoy fresh shrimps, oysters, crabs, lobsters, sea bass, squid and mullet, for which chilled dry sherry is a happy partner.

Two days gives you time for a cursory look, using the N340 (notorious for accidents, but much improved) along the coast between Málaga and Cádiz, and the four-lane A4, for the Cádiz-Seville stretch.

The alternative route between Málaga and Jerez is inland via Ronda (see Local Explorations: 14). The fastest route between Málaga and Seville is the N331 via Antequera and then the A92.

TRANSPORT
Buses run quite frequently between all the major coastal towns. There are long-distance services between Málaga and Cádiz along the coast, and there are direct services inland via Antequera to and from Seville. Modern commuter trains run frequently between Málaga and Fuengirola. There is a mainline rail service between Bobadilla (the junction for Málaga), Ronda, and Algeciras.

1:2,500,000

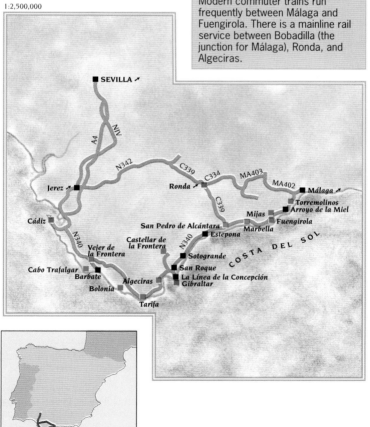

SIGHTS & PLACES OF INTEREST

ALGECIRAS ⊨

On the N340, 120 km SE of Cádiz. Tourism Office, Juan de la Cierva; 956 57 26 36.
Pronounce this tongue-twister 'Al-heth-EER-ass', with the emphasis on the second to last syllable. The somewhat sleazy port is a gateway between two continents, where drug-smugglers, illegal immigrants, tourists, and fishermen mingle. The railway from Madrid terminates here and there are frequent ferry and hydrofoil services to and from Ceuta and Tangiers. Travellers should avoid these services around the end of June and the first weeks of July and August, when hundreds of thousands of Moroccans queue to cross the Straits.

There is a beautiful view across the Bay of Algeciras to Gibraltar, but the shores of the bay have been scarred by industry, including an oil refinery.

Ceuta (a Spanish enclave on the African coast) has little interest except as an entry point into Morocco. If you should be stranded there, a macabre treat awaits you in a museum dedicated to the Spanish Legion, a regiment legendary for its toughness. On my visit, while martial music blared out, a shaven-headed legionnaire talked about the 'War of Liberation', meaning Franco's war. On show were the last blood sample taken from Franco before he died and an eye in a bottle. The eye was lost in battle by Millán Astray, founder of the Legion, the same gentleman who invented the Legion's chilling slogan *Viva La Muerte!* (Long live Death!).

ARROYO DE LA MIEL ✕

See Recommended Restaurants, page 141.

BARBATE

Off the N340, 63 km S of Cádiz. Down at the quayside of this nondescript fishing town, in spring and early summer, you may see the morning's catch of bluefin tuna being unloaded. Some weigh 300 kg or more. Once I noticed a dump-truck delivering a fish so big that it completely blocked a restaurant doorway.

The tuna are caught (in diminishing numbers) about 3 km off-shore in the *almadraba*, an Arab word for netting nailed to the sea-bed by huge anchors. Shoals of migrating tuna swim into this trap and are hooked into lighters as the sea turns to bloody foam. The method has not changed in 2,000 years, but these days most of the tuna are frozen and shipped to Japan.

A road climbs over pine-clad hills north of Barbate to the **beaches of Los Caños de Meca**, popular with windsurfers and nudists. Nearby, marked by a lighthouse, is **Cabo Trafalgar**, the cape off which the English under Admiral Nelson defeated a Franco-Spanish fleet in 1805. Both he and the Spanish commander were killed in the battle.

BOLONIA

Off the N340, 94 km SE of Cádiz. A side-turning 15 km north of Tarifa leads to the delightful little bay of Bolonia and the Roman ruins of **Baelo Claudia**. Guided tours allow you to explore the remains of a theatre, temples, and streets. A fish factory existed here where the Romans concocted *garum*, a paste prized as a delicacy. There is a pleasant beach and bars serving food and refreshments.

CABO TRAFALGAR

See Barbate, this page.

CADIZ ⊨ ✕

On the NIV, 123 km S of Seville.
Tourist information, Avda Ramón de Carranza; tel. 956 21 13 13. Cádiz's unique history and geographical location give it a special character, unlike that of any other city in southern Spain. Gadir, the name given by the Phoenicians to the settlement they founded 3,000 years ago, claims to be Europe's oldest city. An appropriate air of age and decadence pervades the narrow dark streets, crushed together on a narrow peninsula. Despite the Atlantic breezes, it is easy to feel claustrophobic in the old quarter which packs in 14,600 inhabitants per square kilometre.

Ancient Gadir was renowned for sensual activity – the local girls were renowned for their lascivious dances – and today's *gaditanos* are noted for their exuberance, wit and enthusiasm for flamenco. To see them really let their hair down, visit during February when **Carnival** is riotously celebrated.

Treasure-laden galleons sailed into Cádiz Bay and in 1587 so did the English admiral Sir Francis Drake, to 'singe the king of Spain's beard'. Later the port monopolised trade with the New World. Loss of American colonies and the dis-

RECOMMENDED HOTELS

ALGECIRAS
Reina Cristina, PPP; *Paseo Conferencias, s/n; tel. 956 60 26 22.*

Overlooking the bay, this piece of Victorian grandeur was built in the 19thC to accommodate passengers using the Ronda-Algeciras railway, constructed by English engineer John Morrison. In the Second World War, German and British spies stayed here, each checking on the others, also on activity through the Straits. Tea on the terrace and an appropriate old world air.

CADIZ
Francia y Paris, PP; *Plaza San Francisco, 6; tel. 956 21 23 19.*

Old three-star hotel recently renovated, handily situated for the sights.

Meliá La Caleta, PPP; *Amílcar Barca, s/n; tel. 956 27 94 11.*

A new four-star hotel, welcome in a city deficient in quality accommodation. On the beach.

GIBRALTAR
Accommodation on The Rock tends to be more expensive than in Spain. Probably the best value for money is the **Eliott Hotel (PPP**; *2 Governor's Parade; tel. 956 77 05 00*). For a more traditional atmosphere, try the **Rock Hotel (PPP**; *Europa Road, 3; tel. 956 77 30 00*), set in expansive grounds.

MARBELLA
Marbella Club, PPP; *Boulevard Principe Alfonso de Hohenlohe, Ctra Cádiz, km 172; tel. 952 82 22 11.*

The first luxury hotel built on the coast. From the single-storey accommodation it is a short walk through beautiful gardens to the beach.

Refugio de Juanar, PP; *Sierra Blanca, 19 km N of Marbella via Ojen; tel. 952 88 10 00*

A former hunting lodge offering peace among forested mountains. Would suit hikers and nature-lovers.

SOTOGRANDE
Club Marítimo, PPP; *Puerto Sotogrande,* Cádiz province; tel. 956 79 02 00.

Well-appointed hotel on the marina of Sotogrande, a luxury tourist complex with three golf courses, riding and other diversions, at the western edge of the Costa del Sol.

TARIFA
Dos Mares, PP; *Ctra Cádiz-Málaga, km 79; tel. 956 68 40 35.*

Right by the beach and a favourite spot for windsurfers.

Hurricane, PPP; *Ctra de Cádiz, km 77; tel. 956 68 03 29.*

English-owned, designed on elegant lines, with gardens and windsurfing school.

VEJER DE LA FRONTERA
Convento de San Francisco, PP; *La Plazuela; tel. 956 45 10 01.*

A 17thC convent tastefully converted into a hotel, preserving many of the original architectural features. Sophisticated modern cuisine is offered in the restaurant, the old refectory. Vejer is a gleaming white hill-top town on the N340, 54 km south of Cádiz.

BUDGET ACCOMMODATION

MARBELLA
El Castillo, P; *Plaza de San Bernabé; tel. 952 77 17 39.*

Two-star *hostal* in town centre.

TARIFA
100% Fun, P; *Ctra Cádiz-Málaga, km 76; tel. 956 68 03 30.*

An unlikely name, but value for money in bungalows.

Tarik, P; *San Sebastián, 36; tel. 956 68 06 48.*

Simple pension.

TORREMOLINOS
Miami, P; *Aladino, 14; tel. 952 38 52 55.*

A cousin of Picasso designed this small, tranquil hotel, with pool and banana palms. Mercedes, who has run it for 40 years, says 'This is my home and I treat clients as invited guests.'

astrous War of Cuba in 1898 brought decline. Today the bay is important as a naval base, particularly neighbouring San Fernando, and for ship repair. Ferries leave for the Canaries.

A stroll throught the **old quarter** begins at the Puerta Tierra, the entrance gate in the old ramparts. To the west, near the seafront, you encounter the yellow-domed **cathedral**. Construction began in 1702 and they don't seem to have finished yet. Its massive Greco-Roman style provokes disdain among many visitors – 'a stranded wreck on a quicksand', according to one English writer, but the stalls, the crypt and the treasury are worth seeing.

Manuel de Falla, the Cádiz-born composer of some of Andalucía's most evocative works, including *The Three-Cornered Hat*, is buried here. The **cathedral museum**, through which you can gain access, is open mornings.

Further west, beyond the central market, stands the Baroque, oval-shaped **Oratorio de San Felipe Neri**. During the Napoleonic Wars, Cádiz was briefly capital of all Spain not under French control and here in 1812 Spanish patriots proclaimed a liberal constitution, upholding the sovereignty of the people. A national monument, it is only open during evening services.

Phoenician tombs and works by Zurbarán are on view in the **Museo de Bellas Artes y Arqueológico** on Plaza de la Mina.

Everywhere there are small neighbourhood bars serving sherry from the barrel and seafood **tapas**. For a fine sandy beach and summer resort life, head for the modern zone and the **Playa de la Vitoria**, unfortunately lined by graceless apartment blocks.

CASTELLAR DE LA FRONTERA

Off the C 3331, 27 km N of Gibraltar. Until comparatively recent times, the gates of this remarkable 13thC hill-top fortress were closed every night. In the early 1970s, the 2,000 inhabitants abandoned their houses inside the walls to move to a new village in the valley below. A number of hippies took their place. It is a ghostly place these days, although the houses are gradually being bought up and restored. You can enjoy spectacular views of Gibraltar and of the Guadarranque reservoir.

COSTA DEL SOL ⌨ ✕

The Costa del Sol embraces the 148 km of the Málaga province coast, stretching from just east of Nerja to near Manilva, a short distance from Sotogrande and Gibraltar. Its pleasant year-round climate, with Europe's mildest winters, has lured both mass tourism and thousands of expatriates who have settled permanently on the coast, many of them retirees. The 'Costa' has also become synonymous with jet-set shenanigans and drug traffic scandals, due to its proximity to the hashish fields of North Africa.

Although developers have done their best to blitz the charm out of what the British writer Laurie Lee once described as 'salt-fish villages, thin-ribbed, sea-hating' and there is no shortage of tackiness, the coast retains its appeal with some dazzling vistas and innumerable opportunities for sport and entertainment. Every facility exists for tennis, horse-riding, and water-skiing. There were six marinas and at least 15 golf courses west of Málaga at the last count.

Tropical fruit such as avocadoes, mangoes, oranges, lemons, and custard apples flourish along the coast and in the hinterland. It is worth exploring the mountainous **interior**, where you will find old villages crowning ridges or tucked into valleys amid vineyards and olive groves.

The main towns are (east to west) **Nerja**; **Torre del Mar**; **Torremolinos**, a throbbing package tour centre; **Fuengirola**, a rather staid, family resort; **Marbella**, the jetsetters' paradise, and **Estepona**, more relaxed but gradually succumbing to the tourist flood. It can be pleasant to linger over a meal at one of the scores of *chiringuitos* (beach restaurants).

ESTEPONA ✕
See Recommended Restaurants, page 141.

FUENGIROLA ✕
See Costa de Sol, above, and Recommended Restaurants.

GIBRALTAR ⌨
Off the N340, 116 km W of Málaga, 150 km SE of Cádiz. Tourism Offices, 158 Main Street; tel. 9567 74982, and in kiosks at the frontier and at other points, tel. 9567 76400 (dial the prefix 9567 only when calling from

Spain). One day this tiny British colony could be a second Hong Kong, but it has a way to go. Gibraltar – often compared to a crouching lion – is changing its spots. It has lost much of its strategic importance, even though the Rock itself, a mass of Jurassic limestone rising 426 m, is honeycombed with secret installations, and is busy trying to reinvent itself as an offshore financial centre.

Visiting the tiny territory of only 6.5 square km induces feelings of curiosity, nostalgia, and claustrophobia. You can stroll past such symbols of imperial power as the **Hundred-Ton Gun** which needed 35 men to fire it, eat steak-and-kidney pie with tepid English beer, and listen to the inhabitants – known as *llanitos* to Spaniards – mixing English and Spanish in their talk.

Main Street, crowded with shoppers, presents a bewilderingly cosmopolitan atmosphere. The local population – true Gibraltarians number around 20,000 – has Spanish, British, Moroccan, Jewish, Maltese, and Genoese origins. To this add visitors and other residents of at least 44 nationalities, making a total population of 30,000.

The name Gibraltar comes from Jebel Tarik (Mount Tarik), after the Berber warrior Tarik who landed on the Rock in 711 to begin the Moorish invasion of the Spanish peninsula. In 1704, during the War of the Spanish Succession, an Anglo-Dutch fleet captured Gibraltar and the Treaty of Utrecht (1713) ceded it to Britain.

Spain has been trying to get it back ever since. The blockade started by General Franco in 1966 and lasting until 1985 only made the Gibraltarians more determined to avoid Spanish sovereignty. Spaniards claim that the Rock has always provided shelter for smugglers and certainly sneaking cheap tobacco out of Gibraltar into the border town of La Linea is a local pastime.

The main sights can be seen in two to three hours. These include: **massive walls**; the **Upper Galleries**, caves hacked out of the rock to make gun emplacements during the Great Siege of 1779-83; the **Convent**, the Governor's residence where the Gibraltar Regiment stages guard-mountings; and **Trafalgar Cemetery**, the last resting place of men who died in the 1805 sea battle.

Take the **cable car** for magnificent views from the top of the Rock. If you want to visit the **Apes' Den**, get out at the middle station. Legend says that when the Barbary Apes – believed to have first arrived with the Moors – leave the Rock, the British will go too. But Winston Churchill made a monkey out of that story during the Second World War. Hearing that numbers were diminishing, he ordered that they should never fall below 35.

More than 70 of these not exactly lovable creatures now live on the Rock, in two packs. Actually they are not apes but tail-less monkeys (*Macaca sylvana*), the only breed living wild in Europe. Feeding by visitors is carefully supervised and restricted to healthy green stuff, because the junk food given them by tourists was making them overweight and lose interest in breeding. Keep a tight grip on cameras and handbags as the apes are born thieves.

Although no value added tax is payable in Gibraltar, not all the goods on sale are bargains. Visitors entering Spain from Gibraltar can take in goods worth 35,000 pesetas (note, until recently it was 6,000 pesetas), provided they are not resident in Gibraltar or the Campo de Gibraltar, the area adjacent to the colony. Also, they may do so only once a month. Because of the arguments over sovereignty, Spain is not treating the colony as part of Europe, so all nationalities should carry passports.

Parking is difficult in the colony and traffic often has to queue when leaving, so leave your car in La Linea and walk in. Currency is in pounds (British or Gibraltar), but pesetas are accepted.

JEREZ
See Local Explorations: 15.

LA LINEA DE LA CONCEPCION ✕
See Recommended Restaurants, page 141.

MALAGA
See Spain Overall: 10.

MARBELLA ⇌ ✕
On the N340, 57 km W of Málaga. Tourism Office, Glorieta de la Fontanilla; tel. 952 77 14 42. This is where the money gathers. Marbella is the Costa del Sol's up-market resort, its marinas, golf courses, casino, and nightlife attracting a mixture of celebrities, playboys, con-men and boring old tourists. Last century its main claim to fame was iron mines and blast

furnaces. Now conspicuous consumption fights a losing battle with good taste. Luxury villas sprinkle the hills and the King of Saudi Arabia has built himself a palace.

The **Casco Viejo** (old quarter) preserves its whitewashed houses hidden away in a network of flower-decked alleys, where there are some trendy shops. The focal point is the **Plaza de Naranjos**, a pleasant spot to stop for an expensive cup of coffee.

The **Golden Mile** west of town leads to **Puerto Banús**, a pleasure port crammed with costly craft, some of which do put to sea now and then. It's a great place for poseurs and people-watchers. Bars, disco-pubs and restaurants proliferate, and in season, when the action really starts after midnight, you can't move for the hedonist crowd.

A little further west is **San Pedro de Alcántara**, another ambitious resort, but much less hectic than Marbella.

MIJAS

On the MA485, 8 km from Fuengirola. Postcard-pretty Mijas is too cute and too close to the coast not to be over-run with trippers. The dramatic changes that tourism brought to this village, a cascade of white against the mountainside 400 m above the coast, are described in Ronald Fraser's book, *The Pueblo.* Souvenir shops line the area round the main square where donkey taxis ply their trade, but the back streets are still typically Andalucían.

RONDA

And other places of interest nearby, see Local Explorations: 14.

SAN PEDRO DE ALCANTARA

See Marbella, page 139.

SAN ROQUE ✕

See Recommended Restaurants, page 141.

SEVILLE

See pages 201-207.

SOTOGRANDE 🛏

See Recommended Hotels, page 137.

TARIFA 🛏

On the N340, 100 km SE of Cádiz. The road from Algeciras to Tarifa offers fine views over the Straits of Gibraltar to the mountains of Morocco. On clear days,

you can see the white buildings of Tangiers from Tarifa, always a strategic spot but now converted into the Windsurf Capital of Europe.

Hundreds of windmills spin on the surrounding hills, generating electricity. The relentless winds, particularly the Levante which can blow for a week at a time, have frightened off developers from the magnificent beaches of the Atlantic coast north of Tarifa, but attract thousands of windsurfers.

Tarif Ben Malik landed at Tarifa in 710 to reconnoitre for the Moorish invasion that came one year later. Ancient walls, within which are located several of the most popular bars, protect the old town and the 10thC **castle** can be visited.

This is where the Christian leader Pérez de Guzmán withstood a Moorish siege. A treacherous Christian brought Guzmán's son to the castle and threatened to cut his throat unless the garrison surrendered. Guzmán replied in contemptuous manner, tossing down a dagger, 'I prefer honour without a son to a son with dishonour'. (A remarkably similar incident involving the Nationalist commander of Toledo's besieged Alcázar occurred in the Civil War.)

The besiegers were so impressed that they spared the boy. However, another version insists the boy was killed, which is perhaps why Guzmán (later dubbed 'el Bueno') appears so foul-tempered in his statue on the nearby esplanade .

Tarifa is strategically placed to view thousands of birds migrating to and from Africa. The best seasons are February to June and July to October.

A ferry runs daily to Tangiers.

TORREMOLINOS 🛏

On the N340, 12 km W of Málaga. Tourism Office, Plaza de las Comunidades Autónomas; tel. 952 37 19 09. A friend of mine, a sensitive, intellectual type who had lived a sheltered life, once asked me to show him around this package tour heaven. After examining skyscraper developments, gay bars, English pubs, and German *bierkellers*, he stuttered: 'Incredible! But, in a funny sort of way, I quite like it.'

Down-market, garish, noisy... Torremolinos has no pretensions. It is Coney Island and Blackpool with a touch of Spanish *brio*. Forty years ago it was a fishing hamlet, with 19 water mills for grinding wheat (thus its name). First it was discovered by artists and escapees, then celebrities, then tour operators. Today there are 100 hotels and thousands of apartments, and **San Miguel**, its main pedestrian thoroughfare, is filled with as bizarre a range of fauna as one could wish for.

There are four beaches, a humming nightlife, and a sufficient variety of bars and restaurants to satisfy the most demanding. Along **La Carihuela beach** you will find a series of fish restaurants, some offering excellent value. Much of the nocturnal activity is concentrated in the **Montemar** area.

VEJER DE LA FRONTERA ⊨

See Recommended Hotels, page 144.

RECOMMENDED RESTAURANTS

ARROYO DE LA MIEL

In this town between Torremolinos and Benalmádena, two traditional inns offer local dishes and value for money, with open-air dining in summer. They are: **Ventorillo de la Perra, PP**; *Avenida de la Constitución; tel.* 952 44 19 66; *credit cards* AE, DC, MC, V; *closed Mon and Nov*; and **Mesón del Virrey**, *Ctra Benalmádena, 87; tel.* 952 44 35 99; *cards* AE, DC, MC, V; *closed Wed and Oct*.

CADIZ

El Faro, PPP; *San Félix, 15; tel:* 956 21 10 68; *credit cards* AE, DC, MC, V.

If you seek the best seafood Cádiz has to offer, this restaurant deep in the old quarter is the place. It offers regional cooking with a dash of French influence. Advisable to book. Try *Lomos de urta en salsa de camarones* (sea bream in shrimp sauce).

Ventorillo El Chato, PP-PPP; *Ctra NIV, 3 km along San Fernando Road; tel.* 956 25 00 25; *credit cards,* AE, MC, V; *closed Aug.*

A 200-year-old inn with abundant atmosphere. The first owner, a bandit, smuggled salt through a passage under the building to a waiting vessel. Fernando VII was an early customer. Specialities include bull's tail and sole.

ESTEPONA

Robbies, PP; *Jubrique,* 11; *tel.* 952 80 21 21; *credit cards* MC, V; *eve only, closed Mon, first two weeks Dec, all Feb.*

Australian management. International dishes served in the intimate atmosphere of an old converted house. Speciality: Frank Sinatra steak.

FUENGIROLA

Lew Hoad's Tennis Ranch, PP; *Ctra de Mijas, km* 3.5; *tel.* 952 47 48 58; *credit cards* AE, MC, V; *closed Mon.*

For those who want to combine a hard game on the courts, run by the retired Australian champion, with a hearty steak or baby lamb.

LA LINEA DE LA CONCEPCION

La Marina, PP; *on the border with Gibraltar - Paseo Marítimo; tel.* 956 76 96 06; *credit cards* AE, MC, V. Excellent seafood at this establishment on La Atunara, the fisherman's beach that runs towards the Gibraltar frontier.

MARBELLA

La Meridiana, PPP; *Camino de la Cruz, s/n (near the mosque); tel.* 952 77 61 90; *credit cards* AE, DC, MC, V; *closed Mon, Tues lunch.*

Hundreds of restaurants of all classes compete on the Costa del Sol, but the Meridiana stands out. Don't step inside the door if you are on a tight budget. Supervised by Paolo Ghirelli, it offers sophisticated international cuisine in a charming setting amid luxuriant vegetation, with outdoor dining in summer. Try basil-flavoured tomato vichysoisse and duck roasted with cherries. Booking essential.

SAN ROQUE

Claus en El Benito, PP; *on the N340, 13 km E of Algeciras - Plaza de Armas,* 10; *tel.* 956 78 23 42; *credit cards* V; *closed Sun midday.*

Attentive service and international dishes served in a gracious 18thC house in a town founded by Spaniards who fled Gibraltar when the British conquered it.

South-Central Spain

Between Madrid and Seville
Extremadura and Sierra de Gredos

630 km; maps Michelin 444 & 446

In early summer the plains of Extremadura are an ocean of rippling green and golden crops. Wild flowers carpet the roadsides and posses of black pigs root about under oak trees. Watching over the towns and villages are the storks: every church tower and chimney-top seems to house one of their untidy nests. By midsummer, when the landscape is turning brown, the ruined castles jut above the shimmering heat like mirages and any movement is almost imperceptible against the wide horizons and big skies. In winter, the landscape has the bleakness of the steppes.

Extremadura (composed of the two provinces of Cáceres and Badajoz) communicates a sense of timelessness, as though any moment a Roman legion or a stray Conquistador will come tramping into view. It is a hard land and a largely empty one. One million people live in the 42,000 square kilometres, stretching from La Mancha to the Portuguese border, from the trout streams of the Gredos Mountains to the hills of Andalucía. There are many unspoilt areas excellent for wildlife, such as the Cijara Nature Park in eastern Badajoz province, which shelters wild boar, lynx and deer.

Reminders of times past are everywhere, but especially in such towns as Guadalupe, Medellín, and Trujillo, which have counterparts bearing the same names across the ocean; and in the numerous monuments built with plunder from the Americas.

Extremadura retains a leisurely rural atmosphere and you can witness old customs which have died out in other parts of the country. Splendid architecture has been preserved, not least the monuments to grandeur at Mérida, once a showplace of the Roman Empire when it was the capital of a large chunk of the Iberian peninsula, including modern Portugal. Lack of development has saved priceless examples of medieval architecture, such as the old town at Cáceres.

If your starting-point for exploring the region is Madrid, Avila, or Salamanca, a highly-recommended detour will take you via the Sierra de Gredos, where you can enjoy various outdoor pursuits.

The main highway crossing Extremadura from north-east to south-west is the Madrid-Badajoz road, the four-lane NV. Connecting Trujillo and Mérida, and allowing detours to Cáceres and Guadalupe, it is ideal if you want to travel 'red', seeing the main sights only. Allow about three days. By following the N630, which runs north-south from Salamanca to Seville, you can also visit some of the major sights.

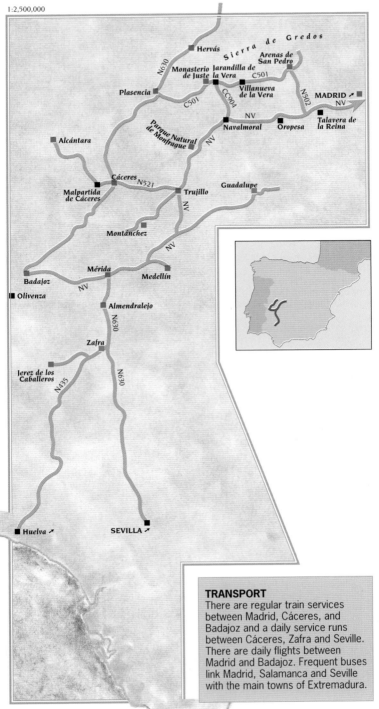

1:2,500,000

TRANSPORT

There are regular train services between Madrid, Cáceres, and Badajoz and a daily service runs between Cáceres, Zafra and Seville. There are daily flights between Madrid and Badajoz. Frequent buses link Madrid, Salamanca and Seville with the main towns of Extremadura.

OLD WAYS PERSIST
One of the most unchanging features of life – and landscape – in Extremadura is the annual movement of cattle and sheep between summer upland pastures and winter shelter. Wide tracks cut across the country, following rights of way established in the Middle Ages. Shepherds and cowboys live for weeks on the trail with their animals.

SIGHTS & PLACES OF INTEREST

ALCANTARA
On C523, 65 NW of Cáceres. Crusading knights established the Order of Alcántara here to promote the fight with the Moors. Ruins of their castle and part of their **Monasterio de San Benito** remain. Tombs of the Grand Masters are in the village's 13thC parish church.

The most striking sight, however, is an amazing example of Roman engineering on the road to Portugal, 18 km out of town. The Romans spanned the River Tajo (Tagus) with a 194 m-long **bridge** (al kantara is Arabic for bridge), completing work in 106 AD. A triumphal arch stands in the centre of the granite structure, which reaches a maximum height of 70 m and is still used by traffic. Restoration work was necessary when it was damaged, first by the Moors, then by the English in 1809.

The **Alcántara Reservoir** on the Tajo can claim to be the biggest in Western Europe.

ALMENDRALEJO ⇔
On the N630, 33 km S of Mérida. This prosperous but unremarkable town, where José de Espronceda, the 19thC Romantic poet and novelist was born, lives from its wine and olives, produced in the fertile clay soils of the Tierra de Barros region. Probably the most outstanding building is the 16thC **church**

RECOMMENDED HOTELS

ALMENDRALEJO
La Perla, P; Plaza de la Iglesia, 7; tel. 924 66 10 03.
Pleasant, low-cost hostal in the centre. Take the plastic cover off the mattress to improve your night's rest.

CACERES
Meliá, PPP; Plaza San Juan, 11; tel. 927 21 58 00.
A classy conversion of a 16thC palace, close to the old quarter. Two carved Gothic lions, elegant ironwork, oil paintings, and vaulted brick ceilings create a distinguished atmosphere. The restaurant is recommendable.

GREDOS, SIERRA DE
Parador de Gredos, PP; Navarredonda de Gredos, Avila; tel. 920 34 80 48.
Panoramic views of the Gredos Mountains are among the attractions of this hotel, Spain's first parador, established in 1928.

GUADALUPE
Hospedería Real Monasterio, PP; Plaza Juan Carlos, 1; tel. 927 36 70 00.
No-frills hotel forming part of the

monastery. Well-prepared food at reasonable prices in the restaurant. Worth staying and eating here just for the setting.

HERVAS
Europa, P; Ctra 630, km 433; tel. 927 47 30 20.
A useful, low-priced stop-over option on the highway. Characterless but immaculate two-star hostal, with a handy restaurant.

JARANDILLA DE LA VERA
Parador de Jarandilla de la Vera PPP; on the C501, 56 km E of Plasencia; tel. 927 56 01 17.
Emperor Charles V lodged in this 14thC fortified palace before moving to the nearby Yuste monastery. A swimming-pool and tennis courts are among the facilities.

JEREZ DE LOS CABALLEROS
Oasis, PP; El Campo, 18; tel. 924 73 12 44.
Spacious tiled rooms with solid wood furnishings in a modern, tastefully-decorated hotel. Reservations advisable. Tapa bar and restaurant, serving Extremaduran specialities.

of the Purificación, a mixture of Gothic and Plateresque. But the **bull-ring** is also worthy of note: beneath the seating one million litres of wine are stored.

Of the several local *bodegas*, one has achieved considerable prestige, particularly among American wine critics. 'Rich, mature, velvety' are some of the epithets applied to Lar de Barros and Lar de Lares, the reserve reds of Bodegas Inviosa. You can buy direct from the *bodega's* retail outlet at Avenida de la Paz, 19. To visit the winery itself, call Marcelino Díaz, who with his five brothers owns the company, on 924 66 09 77.

Tapa bars are your best course for food. The **Mesón Agustín** (Frailes, 8) is recommendable; it has a restaurant serving roast lamb. Behind the bar, a sign advises: 'Ask for broth, we put the bone in today.'

BADAJOZ
On *the* N V, 87 *km* SW *of Cáceres. Tourism

EXTREMADURA AND THE NEW WORLD
It is hardly surprising that so many of the conquerors of the New World came from here, nor that they were so tough nor so ruthless. Fleeing the cruel poverty of their homeland, they were ready for anything. Balboa, Cortés and Pizarro were among the Conquistadors raised in Extremadura.

Office, Plaza de la Libertad, 3; tel. 924 22 27 63. Badajoz is the sort of place you go to by accident rather than design. It commands the main route into Portugal and is Extremadura's largest city, a busy commercial centre. However, it has little to excite the visitor.

It has been plundered and pillaged so many times that little is left except a few narrow streets, the **cathedral,** started in the 13thC, and the remains

MERIDA
Emperatriz, PP; *Plaza de España; tel.* 924 31 31 11.

Empress Isabel of Portugal and Philip II are among the illustrious to have stayed in this noble edifice, now a three-star hotel, built as a palace in the 16thC by Luís de Mendoza. Suits of armour, stone arches, and a three-tier Renaissance patio add to the medieval atmosphere. Renovation has been in progress.

OROPESA
Parador Virrey de Toledo, PPP; *on the* NV, 33 *km* W *of Talavera –* Plaza Palacio, 1, *Oropesa, (Toledo); tel.* 925 43 00 00.

Emperor Charles V and Santa Teresa de Avila stayed in this 16thC Gothic-Mudéjar castle in the old town of Oropesa. Totally renovated, the parador looks out towards the Sierra de Gredos.

PLASENCIA
Rincón Extremeño, P; *Vidrieras, 8; tel.* 927 41 11 50.

A small hotel just off the Plaza Mayor. Cosy rooms, red check bedspreads.

TRUJILLO
Parador de Trujillo, PPP; *Plaza de Santa Beatriz de Silva, 1; tel.* 927 32 13 50.

A Renaissance cloister replete with orange and lemon trees is an outstanding feature of this converted convent. Your room may well be in the modern extension, but it's a peaceful overnight spot. A reliable restaurant.

ZAFRA
Las Palmeras, P; *Plaza Grande, 14; tel.* 924 55 22 08.

Newly-renovated old building, with all modern conveniences, looking out on a pleasant square. Classical music plays in the *tapa* bar, with its vaulted ceilings and stone walls.

Parador Hernán Cortés, PPP; *Plaza Corazón María, 7; tel.* 924 55 45 40.

Cortés slept here before departing for the conquest of the Aztecs. Beneath the 15thC castle lie Moorish fortifications and beneath those Roman remains. If you want a night in baronial splendour, look no further. The restaurant is recommended.

of its **Arab fortress**. The 628 m-long granite bridge, **Puente de las Palmas**, on the Cáceres road, was built by Philip II's favourite architect, Juan de Herrera, he of the Escorial.

Badajoz has suffered many sieges. Six thousand men died when Wellington took it from the French in 1812. More carnage occurred in the Civil War, when Republican prisoners were massacred by Nationalist troops in the bullring (nobody will ever know exactly how many died, although figures of up to 2,000 have been quoted).

Conquistadors who were born here include Pedro de Alvarado, one of Cortés's men, and Sebastián Garcilaso de la Vega, who married an Inca princess.

Although Badajoz has more than 100,000 inhabitants, there is little variety in the way of restaurants. For *tapas*, try **Mesón El Tronco**, at Muñoz Torrero, 16 and **El Sótano**, on Virgen de la Soledad.

To visit a town with a very Portuguese atmosphere without actually

• *Lace-making, Extremadura.*

setting foot across the border, head 25 km south on the C436 to **Olivenza**. Several buildings, including the **library** and **church of Santa Magdalena** are in the distinctive Manueline style, a decorative design marking the transition from Gothic to Renaissance, which developed in Portugal in the 16thC.

Olivenza passed five centuries within the Kingdom of Portugal, from the end of the 13thC until 1801. Spain regained it after a farcical conflict dubbed the War of the Oranges. Manuel Godoy, an unpopular Badajoz upstart, who had wormed his way to the office of chief minister through an affair with Spain's Queen María Luisa, invaded Portugal and sent back to the queen a symbolic gift of Portuguese oranges. After a three-week war, Portugal, to stave off a bigger conflict, agreed at the Peace of Badajoz to hand over Olivenza.

CACERES ⊨ ✕
On the N630, 96 km NE of Badajoz.

Tourism Office, Plaza Mayor; tel. 927 24 63 47. Wealth from the New World helped create the city's *casco antiguo* (old quarter), which can have changed little since such locally-born Conquistadors as Francisco Hernández Girón, who battled his way through Peru, strode its cobbled streets. The whole complex of ramparts, palaces, convents, and churches is a jewel of medieval architecture and frequently attracts film makers in search of authentic background. Part of Ridley Scott's Columbus epic, *1492,* was made here.

The Romans constructed the first fortifications in 35 AD and the colony became one of the five major cities of Lusitania. The Moors rebuilt the walls and later the military Order of Santiago was founded here. When the knights of Cáceres clashed in violent struggles for supremacy, Isabel the Catholic feared that they were becoming too powerful and ordered the destruction of all fortified towers on private mansions. However, the nobles' Gothic and Renaissance palaces have survived, each with its coat of arms and generally somewhat austere lines. Many are still inhabited.

Don't try to drive around the old quarter. I did so once and found myself trapped in a corner so tight that my car had to be lifted clear. Get a map from the Tourism Office on the Plaza Mayor, around which you will find many bars and restaurants, and walk up the adjacent steps to penetrate the walls via the Arco de la Estrella.

One mansion, the **Casa de Toledo-Moctezuma**, was built by Juan Cano, a Conquistador, apparently using the fortune bought to him by his bride, the daughter of Mexico's last Aztec ruler. In another, **Los Golfines de Abajo**, lived French warriors who seem to have been 12thC equivalents of soccer hooligans to judge by the fear in which they were held. The **Casa de las Cigüeñas** (Storks' House), occupied by the military, retains its lofty tower. Storks wheel about the roof tops. Active efforts are being made to protect these birds, which have come to symbolize Extremadura.

Many scions of knightly families including the Ovandos, the Ulloas, and the Saavedras, have tombs in the Gothic **cathedral of Santa María** or the **church of San Mateo**. Across a plaza from San Mateo is the **Museo Arqueológico**, housed in the Casa de las Veletas, built over the ruins of a Moorish fort. Descending to the basement, you can view a large 11thC Arab cistern into which water still trickles. In an adjoining building paintings by leading contemporary Spanish artists are well displayed.

Cáceres is a university town with a lively cultural life and during summer festivals classical drama is presented. The patron saint is San Jorge (St George) and on April 23 a dragon is burned on a bonfire in the Plaza Mayor to excited celebrations.

A worthwhile excursion nearby is the village of **Malpartida de Cáceres**, 12 km west of the city. Just outside it is **Los Barruecos**, a strange landscape of massive boulders, like giant marbles, on top of which scores of storks make their nests. Wolf Vostell, a German artist, has created an avant-garde museum here and half-buried a car among the boulders. The locals are bemused.

GREDOS, SIERRA DE ⌘

Mountain range running some 100 km across the centre of Spain, W of Madrid. Walkers, climbers, fishermen, and equestrians find abundant challenges in this mountain rampart. Its abrupt escarpments shelter a rich variety of wildlife, including thousands of wild goats, black storks, golden orioles, and five species of eagle.

The north- and south-facing sides of the mountains have strikingly different vegetation. The northern slopes are gentler, but open to icy blasts: here you will find large pine forests and green

---

THE FRANCO CONTRIBUTION
Poverty and depopulation don't go away from Extremadura, although the Franco regime helped somewhat, introducing the Badajoz Plan which, by damming the Guadiana river, brought irrigation to large tracts of previously arid land. Tobacco, cotton and other crops flourish, but otherwise the region has little industry and huge feudally-run estates still dominate those who work the land.

pastures. The south-facing southern slopes have a milder climate, encouraging the growth of Mediterranean-type vegetation, including holm oaks and lemon trees. On this side you will find some pretty villages retaining their traditional architecture in the area known as La Vera (see **Villanueva de la Vera**, page 152).

The Gredos, straddling the division between Avila and Toledo provinces, can be most easily approached from Avila or by branching north from the NV highway which runs from Madrid to Extremadura. Daily buses run from Talavera and Avila to **Arenas de San Pedro** (47 km north-west of Talavera), a focal point for Gredos visitors.

Nearby you can explore the **Aguila Caves**, near the village of Ramacastañas, and Mombeltrán, with its impressive 14thC castle.

From Mombeltrán, the C502 climbs up the **Puerto del Pico** – look for the original road built by the Romans. On the descent, turn left in the direction of the Parador de Gredos and Navarredonda de Gredos; just before Hoyos del Espino, a road heads southwards to the **Plataforma**, giving access to spectacular scenery. You can hike to the **Laguna Grande**, a large lake, surrounded by peaks, including the highest peak in the range, Almanzor, 2,592 m. Avoid summer weekends, when campers and picnickers crowd the paths.

GUADALUPE ⇔ ✕
On the C401, 78 km E of Trujillo, 87 km S of Oropesa on the NV. Surrounded by wild moorland, the lush wooded valley which shelters Guadalupe comes as a surprise. In this remote spot stands one of the most important shrines in the Spanish-speaking world. The Conquistadors revered the **Virgen de Guadalupe** and built shrines in her honour in the New World; Columbus named a Caribbean island after her and kings and queens have endowed the shrine with great treasures.

The fortress-like **monastery,** founded in the 14thC by Alfonso XI in thanks for a victory over the Moors, stands boldly above the village. The village is a picturesque jumble of alleys lined with balconied houses and often crowded with pilgrims snapping up religious souvenirs. Articles of brass and copper are

traditional local products. Two native Americans brought back by Columbus were baptized in the fountain before the monastery.

The monastery was sacked by the French during the Napoleonic Wars (a familiar story as you travel about Spain). Later abandoned, the building has been occupied since 1908 by Franciscan monks. Among the features worth noting are **Zurbarán's paintings** in the ornate sacristy; the **Mudéjar cloister**; and the **embroidery museum** in the former refectory.

In a richly-adorned room behind the altar known as the **Camarín** is the Virgin herself: a diminutive, blackened image contrasting sharply with the sumptuousness of her robes. I spent so much time scrutinizing the Virgin and her treasures, a fortune in precious stones and metals, that when I came to leave I found the church exit blocked by a firework bombardment. Crackers, rockets and other explosive devices were whizzing about the church façade to celebrate September 8, **the Virgin's annual fiesta** and a holiday in all Extremadura.

HERVAS ⇔
Off the N630, 40 km NE of Plasencia. Oak and chestnut forests, cattle pastures, and the Gredos Mountains are the backdrop to Hervás, a village of twisting medieval alleys straggling over a hillside. A flourishing Jewish community lived here until their expulsion from Spain in the 15thC. Although traditional crafts such as woodwork and basketmaking continue, I found the dark streets of the Jewish quarter, the Barrio Judío, cheerless rather than charming.

JARANDILLA DE LA VERA ⇔
See Recommended Hotels, page 144.

JEREZ DE LOS CABALLEROS ⇔
On the N435, 77 km S of Badajoz, 40 km W of Zafra. Hills studded with cork trees surround Jerez, a pretty whitewashed town which owes its name to the Knights Templar, who ruled supreme here. After the Templars were bloodily suppressed (their throats cut in the castle's Bloody Tower), Enrique II handed the town over in 1375 to the Order of Santiago and many of the finest buildings were constructed.

The towers of four churches break

the skyline. **San Bartolomé's** is richly decorated with ceramics; the slender, red brick tower of **San Miguel**, founded in the 14thC, rises 64 m above the main square; and that of **Santa Catalina** is neo-classical in style. The oldest church, **Encarnación**, combines Renaissance and Baroque, but an inscription on one of the pillars reminds you that it was consecrated as far back as 566.

At number 12 on Calle Capitán Cortés, one of the many narrow streets, is the birthplace of Vasco Núñez de Balboa, who discovered the Pacific. A statue recalls that another famous Conquistador, Hernando de Soto, was a local man. He fought in Peru and Florida and when he died from fever in 1542 his body was put in a hollow log and consigned to the waters of the Mississippi.

Jerez claims to be 'the cradle of Iberian ham' and the town is crowded during the first weekend of May for the **Feria de Jamón**.

MADRID

See pages 170-192.

MALPARTIDA SE CACERES

See Cáceres, page 146.

MEDELLIN

On the C520, off the N430, 40 km E of Mérida. This insignificant village is wealthier now than when its most famous son, Hernán Cortés, conqueror of Mexico, left it to seek his fortune, but not by much.

In recent years, it has been considerably cleaned up and has acquired a library and an old folks' club. Neat gardens surround the statue of Cortés planting the banner of Castile on a pedestal engraved with names that figured in his Mexico campaign. Born in Medellín in 1485, Cortés was ruthless, haughty and astute. With only 500 men and 16 horses plus the aid of his Aztec mistress, he conquered the Aztec Empire and became so powerful that some Spanish leaders feared he would set up an independent kingdom in Mexico.

Medellín stands in flat, fertile land of the Guadian Valley, where irrigation schemes have increased prosperity and created new towns. Fifteen km to the east is workaday Villanueva de la Serena, outside whose Town Hall

---

> **'THE SILVER ROUTE'**
> The N630 follows the Vía de la Plata – the Silver Route – built by the Romans to link Augusta Emerita (Mérida) and Asturicum (Astorga), now in León province. Although a considerable amount of silver travelled this route, the name is actually believed to derive from the Latin word for a public road.

---

stands a statue of Pedro de Valdivia, born here, who was killed in the conquest of Chile.

MERIDA ⊨ ✕

On the N630, 62 km E of Badajoz. Tourism Office, Paseo de José Alvárez Sáenz de Buruaga; tel. 924 31 53 53. Significant traces remain in and around Mérida of its golden age when it was a flourishing Roman city. Founded by the Emperor Augustus in 25 BC to accommodate veterans of the Roman legions, Augusta Emerita became the capital of Lusitania. It commanded two important roads, the Vía de la Plata between Seville and Salamanca (see 'The Silver Route', this page), and that from Toledo to Lisbon.

The River Guadiana is spanned here by a 60-arch Roman bridge, well used for 2,000 years, until a new bridge was constructed recently; now the Roman bridge is open only to pedestrians.

But perhaps the most impressive Roman relic is the **theatre** built by Agrippa in 18 BC to accommodate 5,500 spectators. Statues have been restored to the colonnaded back-drop of the stage. Classical drama is presented here every summer.

Next to the theatre is a vast **amphitheatre**, scene of gladiatorial struggles and other spectacles. Below it is the excavated remains of a **patrician's house**, with interesting mosaics.

Don't miss the magnificent **Museo Nacional de Arte Romano**, a soaring modern brick structure which does full justice to its rich collection of statuary, tombs, tools, and art. Outside Italy there can hardly be a more dazzling display of the splendour of Ancient Rome. Here are the gods and emperors of the ancient world and intricate mosaics, still glowing with colour, rescued from the houses and temples of Mérida.

Scattered about the city are other relics: **Trajan's Arch**, a **temple of Diana**, the **Milagros Aqueduct** and a Roman circus.

Just to the north of Mérida, the **reservoir of Proserpina**, with the original dam, is still in use. It is a favourite picnic spot.

A **temple** to Mérida's patron saint, Eulalia, is built on the site of a 4thC church honouring her. In front of the church is a **chapel** known as the *hornillo* (little oven). The teenage martyr was apparently baked alive by those pagan Romans.

MONFRAGUE, PARQUE NATURAL DE

Entry by the C524, 20 km S of Plasencia. This 18,000-hectare park of jagged hills follows the course of the Tajo (Tagus) River to its junction with the Tiétar. A rich variety of birds can be seen around the reservoirs and the hills, covered with holm oaks, cork oaks, and Mediterranean evergreens. Species include black storks, imperial eagles

---

FOOD AND DRINK

Extremadura is hardly a gourmet's paradise. There is little subtlety or variety in the cooking and interesting restaurants are far between. However, you can still eat well by sticking to the hearty local dishes – though if you are worried about your cholesterol level, abstain.

A true rustic belly-filler is *migas extremeñas* (breadcrumbs fried with ham, olive oil and garlic). There is always lamb – *caldereta de cordero* (lamb stew with paprika) is a favourite. Game, trout, and frogs' legs are popular. Black Iberian pigs roam by the thousand through cork oak forests, feeding on acorns and ensuring plentiful supplies of *pata negra*, the prized cured ham. And there are excellent cheeses, particularly the soft *queso de la Serena*.

Extremadura produces large quantities of wine, most of it drinkable but undistinguished. Pitarra, a red served from the barrel, is a favourite. But one or two *bodegas* produce some first-rate vintages – see Almendralejo, page 144.

---

and a large colony of black vultures. There are also 15 species of bat. Tracks lead into the park interior. Birds of prey are to be seen in the vicinity of Peñafalcon, a rock pinnacle. An information office is located in the hamlet of Villarreal de San Carlos (tel. 927 45 51 04), but may only be open at peak times. Nearby a crag is crowned by a castle and the **Monfragüe sanctuary** houses a 12thC Virgin.

MONTANCHEZ

Off the N630, which is off the N630, 50 km SE of Cáceres. Black pigs snuffle about the oak trees and granite boulders beside the road which climbs to this village, famed for its cured ham.

Granite frames the doors of the houses with their whitewashed upper storeys. In the main square the Bar Labrador will serve you local wine and ham that melts in the mouth at reasonable prices. For fine views, climb to the partly-restored castle, where the Virgen de Consolación presides over her shrine in gold and silver embroidered robes. A plaque notes that in 1956 the town council named the Virgin honorary mayoress.

OLIVENZA

See Badajoz, page 145.

OROPESA ⇔

See Recommended Hotels, page 144.

PLASENCIA ⇔

On the N630, 83 km NE of Cáceres, 237 km W of Madrid. Tourism Office, Plaza de la Catedral; tel. 927 42 38 43.
Although Plasencia's population is barely more than 30,000, the pleasant old town boasts two cathedrals, interlocked.

Five centuries ago, when the town was prospering from the wool trade, work began on a new cathedral. Great names such as Diego de Siloé and Juan de Alava were employed, but cash ran out before work could be finished. The delicate Gothic vaulting and Rodrigo Alemán's choir stall carvings, including some erotica, are outstanding features of the **Catedral Nueva**. Note iron rings in the floor used to lift slabs for the burial of local bishops. A marble plaque pays forbidding tribute to the Bishop of Plasencia who died in 1906, thus: 'He was a model shepherd, father of the

• *The Roman theatre at Mérida.*

poor, hammer of liberalism, admired by all and feared by those who walk in the shadows.'

What remains of the old Romanesque cathedral adjoining is now a spacious **museum**. It displays religious raiment and some unusual carvings, including a silver-plated Virgin and Child and a polychrome 18thC sculpture of San Hermenegildo. He was a Visigoth king whose conversion to Christianity resulted in his martyrdom: note the axe buried in his head.

Plasencia has a number of fine buildings, one of which, the Renaissance **Palace of the Marqueses de Mirabel**, houses a museum on hunting. In and around the **Plaza de España**, the hub of local life, you will find bars and restaurants. For reliable *tapas*, down an alley named Vidrieras, you will find El Rincón Extremeño and **La Taberna**. The Taberna restaurant, in a brick-arched cellar beyond the bar, offers a cheap fixed meal and reasonably priced lamb stew and roast pork.

Plasencia stands above the Jerte and a pleasant expedition can be made north-west along this river valley via the N110. It is especially attractive in spring when thousands of cherry trees are in blossom.

SEVILLE

See pages 201-207.

TALAVERA DE LA REINA

On the NV, 116 km SW of Madrid. While not an inspiring town, Talavera will interest ceramics enthusiasts. Its pottery has enjoyed well-merited fame for centuries and traditional designs are available from the many factories. For an idea of the splendour of the local products, examine the tiling in the **Ermita del Prada**, in a park at the town entrance.

The **Museo de Ruíz de Luna**, on Plaza Primo de Rivera, traces the history of Talavera ceramics. To see more hand-painted pottery, you should visit **Puente del Arzobispo**, a village on the Tajo river 35 km to the southwest, where there are many small workshops.

TRUJILLO 🚪 ✕

On the NV, 48 km E of Cáceres. Tourism Office, Plaza Mayor, tel. 927 32 26 77. If you only have time to visit one town in Extremadura, Trujillo should be it. From this 'nest of conquerants' – as one old brochure declares – came 'a hundred of captains which spray the names of their native city across all the American lands... what a grandness, what a great nobleness, what a strong colour in this little city that brings us so vigorous sensation so much the more astonishing that it is unforeseen.' Yes, indeed. Trujillo produced some of the most famous and notorious adventurers to leave their mark on the New World.

Take a seat at one of the café terraces in the magnificent **Plaza Mayor** and survey the scene. The first item to catch the eye is an imperious, bronze equestrian **statue of Francisco Pizarro**, created by American sculptors Charles Rumsey and Mary Harriman; an identical one stands in Lima, Peru. Pizarro was one of the illegitimate children of a rascally old soldier known as El Tuerto (the one-eyed). Born in 1477, Pizarro is said to have been dumped at a church door when he was born and only survived by sucking milk from a sow. But it was a taste for gold and power that made him one of the great conquistadors (conquerors) of Latin America.

He was with Balboa (see page 145) when he discovered the Pacific. Later, with four brothers and fewer than 200 men, he battled his way through jungles and mountains to conquer the Incas, becoming the Governor of New Castile. Cunning, ruthless, and illiterate, he was finally murdered in 1541.

His brother Hernando, just as charming in his way, was described as 'uncertain in his friendships, implacable in his vengeance'. He rose high as a colonial administrator in Peru, but spent 20 years in jail for having a rival executed. After release he seduced Pizarro's beautiful daughter Francisca and made her his wife. With Francisca's vast fortune he constructed the **Palacio de la Conquista** in Trujillo. And there it is on the main square. An enormous coat of arms on one corner shows the chained heads of conquered native rulers. Below are carvings which represent Francisco Pizarro, the Inca princess he married, his daughter Francisca, and Hernando. You can enter to inspect the (unfurnished) interior.

Across the plaza is the **Chaves-Orellana Mansion**, known as the Casa de la Cadena because of the chain across the front. One of the Orellana family, Francisco, was the first Euro-

pean to travel down the Amazon. The 16thC **church of San Martín** stands in a corner of the square and near it the **Palacio de los Duques de San Carlos**, with its Baroque façade. This is now an enclosed convent, but you can visit the inner court.

From the Plaza Mayor stroll up to the ancient **walled quarter**, where the Moorish fortress straddles a granite crag. You pass through the Puerta de Santiago, one of seven original entrances, alongside which is the **church of Santiago** with its Romanesque belfry. The **church of Santa María**, dating from the 13thC, is the last resting place of notable Trujillo citizens and has a carved and gilded high altar reredos (decorative screen behind altar) with paintings attributed to Fernando Gallego.

Nearby you can inspect the **Casa-Museo Pizarro**, an old house of the Pizarro family which has been furnished in medieval style. Spaniards from outside Trujillo have recently bought and restored a number of palatial dwellings in this quarter.

VILLANUEVA DE LA VERA

On the C501, 39 km NW of Oropesa on the NV. Villanueva is one of a series of beautiful villages in **La Vera**, an area of mild climate on the banks of the Tiétar river in the foothills of the Sierra de Gredos. The villages conserve their typical medieval architecture and you can stroll through porticoed *plazas* and cobbled streets, the wooden balconies of the stone houses sometimes almost meeting overhead and often festooned with flowers.

On Shrove Tuesday a straw figure known as Pero Palo, symbolizing old bogeys, is paraded around Villanueva, before being destroyed to general jubilation. Spice was added in the 1980s when the British tabloid press launched an hysterical campaign against the celebrations, alleging that a donkey was crushed to death as part of the ritual. The only real casualty in this press campaign was the truth. Villanueva was angered, and the fiesta goes on.

YUSTE, MONASTERIO DE

Off the C501, 12 km W of Jarandilla de la Vera, 48 km E of Plasencia. To this peaceful spot a weary Charles V (Charles I of Spain) was carried in 1557 after his abdication as Holy Roman Emperor to end his days far from affairs of state. Wait at the entrance to the Hieronymite monastery for a tour of the premises, including the royal bedroom and two fine cloisters. The road beyond the monastery runs through rocky hills with wooded valleys to **Garganta la Olla**, where a stream cascades down from the Gredos.

ZAFRA ⊯ ✕
On the N432, 73 km SE of Badajoz. Tourism Office, Plaza de España; tel. 924 55 10 36.

Zafra, in the southern part of Extremadura, has an Andalucían feel. Its two squares are particularly charming. The arcaded **Plaza Grande** was once used as a bull-ring. Note the columns of local marble and the balcony ironwork, typically Extremaduran in its severe, unadorned style. Passing under some arches you reach the more intimate **Plaza Chica**, which dates back to Moorish times. This is where markets were held; a groove cut in one of the columns served as a yardstick to settle traders' arguments over measurements.

The most impressive structure in Zafra is a 15thC **Alcázar** complete with crenellated walls, round towers, and a stylish patio by Juan de Herrera. It is now a parador (see Recommended Hotels, page 145).

Local shops sell typical earthenware ceramics produced in the region of Los Barros, north and west of Zafra. For high-quality leather clothing, a 28-km detour to **Salvatierra de los Barros** is worthwhile.

RECOMMENDED RESTAURANTS

CACERES
Atrio, PPP; Avda España, 30; *tel.* 927 24 29 28; *credit cards* AE, D, MC, V; *closed Sun eve.*

You may have to dodge children playing football in the little square - the restaurant is situated among apartment blocks off the Avenida España. It's the place to go if you have had enough of rustic charm and want a touch of elegance – plus exquisitely prepared dishes such as sirloin cooked in port with truffles. There is a substantial wine list.

Bodega Medieval, PP; Orellana, 1; *tel.* 927 24 29 28; *credit cards* AE, DC, MC, V; *closed Wed.*

Regional dishes, medieval atmosphere.

GUADALUPE
Mesón del Cordero, PP; Alfonso Onceno, 27; *tel.* 927 36 71 31; *lunch only, closed Mon and Feb.*

Home cooking.

MERIDA
Nicolás, PP; Félix Valverde Lillo, 13; *tel.* 924 31 96 10; *credit cards* AE, MC, V; *closed Sun eve and last fortnight Sep.*

Yellow awnings and an impressive entrance welcome you to this restaurant serving unpretentious food at reasonable prices. Lamb with plums, and orange tart, are worth your attention. Alongside, the same family runs El Antillano *tapas* bar (try the frog's legs fried in butter).

TRUJILLO
Aljibe, PP; Plaza Mayor, 27; *tel.* 927 32 20 08; *credit cards* AE, MC, V; *closed Wed & Nov.*

Squeezed between two bars, a few metres from the Pizarro statue, this place offers such local dishes as *caldereta de cordero* (lamb stew) and stuffed partridge at reasonable prices. Friendly service.

Hostal Pizarro, PP; Plaza Mayor, 13; 927 32 02 55; V; *closed Sun eve.*

Solid home cooking and a family atmosphere created by the owner, Doña Manuela.

ZAFRA
Barbacana, PP-PPP; Travesía López Asme; *tel.* 924 55 41 00; AE, MC, V; *closed Sun lunch & Mon.*

More sophisticated food and decoration than you might expect in southern Extremadura. Located in the attractive three-star **Hotel Huerta Honda (PP)**. As a starter try the cream cheese with smoked salmon.

South-Central Spain

Between Madrid, Córdoba and Seville
La Mancha and Andalucía

550 km; map Michelin 444 & 446, 1:400,000

There is no better way to savour the essence of Spain than by travelling between the capital and its most romantic city. You will witness a timeless Spain so close to the travel-brochure image of the country that you may shake your head in disbelief.

South of Madrid is La Mancha, a vast region of sun-bleached plains and slumbering villages, immortalized in Miguel de Cervantes' *Don Quixote*. There are still windmills in La Mancha, although they are no longer employed to grind grain. (See Footsteps of Don Quixote, below.) There are also, in the Manzanares-Valdepeñas area, vineyards stretching as far as the eye can see, and *bodegas* where you can sample the wine. *Queso manchego,* cheese from ewes' milk, is a famed La Mancha product.

Separating north and south is a formidable natural barrier, the rounded mountains of the Sierra Morena. You cut through by means of the Despeñaperros Pass, entering, on the south side, another world. Andalucía,

---

FOOTSTEPS OF DON QUIXOTE

After the Bible, *Don Quixote* by Cervantes is the world's most translated book. A masterpiece of irony, it illuminates the human condition by recounting the absurd adventures of a country squire, who, 'his brain dried up', sallies out in rusty armour to right wrongs.

All across the region you will encounter reminders of Quixote. Almost every dusty hamlet claims to be the scene of one of the gallant knight's misadventures or at least where Cervantes paused for lunch. For those eager to retrace the footsteps of Quixote and his faithful companion Sancho Panza, here are some key spots:

Alcázar de San Juan (on the N420, 150 km SE of Madrid): Quixote may have tilted at the windmills here, mistaking them for giants.

Argamasilla de Alba (on the N310, 29 km NE of Manzanares), is the birthplace of the *hidalgo* Rodrigo Pacheco on whom Cervantes

allegedly based Quixote. A painting of Pacheco is in the church and you can visit the Cueva de Medrano (keys at the Town Hall), where Cervantes may have started work on his book.

Campo de Criptana (on the N420, 10 km E of Alcázar de San Juan) has some of La Mancha's oldest windmills (see page 157).

Consuegra (on the C400, off the N1V, 79 km S of Aranjuez): windmills and a castle perch picturesquely on the ridge above the town, once a seat of the Order of St John.

Montiel (on the CR631, 49 km E of Valdepeñas), near the ruined castle, scene of Pedro the Cruel's assassination in 1369, is where Don Quixote freed the galley slaves.

Puerto Lápice (on the N1V, 36 km N of Manzanares): Don Quixote was dubbed a knight at one of the inns in this halt for travellers.

El Toboso (on the TO104, 30 km NE of Alcázar de San Juan): a Cervantes museum is installed in the house of Dulcinea.

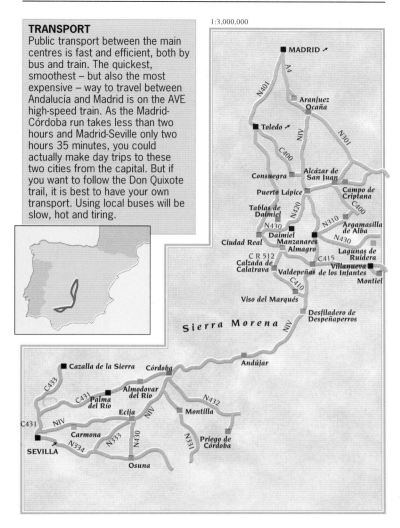

TRANSPORT

Public transport between the main centres is fast and efficient, both by bus and train. The quickest, smoothest – but also the most expensive – way to travel between Andalucía and Madrid is on the AVE high-speed train. As the Madrid-Córdoba run takes less than two hours and Madrid-Seville only two hours 35 minutes, you could actually make day trips to these two cities from the capital. But if you want to follow the Don Quixote trail, it is best to have your own transport. Using local buses will be slow, hot and tiring.

a region that in many ways sums up all our ideas of Spain, opens before you. The fertile valley of the Guadalquivir (from Wadi al-Kabir, the great river, as the Moors knew it) leads you to Córdoba. Its past magnificence lingers on: under the caliphs, it outshone Baghdad and Damascus.

On the surface at least, Andalucía is a place where a romanticized image of Spain is justified. Whitewashed farmhouses in a sea of sunflowers, olive groves, fighting bulls, aristocratic sherry barons, colourful fiestas... all are here. But it is also changing swiftly from medieval to 20th century values.

The N1V *autovía* allows you to travel between Madrid and Seville in a day, briefly dropping in on Córdoba (red route). Take two days if you want to see Almagro too and have more time to explore Córdoba. To linger over *bodegas* and pursue Don Quixote, visit the sights marked green.

SIGHTS & PLACES OF INTEREST

ALMAGRO ⊭ ✕

On the C415, 25 km SE of Ciudad Real. Fine buildings crowd the cobbled streets of this small town, dating from the time when it was the headquarters of the powerful Knights of Calatrava. Head first for the beautifully harmonious **Plaza Mayor**, lined by arcades, supported by 85 stone columns, with two upper storeys of glassed-in, green-framed balconies. Flemish families influenced the square's design: it was enlarged when the Fugger banking house was based in Almagro in the 16thC.

On the square you will find the **Corral de Comedias**, a charming example of an intimate 16thC theatre, where summer seasons of classical drama are staged. Also the **Convento de Asunción de Calatrava**: an outstanding Renaissance cloister and former Franciscan convent converted into a Parador (see Recommended Hotels, page 160). The Calatrava knights founded a university in Almagro in 1535.

The local speciality, eggplant well steeped in herbs and spices, should be available in the *tapa* bars around the Plaza Mayor.

It's worth making a detour to the **fortress of Calatrava la Nueva** (off the CR504, 32 km south of Almagro). This is a massive, forbidding structure crowning a hill just south of Calzada de Calatrava. Raimundo, Abbott of the **Monasterio de Fitero** (see Spain Overall: 6), founded the Order of Calatrava here in 1158 to do battle with the Moors. Al Mansur, the Moorish warlord, conquered the castle, but after the routing of the Moors at Las Navas de Tolosa it was recovered and the present ramparts constructed. The fortress's three-nave **convent church** is built in severe Cistercian style with a 12-lobule rose window.

Closed Mondays; under restoration; guarded by a dour watchman.

ALMODOVAR DEL RIO

On the C431, 25 km W of Córdoba. An impressive Moorish castle, once occupied by the Order of Calatrava, stands above the town.

ANDUJAR

On the N IV, 76 km E of Córdoba. An Iberian settlement named Iliturgi once stood near this town. Look for the 14-arch **Roman bridge** across the Guadalquivir. One or two potters carry on their craft and among the churches the Gothic **Santa María** is worth a visit. It has a Plateresque façade and a *reja* (iron grille) by Maestro Bartolomé, also an El Greco.

A pleasant excursion takes you to the sanctuary of **La Cabeza** (on the J501, 33 km N of Andújar), which tops a rocky outcrop among the pastures and oak forests of the Sierra Morena. In the Civil War, 230 Civil Guards held out here for nine months against attacking Republicans. Finally, on May 1, 1937, the sanctuary went up in flames. On the last weekend in April, several hundred thousand people flock to the re-built temple to pay homage to a small brown image of the Virgin, known as the Queen of the Sierra Morena. It is a stirring, if somewhat disturbing, event. Pilgrims clatter up on horseback, others crawl on their knees, as a priest's voice bellows unceasingly over loudspeakers and flames leap up from a huge torch outside the shrine.

ARANJUEZ

On the A4, 49 km S of Madrid. The Spanish Bourbons loved ornate palaces, and looked to Versailles for their ideas. Aranjuez was the obvious choice for one of their overblown country retreats (La Granja, page 243, was built at around the same time) being an oasis of greenery at the confluence of two rivers. Then, as now, the valley makes a refreshing sight as you approach across the stark plain of La Mancha: trees and vines proliferate, and asparagus and strawberries are grown in abundance. Royalty had long been attracted to these delights: the present **Palacio Real** was built on the site of an earlier one commissioned by Philip II which burned down in 1727. Rebuilding started immediately.

The obligatory guided tour wends through the usual chain of pompous rooms, decorated by vast chandeliers from the glassworks at La Granja, and by items from Charles IV's clock collection which numbered some 2,500. Worth the slog, however, is the **Sala Porcelana**, a dressing room whose walls and ceiling are entirely covered by Chinese-inspired decorative porcelain from the Buen Retiro factory in Madrid. Other diversions include a smoking room done out in painted plaster to resemble the Hall of the Two Sisters at the Alhambra, and a room covered in rice paper paintings depicting different tortures.

The **palace gardens** comprising the **Parterre, Jardín de la Isla** and the vast, park-like **Jardín del Príncipe** make pleasant strolling.

At the eastern end of Aranjuez, standing in the 'prince's garden', is the charming **Casa del Labrador** (farmer's cottage). This little fancy of Charles IV (notice in the last room the fresco of the king coming across the tumbledown farm which provided the site) has remained unchanged since it was built in 1803 (it was never lived in, but used for banquets and other formal occasions). It is sumptuously decorated in the neo-classical style that was the rage of the day.

Back towards Aranjuez, on the river, is the **Casa de Marinos**, a boathouse where royal pleasure craft are on display.

CALZADA DE CALATRAVA
See Almagro, page 156.

CAMPO DE CRIPTANA
On the N420, 10 km E of Alcázar de San Juan, 159 km S of Madrid. A golden photo opportunity. Just as in the time of Cervantes, windmills ride across the skyline above this town with its whitewashed, blue-edged houses. The windmills date from the 15thC and once there were 36; ten remain, all with names, such as Pilón and Quimera. Inside Poyato, you find a Tourist Office with a young man named José Luis eager to answer any questions. 'These were the first mills in Spain and everybody came here to grind their grain,' he says. Three, including El Infante, have the original wooden mechanism.

Next to the windmills is Las Musas, an open-air disco.

CARMONA ⇔
On the NIV, 33 km E of Seville. You enter the town, girdled by walls, by one of the four Roman gates, some with Moorish additions. Wandering through the streets, you will come across a suc-

cession of churches, convents and fine old mansions. The tower of **San Pedro** resembles the Giralda in Seville, while Gothic **Santa María** incorporates a Moorish patio from the mosque that was formerly here.

Further east, the **church of Santa Clara** has fine coffered ceilings. On the eastern edge of the old town is the much-restored Moorish castle, now a parador, where Pedro the Cruel once made himself at home. While enjoying a drink, you can look out over fields of the treeless plain, where Scipio defeated Hasdrubal and his Carthaginians in 206 BC.

Leaving town, towards Seville, look for the sign to the **Necropolis Romana**. This remarkable burial ground, hewn from the rock, was brought to light between 1881 and 1915 by George Bonsor, a British archaeologist. Among the most interesting of the 900 graves which date back more than 2,000 years are the Elephant Tomb, which has an elephant statue, and the Servilia Tomb, an elaborate affair with a galleried patio.

CAZALLA DE LA SIERRA ⇔
See Recommended Hotels, page 160.

CIUDAD REAL
On the N401, 203 km S of Madrid. Ciudad Real, wrote Cervantes, was 'the seat of the god of smiles', but most people just find this nondescript provincial capital dull. It was founded in the 13thC by Alfonso The Wise, but few monuments remain. At least, the arrival of the high-speed train (the AVE) allows you to escape quickly to Seville or Madrid. Between trains, you can view the Mudéjar northern gate, the **Puerta de Toledo**, built 1328.

The 16thC **cathedral of Santa María del Prado** has a beautiful Baroque altarpiece by Geraldo de Merlo, while the Gothic **church of San Pedro** has two fine façades.

CONSUEGRA
And other places south and south-east of Madrid not given separate entries, see Footsteps of Don Quixote, page 154.

CORDOBA ⇔ ✕
On the NIV, 129 km NE of Seville. Tourism Offices, Torrijos, 10 (opposite the Mosque), tel. 957 47 12 35; and Plaza de

Judá Leví, Judería, tel. 957 20 05 22. Córdoba people are often said to be 'Senecaesque', suggesting that they have much in common with Seneca, the cynical, stoical philosopher who was born here in 4 BC and went to Rome to become influential in the court of Nero. If the cordobeses are cautious, they have reason to be, considering the vagaries of history. Once capital of the Roman province of Baetica, the city reached its zenith in the 10thC when Abd-ar-Rahman III declared himself Caliph of the West. For a short time, it was Europe's largest city, where, so the story goes, the fountains ran with quicksilver and there were 300 mosques. Jews, Muslims and Christians lived in harmony while crafts, trade and culture flourished. The great Islamic thinker Averroës and the Jewish philosopher-physician Maimonides were born here.

Intrigue and revolt began Córdoba's decline, accelerated when Ferdinand III conquered it in 1236. Many inhabitants fled and Christian indifference created a dull and torpid provincial city.

In recent years Córdoba, at the point where the Sierra Morena meets the fertile plain known as La Campiña, has reawakened. Ugly apartment blocks have sprung up, but the old quarter remains a fascinating labyrinth of narrow streets, white walls, and flower-decked patios. Traditional crafts such as silver and gold filigree work and embossed leather continue.

By the Guadalquivir in the old quarter stands Spain's most important legacy of Moorish rule, next to the Alhambra of Granada: **La Mezquita**, the Mosque. It is open every day. Pay at least one visit early in the morning, before the tour groups start circulating, to capture the serene atmosphere of this remarkable structure. The main entrance is on the Patio de los Naranjos, but early worshippers enter free by a side door. You penetrate a twilight forest of columns (more than 1,000 were used in the original building), supporting red-and-white arches in two tiers, unprecedented in Arab architecture.

At the end of the main aisle, Caliph Hakam II built the dazzling, richly decorated *mihrab* (prayer niche), with a ribbed dome supported by eight arches. The *mihrab* was intended to amplify the voice of the *imam* (priest) and to indicate the direction of Mecca, but this one is a little off course. The room alongside is the **maqsura,** a royal enclosure built so that those at prayer had no need to rise when the caliph entered. Abd-ar-Rahman I founded the mosque in 785, using Roman and Visigothic columns. Later rulers enlarged it, Al Mansur extending it to its present size in 987.

In the 16thC Christian fervour resulted in the mosque's centre being ripped out to accommodate a Gothic-Renaissance cathedral. On seeing the result, Charles V commented: 'You have destroyed something unique to build what could have been built anywhere.' In fact, the cathedral is sumptuous in its own right and the mosque so vast you barely notice its intrusion unless you look for it.

A **Roman bridge** crosses the river by the mosque to the **Torre de la Calahorra**, a Mudéjar tower housing a museum of Christian, Islamic and Jewish cultures. West along the river is a ruined **Moorish mill** with a colossal water wheel, featured in the city's coat of arms since 1236. The present wheel, of teak and weighing 18,000 kilos, replaces an older wheel which went up in flames in 1993. Nearby is the **Alcázar**, the palatial fortress rebuilt by the Catholic Monarchs. It has some beautiful gardens, particularly impressive when floodlit in summer.

Adjacent is the **Judería**, the old Jewish quarter. Among its souvenir shops and narrow streets you will find one of Spain's three remaining synagogues (the others are in Toledo), though there is little to see. Close by is the **Museo Taurino**, with bullfighting relics including a replica of the tomb of the local matador Manolete, killed in the Linares (Jaén) bullring in 1947. East of the mosque is the Plaza del Potro, where you find a **museum** with heavy-breathing paintings of nudes by Julio Romero de Torres and the **Posada del Potro**, an old inn mentioned by Cervantes.

The **Palacio del Marqués de Viana**, on Plaza Don Gome, 2, is a palatial mansion with 14 patios and valuable works of art. The Viana palace is closed Wednesday, the other monuments Monday, except the mosque which does not close.

Córdoba has several excellent restaurants and numerous *tapa* bars, serving Montilla, a wine similar to sherry (but cheaper) from the district south of Córdoba. An old-time favourite is the **Taberna San Miguel**, also known as El Pisto, on Plaza San Miguel, which has an inner patio and specializes in bull's tail. Bars near the mosque include La Mezquita, on Cardenal Herrero, where a favourite snack is anchovies in vinegar.

May is the liveliest time to be in Córdoba. Festivities include: the **Cruces de Mayo fiesta**, when floral crosses decorate public places; the **Festival de los Patios**, May 5-12, when patios of the old quarter are on view; the **annual fair**, between May 25 and 28, a whirl of flamenco, funfair, bullfights and other events. Montilla wine flows freely.

An essential excursion takes you to **Medina Azahara** (off the C431, 9 km W of Córdoba), a palace out of *A Thousand and One Nights* built by Abd-ar-Rahman III in the 10thC and named after his favourite wife. Thousands of eunuchs and dancing girls attended to his whims amid sumptuous surroundings. Outlined by the dark hills of the Sierra Morena, it was described by an Arab poet as 'a concubine in the arms of a black eunuch'. Not long after the Caliph's death it was sacked. Work goes on to restore some of the grandeur.

DAIMIEL, TABLAS DE

On the N430, 24 km W of Manzanares on the N IV. An EC-backed project is under way to try to save the **Parque National Tablas de Daimiel**, wetlands formed by the waters of the Guadiana and Cigüela rivers and formerly rich in birdlife. There is a visitors' centre 11 km from the village of Daimiel. Summer is not the best time to visit. Take binoculars.

DESPEÑAPERROS, DESFILADERO DE

On the N IV, 48 km S of Valdepeñas. Road and rail thread their way through this rocky pass in the Sierra Morena, a strategic point in communications between Castile and Andalucía. According to an 18thC English traveller, monkeys, parrots and married women unaccompanied by their husbands had to pay a toll. Just south of the pass, on the N1V, is **Las Navas de Tolosa**, scene of an epic battle in 1212, when Alfon-

• *Statue of Manolete, in Córdoba.*

so VIII crushed the Moors. Nearby is **La Carolina**, colonized by Flemish and German settlers 200 years ago in the reign of Charles III.

ECIJA

On the N I V, 89 km E of Seville. Eleven towers and 15 belfries pierce the blue skies over Ecija, known as the City of Towers. However, this area is also called the Frying Pan of Andalucía, because of the torrid summers when temperatures can rise to 45° C.

Although the site of early settlements, Ecija's monuments date mostly from the 18thC. Start your exploration from the Plaza Mayor. The army, which maintains horse ranches on the surrounding plain, occupies the splendid 18thC **Palacio de Benamejí**, known as La Comandancia, which you can enter to view the patio and old stables. Another palace worth viewing is that of **Peñaflor**, which has an unusual curved façade, decorated with paintings. The patio and ground floor can be visited (closed weekends).

A number of churches with ceramic-adorned belfries are in ruins. **Santiago** has a pleasant orange-tree-shaded patio and an altarpiece.

By the way, if you can say Ecija correctly, you are on the way to fluency in *castellano*. The accent falls on the first syllable: "ETH-eeha".

MADRID
See pages 170-192.

MANZANARES 🛏
See Recommended Hotels, page 160.

MONTILLA
See Córdoba, page 157.

OCAÑA
On the N1V, 59 km S of Madrid. Ocaña's prison attracts some visitors, but you may prefer to see the neo-classical **Plaza Mayor** and the **Carmelite Convent**. In the side streets of the old town you will find several potters creating traditional earthware vessels.

OSUNA
Off the A92, 86 km E of Seville. Splendid mansions grace the narrow streets of Osuna, one of Andalucía's best-preserved old towns. Philip ll created the title Duque de Osuna in 1562 and the family became immensely rich and powerful. Their pantheon is in the crypt of **the collegiate church of Asunción**, a fine example of 16thC Renaissance architecture with outstanding Mudéjar ceilings and five paintings by Ribera. Just below the church is the **Monasterio de Encarnación**, where nuns will show you religious treasures and a pleasing cloister. Houses with elaborate façades are prominent on Calle San Pedro, while above the town stands the university founded in 1549, now a secondary school.

PALMA DEL RIO 🛏
See Recommended Hotels.

PRIEGO DE CORDOBA
On the N321, 97 km SE of Córdoba. This whitewashed gem makes a worthwhile detour. It contains some splendidly extravagant Baroque churches: **La Asunción** is outstanding, especially the sacristy. Stroll past the mansions on Calle del Río to the Fuente del Rey, where more than 130 spouts gush.

PUERTO LAPICE ✕
See Recommended Restaurants, page 161.

RECOMMENDED HOTELS

ALMAGRO
Parador, PPP; *Ronda de San Francisco, 31; tel. 926 86 01 00.*
Chapels, paintings and other medieval features recall that this building was once a Franciscan monastery, dating from 1596. Local dishes are served in the former refectory.

CARMONA
Parador Alcázar del Rey Don Pedro, PPP; *tel. 954 14 10 10.*
Magnificently located in a medieval castle, with views over the plain.

CAZALLA DE LA SIERRA
Villa Turística, PP; *on the C433, 108 km NE of Seville, Ctra de Constantina, km 3.5; tel. 954 88 33 10.*
Among rolling hills covered with cork oaks in the tranquil heart of the Sierra Morena. A stone-built village complex with cooking facilities, restaurant and swimming-pool. Nearby is a semi-restored Carthusian monastery.

CORDOBA
Albucasis, PP; *Buen Pastor, 11; tel. 957 47 86 25.*
This delightful place, beautifully-converted from gold- and silversmith workshops, is handily situated in the Jewish quarter close to the mosque.

Andalucía, P; *José Zorrilla, 3; tel. 957 47 60 00.*
Comfortable one-star hotel.

González, PP; *Manríquez, 3; tel. 957 48 61 87.*
A tranquil small hotel in the old quarter with a restaurant in its patio.

MANZANARES
Parador, PP; *on the N1V, 174 km S of Madrid, Ctra N1V, km 175; tel. 926 61 04 00.*
Useful overnight stop: a modern hotel with pool; restaurant serving regional specialities.

PALMA DEL RIO
Hospedería San Francisco, PPP; *Avenida Pío XII, 35; tel. 957 71 01 83.*
A former monastery has been tastefully converted into a hotel, with a recommended restaurant in the old refectory. Hand-painted tiles and old beams lend atmosphere and the rooms are named after Californian missions – Fray Juniper Serra is believed to have stayed here before heading for the New World.

RUIDERA, LAGUNAS DE

On the N430, *52 km* E *of Manzanares.* The Lagunas, which figure in *Don Quixote,* come as a delightful surprise after travelling across the dessicated plains of La Mancha. Straddling the border between Ciudad Real and Albacete provinces, a series of lakes form a tree-fringed oasis of rivulets, streams and tumbling water, where large numbers of waterfowl find refuge. On a golden autumn morning I awoke here to the whisper of wind through the poplars, the murmur of a cascade and a chorus of birdsong. Under siege from an influx of visitors and illegal building, the Lagunas have been declared a Nature Park, which in theory should ensure protection.

SEVILLE

See pages 201-207.

TOLEDO

See Local Explorations: 7.

VALDEPEÑAS ×

Off the N1V, *200 km* S *of Madrid.* Half the wine produced in Spain comes from La Mancha, and Valdepeñas is its biggest centre. Quantity rather than quality remains a problem, but more progressive wineries are upgrading their products. Most *bodegas* welcome visitors (not weekends) if contacted in advance. A big wine festival is held in the first week of September.

The Gothic **church of Asunción's** façade features a Plateresque gallery and has a 17thC altarpiece.

Some 15 km south, off the N1V, is **Santa Cruz de Mudela**. This square bull-ring built in 1641 is claimed to be Spain's oldest. Continue 18 km southeast to **Viso del Marqués**, where – about as far away as you can get from the sea – a Renaissance palace houses the **archives of the Spanish Navy**. The building belonged to Alvaro de Bazán, one of Spain's greatest sailors. He would have commanded the Spanish Armada had he not died in February 1588, inspiring England's Sir John Hawkins to exclaim 'May God be praised.' To inspect the archives you need permission from the Navy Ministry in Madrid.

VISO DEL MARQUES

See Valdepeñas, above.

RECOMMENDED RESTAURANTS

ALMAGRO
El Corregidor, PP; *Plaza Fray Fernando Fernández de Córdoba,* 2; *926 86 06 48; credit cards* AE, DC, MC, V; *closed Mon and first week of Aug.*

Carefully restored old-world charm close to the Plaza Mayor. It offers well-prepared La Mancha dishes: try the venison stew and the beans with partridge.

CORDOBA
El Caballo Rojo, PP-PPP; *Cardenal Herrero,* 28; *tel 957 47 5375; credit cards* AE, DC, MC, V.

An avalanche of tourists sometimes provokes hiccups in this classic Córdoba restaurant, but it is still the place to try traditional dishes, especially those with Arab influence. The *Rabo de toro* (bull's tail) is famous.

El Churrasco, PP-PPP; *Romero,* 16; *tel 957 29 08 19; credit cards* AE, DC, MC, V; *closed Aug.*
An agreeable place, extremely popular with both locals and tourists. Dine in the patio and enjoy such traditional Córdoba dishes as fried eggplant with *salmorejo* (Córdoba's version of *gazpacho*).

PUERTO LAPICE
Venta del Quijote, PP; *on the* N1V, *136 km* S *of Madrid, El Molino,* 4; *tel. 926 57 61 10; credit cards* AE, DC, MC, V.

A favourite tourist lunch spot, thanks to the Quixote theme. You eat around the 18thC patio. Typical dishes and wines of La Mancha.

VALDEPEÑAS
El Tigre en el Peral, P-PP; *Ctra La Solana,* 7 *km* NE *of Valdepeñas; tel.* 926 32 50 00; *credit cards* AE, MC, V.

Surrounded by vineyards, filled with hunting trophies, this restaurant offers large portions at reasonable prices. Try lamb cutlets grilled over vine shoots. The husky owner was a wrestler, whose stage name was The Tiger.

Between Madrid and Alicante
Cuenca and Teruel

450 km; maps Michelin 444 and 445, 1:400,000

Flat and generally monotonous, La Mancha, the region south and east of Madrid, hardly tempts the traveller to linger. But, if you travel its eastern fringe, the scenery changes and you enter mountain wildernesses on the border of Cuenca and Teruel provinces. Because these are not on the main routes to the coast, they are often by-passed by visitors, which is as good a reason as any to dally.

Several imposing castles dot the plains, while Cuenca is worth a visit for its magnificent setting alone. If you detour further east towards comparatively little-visited Teruel, you pass through depopulated zones where outdoor types can revel in the clear air and vistas of crag and forest.

Approaching Alicante, the landscape alters once again and the climate grows milder. You are entering the typically Mediterranean coastal belt, seat of ancient cultures, where vast plantations of citrus fruit flourish in the sub-tropical climate. The food in Alicante and Valencia provinces is mainly rice-based dishes. In the interior you can eat game, roast lamb, trout, the *anise* of Chinchón and such unusual specialities as the *zarajos* of Cuenca (see page 167).

With your own transport, sticking to the N111 and N430, it is easy enough to cover the Madrid-Alicante journey in less than a day. However you will get much more out of it if you deviate to Cuenca for at least half a day. If you include the Teruel detour, count on three days.

DEVIL DANCERS AND HUMAN WALLS

If you are in Cuenca province around the Day of San Blas, at the beginning of February, head for **Almonacid del Marquesado** (on the CU312, off the N111, 33 km SE of Tarancón) to see the **devil dancers**. The 'devils', in baggy trousers with sheep-bells jangling at their waists, dance before the parish church altar and accompany the images of the Virgin and San Blas in procession. After many hours of this ritual, some may fall into a trance.

Another unusual fiesta takes place on December 7 and 8, at **Horcajo de Santiago** (20 km south of Tarancón, on the C302) where an annual battle accompanies the festivities of the Immaculate Conception. As the Virgin's standard is being carried out of the church, one group tries to retain it and another to remove it, the struggle lasting several hours and reaching such intensity that local priests have declined to participate. Finally, Knights of the Blessed Virgin take the standard and parade it through the streets. When they return to the church, another human wall attempts to prevent them entering with the standard.

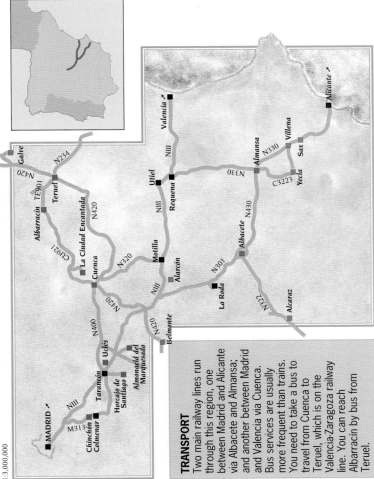

1:3,000,000

TRANSPORT

Two main railway lines run through this region, one between Madrid and Alicante via Albacete and Almansa; and another between Madrid and Valencia via Cuenca. Bus services are usually more frequent than trains. You need to take a bus to travel from Cuenca to Teruel, which is on the Valencia-Zaragoza railway line. You can reach Albarracin by bus from Teruel.

SIGHTS & PLACES OF INTEREST

ALARCON ⚓

Off the N111, 83 km S of Cuenca. A narrow land bridge is the only access to this strikingly situated hamlet and castle in a bend of the Júcar gorge. A Visigoth prince named Alarico is said to have ejected the Romans and given the place its name. In 1184 it was the Moors' turn to be kicked out. The fortifications were strengthened by the Knights of Santiago and later they passed to the Marqués de Villena, an all-powerful 15thC potentate. The castle is now a parador.

ALCARAZ

On the N322, 79 km SW of Albacete. From the highway you see the silhouette of Alcaraz's castle walls and the twin steeples of the Sanctuary of Nuestra Señora de Cortés. It is worth investigating this pleasant town with handsome buildings.

At one end of town stand the ruins of a Gothic church. A number of houses parade beautiful façades, but the high point is the splendid **plaza**, flanked by the 16thC Town Hall. Some of the finer structures were designed by Andrés de Vandaelvira, whose most outstanding work can be seen in Baeza and Ubeda (pages 297 and 299).

ALBACETE ✕

On the N322, 72 km W of Almansa. Tourism Office, Tinte 2-edificio Posada del Rosario; tel. 967 58 05 22. Until its soccer team produced some giant-killing performances (see this page), all anybody could recall about Albacete was that it produced Spain's finest knives. Squatting on the monotonous flatlands of La Mancha, the city's undistinguished architecture has a uniform dullness, reflected even in the name (Albacete comes from the Arab *Al Basit*, meaning the plain).

Wickedly sharp **tools and weapons**, for use or for decoration, are on sale at reasonable prices: you can buy them at several shops not far from the 16thC **cathedral**. The **Museo Arqueológico** in the pleasant Abelardo Sánchez Park has Roman mosaics and relics from Iberian settlements.

Albacete's **Plaza de Toros** was the scene of tragedy in 1981. When a man leaped from the crowd and tried to play the bull, the matador El Cordobés

---

POSSIBLE GOAL

In 1991 the Albacete football team, which had never won a trophy in its whole career, achieved the impossible by gaining promotion to Spain's premier league. The whole population (125,000) shared in the glory and the euphoria has still to subside. The team has managed to hold its own against such giants as Real Madrid and Barcelona.

---

allowed him to continue: he had started his career the same way. But the bull hooked an artery and the amateur bled to death before the eyes of the horrified spectators. El Cordobés was so shaken that he quit bullfighting.

For snacks, try a traditional meeting place, the **Café Milán**, at No. 4 on Paseo de la Libertad.

Twice a year a curious *romería* (pilgrimage) takes place at **Peñas de San Pedro**, 33 km south of Albacete on the C3211. On the Monday of Pentecost, an image of Christ, the Cristo del Sahuco, is placed in a wooden coffin and carried at the run for 15 km to a sanctuary. Hundreds of young men and women, dressed in white with red sashes, compete to carry the image, urged on by crowds along the route. Near the sanctuary Christ is removed from his box and meets the Virgin, who is brought out of her chapel for the emotional encounter. On August 28 Christ is returned to his home chapel.

ALICANTE

See Spain Overall: 9.

ALMANSA ✕

On the N430, 79 km NW of Alicante. Jutting above the surrounding plain, Almansa's **castle** breathes invulnerability and arrogance from its limestone pinnacle. The Knights Templar occupied the fortifications, but most of the present structure was built in the 15thC. Its daunting appearance no doubt put off attackers and the only significant siege occurred in 1475, by Queen Isabel. Plague broke out among the defenders and the castle fell.

Close to the walls of the castle, on Plaza Asunción, is the **Casa Grande**, an ancient mansion with a finely-carved façade and galleried courtyard. Here, it is said, the Duke of Berwick planned strategy with his generals in 1707 before a battle in the War of the Spanish Succession, which led to the Bourbons acquiring the Spanish throne. Berwick's 9,000 cavalry thundered across the Almansa plain to rout the army of Henri de Ruvigny. The Duke led a force of French and Castilians, while under the French general's command were English, Dutch, Catalans, Germans, Huguenots and Portuguese. Confusing, but it was a famous victory.

BELMONTE

On the N420, 100 km SW of Cuenca. In the 15thC, the mighty Marqués de Villena ruled supreme around here. He built the imposing castle, in which the **Mudéjar coffered ceilings** are worth study. Juana la Beltraneja took refuge in the castle during a bitter dispute (involving the crowns of Aragón, Castile and Portugal) with her aunt, Isabel, later known as Queen Isabel the Catholic, conqueror of Granada.

Villena also built the **collegiate church**, which contains his tomb. The choir stalls, which illustrate Bible scenes, were originally in Cuenca's cathedral. Fray Luis de León, the 16thC theologian who taught at Salamanca University (see Spain Overall: 4) came from Belmonte and was baptized here.

CHINCHON ⌂

On the M313/404, 54 km SE of Madrid. Chinchón's picturesque appeal and its proximity to Madrid means that packs of sightseers are regularly disgorged from tour buses, while at weekends the little village is overrun by *madrileños* intent on lunch in one of the many restaurants. Tourists apart, the circular **Plaza Mayor** is a fine sight, with its two tiers of wooden balconies supported on stone columns. These balconies are rented out to spectators at the occasional bullfight or summer concert which takes place in the plaza.

RECOMMENDED HOTELS

ALARCON
Parador Marqués de Villena, PPP; *Avda Amigo de los Castillos; tel. 969 33 03 15.*
  Guarded by a gorge and mighty ramparts, you should sleep securely in this state-run hotel converted from a medieval castle. The magnificent banqueting hall serves local specialities.

ALBARRACIN
Albarracín, PPP; *tel. 978 71 00 11.*
Seigneurial mansion of stone and timber with swimming-pool and fine views over the valley. Regional dishes in the restaurant.

Arabia, PP; *Bernardo Zapater, 2; tel. 978 71 02 12.*
  Located in a restored 300-year-old building. Comfortable and friendly.

CHINCHON
Parador de Chinchón, PPP; *Avda Generalisimo 1; tel. 918 94 08 36.*
  In the village, close to the Plaza Mayor. One of the more luxurious paradors with a charming, peaceful internal courtyard made from an arcaded, glazed-in cloister – the building was a monastery. There's a blue tiled *taberna* and an expensive restaurant serving French dishes.

CUENCA
A new parador (**PPP**; *tel. 969 23 23 20*), has been installed at enormous cost in the 16thC San Pablo Convent, just below the Casas Colgadas. By comparison, these hotels in the old quarter are bargains:

Leonor de Aquitania, PP; *San Pedro, 60; tel. 969 23 10 00.*
  Behind the façade of an old palace is this modern three-star hotel, tastefully decorated, with a large tapestry in the foyer and antique furnishings. The restaurant serves regional dishes.

Posada de San José, P-PP; *Julián Romero, 4; tel. 969 21 13 00.*
  A creaky 16thC house hanging on the edge of the chasm, with enough character to let you forget the threadbare carpets.

TERUEL
Parador de Teruel, PP; *Apartado, 67; tel. 978 60 18 00.*
  A modern building in a peaceful part of town with a restaurant of respectable quality.

• *The hanging houses of Cuenca.*

DETOUR – **TERUEL PROVINCE**
Removed from the usual tourist trails, Teruel province (part of the Aragón region) offers a view of pre-industrial Spain, with unspoiled villages and uninhabited mountain areas, ideal for hiking or biking, as well as hunting and fishing. It includes part of the Maestrazgo region (for details see Spain Overall: 8).

An attractive approach from Cuenca is via the CU921, on narrow roads with light traffic or none at all. You pass through largely uninhabited country, following the Júcar Valley first north, then east, and climbing through the rugged **Serrania de Cuenca**, passing over the Puerto de El Cubillo, 1,620 m high, to enter the pine forests of the Montes Universales of Teruel province.

Off the TE903 you find the **source of the Río Tajo** or Tagus, which flows across northern Spain to the Atlantic coast of Portugal. A fancy monument marks the spot, but graffiti artists have been at work on the rusting metal sculptures.

Albarracín (below) lies 35 km to the north-east, reached through a narrow gorge with a trout stream gushing through.

Albarracín 🛏
On the TE903, 39 km W of Teruel. If you only have time for one medieval town, red-hued Albarracín will be ideal.

Spilling picturesquely down a hillside, it offers old walls, a handsome porticoed plaza, coats of arms, wooden balconies, eccentric houses leaning over steep, narrow streets, plus a 16thC Renaissance **cathedral** with a collection of Flemish tapestries. The only problem, a common one in these showplace towns, is that there is a singular lack of life in the cobbled streets, except when avalanches of visitors descend and slumbering bars and shops spring open for business. Twice in its long history, the town was independent, first as capital of the fiefdom of the Aben Razin dynasty in the 11thC, then in the 13thC when its rulers briefly resisted the dominance of the king of Aragón. In the 17thC, Albarracín and district were important for woollen goods, timber and iron-work. La Taberna in the Plaza Mayor is a pleasant spot for drinks and *tapas.*

Teruel 🛏 ✕
On the N234, 181 km SW of Zaragoza. Tourism Office, Tomás Nogués, 1; tel. 978 60 22 79. The small provincial capital, surrounded by ravines and eroded heights, is particularly rich in Mudéjar architecture, a legacy of the skilled Moorish craftsmen who lived here until their disastrous expulsion from Spain in the early 17thC.

Notorious as one of the coldest places in Spain, Teruel was the scene of one of the Civil War's bitterest battles during the murderous winter of 1937-38.

Begin at the **Plaza del Torico**, in which stands a tiny **statue of a bull**. It recalls an incident when Alfonso I of Aragón's attack on Teruel was blocked by stampeding bulls. In a country of grandiose monuments, the Torico is highly understated, but it suits Teruel, which is an understated sort of place. Of course, you can buy clay models of the bull as souvenirs.

Four **Mudéjar towers** displaying marvellous brickwork and multi-coloured tiles rise above the city. Two brothers, competing for the hand of the same damsel, are credited with building the two finest towers, that of San Martín and Salvador, in the 13thC. More Moorish art crowns

Teruel's **cathedral**, which has a magnificent *artesonado* (coffered) ceiling, intricately carved and painted.

Near the former Jewish quarter is the **church of San Pedro**, which also has a Mudéjar tower and, in a separate chapel alongside, the alabaster **tomb of the Lovers of Teruel** (small entry fee). According to legend, in the early 13thC an impoverished young man named Juan Diego and the teenage Isabel de Segura fell in love. Her family were against the match, the father insisting that he make his fortune first. Off he went to war. When he returned he found that Isabel was to marry someone else that day. He visited her and asked for a kiss. When she refused, he died of grief. At his funeral Isabel approached his coffin, gave her lover the kiss she had denied him in life and fell dead. In 1555 two bodies were discovered and a document relating this story. The theme has attracted many writers and artists and Juan de Ávalos sculpted the recumbent statues, under which you can glimpse two mummified figures.

An interesting excursion from Teruel takes you to the remote hamlet of **Galve** (off the N420, 60 km north-east, via Perales del Alfambra), where prehistoric remains of mammals, reptiles, fish and birds, some of species previously unknown, have been discovered by amateur archaeologist José María Herrero and his family.

If you arrive here late on a stormy evening, as I did, it is easy to imagine dinosaurs wandering about the eerily bleak landscape. In Galve, through which trucks rumble loaded with clay, a well-lit **museum** displays some of José's finds, including a dinosaur's 134-kg femur. Monsters up to 8 m long tramped the area when it was swamp some 150 million years ago. Signs point down a track to a slab of rock where their fossilized footprints can clearly be seen. If you show interest, José will be delighted to tell you more. (For dinosaurs, see also Spain Overall: 5).

Beyond the plaza you can see the church; Goya's brother was the village priest. All around the plaza are little food shops, bars and restaurants specializing in hearty Castilian fare. **Mesón de la Virreina** (No. 21), its bar hung with hams, is one of the best known. Close by is a bakery, its oven visible at the back, selling bread in fancy shapes.

CUENCA 🛏 ✕

On the N400, 167 km SE of Madrid. Cuenca's old quarter is splendidly situated on a narrow beak of rock separating the Júcar and Huécar rivers. Cliffs surround it on three sides, with the less interesting modern town far below. In case you haven't noticed, a brochure stresses: 'This has been officially declared a Picturesque Spot.'

Cuenca, with only 40,000 inhabitants, is a useful centre for exploring its province, which forms the eastern boundary of La Mancha and varies from broad, empty plains to spectacularly craggy sierras, thickly wooded and threaded with trout streams.

Conca, as the Romans called it, has had its ups and downs. A Moorish ruler of Seville gave it as a dowry when his daughter Zaida married Alfonso VI of León and Castile. The town rebelled and to subdue it there was nine-month siege in 1177. Cuenca prospered from the wool trade in the Middle Ages, but the French sacked it three times in the Napoleonic Wars and it was sacked again in the Second Carlist War. The Civil War brought more plundering and 10,000 priceless volumes from the cathedral library went up in flames.

Follow the signs for the old quarter (Barrio Antiguo), although you will surely get lost. But don't worry: eventually you end up in the cathedral square, near which there is parking. The best way to tackle Cuenca is to wander about soaking up the medieval atmosphere. The **Casas Colgadas** (Hanging Houses), balancing on the precipice edge, are the outstanding sight. Three of these accommodate the **Spanish Abstract Art Museum**, which exhibits works by leading contemporary artists including Chillida, Guerrero, Saura, Tapiés and Zóbel. Built of pine and plaster, reinforced with stone, the houses date back at least 500 years although their balconies are a 1927 addition.

DETOUR – **LA CIUDAD ENCANTADA**
You should find time for this attractive expedition from Cuenca along the poplar-lined **River Júcar** to the pine-forests around the **Ciudad Encantada** (Enchanted City), off the CU921, 35 km north-east of Cuenca. On the way you can stop at the **Ventano del Diablo** (Devil's Window) to inspect the river's imposing cliffs and gorge. The Ciudad Encantada (entry fee, open daily 9.30 am until sundown) is an area of strangely-eroded rocks, most eerily impressive at twilight or when a mist swirls around them. It takes about an hour to stroll around the formations, which somebody with a well-developed imagination has given such names as The Bear, Roman Arch and so on. A bar near the entrance serves refreshments.

On the square opposite the Hanging Houses is the **Museo Provincial**, which has an interesting collection of archaeological discoveries.

Pass through the archway by the Hanging Houses and descend the narrow road to the footbridge, dizzily spanning the gorge, for the best views. The 40 m-high iron bridge leads to the San Pablo Convent, now a parador.

The **cathedral**, of solid Gothic construction with Anglo-Norman touches, has suffered from tinkering by later architects. Of particular interest are the Knights' Chapel, with delicately carved tombs, a Byzantine diptych and two paintings by El Greco in the treasury, the tombs of the Hurtado de Mendoza family (once immensely powerful and viceroys of Chile and Peru), and the east chapel's beautiful coffered ceiling.

Near the cathedral are several bars serving snacks. You should definitely try *zarajos*. They look like golf ball innards: in fact, they are lamb's tripe cut in strips, twisted about vine twigs and baked. They go well with *vino de la sierra*, a strong red wine. Also worth trying is *alajú*, a mouth-watering confection of breadcrumbs, honey and almonds.

In the noisy, beamed Bar La Tinaja, you can entertain yourself with, or be enraged by, the rhyming wall plaques, such as 'Women and sardines belong in the kitchen'; 'The best milk in the world is from a woman/You know that just by looking at the container'.

Cuenca's **Santa Semana** (Easter Week) features impressive processions and a series of concerts of religious music performed by musicians of repute. For four days around September 21, San Mateo is honoured and the ousting of the Moors is celebrated. On two days, young cows career through the streets, hooking at those who dare challenge them.

CUIDAD ENCANTADA, LA
See left.

GALVE
See Teruel, page 166.

REQUENA
On the N111, 70 *km* W *of Valencia.* Requena, unimpressive on first sight, has some fine old mansions and several medieval churches, including that of Santa María and El Salvador. The Utiel-Requena area has one of Spain's biggest grape harvests and its *rosé (rosado)* wines are gaining in reputation. A **wine harvest fiesta** is celebrated at the end of August.

SAX ✕
Off the N330, 46 *km* NW *of Alicante.* This small agricultural town sits below a crag crowned theatrically by the ruins of a Moorish fortress. One of the towers is Roman. Sax's **Museo del Traje** exhibits costumes worn during the annual Moors v Christians fiesta in the first week of February (open at weekends or contact the Town Hall).

TARANCON
On the N111, 80 *km* SE *of Madrid.* There is not much to detain you here, unless you want to see the Gothic **church**, with its outstanding altar screen.

However, 15 km to the east (turn left off the N111 on to the CU120) is the **Monasterio de Uclés**, called the Escorial of La Mancha, because its architect Francisco de Mora was a disciple of Herrera, who designed the Escorial. The church has tombs from the 15th and 16thC including that of the Infanta Doña Uraca and the poet Jorge Manrique.

Further along the N111, turn right to reach the **Roman ruins of Segóbriga** (on the CU304, 26 km SE of Tarancón). There is a small museum.

UCLES
See Tarancón, page 168.

UTIEL
See Requena, page 168.

VALENCIA
See Spain Overall: 8.

VILLENA
On the N330, 57 km NW of Alicante. Moslem and Christian elements form the **Atalaya**, a castle with a square keep known as the Torre del Homenaje which was embellished in the 15thC with a series of circular turrets. The town's **Museo Arqueológico**, on Plaza Santiago, has an interesting collection of Bronze-Age silver and gold articles. Look for the twisted columns in the 16thC **church of Santiago**.

Some 7 km from Villena lies the well-preserved **Biar Castle**, which was seized from the Moors by James I of Aragón in 1245. It has vast dungeons and a triple ring of fortifications.

YECLA
On the C3314, 22 km W of Villena. This town, in the northern corner of Murcia province, is best known for wine production and furniture manufacture. The **church of San Francisco,** badly damaged in the Civil War, has one of the life-like images characteristic of Murcia sculptor Salzillo. The **Ayuntamiento**, once the Marqués de Villena's residence, is distinguished by a Mudéjar roof and a Renaissance façade.

In the **Museo Arqueológico** sculptures and other artefacts are displayed from the Bronze Age and from an Iberian town which existed in the 4thC BC in the hills to the north-west. Yecla celebrates the **fiesta of the Immaculate Conception** on and around December 8 in spectacular style. Deafening shotgun blasts accompany the progress of the Virgin from her castle sanctuary to the parish church. Public fervour reaches a climax on the Sunday of the fiesta when the image is returned to her temple.

RECOMMENDED RESTAURANTS

ALBACETE
Nuestro Bar, PP; *Alcalde Conangla,* 102; *tel.* 967 24 33 73; *credit cards* AE, DC, MC, V; *closed Sun eve and Jul.*

There is a special menu featuring traditional dishes of the region. The prices are very reasonable.

ALMANSA
Pincelín, PP; *Las Norias,* 10; *tel.* 967 34 00 07; *credit cards* AE, DC, MC, V; *closed Sun eve, Mon, mid-Jul to Aug 6, Holy Week.*

An oasis in a culinary desert. It can be noisy, but the service is efficient. Apart from fresh fish, you should try the *gazpacho* La Mancha-style, the rice with rabbit, snails and chicken, and the home-made desserts.

CUENCA
Casas Colgadas, PP; *Canónigos, s/n;* *tel.* 969 22 35 09; *credit cards* AE, DC, MC, V; *closed Tues eve.*

Living dangerously can be expensive: this timber-and-stone restaurant, teetering on the edge of the gorge, has a stupendous view and somewhat giddy prices. A good place to try such Cuenca specialities as *morteruelo* (a hot paté of minced pork liver, chicken, hare and other ingredients) and *resolí*, a liqueur.

SAX
La Bodega de Don Gil, PP; *Casa Los Giles, Colonia Santa Eulalia; tel.* 965 80 00 21; *credit cards* MC, V; *closed Mon and eves, except for reservations Fri and Sat.*

Roast lamb and pork are the specialities in this restaurant in a 200-year-old wine cellar. An extensive wine list.

TERUEL
Ovalo, PP; *Paseo del Ovalo,* 2; *tel.* 978 60 98 62; *credit cards* AE, DC, MC, V; *closed Mon, Jan 8-28.*

Luis and Teresa, the generously proportioned owners, guarantee a substantial meal in this efficiently run restaurant. Recommended: venison stew or *Jarretes de ternazo con setas* (lamb hocks with mushrooms).

Madrid:
introduction

To the occasional visitor, Madrid has two great assets: its paintings and its vitality. The former, housed principally in the Prado, but in several other great museums as well, are alone worth the journey. Then, after a day in the serious pursuit of art – or business, or shopping or whatever – night comes along and you can change gear completely: Madrid is made for night birds. And should you care to look, there is much more of interest besides, as this section will reveal.

Madrid lies at the centre of the Iberian peninsula, at 650 m the highest capital in Europe. Surrounded by the great Castilian plain, it is sheltered to the north by the Sierra de Guadarrama, whose snow-capped peaks may be glimpsed from several vantage points. The city can be bitter in winter, scorching in summer; the main streets teem with people and the traffic is choking. The need to escape is integral to a *madrileño's* existence: weekends see a huge exodus to the surrounding countryside and in August the place empties, with many museums and offices shut completely.

Madrid did not grow naturally to eminence as do most great cities. Philip ll decided that it should be the nation's capital a mere five centuries ago, making it Europe's youngest. Perhaps this – together with the Spanish character – explains the devil-may-care air of frivolity which has been in evidence ever since.

After a long fallow period, Madrid has once again become a major international centre with a thriving business community, as witnessed by the rows of glinting high-rises which march northwards from the centre. Yet Madrid remains essentially Spanish. Visitors and residents from overseas find themselves with little choice but to adjust their body clocks to suit the sleep-defying *madrileño* day: breakfast on coffee and *churros*; work from 8 am until lunchtime; break for a leisurely lunch – many still go home for the main meal of the day and a *siesta*; work again from 4 pm until evening, perhaps pausing for *merienda* (tea); then out to the cafés and bars, perhaps for an extended *tapas* crawl. Dinner is never started before 10 pm and the streets, the bars and the discos are thronged until dawn.

• *Cervantes.*

Sundays are for strolling in the parks and plazas, visiting the Rastro flea market or lunching *en famille* in the countryside. Visitors should set aside Monday for shopping because most museums are closed. Above all, catch up on sleep before arriving.

USING THIS SECTION

The most important sights of Madrid – major museums, galleries and so on – are covered in detail in the alphabetical gazetteer of Sights & Places of Interest starting on page 185, together with some further sights and districts.

Once the great art museums of Madrid have been accomplished, your list of sightseeing 'musts' quickly runs dry. Thereafter, the history, architecture and all-important atmosphere of the city is best discovered on foot, so we offer you four walks which together cover many of Madrid's most interesting features, including the nightlife. As with all the itineraries in this guide, you don't have to follow them at all. The information can just as well be absorbed at a café table; and of course, the hotel and restaurant recommendations, pages 188-190, can also be consulted as and when needed.

ARRIVING

Madrid's Barajas Airport is 12 km east of the city. A frequent (every 15 min-

> ### EXCURSIONS FROM THE CAPITAL
>
> For sights and places of interest within easy reach of Madrid, and usually visited from the capital, see especially Local Explorations: 7 (Around Madrid), and don't overlook Local Explorations: 8. Spain Overall: 4 and 5 also have several interesting entries close to the capital.

utes between 5.40 am and 2 am) and very inexpensive bus service leaves from right outside the main exit and takes about 20 minutes to Plaza Colón. From this subterranean terminus (watch your belongings) you'll probably want to take a taxi to your hotel. A taxi from the airport to the city should cost around 2,500 pesetas. For flight and airport information, call 91 393 60 00. If you come by train, you will arrive at one of three stations: the recently glamourized iron-and-steel **Atocha** (serving the south and east); **Chamartín** (serving the north); and **Norte** (which handles mainly local traffic). Taxis, buses or metro are available from all three. RENFE is the state-owned rail company: tickets can of course be purchased from these stations; they also have information counters; tickets and information also at the main ticket office, Calle Alcalá, 44.

Arriving by bus, you will probably find yourself at either **Estación del Sur** (Canarias 17) or **Auto-Rés Estación** (Plaza Conde de Casal 6). Money is well spent on a taxi to escape from either of these busy places.

Useful telephone numbers: visitor information is available from these Tourism Offices: Plaza España, 91 541 23 25; Barajas Airport, 91 305 86 56; Chamartin Station, 91 315 99 76; Duque de Medinaceli 2, 91 429 49 51.

PUBLIC TRANSPORT
The metro is fast, efficient, cheap and relatively safe. As in Paris, each line is given a different colour, and named by its final destination. One flat-fare ticket enables you to travel anywhere on the network, but it is best to buy a *billete de diez*, allowing ten trips for much less than ten single tickets would cost. A digital clock shows how long ago the last train left, and a poster on the wall tells you how many minutes it should be between trains at that time of day.

Madrid's red buses are also cheap to ride on, and plentiful. Either pay the driver the flat fare for a single ride, or buy a ten-ride ticket called a *bonobus* at EMT kiosks on Plaza de la Cibeles or Puerta del Sol (where route maps are also available). If you have a *bonobus* ticket, you must endorse it by inserting it in the punch machine near the driver. Each bus stop (named for the streets they are on) displays a route line for the

buses which stop there, showing all the stops. Buses are numbered, except for the one called 'Circular'.

Taxis can be hailed in the street: watch for the *libre* sign during the day, the green roof light at night. Make sure the fare is decided by the meter and that the meter is set correctly at the start of the journey. The numerous supplements which may apply should be posted in the cab. To order a taxi, telephone 91 445 32 81 or 91 447 32 32.

ACCOMMODATION GUIDELINES
Madrid is not a city noted for charming or inexpensive accommodation. There are none of the gem-like 'private house' hotels of Florence, Venice, Paris or London. It is generally a choice between the luxurious and outrageously expensive, the soulless and merely expensive or the scruffy and cheap. Having said that, there are plenty of perfectly acceptable hotels in each price bracket (see page 188) and one or two notable ones (in particular, the Ritz, one of the world's great hotels).

Hotels are not confined to particular areas (except the centre) but are scattered across the city. You will find hotel booking services at the airport and at Chamartín Station.

La Brujula agency will also find you a room for a very modest service charge and can book rooms and tours countrywide. Contact them at 6th floor, Torre de Madrid, Plaza de España; tel. 91 248 97 05.

NEIGHBOURHOODS TO AVOID
At any time: vicinity of Calle de la Ballesta and around Plaza de Tirso Molina.

At night: Plaza de Santa Ana; the area between Puerta del Sol and Gran Vía; and around Plaza Dos de Mayo, north of Gran Vía.

Women may be harrassed when wandering Sor Angela de la Cruz and Capitán Haya streets in the area of Hotel Meliá Castilla, northern Madrid, a notorious red light district. Leave all documents and valuables in the hotel safe before wandering Madrid's streets. Especially at night, leave handbags in the hotel. Cash-hungry drug addicts often work in pairs: one asks you for a light while the other cuts your handbag strap.

Madrid's Historic Heart

Orientation The municipality of Madrid covers some 375 square kilometres, but its focus of interest is usefully contained within a small chunk at the heart of the city. You will find most of what you want to see, including the major museums and the oldest (Habsburg and Bourbon) quarters, in the area bounded to the east by the Parque del Retiro and to the west by the Palacio Real and its gardens, Campo del Moro. Right in the middle is the city's hub, Puerta del Sol: you will keep coming back to it.

Another important aid to orientation is the main north-south drag, Paseo de la Castellana, becoming Paseo de Recoletos, then Paseo del Prado. Being Madrid, this is no mere traffic conduit, but an essential ingredient in the city's *joie de vivre*. From the centre, it leads north to Chamartín railway station and the gleaming, multiplying high-rise blocks of the business district.

All four walks on pages 173-185 are set within the centre (*centro*), and radiate from Puerta del Sol. The first two, starting respectively on pages 174 and 177, are devised as a figure of eight, so you can tackle them as one longer walk or two short ones. *To do the first two walks as one figure of eight route, follow the italicized instructions.*

Remember, when you are planning your time, that the walking routes pass sights which you may wish to spend several hours visiting. They also give you advice on **shopping**, so decide in advance what to include on the walk and what to leave for a separate visit.

By the way, if it is sunny the Plaza Mayor makes a great place for leisurely consulting guidebooks over a cup of coffee or a beer.

Unless you are making prolonged stops, each walk should take a morning or afternoon to accomplish. If you do them all, your feet may be sore, but Madrid will be a mystery no longer.

AROUND PLAZA MAYOR

This walk covers the oldest part of Madrid, **La Cuidad Antigua**, which lies to the south and west of Plaza Mayor.

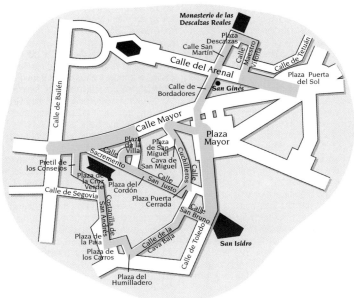

173

Start In Puerta del Sol. Geographical centre of Madrid, **Puerta del Sol** is also regarded as the centre of Spain, which it almost is. All roads radiating from Madrid are measured from here: you can see the *kilométrico 0* plaque set in the pavement outside the Communidad de Madrid building. A wide, recently reorganized urban space besieged by ten oncoming streets, its other noteworthy features are the statue of the bear guzzling fruit from a strawberry tree, Madrid's emblem, and **La Mallorquín**, the famous tearoom/pastry shop. Battle your way through the apparently starving crowds in the shop – especially in the morning and during afternoon tea (*merienda*) – and shout 'un neopolitana'. You will be rewarded with a delicious custard pastry.

May 2, 1808 saw bloodshed in Puerta del Sol when desperate *madrileños* clashed hopelessly with their French occupiers. The events were memorably captured by Goya in his famous *Dos de Mayo* and *Tres de Mayo* paintings in the Prado. Later, in 1870, Italian writer Edmondo de Amicis described Puerta del Sol as '...a mingling of *salon*, promenade, academy, theatre, garden, a square of arms and a market.' The rigours of modern life may have diminished the effect, and the outdoor cafés have all gone, but this is still a natural meeting place and the city's heart.

Leave by Arenal to the right of La Mallorquín. Take the first right, Plaza de Celenque. On the corner of Tetuán notice **Maty**, where you can buy children's flamenco dresses and matador outfits – and you can kit yourself out at the same time. Carry on up the Maestro Vitoria past **El Corte Inglés**, a rambling branch of Madrid's best department store chain (Galerías Preciados are the rivals); excellent foodstore in the basement. Turn left into Plaza Descalzas. On the right is the **Monasterio de las Descalzas Reales**; a visit here is highly recommended, so note the opening hours (see page 12).

With the monastery behind you, walk downhill along the San Martín. On the left, you may spot your first evidence of two of the capital's great gastronomic loves displayed in the window of a restaurant/*marisquería*: perfect little skinned piglets dangling alongside great gaping fish. Roast sucking pig is a Madrid speciality, as are fish and shellfish, despite the fact that Madrid is far from the sea. Reaching Arenal notice, on the opposite corner, the charming **church of San Ginés**, one of the city's oldest parishes. What you see was built in 1645, during the reign of Felipe IV, but much restored over the years. The playwright Lope de Vega, whose home you can visit on the Carrera San Jerónimo walk, page 180 was married here. Next door is **Joy Eslava**, a large, well-known disco in a converted theatre. Round the corner, in Paseo San Ginés, is the **Chocolatería San Ginés** which serves hot chocolate and *churros* through the night.

More tempting sights and smells emanate from fish restaurants and *tapas* bars along Bordadores. Here also is **Asidra**, which sells religious objects. Across Mayor, **Plaza Mayor** can be glimpsed through one of its eight arched entrances ahead. Like Puerta del Sol, Plaza Mayor's importance in the life of the city has never waned. Harmonious, almost beautiful, its enclosing tiered and arcaded buildings, red-painted, white-shuttered and mostly uniform in height, are embellished by the Casa de la Panadería on the north side. Decorated in allegorical murals (a recent addition – it used to be white) with turrets designed by the great Habsburg architect Juan de Herrera (of Escorial fame), it was from here that the royal family watched the various spectacles for which Plaza Mayor has always been renowned. It might have been a pageant, a bullfight, an execution (beheading on the north side, hanging on the south) or an *auto-de-fé*, a speciality of the Inquisition which involved the trial, torture and killing of heretics. Nowadays it's more likely to be a pop concert, a play or a happening during the **Fiesta de San Isidro** (Madrid's patron saint) in May. During quiet times, *madrileños* tend not to congregate here, but tourists find the cafés and outdoor tables in the peaceful square alluring, beggars being the only irritant. The equestrian statue in the centre is of Philip III, in whose reign the square was constructed (1619). On the south side there is a small **Tourist Office**, (tel.91 429 49 51). Every Sunday morning a stamp market is held in the plaza.

After a pause, take the north-west exit into the Plaza San Miguel with its attractive iron, glass and ceramic tiled

market – **mercado San Miguel**. Most food shopping is done in Madrid's covered markets, also great places to exchange news and gossip. This one is typical, with wonderful displays of top quality fresh produce (open mornings). Now take the **Cava San Miguel** which curves round to the right past a corner building with finely ornamented windows. On the left are the dark little *tascas* (*tapas* bars) known as **cuevas** for the way they are set right into the curved retaining wall of the arcades.

Beyond this strangely bulging arc of buildings the steep steps of the **Arco de Cuchilleros** (knife-grinders' arch) lead back to Plaza Mayor. Carry on along **Cuchilleros** – you can feel that you are in the city's core, the *ciudad antigua,* around here. There are tiny old-fashioned shops, such as the one selling dried fruits and boiled sweets, and the antedeluvian radio shop next door.

• B*arbers shop,* M*adrid.*

There's a shop selling straw and cane work, a guitar shop, a traditional barber's, a brick-lined Mesón de Cerveza, and the famous restaurant **Botín** (see Recommended Restaurants, page 190). There is also **El Gourmet de Cuchilleros**, a good delicatessen: saffron, smoked fish, olives and so on. A marble cross marks the little square called Puerta Cerrada ('closed gate'), once an entrance into the town and a market place. Look back down Latoneros to see one of Madrid's splendid tile bars, **Casa Antonio**. You may be daunted at the thought of going in: these local bars, filled with regulars, can be intimidating for tourists. More welcoming is **Casa Paco**, another old favourite (see Recommended Restaurants, page190). Leave Puerta Cerrada by San Justo, lined by buildings with attractive wrought iron balconies. In the **church of San Miguel**, with its imposing curved Baroque façade (it was designed by Italians) one is aware, as so often in Catholic churches, of the contrast between the lavish, overwrought interior, and the silence and contemplation of the worshippers, housewives and shoppers taking stock before carrying on with the day.

Continue through Plaza Cordón along Sacramento, passing the lovely façade of the Casa de Cisneros, (see below) a rare example of Madrid Plateresque (late Gothic) decoration. Ahead, the grey and white dome floating above the roof tops makes Almudena Cathedral look more promising than it is. Beyond the refreshing modern fountain – or rather water sculpture – head diagonally across the concrete space above the underground car park, and so through the arch into **Plaza de la Villa**. This small-scale, harmonious square, with architectural elements from the Middle Ages, the Renaissance and the Baroque, has always been the seat of city government. The charming **Ayuntamiento** (City Hall) contains Goya's *Allegory of Madrid* and the pretty Patio de Cristales (open Mon-Fri 9 am-2 pm). To the south is the rear façade of **Casa de Cisneros**, official residence of the mayor, dating from 1537. To the east, the **Torre de los Lujanos**, dating from the 15thC, is one of Madrid's oldest buildings. The chap in the middle was the hero of the great sea battle of Lepanto, 1571.

Now turn left into Mayor. Opposite Pretil de los Consejos is No. 88, from where, in 1906, a bomb disguised in a bouquet of flowers was thrown at the wedding procession of King Alfonso XIII and his English bride, Queen Victoria Eugenia. Though the couple escaped death, the Queen's bridal gown was spattered with blood, and the coachman and two horses were killed.

To complete this walk, read on. To combine this walk with the next as one figure-of-eight route, turn to the start of the Palacio Real walk, page 177.

Turn left down Pretil de los Consejos, dipping if you like into the 18thC **Sacramento** church on the corner, now the church of the military chaplains, with its glitzy and pristine white and gold interior. Plaza de la Cruz Verde was named for a great green cross used by the

Inquisition at the last *auto-de-fé* which stood here until it rotted away. The Fuente (fountain) de la Cruz Verde, erected in 1850, is rather a sad sight now, without water. To your left, up a broad flight of steps, is an inexpensive restaurant, **El Corgo**, with a shady outdoor terrace where you might like to stop for lunch. Either way, cross over Segovia, and prepare for a steep climb to the charming **Plaza de la Paja**, a silent, dusty space which was, in medieval times, the city's principal (straw – *paja*) market. The square is surrounded by elegant rows of houses, with the **Capilla del Obispo**, which adjoins San Andrés, on its south side. It was built in the early 16thC to house the shrine of San Isidro, and contains Plateresque tombs and a fine high altar of the same period.

Continue up the Costanilla de San Andrés into Plaza de Carros and then left to stand in front of the early Baroque church of **San Andrés**, which also incorporates the **Capilla de San Isidro**. The saint, a labourer in the fields, was a parishioner of San Andrés and the church assumed great importance after his canonization and adoption as Madrid's patron saint, hence the addition of the two chapels to house his relics. Turn right at Plaza del Humilladero and immediately left down **Cava Baja**. In 1083, when Madrid was reconquered by the Christians, Cava Baja was just that, a 'low ditch' running away from the town through which fleeing Moors made their escape. Over the years it became a back way into the city for salesmen, servants, soldiers and the like and was lined with *posadas* and *tabernas* as well as merchants' shops. Not much has changed: you can still tell it was a curving ditch, and little shops, heavily shuttered during *siesta* time (coal merchants, coopers, guitar makers, cordwainers), bars and restaurants still line the street.

Turn right off Cava Baja down San Bruno. Across Toledo, a busy shopping street, is **San Isidro**, which served as Madrid's cathedral pending the completion of Almudena (see Walk Two, page 177). It is a clodhopping construction of the Baroque period and you can swiftly turn left and head back to Plaza Mayor, and thence along Mayor to Puerta del Sol.

AROUND PALACIO REAL

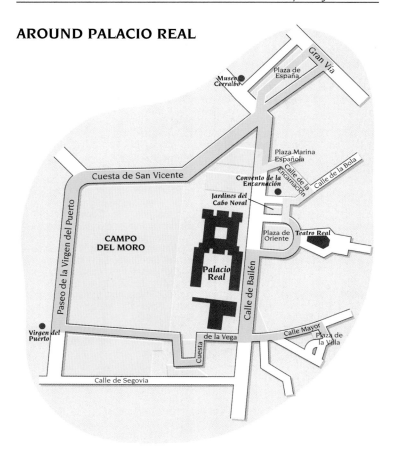

Passing some Moorish ruins *en route*, this walk moves from Habsburg to Bourbon Madrid in the area around the Royal Palace.

Start Plaza de la Villa. From there walk west along Mayor past the military headquarters on your left. At Balién walk straight across, down Cuesta de la Vega. Suddenly you are on the crest of a steep hill: it feels like the edge of the city, which indeed it once was. On the left are the excavated remains of **defensive walls** dating from Madrid's earliest days as a small Moorish stronghold. Ahead there are distant views of the **Casa de Campo** (see page 185). On the right, the great stone bulk of Nuestra Señora de Almudena piles up to its golden pinnacle (see 179).

The road zigzags down. Continue to the bottom, past the playground, and turn right into Paseo de la Virgen del Puerto. The spires of the church of the same name, built by Pedro Ribera in 1718, are visible across the road. Beyond that is the River Manzanares. The lush greenery on the right is the **Campo del Moro**, the grounds of the Palacio Real which can be seen frothing above the trees on top of the hill.

Walk alongside the railings, and suddenly a gate opens on to a magnificent avenue which sweeps past graceful fountains towards the centre of the palace. On a warm day dozens of feral cats can be seen sunning themselves near the gate (which is the only access to the park, so return there when you wish to leave). You can walk along the avenue, and in the carefully tended grounds, perhaps stopping to eat your *bocadillos* (filled rolls) on a bench. It's a pleasantly under-used open space, and attracts a rather sophisticated clientèle. Also in the grounds are the converted royal stables housing the **Museo de Carruajes** (see Sights & Places of Interest, page 185).

On leaving Campo del Moro, turn right, and to avoid a tedious, traffic-choked stretch on foot, make for the bus stop. Catch one of the frequent 'Circular' buses; pay the driver the flat fare and look out for **Plaza España**, which is the first stop after the underpass. Alight in front of the Plaza Hotel, and walk across the Plaza through gardens and past the ostentatious monument to Cervantes, with Don Quixote and San-cho Panza cowering beneath on their steeds.

Having thus far wandered in Habs-burg and Bourbon quarters, 20thC Plaza España makes a somewhat rude appearance. The tiered building on the east side, where you got off the bus, is the Edificio de España (1947). Even taller is the Torre de Madrid on the north side (1957). At the time of building they were the tallest skyscrapers in Europe; both have bars at the top with panoram-ic views. Off to the east sweeps **Gran Vía**, one of the city's principal routes, which in 1928 began ploughing its way through a district mainly of slums, but whose buildings at this end mostly date from the 1930s. Meant to be 'grand' but in fact lined by a motley succession of indifferent shops, fast food outlets, hire car companies, travel agents and so on, its main interest to the passer-by is its cinemas, decorated by huge hoardings advertising their latest offerings. These employ not stills from the film, but lurid paintings of the stars, usually in the act of some passionate embrace, which remind me of those in India.

North-west of the Plaza lies the attractive **Parque del Oeste**, with a lovely rose garden and the start of the cable car to **Casa de Campo**, and north of that the **Ciudad Universitaria**. Closer to hand, the southerly tip of the park, just off chic **Paseo Pintor Ros-ales**, with its expensive apartment blocks and terrazas, is called **Parque de Montaña**, and occupies ground as high as that of the Palacio Real. This area saw the 1808 massacre depicted in Goya's Tres de Mayo as well as vicious fighting during the Spanish Civil War. Nowadays you will find an incon-gruous 4thC BC Egyptian temple, the

Templo de Debod, which was trans-ferred from the banks of the Nile during the creation of the Aswan Dam.

Also near here is the **Museo Cerral-bo**: see page 187.

Leaving the Plaza to the south-west (left), walk over the underpass and south down Bailén towards Plaza Ori-ente. Turn first left along Plaza Marina Española, passing the renowned mesón de jamón, **Mi Venta**, decorated by scores of dangling hams. On the left is the **Palacio del Senado**, seat of the upper house of the Spanish parliament (cortes). Turn right down Encarnación, and in a few moments you will find your-self outside the **Convento de la Encarnación** (see Sights & Places of Interest, page 185). Now modern Madrid seems far away; like Descalzas Reales (see page 174) this is another of the Habsburgs' calm and elegant monastic foundations. Its frame of cypress trees and the sudden air of quiet gives the building a pensive, serene quality.

At No. 2 in the Plaza is a famous cookware shop and cookery school, **Alambique**. Now turn, via the little Jar-dines del Cabo Noval, into the dignified **Plaza de Oriente**, which, together with the surrounding Palacio Real and Teatro Real, takes us firmly back into the Bour-bon era (although it is a Habsburg whose marvellous equestrian statue dominates the space). The Plaza was conceived by Joseph Bonaparte, Napoleon's brother, during his brief reign as King of Spain (1808-13). The statue dates from 1640 and portrays Philip IV, whose features are so well known to us thanks to Velázquez, in spritely leap, his sash flying in the breeze. A far cry from the man he real-ly was – a third-rate ruler who shirked his responsibilities and allowed Spain's fortunes to slide. Commissioned by the king, it was sculpted by the Tuscan Pietro Tacca. To help him, Velázquez sent a portrait of Philip and none other than Galileo advised on weights (load the back of the horse with solid metal and keep the front hollow).

On one side of the Teatro Real you will find the offices, and departure point of **Pullmantours** (for sightseeing excur-sions), and the **Patrimonio Nacional** (government heritage body) bookshop. On the other side, an oasis: the outdoor terrace of the sophisticated **Café de**

• Plaza España.

Oriente (see Restaurant Recommendations, page 190).

The **Teatro Real**, also known as the Opera, has had a chequered existence. Inaugurated by Isabel II in 1850 with a performance of Donizetti's *La Favorita*, its heyday was during the late 19thC. For many years of this century it was closed because of structural problems, re-opening as a concert hall. Today it is under drawn-out renovation to recreate an opera house. Madrid's newest concert venue is the **Auditorio Nacional de Música** (Príncipe de Vergara, 136).

The Teatro Real faces the **Palacio Real** (see Sights & Places of Interest, page 185), or rather its restrained east façade which gives no hint of the excesses contained within. The entrance lies a little along Bailén, on the right. Facing the main façade, across a huge and colourless courtyard is the **Nuestra Señora de la Almudena**, which has finally been completed (the foundation stone was laid in 1883) and consecrated as Madrid's cathedral. Perhaps this is Spain's worst case of

mañana, mañana? In 1870 its predecessor, an apparently handsome church dating from the late 16thC, was demolished for no good reason.

You have now almost completed this route. The shortest way to a drink from here is across the road at **El Anciano Rey de los Vinos**, an old and atmospheric *taberna*. It suffers, however, from a common drawback for footsore tourists in Madrid – lack of seating. A better bet is **El Ventorillo** along Bailén on the far side of the **viaduct**, with little *terrazas* set up in the **Jardines de las Vistillas** and views stretching as far as the Sierra de Guadarrama. Those willing could continue on to the 18thC church of **San Francisco el Grande**, whose great dome boasts a larger diameter than even that of St Paul's in London. Had it been more central, it would have made a fine cathedral. *If you wish to combine this walk with the first one as a figure-of-eight, turn to page 176 and follow it from Pretil de los Consejos.*

AROUND CARRERA SAN JERONIMO

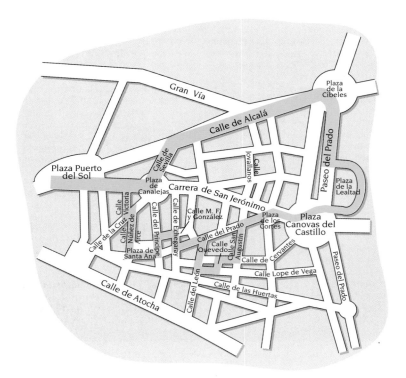

This walk takes in great thoroughfares, a literary backwater and a *tapas* crawl through the heart of the nightlife area.

Start Puerta del Sol, leaving by the Carrera de San Jerónimo. You could stop for a quick pick-me-up in the bustling **Museo de Jamón** where the *tapas* consist of cured ham (*jamón serrano*), of which dozens of regional examples are on offer. *Ibérico* is one of the most highly prized, and expensive. By the way, if you are shocked by the state of the floor – littered with papers, cigarette ends and so on – you will soon get used to it. It's a Spanish trait to drop everything while standing at the bar, and not to sweep it up until closing time.

Next door is **Lhardy**, established in 1839. Roll back the years by a century or so, think elegant and pop into the dark wood and mirrored delicatessen for a patisserie and hot chocolate or a dainty sandwich and a cup of *caldo*

(broth) served from a silver urn. The panelled dining rooms upstairs are a delight; only a pity that the food doesn't match up. In Plaza Canalejas, bear left down Sevilla, past imposing turn-of-the-century edifices (mostly banks) typical of the buildings which grew up along **Alcalá** in the days when it was regarded as one of the most fashionable streets in Europe, certainly the most majestic in Madrid. In those days, café life thrived and *tertulias* (daily meetings of a group of people, often intellectuals) were regular features.

Almost opposite the junction of Sevilla and Alcalá is the gracious (private) Casino de Madrid building of 1836, a time when, despite the country's declining fortunes and the regular rebellions and restorations, society knew how to enjoy itself (a knack that *madrileños* have never lost). Next door is the **Real Academia de Bellas Artes de San Fernando** (see Sights & Places of

Interest, page 185).

Now turn right for a very noisy walk along Alcalá, passing the junction with **Gran Vía** (see page 178), dominated by the Edificio Metropolis with its winged goddess on top. Across Alcalá, notice the arts complex **Círculo de las Bellas Artes** (Antonio Palacios, 1926) with its theatre and café (very comfortable, patronized by an arty crowd, useful for a rest). Behind, in Jovellanos is the **Teatro de la Zarzuela** which stages traditional *zarzuela* (musical comedy) between January and June. Next to the Círculo are the offices of RENFE where national rail tickets, timetables and information can be obtained. On the other side, the darkened interior of **San José** is a haven of silence and peace. The buildings at the entrance to Plaza de la Cibeles are, on the right, the **Banco de España**, and on the left, almost hidden by its tree-filled grounds, the late 18thC **Palacio de Buenavista**, built for Cayetana, Duchess of Alba. This enigmatic, restless and alluring lady was society queen of the day, quite outshining the real queen, dumpy María Luisa. Compare their portraits by Goya, of whom the duchess was patroness, in the Prado or in the current Alba home, **Palacio de Liria** (see Sights & Places of Interest, page 185). Buenavista is now headquarters of the army's general staff.

Plaza de la Cibeles is a key point in the city, standing at the intersection of two main thoroughfares. Looking across, the huge wedding cake which frames the central fountain must be the world's most over-the-top Post Office (*correos*). Called the **Palacio de Comunicaciónes**, it was built in the early 20thC. It stays open until 8 pm (1 pm on Saturdays), so now is the time to buy your stamps (*sellos*), send a telex or pick up your mail (*lista de correos*). (Stamps can also be bought at *estancos* – tobacconists – but it's easy to walk past them without noticing.)

The imposing central fountain, **Fuente de Cibeles** (the Greek goddess Cybele) always gives me the shivers. Poised in her chariot, she looks about as animated as a society matron taking a cup of tea and a slice of cake. There is certainly no Spanish fire in her marble veins; nevertheless she is a famous symbol of Madrid. The fourth major building in the plaza is the Palacio

Linares, recently restored and now the **Casa de América** (see Sights & Places of Interest, page 185).

Now turn right down **Paseo del Prado**. From the 16thC onwards this erstwhile river bed was a popular promenade, *hoi polloi* on one side, *bourgeoisie* on the other. In the 18thC, Charles III, a king who did much to modernize Madrid, gave it the air of grandeur we see today albeit through a haze of traffic. Juan de Villanueva and José de Hermosilla were responsible for the project which included building the Prado (as a natural history museum) and the botanical gardens, while Ventura Rodríguez designed the three great fountains (Apolo, Neptuno and Cibeles).

On your left is the **Museo Naval** (see page 187). In semi-circular Plaza Lealtad comes first the **Bolsa** (Stock Exchange), and then the inimitable, intimate **Ritz** (see Recommended Hotels, page 188); you need to be well dressed if you want a drink here – jacket and tie for men.

Now cross Plaza Canovas del Castillo. On the corner of **San Jerónimo**, in the neo-classical Palacio Villahermosa, is the **Museo Thyssen-Bornemisza** (see Sights & Places of Interest, page 185). You are now officially in the Golden Triangle, or if you prefer, Museum Mile, with the **Museo del Prado** and **Centro de Arte Reina Sofía** (see Sights & Places of Interest, page 185) close at hand. Across the road, the **Galería del Prado** is perhaps the best of Madrid's clutch of upmarket shopping malls: luxury shopping made easy, plus several cafés.

Galería del Prado forms part of the grand **Palace Hotel** (see Recommended Hotels, page 188), named for the vast Lerma Palace that stood here until early this century. Owned by the Dukes of Lerma, and then of Medinaceli, it covered several acres and had its own churches, schools and tradespeople.

Plaza de los Cortes is another of Joseph Bonaparte's embellishments (he was known as King of the Plazas amongst other less complimentary epithets; the statue is of Cervantes, and the porticoed neo-classical building flanked by two splendid bronze lions, is the **Cortes** (parliament). Here also is the newish luxury hotel, **Villa Real** (see Recommended Hotels, page 188), and next door an example of the many expensive

• *Palatial post office, Plaza de la Cibeles.*

antique shops in this part of town, **Antiguedades Linares**.

Turn left down San Augustín. At the junction with Cervantes, look left towards the well-preserved façade of **Jesús de Medinaceli**. If it's the first Friday in March, you will see long queues of people waiting their turn to venerate the image within known as Jesús de Medinaceli. Turn right. This street, Cervantes, and the parallel one, Lope de Vega, are confusingly named, for Cervantes died in a house on Lope de Vega, while Lope de Vega's house, **Casa de Lope de Vega** (worth visiting if it is open: see Sights & Places of Interest, page 185) is here on Cervantes. Turn left down Quevedo, correctly named for the writer and satirist who lived in the house, marked by a commemorative tablet, at the end. Apparently the shouting matches with his wife frequently disturbed the neighbourhood. Opposite is the charming **Convento de las Trinitarias**, an excellent example of 17thC Madrid architecture. The daughters of both Cervantes and Lope de Vega were nuns here, and Cervantes was buried here, though his tomb cannot now be traced. Spain's golden age is easy to imagine in these old lanes, well known then as Madrid's literary quarter.

Turn right in front of the convent, past the splash of colour afforded by the *frutería*. In season, local strawberries, asparagus and tiny lettuce hearts spill out on to the street. At León, turn right. Shops – interesting little ones – become more frequent, and *tabernas* and *tascas* lie thick on the ground. At Prado turn left, but first notice to the right the **Ateneo** (Atheneum), a hub of literary and political life since the early 19thC. Turn second right into Echegaray. You are now in an area which comes alive at night, its many bars and restaurants crowded with people until the early hours. It has a seedy side, with plenty of low life around, so be vigilant. Forget sightseeing: this quarter, with Plaza Santa Ana at its heart, is dedicated to food, drink and fun. Just south of your route, but not to be missed, is Huertas, where you will find the greatest concentration of bars and music of all kinds.

Turn first left into Calle de M.F. y Gonzáles, passing – or entering – two terrific tile bars (no food): **Viva Madrid** and **Los Gabrieles**. Next comes **La Trucha**, very popular and noted for its smoked fish. Then into **Plaza Santa Ana**, another of Joseph Bonaparte's creations. These days lively and rather scruffy, it used to be an intimate and peaceful spot, well known for its cafés during the Romantic period, where brilliant *tertulias* were held. The **Teatro Español**, one of the city's best theatres, is a landmark; there has been a theatre here since the 16thC. Amongst the bars, the **Cervecería Alemaña** is a landmark of a different sort: Hemingway hung out here. A long draught beer and a few *tapas* sound very appealing at this juncture.

Leave the plaza by Núñez de Arce to the right of **Hotel Reina Victoria** (see Recommended Hotels, page 188) past another tiled façade. **La Casa del Abuelo** along here is a good seafood bar – try its *patatas bravas* too. Turn left on to Cruz and right on to Victoria. More seafood bars, plus the tourist-packed **Passaje de Mathéu**, with its outdoor tables and beckoning waiters. Then – the Museo de Jamón again.

THE PASEO

Walk 4 takes in Madrid's great north-south boulevard, the Paseo del Prado; the city park; and the exclusive shopping district.

Start Paseo del Prado at Plaza Canovas del Castillo. Turn away from the Paseo into Felipe IV and you enter a very proper, mostly residential area of expensive apartment blocks. Ahead is the **Cason de Buen Retiro**, to the left the **Museo del Ejército** (see Sights & Places of Interest, page 185. These buildings are the only bits left of the Habsburgs' vast 17thC country residence, Real Sitio del Buen Retiro (pleasant retreat), which was destroyed by the French after their 1808 occupation. The columned neo-classical building on the corner of Noreto is the **Real Academia Española** where the official dictionary of the Spanish language is updated (very sparingly) by specially elected academicians. Opposite is *the* church for society weddings, **San Jerónimo el Real**.

Walk along this tree-lined street, turning right at the end into Espalter. In Plaza Murillo, **El Botánico** is an attractive café with covered terrace. To the right is the **Museo del Prado** (best done in two visits, so you might consider one of them now; see page 187). To the left is the **Jardin Botánico**, a very pleasant place to wander, where the roar of the traffic becomes a distant blur and there are delicious scents in the air.

• *The boating lake, Parque del Retiro.*

Returning to Plaza Murillo, turn left into Paseo del Prado. The **Centro de Arte Reina Sofía** (see Sights & Places of Interest, page 185) is a short walk further on, but if that is not on your agenda for now, turn left along **Cuesta Claudio Moyano**, lined with second-hand book stalls (open daily, but busiest on Sundays).

Across Alfonso XII is the entrance to **Parque del Retiro**, another survivor of the Real Sitio del Buen Retiro. Unlike some city parks which are regarded as a bonus for a sunny day, Retiro is an integral part of the life of *madrileños*, especially on Sundays, when whole families come here to stroll. There are avenues and grassy paths, statues, fountains and grandiose monuments (notably the one to Alfonso XII by the boating pool); there are two exhibition halls, one made of crystal; a rose garden; and several outdoor cafés. Avenida de Mexico leads you out of the park at Plaza de la Independencia.

Smart Madrid lies ahead. Serious shoppers, or at least window shoppers, will want to investigate, but it must be said that the streets in this part of town, **Salamanca**, are long and straight and the walking is tiring. **Serrano** and its offshoots are lined with *haute couture* and fashion accessory shops. You might try **Goya** which has an interesting mix, not

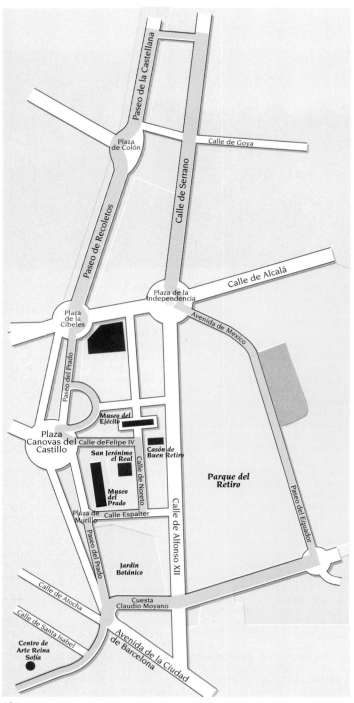

all exclusive, and cafés as well. **El Jardín de Serrano**, another of Madrid's excellent shopping malls, is near the corner. Along Serrano you will pass **Mallorca**, a luxury food store which serves champagne and smoked salmon as well as wonderful chocolates downstairs and delicious titbits and take-out food upstairs. Further along on the left is the entrance to the **Museo Arqueológico Nacional** (see Sights & Places of Interest, below).

Cross to the **Paseo de la Castellana**. This, with its continuations **Paseos de Recoletos** and **Prado**, is the great boulevard which leads northwards towards modern Madrid and its many high-rise office blocks. Across busy **Plaza de Colón** (airport bus terminal; subterranean cultural centre; also the waxworks museum, **Museo de Cera**) Recoletos still retains a handful of the palaces with which it was once lined. Of more immediate interest is **El Espejo** (No. 31), which has a cleverly reproduced Art Nouveau interior; better still, you could take a drink and a *ración* in the café's glass *pabellon*, which stands in the central reservation. In the summer months many more *terrazas* spring up and people love to drink and stroll along the boulevard until the early hours. The traffic never stops (although loud music helps to drown it out). It's possible to sit in a solid traffic jam along here at two in the morning.

Another famous café is the venerable **Gijón** (No. 21), mirrored and smokey. It drove me mad trying to find it the first time – it's on a parallel service road (west side). A little further, and you are in **Plaza de la Cibeles** (see page 172), where there are plenty of buses to whisk you home.

SIGHTS & PLACES OF INTEREST

For guidance on opening times, see page 12

CASA DE AMERICA
Plaza de la Cibeles. Open 9-11.30 am Tues-Fri; 10-1.30 pm Sat, Sun; closed Mon. One of the city's finest palaces, the **Palacio Linares**, previously on the brink of ruin, has been restored to Disneyworldesque perfection and is now home to the **Museo de América**, a cultural centre and art gallery focusing on Latin America. Guided tours only of the late-19thC mansion.

CASA DE CAMPO
The city's out-of-town recreation area which lies across the Manzanares to the west of the centre. Amusement park, zoo (said to be improving), swimming-pool and boating lake. You can get there by cable car (*teleférico*) which starts on Paseo Pintor Rosales near Marqués de Urquijo (nearest metro Argüelles).

CASA DE LOPE DE VEGA
Cervantes. Closed Sun. The restored home of the great dramatist and poet, contemporary of Shakespeare and author of over 1,500 works, is more interesting as an evocation of domesticity in 17thC Madrid than of his larger-than-life personality.

CASON DEL BUEN RETIRO
Plaza de Felipe IV; entrance on Alfonso XII. Same entrance ticket as for Museo del Prado. An annexe of the Prado, just to the northeast. Formerly the rather incongruous home of Picasso's *Guernica* (now in the Centro de Arte Reina Sofía), the Casón is a showcase for post-Goya 19thC Spanish painting. A room devoted to Vincente Lopez catches the eye: compare his over-the-top allegorical portrait of the *Family of Charles IV* to Goya's of the same in the Prado. A grumpy 80-year-old Goya himself is also depicted, as well as a heavily mustachioed *Señora Delicado de Imaz*.

Upstairs, amongst the historical painting so popular at the time, Teofilo de la Puebla's depiction of the fate of El Cid's daughters, *Las Hijas del Cid*, might be of interest as well as *El General Prim* by Eugenio Lucas and some pleasing works by Impressionist Sorolla. (For fans, the **Estudio y Museo Sorolla** is open to the public at Paseo General Martinez Campos, 37.)

CENTRO DE ARTE REINA SOFIA
Santa Isabel, 52; closed Tues. Madrid's answer to the Beaubourg or MOMA, this modern arts complex is housed in a vast, specially converted 18thC public hospital, given street cred by its *de rigeur* exterior glass elevators. In the basement, there is a popular, inexpensive restaurant, pleasant for lunch. An

important feature of the centre is its temporary exhibitions.

The permanent collection is on the 2nd floor, reached by the glass lifts, and traces Spanish painting from the late 19thC to the present day. Picasso, Miró and Dalí predominate, and there are modern works from artists such as Chillida and Tàpies. After a beautiful display of Cubism (No. 4) by Juan Gris and Picasso, comes the centre's highlight and a national icon: Picasso's *Guernica*, brilliantly displayed in a recess of the room so that, as you approach, the wall seems to slide back to reveal it inch by inch, like a curtain being drawn. It's a surprise to find that this famous and furious condemnation of war, and in particular of the bombing of the Basque city of Guernica during the Spanish Civil War, is played out in muted tones of grey and white, yet it has a subtle power – and hidden messages – which bear contemplation.

CONVENTO DE LA ENCARNACION

Plaza de la Encarnación. Open daily 10 am-1 pm; closed Mon; also open 4-5.30 pm Tues-Thur, Sat. Like the earlier Monasterio de las Descalzas Reales (see below), this is a Habsburg convent, founded in 1611 by Queen Margarita, wife of Philip III. Unlike Descalzas Reales it has the austerity commonly associated with monastic foundations, although there are regal flourishes, particularly in the church with its lavish reliquary room. The works of 17thC Spanish artists are displayed in the convent. Guided tours only, in Spanish.

ERMITA DE SAN ANTONIO DE LA FLORIDA

Glorieta de San Antonio de la Florida Confirmed admirers of Goya, as well as newcomers to his art, will be rewarded by a visit to this out-of-the-way little church (best reached by taxi), now the **Pantéon de Goya**. The artist is buried here; and he painted the marvellous dome fresco, *Miracle of St Anthony of Padua*. Though Goya's depiction is grounded in the secular, it has a wonderfully inspiring quality.

MONASTERIO DE LAS DESCALZAS REALES

Plaza de las Descalzas, 3. Even non-Spanish speakers will find the (compulsory) guided tour of this Habsburg monastery – and the wait outside for the tour to begin – well worthwhile. What they won't be allowed to see is the enormous garden which I spied on from a friend's attic window – quite a sight in the middle of the city. Slightly run down now, it was until a few years ago full of fruit and vegetables, even pigs and sheep, to keep the closed Fransiscan order of Royal Barefoot Sisters (Descalzas Reales) self-sufficient; nowadays there are only a handful still in residence. Until the 19thC, when it was opened, the riches inside the monastery were a secret known only to the nuns and their aristocratic patrons.

The convent, built in the traditional red brick and granite of the age, was first a Renaissance palace, birthplace of Juana of Austria, daughter of Charles V. It was she who had the palace converted into a convent and a retreat for ladies of high birth. It was their families who donated its extraordinary riches, not normally associated with monastic life. They take the form of sumptuously painted walls and ceilings by Claudio Coello, many paintings (including some famous names), Flemish tapestries, sculptures, and a riot of ornamentation in the reliquary. Best of all, though, up the magnificent staircase, is the courtyard gallery with its many individual chapels, and altars set into shallow alcoves. They are incredibly ornate and wonderfully pretty, with their Virgins dressed like exotic dolls.

MUSEO ARQUEOLÓGICO NACIONAL

Serrano, 13. For its collection, and for the imposing building which houses it (and the **Biblioteca Nacional**), this museum is second only to the Prado in importance, but it is not on most tourists' busy agendas. It traces the artefacts, art and architecture of the Iberian Peninsula from cave men to the present age and includes some notable treasures. Labels and descriptions are in Spanish, but catalogues are available in other languages.

MUSEO DE CARRUAJES

Campo del Moro. An entertaining collection of sedans, coaches and carriages, including that of Alfonso XIII and his bride (see page 176) and the litter that transported Charles V all the way from the coast to Yuste, where he spent his last years in seclusion.

MUSEO CERRALBO

Ventura Rodríguez,17; closed Aug. The occasionally garish tastes of late 19thC Spanish nobility are reflected in this mix of furniture, sculpture, paintings (El Greco, Zurbarán, a lovely *Jacob with his Flocks* by Ribera), tapestries, armour and archaeological pieces. They were unified by the Marqués de Cerralbo who bequeathed his mansion and his collection to the nation on his death in 1922.

MUSEO DEL EJERCITO

Calle Méndez Núñez, 1. The future of this army museum is somewhat uncertain, since it may be commandeered by the Prado for more desperately needed gallery space, but doubtless its huge collection of weaponry and military regalia will be rehoused elsewhere.

MUSEO DEL PRADO

Paseo del Prado. Nowhere in Spain are the riches of the Habsburgs and the Bourbons put to such good effect as in the Prado. The paintings, commissioned and collected by the Spanish monarchs from the days of Ferdinand and Isabel (and supplemented by the anticlerical laws of 1836 which forced religious institutions to hand over their artworks) make one of the world's great collections. You go to the Prado to marvel at Velázquez, El Greco and Goya, and at Italian and Flemish masterpieces, collected when the Spanish Empire extended thus far.

Once you are inside the Prado it makes sense to know that it was commissioned, by Charles III, as a natural history museum. However, by the time it opened in 1819 it was as a repository for the royal collection.

There are guided tours in Spanish, English and French, but for those who prefer to wander on their own, here is one way of tackling it (paintings may have been moved). Locate the Puerta de Goya (nearest to the Ritz) and walk up the steps to the **upper floor** (*planta principal, primera planta*) entrance. Halfway along the long gallery is a bookshop selling an excellent guide to the collection in several languages. Retrace to the dome, and turn right for Italian Renaissance paintings **(Rooms 2-6)** which include several Raphaels, plus some very nasty things happening to a lady from the *Decameron* by Botticelli.

Next comes a superb collection from the Venetian school: Veronese, Tintoret-

to and, most important, Titian. His works include a wonderful portrait of Titian's patron, Charles V, and *La Gloria*, which Charles V gazed upon from his deathbed at the monastery of Yuste.

After Titian comes El Greco **(Rooms 9b and 10b)**. None of his greatest works are here in the Prado, except perhaps the *Adoration of the Shepherds*, but there is enough to display his extraordinary individuality, as astonishing to us today as it was to his 16thC contemporaries. The endless elongation does become tiresome, but there is an undeniable excitement about all his work.

Now pop out into the long gallery, and then turn left again into the world of Velázquez. **Las Meninas** is simply breathtaking (you should read about it truly to appreciate it), a virtuoso performance in the depiction of light and space. You are standing next to the king and queen in the doorway of a room in the old Alcázar and it seems that you, like them, could step inside at any moment. Other famous canvasses include *Las Lanzas, Los Borrachos* and the portraits of court entertainers and of his royal patrons: Velázquez's genius is gently to convey the truth about hopeless Philip IV, whatever his regal get-up.

Amongst the later Spanish paintings which follow, notice a moving portrait of Charles II, Philip's mentally and physically handicapped son, family chin still intact. One room is devoted to Murillo, a fine draughtsman, despite the saccharine mood of his best pictures.

In the dome at the end of the long gallery you find Goya's famously irreverent portrait of the *Family of Charles IV* to whom he was court painter (and amazingly never lost favour). The awful Maria Luisa was toothless, by the way, but very proud of her well-rounded arms. She crops up several times more, but, whatever her fancy apparel, Goya can never bring himself to flatter her. Here also are the famous pair, *Maja Desnuda* and *Maja Vestida*, supposed to be the Duquesa de Alba, whom Goya adored. In the galleries opposite are Goya's cartoons for a series of tapestries, surprisingly light and bucolic in style, but nevertheless worthy of attention. At the far end **(Room 39)** you will find Goya's greatest painting, *Los Fusilamientos de Tres de Mayo*. The pathetic ragbag of victims in contrast to the hard line of unquestioning executioners, the pure white shirt and crucified stance of the central figure – these things and more help to convey the sense of drama and outrage which makes this such a moving and terrible canvas to observe.

Downstairs you will find Goya's 'black paintings', found on the walls of his *quinta* and painted in obvious despair toward the end of his life.

By now you will need at the very least a cup of tea, and the Prado's dull cafeteria is immediately below in the basement (*sótano*). The nearest alternatives are the **Ritz** (for the smartly dressed),

---

RECOMMENDED HOTELS

Barajas, PPP; Avenida de Logroño, 5; tel. 91 747 77 00.

If you want to combine the leisure facilities of a swimming-pool, gym, gardens and golf course with a visit to Madrid, this could be your hotel. As it is 14 km from Madrid you might think of alternating a day in town with a day at the hotel. It is near the airport.

Carlos V, PP; Maestro Vitoria, 5; tel 91 531 41 00.

Conveniently located closed to Puerta del Sol and round the corner from the Monasterio de las Descalzas Reales. Rooms are adequate, if dull (try for a balcony room), but the hotel is family-run and possesses an elegant first floor salon/breakfast room.

Inglés, PP; Echegaray, 8; tel. 91 429 65 51.

Close to Plaza Santa Ana, in a street packed with bars and restaurants, this is an ideal spot for those who want instant access to Madrid's lively nightlife. It is also rather charming, though faded, and old-established, with large comfy rooms, some with balconies overlooking the street.

Liabeny, PP; Salud, 3; tel. 91 531 90 00.

Run of the mill, though clean and well-equipped with a convenient location and a lively bar and restaurant.

Monaco, P-PP; Barbieri, 5; tel. 91 522 46 30.

In the potentially intimidating Chueca area north of Gran Vía, a one-star eccentricity filled with mirrors, brass and potted plants and an air of slightly shabby gentility.

Palace, PPP; Plaza de la Cortes, 7; tel. 91 360 80 80.

Second only to the Ritz in the league of *grande dame* hotels, and about half the price, the Palace has always attracted a mix of politicians, diplomats and entertainers. Public rooms are impressive, particularly the glass-domed rotunda, although bedrooms are much more muted, and vary considerably in size. Well-equipped bathrooms, though.

Paris, PP; Alcalá, 2; tel. 91 521 64 96.

Old-fashioned two-star hotel, decent value for its prime, though noisy location on the corner of Alcalá and Puerta del Sol. It has a dignified dark wood lobby and a second floor restaurant.

Ramón de la Cruz, P-PP; Don Ramón de la Cruz, 94; tel. 91 401 72 00.

In Salamanca near Alcalá, a short bus or metro ride from the hub of things. Solid value, at least for Madrid, modern and clean but without flourish.

Reina Victoria, PPP; Plaza del Angel; tel. 91 531 45 00.

Famous as a favourite of bullfighters, bohemians and – need it be said

the **Galería del Prado** across the Paseo or the tile bar **La Dolores** along Lope de Vega.

Begin your tour of the **ground floor** (*planta baja*) from the 'black paintings' (Puerta de Murillo end). Pass through the domed gallery devoted to sculpture into the long gallery where endless plump, pink ladies by Rubens and his followers get themselves into various kinds of mythological trouble. The galleries to the right contain many more sumptuous, rollicking Rubens canvasses including *Judgment of Paris*, plus a room devoted to Van Dyck. Tucked away nearby is the small Dutch collection, including a captivating *Artemesia* by Rembrandt.

Back in the long gallery, pass through the small sculpture hall into the Spanish

16thC – retablos and altarpieces. Pedro Berruguete is a name that will crop up as you travel round Spain.

To the right are 15th and 16thC Flemish masterpieces. Rogier Van der Weyden's *Descendimiento* is one of the three unforgettable paintings in the Prado with its frieze-like line of mourners, its limp and weightless Christ and the finely modelled, tear-stained head of the Virgin.

Philip II was fascinated by the

BUDGET ACCOMMODATION

There are plenty of cheap hostas and fondas in Madrid; the trouble is that they are often full up with long-term guests. You could enlist the help of an accommodation agency (see Accommodation Guidelines, page 172) or try your luck at the following: **Hostal Montalvo**, *Zaragoza, 6; tel.* 91 365 59 10; **Hostal Alcázar Regis**, *Gran Vía, 61; tel.* 91 547 93 17.

– Ernest Hemingway – the Victoria is once again an amusing and increasingly popular place in which to stay after a long period of decline. Rescued and renovated by the Tryp chain, it has spacious, smart and well equipped rooms, the pleasantest of which face Plaza Santa Ana.

Ritz, PPP; *Plaza de la Lealtad, 5; tel.* 91 521 28 57.

Probably the best hotel in Spain, certainly one of the best in the world, the Ritz was built in 1910 under the direction of Alfonso XIII. A recent renovation has restored its stunning Belle Epoque decorations to perfection. Exclusivity, intimacy, silky smooth service and minute attention to detail are its hallmarks, all of which come at a cost which even the super-rich might notice: think of a price for a luxury hotel bedroom, double it and you might be somewhere near.

Santo Mauro, PPP; *Zurbano, 36; tel.* 91 319 69 00.

Hotels of the intimate and luxurious type are beginning make a welcome appearance in Madrid. This one, opened in 1992, occupies a late 19thC *palacio*, although the furnishings are contemporary, which makes a refreshing change. There is an indoor pool and a gym and the prices are nearly as high as the Ritz's.

Serrano, PP; *Marqués de Villamejor, 8; tel.* 91 576 96 26.

Well located for inveterate shoppers in the heart of the Salamanca district, the Serrano is another standard Madrid hotel which deserves a mention for its extra touches – including massage showers – and its lack of tour groups.

Villa Magna, PPP; *Paseo de la Castellana, 22; tel.* 91 587 12 34.

If you like up-to-the-minute zip and zing with your ultra-luxury, try the Villa Magna, well placed on the main boulevard mid-way between the city centre and the business district. The building itself is a glinting modern tower, set off by immaculate gardens and, inside, chandeliers, marble floors, elegant furniture and soothing piano music. Another hostelry where you don't bother to ask the price.

Villa Real, PPP; *Plaza de la Cortes, 10; tel.* 91 420 37 67.

Right in the heart of things, next to the parliament building and across the road from the Prado, this sophisticated and extremely comfortable hotel was new in 1989 but already feels part of the scene. Rooms are individually decorated, bathrooms are stuffed with goodies, and prices are a smidgeon less than others in its class.

grotesque, and works by Hieronymous Bosch (El Bosco) are another highlight, along with Pieter Breughel's grisly *Triunfo de la Muerte*. Finish your tour with a vision, not of death, but of the start of life in Dürer's *Adam and Eve*.

MUSEO LAZARO GALDIANO

Serrano, 122; closed Aug. Like Cerralbo, this is another private mansion plus contents bequeathed to the nation after the owner's death. Here, it is the magpie collection of writer, publisher and general culture vulture Lázaro Galdiano (1862-1947), which fills a staggering 30 rooms. One wonders how he found the time. The artworks span many types – jewellery, glassware, enamels, clocks, fans to name but a few – several centuries and three continents; the paintings include almost all the great Spanish names as well as Bosch, David, Rembrandt, Reynolds, Turner.

MUSEO NACIONAL DE ARTES DECORATIVAS

Montalbán, 12. After the unimaginable riches of the various private collections in Madrid, the domestic arts and crafts of the last four centuries displayed here are somewhat a breath of fresh air. Don't miss the beautifully tiled 18thC Valencian kitchen in **Room 46**.

FOR NIGHT BIRDS

You've trawled the *tapa* bars, and ended up in a restaurant for a late dinner, but it's only a little past midnight, so now what? Wander down Huertas, taking in all the different live music on offer in the various bars and clubs; or go to a *flamenco* show at either **Café de Chinitas** (Torija, 7; tel. 91 248 51 35; reserve if possible) or **Corral de la Moreria** (Moreria, 17; tel. 91 265 84 46); or visit a *sala rociera* such as **El Porton** (López de Hoyos, 25; tel. 91 262 49 56) where you can try your hand at the much trendier *sevillanas* dancing. For *salsa* dancing go to **Café del Mercado** (Ronda de Toledo,1, in the Mercado Puerta de Toledo). Finish up in a disco: **Baños** (Escalinata 10) in converted public baths; **Joy Eslava** (Arenal, 11) in a converted theatre; **Archy** (Marqués de Riscal, 11) for the smart set.

MUSEO NAVAL

Montalbán, 2; closed Aug. On the corner of Paseo del Prado, the Naval Museum is worth a visit for its terrific ships' models, navigation instruments and early

---

RECOMMENDED RESTAURANTS

If you want to eat out, be prepared to eat late. At night restaurants open around 9 or 10 pm and usually fill around 11 pm. Reservations are advised. At lunchtime restaurants open at around 1.30 pm; the menu del día is often a safe bet and can still offer value for money.

Asador Frontón, PP; *Plaza de Tirso de Molina, 7; tel. 91 369 16 17; credit cards* AE, DC, V.

Meat and fish are barbecued to perfection over wood in this neighbourhood restaurant south of Puerta del Sol; worth seeking out.

Botín, PP; *Cuchilleros, 17; tel. 91 366 42 17; credit cards* AE, DC, MC, V.

Madrid's most famous restaurant, going strong since 1725 and very much on the tourist route. Don't be put

off, though: it is full of atmosphere with its warren of rooms, beamed ceilings, charming tiles and wood-burning ovens. The food holds up well (house speciality is roast suckling pig) and, considering its popularity, the prices are fair. Be sure to book.

Café de Oriente, PPP; *Plaza de Oriente, 2; tel. 91 541 39 74; credit cards* AE, DC, MC, V; *closed Sat lunch, Sun, Aug.*

Strategically placed opposite the Palacio Real. For passers-by, the outdoor café and the gleaming bar are a delight; the two restaurants, one Belle Epoque, the other brick-lined, are more serious, serving Spanish dishes with French flourishes.

Casa Paco, PP; *Puerta Cerrada, 11; tel. 91 366 31 66; credit cards* DC, V; *closed Sun, Aug.*

Round the corner from Botín (see above), just as atmospheric, but less full of madrileños, rather than tourists.

maps made when Spanish explorers were discovering the world.

MUSEO ROMÁNTICO

San Mateo, 13. Closed Aug. A pleasing collection of objects and paintings from the Romantic period in a little mid-19thC *palacio*. It was the home of the Marqués de la Vega-Inclán and gives a feel for life during the reign of Isabella II.

MUSEO THYSSEN-BORNEMISZA

Palacio de Villahermosa, Paseo del Prado, 8. The private art collection of Baron Thyssen-Bornemisza and his Spanish wife Carmen came to rest in Madrid in 1992, enhancing the capital's reputation as a treasure house of art and creating the so-called 'golden triangle' with the Prado and Reina Sofía. To house it, the lovely neo-classical Palacio de Villahermosa has been superbly converted: paintings are hung spaciously against a background of terracotta pink walls and marble floors, with light filtering through tall shuttered windows.

Take the lift to the second floor, and follow the galleries in numerical order. The collection, probably the most important and extensive private one anywhere in the world, takes you on a trip from medieval Italian painting to the pop art of the 1960s (by which time you are back on the ground floor). The paintings are clearly and sensibly grouped, but although there are plenty of show-stoppers, the spread is perhaps too wide and too thin.

Of special note are the galleries dedicated to Nordic Modernist painting on the first floor – wonderful canvasses by Kirchner, Rottluff and Pechstein, a real eye-opener for those unfamiliar with this movement. Back on the ground floor you are confronted with life-size pictures of the Baron and Baroness. Are they a comment on the state of portrait painting today?

PALACIO DE LIRIA

Princesa, 22. Open Sat am by appointment only; tel 91 247 53 02. The 18thC *palacio* (completed by Ventura Rodríguez) is the residence of the Alba family. Almost destroyed in the Spanish Civil War, it was rebuilt in the 1950s and its treasures, rich in Old Masters, which had been taken to the Bank of Spain for safekeeping, returned.

PALACIO REAL (ROYAL PALACE)

Plaza de Oriente. Compulsory guided tours in Spanish, English, French and German. On Christmas Eve 1734 a great fire burnt Madrid's Moorish Alcázar

---

Not for vegetarians: slabs of prime beef, ordered by weight, are brought to the table still sizzling on the plate.

El Garabatu, PP; *Echegaray, 5; tel.* 91 429 63 90; *credit cards* AE, V.

Characterful restaurant and *tapas* bar serving simple Asturian dishes in a street packed with eating places.

El Inti de Oro, PP; *Ventura de la Vega, 12; tel.* 91 429 67 03; *credit cards, none; closed* Sun *eve,* Mon.

Sound-value, unusual dishes, and a jolly atmosphere make this Peruvian restaurant a popular choice. Try the stuffed potatoes to start with, followed by the rabbit or beef. And don't turn down the offer of the Peruvian aperitif – it is delicious and refreshing.

El Pescador, PPP; *José Ortega y Gasset, 75; tel.* 91 402 12 90; *credit cards* MC, V; *closed* Sun, Aug.

One of Madrid's surprises is its seafood, trucked in nightly from the far-off coast, and a source of great pride to *Madrileños*. El Pescador is considered the best of many seafood restaurants. The setting is rustic, the ambience relaxed, the clientele impressive, and the price steep.

Sanabresa, P; *Amor de Dios,*12; *credit cards none; closed* Sun *eve,* Aug.

Excellent 'greasy spoon' for a hearty Spanish lunch (paella is served on Thursday and Sunday) at minimal cost.

Zalacaín, PPP; *Alvarez de Baena, 4; tel.* 91 561 48 40; *credit cards,* AE, DC, V; *closed* Sat *lunch,* Sun, Aug.

How to take Spanish cuisine to the dizziest gourmet heights (many accolades: 'Spain's best restaurant'; three Michelin stars). The Mercedes' purr outside, the waiters purr inside, the bill freezes the blood in your veins.

(fortress-palace) to the ground. The Bourbon extravaganza which replaced it was commissioned by Philip V, but finished in the reign of his successor Charles III in 1764.

The sheer scale of the place is overwhelming (and beware, all that Rococo opulence, all those fat cherubs and fancy clocks, all those dripping chandeliers, inlaid tables and vast tapestries can become wearisome and disorientating after you have been going for an hour or more). Incredibly, the palace has more than 2,000 rooms, so count yourself lucky that the tour only takes in 50 or so. Since the guided tours are compulsory, detailed descriptions are best left to the experts. However, you will wish to linger longer than they allow in the **Salón de Gasparini**, the **Sala de Porcelana** and the **State Dining Room**. The Biblioteca Real (first edition of *Don Quixote*), Museo de Música (Stradivari), Armería Real and Real Oficina de Farmacía can also be visited.

To the north of the palace complex, the formal Jardínes Sabatini are open to the public, as well as the palace grounds Campo del Moro, though only accessible from the far side, a long walk round.

RASTRO, EL
South from metro Latines, along Ribera de Curtidores and surrounding streets. This is the area where, on Sunday mornings, Madrid's flea market erupts into life. Though most of the stuff is junk, and bargains are a thing of the past, the colour and chaos and the sheer profusion of goods are worth the trip. Guard your wallet.

REAL ACADEMIA DE BELLAS ARTES DE SAN FERNANDO
Alcalá, 13. Open daily. If you want to shut out the roar of Alcalá, you could do worse than step into this little-visited and rather dusty repository, headquarters of the Madrid Academy of Art, especially if you only visit to the first few rooms which contain the cream: excellent examples from **Ribera** and **Zurbarán** and an illuminating selection of **Goyas**.

VENTAS, LAS
Plaza de las Ventas, de Alcalá; metro Ventas. Madrid's bull-ring, one of the most prestigious in Spain. *Corridas* are held on Sunday afternoons, April to November. **Museo Taurino** (open 9 am to 2 pm except Sun) charts the history of bullfighting and spotlights the matadors.

RECOMMENDED BARS
At about 9 or 10 pm it's time to go out and start exploring Madrid's wonderful *tapa* bars, either prior to or instead of a meal. Simply go to an area where bars lie thick on the ground and wander in and out, sampling the different *tapas*. You could explore the little cuevas in Cava San Miguel which borders Plaza Mayor, or go to the area round Plaza Chueca, north of Gran Vía, or to the scruffy but trendy Plaza Dos de Mayo in Malasaña or, most profitably, to the area around Plaza Santa Ana and Calle Huertas. Though it is fun to take pot-luck, the following are particularly interesting. They can all get very crowded, and chairs are a rarity:

Around Chueca: **Bocaíto** (*Libertad*, 6) pleasantly old-fashioned, with excellent *tapas* (or a meal), though expensive.

Around Plaza Santa Ana/Huertas: **La Trucha** (M.F. *Gonzalez*, 3) very well-known, with great *tapas* including deep-fried asparagus and *pimientos padrón* which all look the same though every one in ten or so is a firecracker; **La Venencia** (*Echegaray*, 7) charmingly old-world sherry bar; **Los Gabrieles** (*Echegaray*, 17) and **Viva Madrid** (M.F. *Gonzales*, 7) two justly famous bars, easy to spot for their wonderful pictographic tiles and always filled with a young crowd; **Hermanos Muñiz** (*Huertas*, 29); excellent old-timer; **La Dolores** (*Plaza de Jésus*, 4) great ambience, serving draught beer.

Elsewhere: **Café Gijon** (*Paseo de Recoletos*, 24) venerable institution; **El Espejo** (*Paseo de Recoletos*, 31) with a pleasant pavilion on the Paseo; **Café de Oriente** (*Plaza de Oriente*, 2) great position opposite the Palacio Real, outdoor tables, chic clientele; **El Ventorrillo** (*Bailén*, 14) in the Jardines de las Vistillas, the place to watch the sun go down over the Sierra de Guadarrama.

Barcelona:
introduction

B arcelona was dubbed, by Catalan poet Joan Maragall, *la gran encis-era* (the great enchantress). And so it is. This is a vibrant city, industrious, cultured and pace-setting. You can immerse yourself in art and music, indulge your gourmet dreams, or live it up all night.

Spain's second city, with three million people in its metropolitan area, never lacked in confidence, but the 1992 Olympics set the seal on its pride. The flaming arrow that launched the Games epitomized Catalans' vaulting ambition to be recognized as a progressive nation in their own right, which hardly increases their popularity elsewhere in Spain.

Barcelona people have a longstanding rivalry with Madrid, inhabited in their view by slothful bureaucrats and frivolous upstarts. In contrast, they see themselves as innovative, businesslike and imbued with an almost mystic quality, *seny* (roughly, 'natural wisdom'). Barcelona natives cannot forget that between the 12th and 15thC their city was capital of the Catalunya-Aragón kingdom, exerting great influence all around the Mediterranean before Spain became a united state. The region developed a merchant class and, in the 19thC, flourishing manufacturing industries while much of Spain was locked in feudal ways.

Franco's repression, when the local language and customs were banned, served only to reinforce Catalan national consciousness. One result is an obsession with widening the use of the Catalan language, closer to Provençal French than Castilian. This creates problems for visitors, as everything from museum information to street signs are in Catalan – irritating if you have been keenly studying Castilian.

Fast growth in the 1950s and 1960s ringed Barcelona with some eyesore suburbs, sheltering migrant workers employed in the major industries, producing cars, textiles and chemical products. But huge construction and modernization programmes associated with the Olympics reshaped and refurbished whole sections of the city.

Visitors can gape at the wild imagination of Gaudí and other Modernist architects, visit shrines to such artists as Miró and Picasso and hear opera stars such as José Carreras and Montserrat Caballé. They can indulge themselves in fashionable shops (above all, this is a highly design-conscious city) and in the hundreds of restaurants serving everything from hearty country dishes to the most outrageous *nouvelle cuisine*. And, night or day, there is La Rambla (see page 196), with flower kiosks, pavement cafés and a bewildering variety of human fauna.

USING THIS SECTION

Barcelona's most important sights are covered in the alphabetical gazetteer of Sights & Places of Interest, starting on page 196. To introduce you to the city, a walk is suggested. You will find hotel and restaurant recommendations at the end of the section.

ARRIVING

Drivers are advised to leave their cars at their hotels or in a public car park. Street parking is difficult, and costly if your vehicle is towed away.

From El Prats Airport, frequent trains take 15 minutes to reach Sants station and buses half an hour to reach the Plaça d'Espanya. For information about Iberia flights tel. 93 401 33 81. Estació del Norte, near Ciutadella Park, is the most important long-distance bus station. For information on Madrid buses, call 93 245 88 56, for Valencia 93 245 25 28. Mainline trains arrive at Sants and França stations. RENFE information: for national routes tel. 93 490 11 22, for international tel. 93 490 11 22.

Hotel reservation services are available at the airport and at Sants.

Ferries run between Barcelona and the Balearic Isles (Cia. Trasmediterránea. tel. 93 295 91 07).

The Tourism Office is at Paseo de Grazia, 107; tel. 93 238 40 00. There are also offices at the airport and in Sants and França stations.

Buy the weekly *Guía del Ocio* for details of Barcelona's 24 theatres, 52 cinemas (some showing undubbed foreign films), and more than 100 art galleries. **La Mercè fiesta** on September 24 is the occasion for colourful festivities, including processions of giant figures.

PUBLIC TRANSPORT

Barcelona has an efficient transport system. The metro lines are colour-coded for easy use, although you may have to walk some distance when changing trains. Buy a *multiviatje*, a ticket valid for ten trips on bus and metro, costing half the price for individual tickets. A day ticket for Line 100 lets you stop off at will on a circular tour of most of the interesting sights (Jun-Sept). Outlying areas are served by Ferrocarrils de la Generalitat (FGC).

Taxis are plentiful, but progress can be slow in the dense traffic.

A cable car whisks you across the harbour from Montjuïc to the old quarter of Barceloneta and funiculars run from Paral.lel metro station to Montjuïc and from Plaça Tibidabo to Tibidabo amusement park. Service is daily in summer and at other peak times, but otherwise only on Saturdays and holidays. For information on transport, call 93 412 00 00.

ACCOMMODATION GUIDELINES

The Olympic Games brought an increase in better-class accommodation, but also a boost in prices. To be close to everything, look for a place near the Plaça de Catalunya at the upper end of La Rambla. Some of Barcelona's finest and most expensive hotels are in the Eixample area, north-east of the Plaça. The biggest range of budget hotels is in the Barri Gòtic, the medieval section. However, those in the dark, narrow streets towards the port are not recommended.

NEIGHBOURHOODS TO AVOID

Unless you are looking for local colour at any cost, steer clear of the depressing Barri Xines (Chinese Quarter, the euphemism for the red light district), west of La Rambla's seaward end, to which only the brush of Toulouse Lautrec could do justice. The Plaça Reial has supposedly been cleaned up, but strange characters still drift around here and parts of La Rambla by night. In the Barri Gòtic stick to main, well-lit streets. Leave all valuables in your hotel. A favourite trick of local thieves is to spill liquid on your clothing and then pick your pockets under cover of helping to clean it off.

Thriving Barcelona

Orientation Spread out on a plain between Montjuïc, a hill to the south of the city, the sea and the Tibidabo hills, Barcelona is sliced by broad boulevards. The most stylish is the Passeig de Gràcia, the most lively La Rambla, which bisects the old quarter, running between the port and the Plaça de Catalunya, a focal point; each part of La Rambla has its own name. A few blocks north is the Barri Gòtic, the medieval heart of the old city, where the cathedral and seats of government are found among a warren of narrow streets. North-east along the waterfront is the ultra-modern Olympic Village.

Inland from the Plaça de Catalunya is the Eixample, with some of the best shops and hotels, which was laid out on a grid system in the 19thC. The mighty thoroughfare, the Diagonal, cuts across it. Montjuïc has important museums and the Olympic Stadium.

FROM THE PLAÇA DE CATALUNYA TO THE PORT VIA THE GOTHIC QUARTER

Start The Plaça de Catalunya. Walk towards the sea along **Portal de l'Angel**, a bustling shopping street. Just down the second street on the left, at Carrer Montsió, 3, is one of young Picasso's haunts, **Els Quatre Gats**, where at 18 he exhibited his portraits. This café, a legendary meeting place of bohemians and intellectuals, was reopened in 1986.

Continue along Portal de l'Angel to Plaça Nova, turning left on Avinguda Catedral. On your right, steps lead up to the magnificent Gothic **cathedral** (see Sights & Places of Interest, page 196). Outside the cathedral at midday on Sundays you can see locals performing Catalunya's lilting traditional dance, the *sardana*.

Turn right at the side of the cathedral

195

down Comtes, then left on Santa Clara to enter the **Plaça del Rei** (the King's Square, see Sights & Places of Interest, this page), lined with splendid medieval buildings once occupied by the Counts of Barcelona. They incorporate the remains of Roman walls, visible from Vía Laietana.

Leaving the Plaça del Rei, take Veguer, then turn first right on Llibreteria to emerge in the spacious Plaça Sant Jaume, scene of many a joyous celebration and angry demonstration. On one side of the cobbled square is the 15thC palace of the **Generalitat** (seat of regional government, see Sights & Places of Interest, this page). Facing it, on the seaward side is the Ayuntamiento (City Hall), with a neo-classical façade. On the first floor is the **Saló de Cent**, where from the 13thC Barcelona's representatives, the Council of One Hundred, met in an early semblance of democracy.

Walk southwards from the square along the Carrer de Ferran to reach **La Rambla**, the series of lively tree-shaded promenades running east from the Plaça de Catalunya to the port. Built over a water-course (*rambla* means torrent), it is always full of strollers, vendors and entertainers and its cafés are perfect for people-watching. News-stands, pet shops and flower stalls dot its length.

El Liceu, Barcelona's majestic opera house, just across from the Ferran junction, is being rebuilt, having been destroyed by fire in 1994.

Turn right to view at Nou de La Rambla, 3, the **Güell Palace**, by Gaudí.

Walking towards the port, you see off to your left the **Plaça Reial**, a noble, arcaded square, usually with a few not-so-noble-looking individuals occupying the benches.

At the junction with the waterfront road, Passeig de Colom, soldiers stand guard outside military headquarters.

By the port a 60-m iron **column** bears the bronze figure of Columbus pointing, for some reason, in the opposite direction to the New World. Take the elevator to the top for excellent views. Tourist information available at the bottom. Boats, called *golondrines*, ply from the adjacent quayside across the busy harbour.

The old timber wharf, **Moll de la Fusta**, has been converted into a promenade, with bars and restaurants.

SIGHTS & PLACES OF INTEREST

CATHEDRAL (LA SEU)

Avenida Catedral, Barri Gòtic. The soaring façade of this Gothic pile was actually built in the 19thC, based on drawings by a French architect in 1408. Much of the structure dates from the 14thC. The crypt, beneath the choir, contains the elaborate alabaster sarcophagus of Santa Eulalia, patron saint of Barcelona. In the tranquil cloister geese swim in a pool surrounded by palms and orange trees.

F.C. BARCELONA

Estadi Nou Camp, Aristides Maillol, s/n. On match days up to 150,000 spectators squeeze into the massive Nou Camp stadium, soccer shrine and home to Football Club Barcelona, known as 'Barca'. Attend a Barcelona-Real Madrid game to see just how deep the rivalry goes. Visit the club museum (closed match days, and Mon).

MONTJUIC

South of the Avenida Parallel. The most impressive approach to this hilltop, which offers commanding views of the city, is from the Plaça d'Espanya along Reina María Cristina, passing the trade fair centre. On summer evenings a huge fountain plays, constantly changing form and colour. Steps and escalators lead up the hill, where apart from a park and gardens you find:

Museu Arqueológico, which has outstanding collections of megalithic artefacts and pieces from the Greek and Roman colonies at Empuriés.

Castell de Montjuïc. The castle houses a military museum. Catalunya president Lluís Companys was executed here in 1940. Tombstones from an old Jewish cemetery can be seen (Montjuïc means Mountain of the Jews), a rare vestige of the large Jewish community that once lived in the Gothic quarter. A cable car runs up to the castle via an amusement park.

Fundació Miró. Designed by his friend Josep Lluís Sert, this well-lit building is an ideal showcase for the challenging tapestries, sculptures and paintings of Catalan artist Joan Miró. Film shows and lectures are held. You will see Miró's unmistakable designs in many places, for example as a logo in Spanish tourism publicity.

Estadi Olímpic and Palau Sant Jordi. The former was originally built for the International Exhibition of 1929 and renovated in time for the 1992 Olympics. The latter, a roofed sports stadium, looks like a flying saucer, but Japanese architect Arata Isozaki's daring design has won enthusiastic praise. **Palau Nacional**. This immense building houses the **Museu d'Art de Catalunya**, with a superb collection of Gothic and Romanesque art, which may not be on view until the incorporation of a contemporary art centre has been completed.

Poble Espanyol, a village built for the 1929 International Exhibition to show the country's diverse architectural styles; also a popular nightspot.

MONTSERRAT *60 km NW of Barcelona, off the N11. Take an FGC train from Plaça de Espanya to Montserrat Aeri, then a cable-car.* Soaring to a height of 1,235 m, this dramatic jagged-edged outcrop is Catalunya's holy mountain, a place of pilgrimage for all Catalans. Montserrat is a common girl's name, chosen in honour of La Moreneta (the Little Dark One), the region's patron saint, embodied in a 12thC polychrome carving of the Virgin enshrined in a glass case above the altar in the monastery church. The faithful queue to kiss her right hand. At 1 pm and 6.45 pm you can hear the Escolanía, one of Europe's oldest boys' choirs, founded in the 13thC. Adjacent souvenir shops are packed with religious baubles.

MUSEU MARITIM
Portal de la Pau, 1. The Drassanes, immense medieval shipyards, give an idea of the power which Catalunya's navy once wielded around the Mediterranean. The collection of vessels in the Maritime Museum includes a submarine of 1859, invented by Narcis Monturiol (it worked but drove him bankrupt), and a stunning replica of the 16thC galley of

---

GAUDI AND THE MODERNISTS
If only one thing sticks in your mind after visiting Barcelona, it will surely be the amazing flights of fantasy of Antoni Gaudí. He was the most famous exponent of the Modernist movement, the Catalan version of Art Nouveau, developed around the turn of the century. *Modernisme* was part of the *Renaixenxa*, a drive to restore Catalan culture supported by a new middle class. Sinuous lines, foliage embellishments and the use of ceramics, stained glass and metal are features of the style. The most famous architects were Lluís Doménech i Montaner (see his printing house at Aragó, 25, which houses the **Fundació Antoni Tàpies**, dedicated to Barcelona's leading modern painter); Josep Puig i Cadafalch (**Casa Amatller**, Passeig de Gracia, 41, and **Els Quatre Gats** building, Montcada, 3); and Gaudí (1852-1926).

Some condemn Gaudí's buildings as kitsch or camp, but he was undoubtedly a genius. As art critic Robert Hughes commented in his brilliant book *Barcelona*: 'His work dominates Barcelona as Bernini's does Rome, setting a scale of imaginative effort against which one is apt to measure everything else.' Some outstanding examples:

Temple Expiatori de La Sagrada Família. This crazy, glorious project has become the symbol of Barcelona. A century after work started, construction of the church still creeps along. The soaring spires (18 were planned) and cascades of symbolic sculpture are the pious Gaudí's hymn to the Catholic faith. An elevator takes you up one of the towers and there is a museum.

Casa Batlló, Passeig de Gràcia, 43. The façade is even more spectacular by floodlight.

Casa Milà, Passeig de Gràcia, 92. This corner building is dubbed the Pedrera (quarry) because it appears to have been carved from rock. The interior is equally striking.

Parc Güell, Olot s/n (Metro Lesseps). Gaudí let his imagination run riot when Eusebio Güell, a banker, asked him to design a garden city, never completed. Its bizarre structures make a visit a dreamlike experience. The house where Gaudí lived is a museum (closed Sat).

• In Gaudi's Parc Güell.

Don Juan of Austria. The building itself, with colossal vaulting, is unique, a masterpiece of early industrial design.

MUSEU PICASSO

Montcada, 15 (north of Vía Laietana). Housed in a medieval palace, the museum has more than 3,000 of the artist's paintings, sketches and drawings. Although there are gaps in the collection, it throws an interesting light on his early years, including his Blue Period. Picasso donated a series of paintings showing his interpretation of the masterpiece *Las Meninas* by Velázquez.

PALAU DE LA GENERALITAT

Plaça Sant Jaume. Catalunya's leaders have met here since medieval times. Now it houses the regional government. Enter from the Carrer del Bisbe. Stone stairs rise along one side of an exquisite patio, leading to the flamboyant Gothic chapel of Sant Jordi (St George, patron saint of Catalunya).

PALAU DE LA MUSICA CATALANA

Sant Francesc de Paula, 2. Doménech i Montaner designed this concert hall, 'the temple of Catalan music', a dazzling Modernist mirage of brick, mosaics and stained glass with Wagnerian horses leaping above the audience. Concert tickets are often sold out weeks in advance.

FOR NIGHT BIRDS

Barcelona stays up until dawn, and later at weekends. The *Guía del Ocio* lists countless piano bars, disco-pubs, music halls and jazz clubs. The city has gone bananas on high-tech nightspots, some converted from warehouses or garages. They are expensive and so designer-trendy it hurts. Two of the 'in' places are **Otto Zutz** (Lincoln, 15) and **Torre d'Avila** (Poble Espanyol) of which Barcelona observer Robert Hughes said 'Its sheer awfulness may entitle it to preservation.'

Awful too, in a grotesquely amusing manner, is **Bodega Bohemia** (Lancaster, 2) where ancient music hall performers nightly resurrect the past.

RECOMMENDED HOTELS

Adagio, PP-PPP; Fernando, 21; tel. 93 318 90 61.

Handily situated near La Rambla, off Ferran Street, this two-star hotel is modern and comfortable.

Condes de Barcelona, PPP; Passeig de Gracia, 75; tel. 93 488 22 00.

An expensive luxury hotel located in a unique building, designed in the 19thC by Vilaseca as an opulent private villa in which Modernism meets Art Deco.

Cortés, PP; Santa Ana, 25; tel. 93 317 91 12.

Attractive and functional two-star hotel, near the Plaça de Catalunya.

Gran Vía, PPP; Gran Vía Corts Catalanes, 642; tel. 93 318 19 00.

Fans of faded grandeur will like this one with its grand staircase, chandeliers, gilt furniture and mirrors.

Mercure Barcelona Rambla, PPP; Rambla Estudis, 124; tel. 93 412 04 04.

A three-star hotel with a noble façade, situated on La Rambla.

If cost is secondary, try the plush four-star **Rivoli Ramblas**, (no. 128; tel. 93 302 66 43).

RECOMMENDED RESTAURANTS

Agut d'Avignon, PPP; Trinidad, 3; tel. 93 302 60 34; credit cards AE, DC, MC, V.

Discreetly located down a cul-de-sac near the City Hall, the Agut has a well-established reputation for quality, mixing traditional *cuisine* with modern dishes. Recommended is *Conejo a la ampurdanesa* (rabbit Ampurdan style).

Can Culleretes, PP; Quintana, 5; tel. 93 317 64 85; credit cards AE, MC, V; closed Sun eve, Mon, three weeks Jul.

Founded in 1786, this reasonably priced restaurant (two blocks from La Rambla) serves traditional Catalan dishes. Tiled walls and chandeliers give you the flavour. Try the *Cuixa d'oca amb pomes* (leg of goose with

---

---

apple).

Los Caracoles, PP; Escudellers, 14; tel. 93 302 31 85; credit cards AE, DC, MC, V.

Tourists cannot resist the chickens spit-roasting outside. Inside there's a welcoming atmosphere. *Caracoles* (snails) are a speciality.

The street is rather sleazy: take lunch rather than dinner here.

Quo Vadis, PPP; Carme, 7; tel. 93 302 40 72; credit cards AE, DC, MC, V; closed Sun, Aug.

Fresh ingredients from nearby La Boquería market. Mushroom potpourri and cheese soufflé are on the extensive menu and there's a wide range of sparkling wines.

Salamanca, PP; Almirante Cervera, 34; tel. 93 221 50 33; credit cards AE, DC, MC, V.

Many restaurants compete for your custom in the Barceloneta. This is one of the liveliest; for quieter dining go upstairs. Try such fish dishes as *Sarsuela* (fish stew) and *Rape a la plancha* (grilled angler fish). Service is pushy but friendly.

Siete Portes, PP; Passeig Isabel II; tel. 93 319 30 33; credit cards AE, DC, MC, V.

An excellent-value restaurant with 150 years in the business. A wide range of rice dishes, including *paella*, and traditional Catalan food are served. Book, especially at weekends.

PARC DE LA CUITADELLA AND BARCELONETA

On the Passeig Lluís Companys. A Mudéjar-inspired arch of triumph welcomes you to the park, scene of the 1888 Universal Exhibition. It contains the **zoo** (whose most famous inmate is Snowflake, an albino gorilla), the **Museus de Geologia, Zoologia and Art Modern** and Catalunya's **parliament buildings**.

East of the park, on a spit of land bordering port and sea is the **Barceloneta**, a seething workers' quarter of narrow rectangular tenements built in the 18thC and famous for its seafood restaurants. The waterfront has been spruced up and ramshackle eating places cleared away.

PLACA DEL REI

Barcelona's rulers held sway in the buildings around this austerely handsome square. On his triumphant return from the New World, Columbus came here to receive the congratulations of the Catholic Monarchs, Ferdinand and Isabel, in the Saló del Tinell, the wide-arched throne room. Adjoining is the **chapel of Santa Agata** and opposite is the Casa Clariana-Padellàs, which houses the **Museu d'Història de la Cuitat** and a basement with Roman and Visigoth remains. The 16thC structure was moved here stone by stone when Vía Laietana was built.

SANTA MARIA DEL MAR

Passeig Born, La Ribera. This superb example of 14thC Catalan Gothic has an impressive feeling of spaciousness. An 11-day fire started by anarchists destroyed many treasures during the Civil War. Now society marriages are often held here.

TEMPLE EXPIATORI DE LA SAGRADA FAMILIA

See page 197.

TIBIDABO

Take the FGC railway to Avinguda Tibidabo, or bus 17 from Plaça de Catalunya to Avenida, then the blue tram to the funicular station. They say that on a clear day you can see the Balearics from this 532-m peak northwest of the city. Apart from the view, Tibidabo offers an amusement park. A 260-m telecommunications tower, designed by British architect Norman Foster, spears the heavens. At the foot of the mountain is the **Monasterio de Pedralbes**, *Baixada Monestir, 9,* founded in 1326 and containing part of the Thyssen art collection (reached by bus No. 22 from the Plaça de Catalunya).

A walk south (or bus No. 75) along Avinguda de Pedralabes will bring you to **Palau Reial de Pedralbes**, built for Alfonso XIII in the 1920s and now housing the **Museu Ceràmica**, a treat for fans of Spanish ceramic art (metro: Palan Reial).

VILA OLIMPICA (OLYMPIC VILLAGE)

At Poble Nou, east of the Barceloneta, hotels, apartments and a marina, planned by architects Bohigas, Martorell and Mackay, have replaced a wasteland of warehouses and railway lines. A promenade and new beaches have restored life to the seafront.

RECOMMENDED *TAPA* BARS

Barcelona has an infinite variety. A few suggestions:

Narrow streets in the **Barri Gòtic** labyrinth near the port offer a traditional atmosphere (leave your tiara at home). Try the rowdy, barrel-lined **La Bodega** (*Regomir, 11*), where you sit on wooden benches and order platefuls of food listed on a blackboard, or **La Socarrena**, for cider and goat cheese, one of numerous small bars on Mercè.

The customers can be as interesting as the *tapas* in the **Barceloneta** bars. Fast food has invaded **La Rambla**, but the **Café de l'Opera** (*Rambla Caputxins, 74*) preserves its old decorations. The **Plaça Reial** has popular pavement cafés. Move to **Eixample** for more fashionable bars.

Xampanerías, serving *cava* (sparkling wine), are popular. Try **El Xampanayet** (*Montcada, 22*); the decorations include tiled walls, a '1,000-year-old ham' and giant *porrones* (the typical Catalan glass drinking vessel). *Anchoas* (cured herrings with a spicy sauce) are the house speciality. More up-market is **La Cava del Palau,** (*Verdaguer i Callis, 10*) near the Palau de la Música.

For a Spanish idea of an English pub, try **The Daily Telegraph** (*Pau Claris, 139-141*).

Seville:
introduction

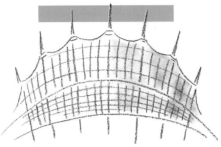

F ew cities have had so many verses, songs, and operas composed in their honour as Seville. Few urban dwellers are so proudly aware of their traditions and their home town's attractions. And in few cities is there such devotion to diversion. Seville's fun-loving image goes back at least to the 13thC when Abu-l-Wali El Sakundi, a Moorish commentator, declared that the people were 'the most frivolous and most given to playing the fool'. Seville's style provokes both admiration and envy among other Andalucíans.'Hijo de Sevilla, uno bueno por maravilla' (If you come across a good *sevillano*, it's a miracle) goes one saying.

Thanks to the impact of the world fair, Expo 92, Seville has never looked better. Huge investment brought a surge of activity and new ideas to a city so in love with itself that it hardly cared what happened else-where. Old buildings have been refurbished, new promenades opened up along the River Guadalquivir and traffic re-routed.

Spain's fourth largest city (population 650,000) retains its magic and the best way to enjoy it is to soak up the theatrical atmosphere of the place and its people. Living up to their legend is a full-time occupation among the *sevillanos,* who love to demonstrate their *gracia,* (a special type of wit and charm). Balmy jasmine-perfumed evenings, flamenco's staccato rhythms, characters who seem to have stepped straight out of Carmen – they are all there.

Summers are oppressively hot, with temperatures up to 45°C. Autumn is pleasant, but winters can be damp. By far the best time to visit is spring, when you can witness Seville at its most colourful and exuberant, during Semana Santa (see page 204) and the Feria (April Fair). The latter is a week-long spectacle when the whirl of *sevillanas* (a fast-moving, light-hearted flamenco dance) never stops. It is a very private public party, for only a member's introduction can get you into the 1,000 or so *casetas* (private booths) where much of the merrymaking goes on. There is, however, plenty to goggle at.

• *The Feria de Sevilla.*

USING THIS SECTION

The most important sights of Seville are covered in the gazetteer of Sights & Places of Interest starting on page 204. A walk is also suggested for those who want a guided tour. You will find hotel and restaurant recommendations at the end of this section.

ARRIVING

San Pablo Airport (tel. 95 451 06 77) is 12 km out of the city off the Madrid road. There is no bus service so you will need a taxi. (For information about Iberia flights tel. 95 422 89 01.)

All trains arrive at Santa Justa Station. At least six times a day the AVE high-speed train connects Seville with Córdoba and Madrid. The journey from Córdoba takes 44 minutes and from Madrid two hours 35 minutes. (For RENFE information tel. 90 224 02 02.)

Most long-distance buses arrive at the Estación de Autobus, on Manuel Vázquez Sagastizabal, Prado San Sebastián (information tel. 95 441 71 11). At least eight buses a day link Seville with Madrid. Buses for Huelva and Badajoz arrive at the Estación Plaza de Armas (tel. 95 490 80 40).

TheTourism Office is at Avenidade la Constitución, 21; tel. 95 422 14 04. To find out what's on, ask for the entertainment guide, *El Giraldillo.*

PUBLIC TRANSPORT

Seville has a good bus network; ask for the *Guía del Transporte* from the Tourism Office. Within the old quarter it is simplest to walk, but four useful buses circle the centre of town. Buy a Bonobus, a ticket allowing ten journeys, on sale at *estancos* (tobacco shops) and newspaper stands. Taxis are reasonably priced as distances are generally short.

A pleasant way to view the city is by hiring a horse-drawn carriage. Fix the price before starting. You will find them at various points, including outside the cathedral and in the Plaza de España.

Several companies, among them Compañia de Cruceros (tel. 95 456 16 92) offer trips on the river, departing from the Paseo Marqués de Contadero, near the Torre do Oro. From April to October Cruceros del Sur (tel. 95 421 13 96) has Saturday trips to Sanlúcar de Barrameda.

ACCOMMODATION GUIDELINES

Hotel prices tend to be higher in Seville than in other parts of Andalucía. Overcharging reached ridiculous levels during Expo '92, but market forces now prevail. Serious overbuilding has resulted in a glut of more expensive accommodation, so that it is worth haggling over room rates. High season runs from Easter until the end of May. During Semana Santa and the Seville Fair, prices are 50 to 100 per cent higher than normal and rooms may be hard to find.

Some of the large luxury hotels are inconveniently distant from the main sights, but numerous hotels of all categories near the cathedral and around the Barrio Santa Cruz cater for tourists. You will find others in or near the Plaza Nueva and Reyes Católicos.

NEIGHBOURHOODS TO AVOID

Seville has a bad name for bag-snatching and theft from cars, often by jobless youths from the dismal new suburbs, although police action has improved the situation. When driving into town, keep all objects of value out of sight. Leave nothing in your car at any time. Leave your passport and valuable items in the hotel safe. Avoid dark narrow streets after dark. Be especially wary around the Alameda de Hércules and the Macarena Basilica.

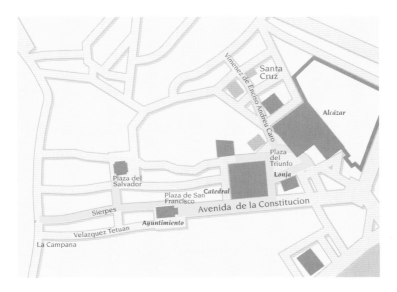

Map labels: Jiménez de Enciso · Andreu Caro · Santa Cruz · Alcázar · Plaza del Triunfo · Lonja · Plaza del Salvador · Plaza de San Francisco · Catedral · Sierpes · Avenida de la Constitucion · Ayuntimiento · Velazquez · Tetuan · La Campana

Mainstream Seville

Orientation Seville's main sights are contained in a triangle within the old quarter, bordered by the Guadalquivir and the streets Alfonso XII and Laraña Imagen (running east from the river), Menéndez Pelayo (running north-east) and the Parque de María Luisa.

If you don't know where to start, try the walk below, designed to give you a taste of some of the main sites in this triangle.

FROM THE CATHEDRAL TO SIERPES

Start The cathedral. At one corner is the **Giralda Tower**, symbol of Seville (see Sights & Places of Interest, page 204). Adjoining it is the **Patio de los Naranjos**, the courtyard of the old mosque.

Turn right on leaving the cathedral to reach the **Lonja** (Exchange) which holds the **Archivo de Indias**, 80 million pages (many now accessed by computer) detailing Spain's dealings with the New World (open mornings, closed Sun).

A few paces beyond, on the Plaza del Triunfo, is the entrance to the **Alcázar**, a magnificent example of Mudéjar architecture (see Sights & Places of Interest, page 204).

From the Alcázar you pass through the Patio de Banderas with its orange trees, then turn right to enter the **Barrio Santa Cruz**, the old Jewish quarter, one of Seville's most attractive corners. You will inevitably get lost in the maze of narrow streets, passing small workshops, intimate little squares and patios glimpsed through iron gates, known as *cancelas*.

Return to the cathedral and proceed north along the broad Avenida de la Constitución to the Plaza de San Francisco, bordered on the west by the **Ayuntamiento** (City Hall), with a magnificent Plateresque façade. From the north side of the square runs Seville's most famous street, **Sierpes**, pedestrians only. Here you can buy everything from ornate fans to lottery tickets. Through the windows of the Círculo Mercantil (a private club) you can see Franco clones sipping their sherry.

Detour east on Sagasta to the **church of El Salvador,** built on the site of a mosque. Behind it is **Plaza Jesus de la Pasión**, where virtually every shop sells wedding gowns. At the bottom of Sierpes is **La Campana**, a cake shop and traditional meeting spot.

SIGHTS & PLACES OF INTEREST

ALCAZAR

Plaza del Triunfo. This sprawling palace-fortress was founded by the Almohads and expanded in the 14thC by Pedro the Cruel. He employed Moorish craftsmen as you will see from the Alhambra-style adornments of intricate plasterwork, tiles and coffered ceilings. When a Moorish ruler came to a banquet, Pedro had him and 37 of his courtiers put to the sword, because he craved a ruby in his turban. In 1367 he presented the ruby to the Black Prince and it ended up in England's Imperial Crown. In the basement are baths where Pedro's courtiers allegedly drank his mistress María's bathwater to show their devotion, except one who slyly observed that 'If I taste the sauce, I might covet the partridge'.

SEMANA SANTA

Pagan roots and piety cheerfully mix during Semana Santa (Holy Week), when more than 100 *pasos* (floats) carrying religious images sway through the streets of Seville, where Easter is celebrated in a more sumptuous manner than anywhere else in Spain. Throughout Andalucía, the week has solemn moments but can also be noisy and festive.

Processions begin on Palm Sunday and reach an emotional climax on Good Friday. They are organized by *cofradías*, brotherhoods which in Seville date back to the 13thC. Each tries to outdo others in the skill with which they bear the floats, weighing as much as a ton, and particularly in the magnificence of their Virgin's attire: millions of pesetas are lavished on jewel-encrusted mantles.

Up to 2,500 *nazarenos*, as participants are called, walk in procession. They wear robes similar to those of heretics condemned by the Inquisition; the sinister appearance appealed to the Klu Klux Klan which adopted the same pointed hoods. Others, sometimes barefoot, join the procession to do penance or to give thanks for some favour conceded by the Virgin.

Especially noteworthy are the **Salón de Embajadores**, where Charles V married Isabel of Portugal, the **leafy gardens** and the **Patio de las Doncellas** (Maidens' Court). Spain's present monarchs stay in the Alcázar on their visits to Seville.

BASILICA DE LA MACARENA

Off Muñoz Léon. This temple, north of the old quarter near the remains of the old walls, houses Seville's most venerated Virgin, La Macarena. Gilded ornamentation enthrones the sumptuously robed, tearful image.

CASA PILATOS

Plaza Pilatos. This Mudéjar-Renaissance palace, property of the Duque de Medinaceli, has a Plateresque entrance, a charming patio embellished with Roman statues, and some beautiful decoration in tile and carved woodwork. The name arises from the belief that the Marqués de Tarifa, who completed the building in 1540, copied features of Pilate's house in Jerusalem.

FABRICA DE TABACOS (TOBACCO FACTORY)

San Fernando. It featured in Bizet's opera *Carmen*. Now the huge building is part of Seville University.

GIRALDA AND CATHEDRAL

Plaza Virgen de los Reyes. Elegant symbol of Seville, decorated with brickwork, arches and niches, the 98 m-high Giralda was built as a minaret in the 12thC, the top storey and weather vane being added 400 years later. Climb the ramp inside to enjoy excellent views. The adjacent mosque was destroyed in 1401 when church elders declared: 'Let us build a cathedral so immense that everyone on beholding it will take us for madmen.' Judge for yourself. The building, which took a century to construct, is the largest Gothic church in the world.

Many Renaissance splendours lie within its gloomy depths. The Capilla Real (Royal Chapel) holds the remains of Pedro the Cruel and Ferdinand III (the Saint), whose tomb is opened three times a year so that the public can view the incorrupt body. Also notable are beautiful grilles by Francisco de Salamanca, superb choir-stalls, a huge retable in the main chapel and the relics in the Treasury, which include a cross said to be made from the first gold brought back from the New World by Columbus. His body is supposed to rest in an elaborate tomb in the cathedral but, in fact, it is almost certainly in Santo Domingo (Dominican Republic).

HOSPITAL DE LA CARIDAD

Temprado; closed Sun. Miguel de Mañara founded the hospital in 1674 to help the needy dying. A dissolute noble, he changed his ways and devoted his life to charity after a nightmare vision of his own funeral. The building contains an important collection of **paintings by Murillo and Valdés Leal**.

ITALICA

Off N630, near Santiponce, 9 km NW of Seville. Itálica was the first Roman colony in southern Spain and the emperors Hadrian and Trajan were born here. You can see mosaics, streets and an amphitheatre. To mark the 2,200th anniversary of its founding, a bullfight was staged in the amphitheatre in 1994.

LA MAESTRANZA (PLAZA DE TOROS)

Paseo de Cristóbal Colón. Seville's bull-ring holds 14,000 spectators and – along with Las Ventas in Madrid – it is the ultimate venue for any matador. The season runs from April to October and there are fights daily during the April Fair. The local idol is Curro Romero: when he is good he is superb and when he is bad (usually the case), he often flees the ring under a hail of cushions.

MARKETS

On Sunday mornings there is a street market in the Alameda de Hercules and a philately market in the Plaza del Cabildo. Andalucían crafts are on sale every day in El Postigo market, on Calle Arfe near the Plaza del Cabildo.

MUSEO ARQUEOLOGICO

Plaza de América. At the south end of Parque de María Luisa, the museum contains treasures of Tartessus, Roman statues and Phoenician ceramics.

RECOMMENDED HOTELS

Casa de los Mercadores, PP-PPP; *Alvarez Quintero, 9-13; tel. 95 422 58 58.*
A stylish modern hotel with a pillared patio, near the Ayuntamiento and Sierpes.

Atenas, PP; *Caballerizas, 1; tel. 95 421 80 47.*
A two-star *hostal* to the rear of the Casa de Pilatos, decorated in typical Seville style, with a flowery patio and tiled walls.

Doña María, PPP; *Don Remondo, 19; tel. 95 422 49 90.*
Antique furnishings and old-world charm just opposite the cathedral.

Hacienda Benazuza, PPP; *Sanlúcar la Mayor (off the N431 Seville-Huelva highway, 12 km W of Seville); tel. 95 570 33 44.*
A palatial residence with an 18thC church has been converted into an exclusive – and expensive – hotel. Patios, fountains, palms, tennis courts, swimming-pools, antique furnishings and impeccable service. The three restaurants include the elegant

Alquería (PPP); try the glazed sea urchins with quails' eggs.

Hacienda San Ignacio, PP; *Real, 194, Castilleja de la Cuesta (off the A49, 8 km W of Seville); tel. 95 416 04 30.*
Palm trees and traditional decoration add atmosphere to this 300-year-old whitewashed country mansion, formerly a Jesuit retreat, now a comfortable hotel.

Los Seises, PPP; *Segovia, s/n; tel. 95 422 94 95.*
An archaeological site with a modern four-star hotel around it. Individually-styled rooms have been slotted into a 16thC palace, part of the Archbishop of Seville's residence. The decoration includes Roman mosaics, Arab tiles and the Inquisition insignia.

Simón, PP; *García de Vinuesa, 19; tel. 95 422 66 60.*
Pleasant old-style hotel with rooms around a central patio.
Reservations for stays in private houses and country houses and hotels in the Seville area can be made by calling (free) 900 21 08 71.

DEATH IN THE AFTERNOON

Spain's *fiesta nacional* is colourful, dramatic, barbaric and usually misunderstood by visitors. Half of Spain's adults have never attended a bullfight, most preferring soccer (Seville has two leading soccer teams, one bull-ring), while angry intellectuals like Manuel Vicent say that if bullfighting is art then 'cannibalism is gastronomy'.

Even so, the *corrida* is as popular as ever. If you see a fight, don't look for a winner or a loser. This is a highly-stylized ritual sacrifice, often deteriorating into farce, occasionally achieving sublime moments. The spectator suffers vicariously the emotions of a puny man faced by a 500-kg beast bred to attack. How the *matador* reacts in the face of possible death or maiming is the essence of the *corrida*.

Anthropologists maintain that animal sacrifice is an ancient celebration of life. Indeed, man has been sacrificing bulls since the worship of Mithra more than 15,000 years ago. Certainly bullfighting appeals to instincts we all share.

Perhaps the strongest argument against the *corrida* is that it may blunt a spectator's sensitivity to suffering. But enthusiasts retort that a bull endures only minutes of pain after four good years on the open range, a privilege not given to millions of chickens, lambs and calves sacrificed to feed other basic instincts. Maybe one day the bulls and chickens will have *their* say.

• *The victor's applause.*

MUSEO DE BELLAS ARTES

Plaza del Museo, 9. Set in a splendid 17thC convent, the museum has works by some of Seville's great artists, including Murillo, Velázquez and Zurbarán.

PARQUE DE LOS DESCUBRIMIENTOS

Isla de La Cartuja; open Fri, Sat, Sun, also Tues, Wed, Thur eves in summer; closed Mon and Jan 10-Feb 24. The science and theme park occupies many Expo '92 pavilions. Tickets are pricey but the park offers a great variety: audio-visual spectacles, street musicians, pavilions devoted to historic voyages, nature, and the environment, fun fair attractions, pop concerts, discos and laser shows.

Adjoining the park is **Monasterio de La Cartuja** (closed Monday), where, in the crypt of the Santa Ana Chapel, Columbus was initially buried before his remains were shipped to the Caribbean. Incongruous bottle-shaped furnaces date from the 19thC when English entrepreneur Charles Pickman, later the Marqués de Pickman, converted the building into a pottery.

Two of the best rooms are the refectory with its fine coffered ceiling and that containing the tombs of the Ribera family who endowed the monastery.

PARQUE DE MARIA LUISA

Avda Isabel la Católica. This leafy park is a pleasant place in which to wander and take refreshment. It was the site of the 1929 Ibero-American Exhibition. The most spectacular relic is the **Plaza de**

España, with a boating canal, bridges and elaborate tilework.

TEATRO DE LA MAESTRANZA

Paseo Colón. Seville's first opera house, opened in 1992. Symphony concerts are staged here but not many operas, mostly for lack of funds.

TORRE DEL ORO (TOWER OF GOLD)

Paseo Colón. Built by the Moors in the 13thC. The tiles that once covered the tower sparkled like gold. Now it houses a maritime museum.

RECOMMENDED RESTAURANTS

Cheap, tourist-orientated eateries line Mateos Gago, which runs from the cathedral square alongside the Santa Cruz quarter. Good food tends to be pricey in Seville. Recommended dishes include *gazpacho*; *Rabo do toro a la sevillana* (ox tails flamed, braised and spiced); and for dessert *tocino del cielo* (heavenly bacon), made from egg yolk and sugar.

La Albahaca, PPP; Plaza Santa Cruz, 12; *tel.* 95 422 07 14; *credit cards* AE, DC, MC, V; *closed* Sun.
On a pleasant little square, this restaurant occupies a house built by one of the architects of the 1929 Ibero-American Exhibition. Chandeliers and tiles lend a sophisticated air to small dining rooms. Recommended: sirloin with green mustard sauce.

Mesón Don Raimundo, PP; Argote de Molina, 26; *tel.* 95 422 33 55; *credit cards* AE, DC, MC, V; *closed* Sun eve.
Plenty of olde Spanish decorative efffects in this former convent, near the cathedral. Angled at tourists, but pleasant. Try the duck Moorish style.

Río Grande, PP; Betis, 70; *tel.* 95 427 39 56; *credit cards* AE, DC, MC, V.
Enjoy the splendid view of the river and the Torre del Oro from the riverside terrace. The restaurant specializes in fresh seafood.

TAPAS AND NIGHT LIFE

Seville's *tapas* are so good you hardly need to set foot in a restaurant. A *fino* (dry sherry) or a *manzanilla* (sherry from Sanlúcar) goes well with plump Seville olives, *jamón serrano* (cured ham), grilled shrimps, or *criadillas* (sautéed calves' testicles). This last was a favourite dish of the dictator Primo de Rivera – when he attended bullfights, he would order up platefuls from the first bull of the afternoon. Also try *huevos a la flamenca* (baked eggs with asparagus, sausage and peppers).

You will soon find your own favourites among the countless *tapa* bars both sides of the river. Two atmospheric traditional spots are **Casa Morales** (*García de Vinuesa, 11*), an old *bodega* with huge barrels, and **El Rinconcillo**, (*Gerona, 42*), founded 1670, with wine from the barrel. For elegance rather than *tapas*, try the bar at **Taberna del Halaberdo**, a mansion at *Zaragoza, 20*, with marble floors and fountain.

Jazz, discos, and classical concerts are all possibilities in Seville, which has a lively student population. **La Carboneria** (*Levies, 18*), a popular meeting place for the younger generation, has exhibitions, sometimes live music. Late nighters relax at **Abades** (*Abades, 13; open from 5 pm, closed Mon*), near the cathedral. Catch some of the fire of flamenco at such night spots as **Los Gallos** (*Plaza Santa Cruz; tel. 95 421 69 81*); **El Patio Sevillano** (*Paseo de Colón, 11; tel. 95 421 41 20*); or **El Arenal** (*Rodo, 7; tel. 95 421 64 92*). They are tourist-orientated but will give you an idea of this constantly-evolving art, derived from Oriental and Byzantine influences brought by the gypsies, with Arab and Jewish elements. Flamenco is divided into three main categories, *cante jondo* (deep song), an outburst of anguish, the blues of America's blacks; *intermedio*, less profound; and *chico* (small), sensuous and frivolous. Night-long summer flamenco festivals are held in many towns nearby.

Northern Spain

Basque Country – Coast and Interior

220 km; map Michelin 442, 1:400,000

B asques have an almost mystic attachment to their land and its customs. To explore the back country give yourself time. Sinuous roads meander along the coast past fishing villages or wander into secluded valleys with their white, snug-looking *caseríos* (farmhouses). Here and there are dour industrial towns, but idyllic scenery is always close. At local fiestas you will have the opportunity to see some of the traditional dances accompanied by music played on drums, the *txistu* (a type of whistle) and the *alboka*, a pipe made of straw, wood and horn. You will also witness such Basque tests of strength as rock-lifting, log-chopping, and races between oxen dragging boulders. You can join the crowds that flock to the *sidrerías* (rustic bars, mostly in Guipuzcoa) where you drink new cider from the barrel and eat simple country fare. Their high season is January 19 to March 19, although they also open in summer.

TRANSPORT

Buses run between all the towns, and there are daily connections with Bilbao and San Sebastían. Their frequency varies and, remember, traffic is slow on the country roads. There are train services to Guernica, Bermeo and Azkoitia.

1:1,000,000

RECOMMENDED RESTAURANTS

BERGARA

Lasa, PP-PPP; *off the C6213, 70 km SW of San Sebastian – Zubiaurre, 35; tel. 943 76 10 55; credit cards MC, V; closed Mon, eves, (except Fri and Sat), Aug.*

Traditional, family-run establishment with some imaginative dishes. Go for the fresh trout or salmon and aspic with truffles.

BERMEO

Artxanda, PP; *Santa Eufemia, 14; tel. 946 88 09 30; credit cards V; closed Dec.* Ultra-fresh fish are served in this restaurant with a terrace overlooking the port. Delicious desserts.

RECOMMENDED HOTELS

More than 100 government-supervised farmhouses in the area offer bed-and- breakfast at very reasonable rates. For more information, call 946 20 11 88/63, fax 946 20 06 66, or write to the Oficina de Agroturismo, at San Miguel Auzoa, 11–1 Dcha, 48200 Garai (Vizcaya).

MUNDAKA

Atalaya, PPP; *near Bermeo on the Guernica road – Paseo de Txorrokopunta, 2; tel. 946 17 70 00.*

A well-kept bay-windowed house, decorated in English style; peaceful atmosphere; overlooks sea and estuary.

ZESTOA

Balneario, PP; *off the N634, 44 km E of San Sebastian – Paseo San Juan; tel. 943 14 71 40; closed Dec 15-Mar 15.*

Belle Epoque atmosphere in a spa amid gardens and mountains. The waters are recommended for the digestion.

209

• The harbour, Lekeitio - see page 211.

SIGHTS & PLACES OF INTEREST

ARANTZAZU
See Oñati, page 211.

AZKOITIA
There are several buildings of note, including the medieval tower of **Idiáquez** and the Baroque **Palacio de Insausti**. Between the town and Azpeitia lies the **Santuario de Loyola**, a huge monastery marking the spot where Ignatius of Loyola was born in 1491. While recovering from battle wounds, he declared he had been called by God, later founding the Society of Jesus. Little remains of the original Loyola manor house, but it has been converted into a permanent exhibition.

The massive **basilica** is surmounted by a 63 m-high cupola, reminiscent of St Peter's in Rome. Thousands of pilgrims attend the **San Ignacio day celebrations** on July 31.

BERGARA ×
See Recommended Restaurants, page 209.

BERMEO ×
With the largest trawler fleet on the whole Cantabrian coast, Bermeo is worth visiting if only to see the auction of the night's catch when the craft return in the early morning. Founded in the 13thC, the town competed with Bilbao in importance and Santa Eufemia Church was one of four where the Castilian kings, as lords of Biscay, used to swear to uphold the Basque privileges. A **fishing museum** is located in the Gothic Ercilla tower. Each June 22 Bermeo and nearby Mundaka take part in a **regatta**, an event that arose from an age-old argument over who owns the island of Izaro. There are fine views along the coast, one of the most spectacular being to the west where a shrine to St John the Baptist tops the Gaztelugatxe islet, scene of a June 24 pilgrimage.

GUERNICA (GERNIKA)
Guernica holds a special place in Basque hearts because, since the Middle Ages, the Basque parliament came to debate here, in the shade of a tree; the Spanish monarchs also came to swear to respect the *fueros* (local privileges) of the Basques. Thus, the bombing of the town on April 26, 1937, by the Condor Legion in support of Franco's rebels was a psychological attack on Basque resistance. Regarded as a trial run for the horrors of the Second World War, the attack inspired Picasso's famous anti-war painting, *Guernica*, which hangs in Madrid.

Most of the town has been rebuilt and

the only true relics of the past are the Assembly Hall, the **Casa de Juntas**, which houses a museum, and the adjacent **sacred oak tree**. A pillared temple shields the stump of the original oak, while a new tree grown from a seedling in the 19thC arches upwards behind iron railings.

About 7 km north-east of Guernica, near Kortezubi, are the **Santimamiñe Caves**. Prehistoric wall paintings depict bison, bears, stags, and a red-haired bull which is said to have guarded Mari, a beautiful goddess. According to ancient Basque legend, she lived in caves and hopped from one mountain to another like a fireball.

Another worthwhile excursion from Guernica is to the **Balcón de Bizkaia**, 18 km south-east, from where you can admire a sweeping view of green fields, woods, and mountains.

LEKEITIO

This pleasant little fishing town has an attractive, well-protected bay and there are several pleasant beaches in the area. Lekeitio earned notoriety among animal rights activists because of an ancient **fiesta** held in the first week of September. Youngsters in rowing-boats snatched at geese suspended on a line above the harbour, yanking their heads off. A public outcry has, apparently, condemned this custom to oblivion.

• *Basque country contests.*

MUNDAKA ⌂

See Recommended Hotels, page 209.

OÑATI

Birthplace of Lope de Aguirre, the conquistador, Oñati in its tranquil valley has splendid old buildings, including a **former university** founded in the 16thC and a Baroque **Ayuntamiento**. The university's Plateresque façade was sculpted by a Frenchman, Pierre Picart. The fall of the town, headquarters of the pretender Don Carlos, led to the end of the bloody First Carlist War in 1839.

An excursion to the **Arantzazu Shrine** takes you above a narrow gorge to a point 800 m above sea-level with magnificent views of the mountainous terrain.

A choir of Franciscan friars sings at Arantzazu's Sunday morning Mass. I found their voices more uplifting than the grey slab-like 1950s church, although noted Basque artists worked on it, including architects Javier Saenz de Oiza and Luis Laorga, sculptor Eduardo Chillida (who designed the doors), and Jorge Oteiza, who carved the Apostles on the façade.

ZESTOA ⌂

See Recommended Hotels, page 209.

Picos de Europa

250 km, map Michelin 442, 1:400,000

Jagged, snow-brushed *sierras*; deep, forested valleys; salmon and trout streams; and wildlife that includes bears, wolves, rare butterflies, chamois, wild boar, and a rare wild horse called the *asturcón*: These are the Picos de Europa, a wilderness zone with highly changeable weather (because of its closeness to the sea) that strays into three provinces, Asturias, Santander, and León.

The daunting limestone massif rises with amazing abruptness to a height of more than 2,600 m, offering some of Spain's most spectacular scenery. Climbers, walkers, fishermen, mountain bikers and canoeists all find challenges in the Picos. But you don't have to be super-fit to enjoy the panoramic views.

Mountain refuges are there on the heights for those exploring on foot and you will find a number of pleasant small hotels in the villages, with their wooden-balconied houses. Familiar sights are cows drawing carts stacked with hay and the *hórreos*, wooden storehouses raised on pillars

TRANSPORT
There are bus services from
Santander along the Deva valley. From
Oviedo buses run to Cangas de Onís,
Covadonga, Arenas, and Riaño.

1:500,000

to prevent rats and mice from eating the grain. More than 20,000 *hórre-os* dot Asturias and are protected by a 1973 edict.

The livestock grazing the mountain pastures produce numerous cheeses. The most famous is Cabrales, a pungent blue cheese made from the milk of cows, ewes, and goats. Trout is usually served fried with ham, while a filling country dish is *pote asturiano* (a stew of potatoes, sausage, blood sausage, beer, cabbage, and beans).

If you are approaching the Picos from Santander, the best access by car is from the N634 along the Deva Valley, following the N621 to Potes and then Fuente Dé. Alternatively, you can branch right from the N621 at Panes and continue along the Cares valley to Arenas de Cabrales. From Oviedo, you can turn off the N634 at Arriondas towards Cangas de Onís and Covadonga. From León, head for Riaño, from where several roads penetrate the Picos.

SIGHTS & PLACES OF INTEREST

ALLES ⌨
See Recommended Hotels, page 216.

ARENAS DE CABRALES
Tourism Office Ctra. General, tel. 98 584 52 84. Arenas is a handy base for exploring the **Cares Valley** and making an excursion to the **Bulnes** and the **Naranjo de Bulnes** (right). It has some small hotels and a good camp ground by the river, where you can obtain information about excursions and local guides.

This is the home of Cabrales cheese, sold in many shops, also direct from

WALKING IN THE PICOS
The **Federación Asturiana de Montañismo**, Calle Melquiades Alvarez 16, Oviedo; tel. 98 525 23 62 provides up-to-date information on maps, guides, walking routes and mountain huts where you can stay overnight. (Most Picos villages have a campsite.)

Non-Spanish language guides to walking the Picos are somewhat scarce: West Col of Reading publish one for the ordinary walker, Picos de Europa, by Robin Collomb; and Cicerone Press have a 'tough' guide describing climbs, scrambles plus a few easy/intermediate walking routes.

Maps
Local walkers and climbers recommend maps published by Miguel Angel Adrados, of Oviedo, scale 1:25,000, available in the Picos area and all over Spain in specialized bookshops. Editorial Alpina publishes two guides on the Picos with maps at 1:25,000. The Instituto Geográfico Nacional and the Servicio Geográfico del Ejército both issue maps at scales of 1:25,000 and 1:50,000, although these are not always up to date.

More information on and suggestions for easy and challenging walks is given under Bulnes, this page; Fuente Dé, page 216; Naranjo de Bulnes, page 216; and Cares Gorge, this page.

farmhouses. You will never forget your first taste: like eating port. Ideally, the cheese should be accompanied by local cider. Locals claim that there is no truth in stories that Cabrales is matured in cow-byres.

BULNES
There is no road to this tiny hamlet, only a path leading through the deep valley to the awe-inspiring peak, **El Naranjo de Bulnes**. The handful of inhabitants would appreciate a surfaced road, but the potential damage to the environment – and the cost – has blocked the project. Instead, you escape the sounds of the 20thC as you trek up the path from the road at Poncebos to the mist-shrouded stone houses by a tumbling stream. It takes about 90 minutes.

There are one or two bars and the **Albergue de Bulnes** (tel. 98 536 69 32), a refuge with basic, cheap accommodation in a three-storey house built in 1906. It has 20 bunk beds in two dormitories (bring your own sleeping bag). This is the place to wise up on walking and climbing routes, by talking to other visitors, and to Alberto, who runs the Albergue. He knows the Picos well and can arrange for professional guides. There is a library with books and maps of the region.

CANGAS DE ONIS ✕
See Spain Overall: 1 and Recommended Restaurants, page 217.

CARES GORGE
Accessible from Arenas de Cabrales in Asturias or Posada de Valdeón in León province.

The walk along La Garganta Divina (the Divine Gorge) is a highly recommended expedition. It is not as strenuous as most hikes through the Picos because an adequate path, which services hydro-electric installations, follows the gorge, tunnelling through the rock at points and climbing high above the tumbling waters of the Cares. Waterfalls and cliffs towering more than 2,000 m delight the eye, while buzzards and falcons swoop around the crags. It is a 12-km walk through the gorge, between Caín, a picturesque cluster of houses just south of Posada de Valdeón, and Poncebos, reached by road from Arenas.

• *Abrupt limestone cliffs of the Picos.*

COSGAYA ⊨
See Recommended Hotels, page 217.

COVADONGA ⊨
In a valley of sturdy oaks, chestnut trees and green meadows, Covadonga is a sacred place for Spaniards. It is hailed as the cradle of the nation for here, in 722, began the Reconquest of Spain from the Moors. Virtually the whole peninsula was in Moorish grasp when the Emir of Córdoba sent an army to crush 300 or so Visigoth nobles and officials who had taken refuge here. What exactly happened next is as obscure as the mist which often shrouds the mountains. Led by Pelayo, a tribal leader, the defenders are said to have rolled down rocks on the attackers' heads, the Virgin also lending a hand. For the first time the Moors suffered defeat and Pelayo and Covadonga became symbols of resistance. Pelayo was elected the first Christian king of Asturias and established his capital at Cangas de Onís.

Pelayo's statue stands on the esplanade before the neo-Romanesque **basilica**, an uninspiring, twin-steepled structure less than a century old. On the hillside is the **Santa Cueva** (Holy Cave), allegedly the grotto where the

---

GUIDED EXPLORATION
A number of companies organize expeditions through or around the Picos by horse, mountain bike, canoe, raft and on foot. One is **Rutastur**, based in the coastal town of Llanes (tel. 90 210 7070). Four-wheel drive trips can be made with Rutastur and other companies. Information on guides for climbing trips and climbing instruction is available at Arenas de Cabrales (at the camping ground, tel. 98 584 65 78, also on tel. 98 584 55 45). Information on all aspects of the Picos is available from the Centro de Investigacíon de los Picos de Europa, based in Panes on the N621.

Christian defenders took refuge. Here you will find an altar and the image of the Virgen de las Batallas, who is patron of Asturias. Solemn homage is paid to her in religious festivities on September 8. Also in the cave are the tombs of Pelayo and Alfonso I. A spring nearby has special powers, for girls who drink from it will be cured of 'the ills of spinsterhood'.

From Covadonga a road curls upwards to a beautiful Alpine landscape of cow pastures and lakes backed by mountains. **Lakes Enol** and **Ercina**, formed by glaciers, lie within the 17,000-hectare **Parque National de Covadonga**, the first of Spain's National Parks, founded in 1918. Holly and beech trees grow on park slopes and the streams are rich in trout and salmon.

FUENTE DE 🛏

Rock walls rise sheer from a green valley to form a magnificent amphitheatre, where the Deva River has its source. On the valley floor is a campsite, a parador, and the starting-point for a cable car which swings you up 800 m in three minutes to a look-out point known as the **Mirador del Cable**.

The service operates every day from 10 am until 6 pm, but sometimes closes in winter. Arrive early in high season as long queues form; there may also be a long wait to descend in late afternoon.

From the upper station you can tramp into the mountains towards the tiny **refugio de Cabaña Verónica** (a two-hour expedition), where you can view the Naranjo de Bulnes (see page 214).

An easier walk is to the **refugio de Aliva**, about 4 km, from where a dirt track leads down to Espinama, which is on the paved road to Fuente Dé.

Non-walkers can do it the easy way, by hiring a four-wheel drive car with driver (available in Espinama and Arenas de Cabrales). You will be taken along some hair-raising tracks through the mountains. One route runs from Espinama near Fuente Dé to the Aliva Refuge, then to the village of Sotres and thence to Arenas de Cabrales.

LLANES
See Spain Overall: 1.

NARANJO DE BULNES
This impressive rock tower in the heart of the Picos, also known as Pico Uriellu, has been called the Spanish Eiger,

---

RECOMMENDED HOTELS

ALLES
La Tahona de Besnes, PP; Besnes, Peñamellera; tel. 98 541 42 49.

In a leafy valley, just off the C6312 road to Arenas de Cabrales, this old stone building is a cosily rustic hotel, replete with stonework and solid beams, next to a rushing stream. Once it was occupied by the local miller and baker. It is one of a number in Asturias, converted with government and EC aid. Facilities are available for walking, horse-riding, cycling, and excursions into the Picos. The restaurant offers paté with mushrooms and Cabrales cheese and fresh trout or salmon.

COSGAYA
Del Oso Pardo, PP; Ctra Espinama; tel. 942 73 30 18; closed Jan 7-Feb 15.

In the beautiful Deva River valley, near Fuente Dé. Hearty country soup and roast lamb in the restaurant, **Mesón del Oso** (**PP**; credit cards DC, MC, V), which has an extensive wine list.

COVADONGA
Peñalba, P; La Riera; tel. 98 584 61 00.

A small, family-run hotel in a restored 18thC house, 3 km from Covadonga. Home cooking.

FUENTE DE
Parador Río Deva, PP; Fuente Dé; tel. 942 73 66 51.

A modern building magnificently located amid the mountains.

Refugio de Aliva, PP; tel. 942 73 09 99; closed mid Oct-Jul.

This 27-room refuge in the heart of the Picos can be reached by four-wheel-drive from Fuente Dé, or by taking the cable car and walking about 3 km.

a challenge that no mountaineer can resist. You don't have to be a climber to appreciate it, however. From any angle it is a daunting pinnacle of bare limestone, jutting 2,519 m into the sky. It was first climbed in 1904, when Pedro Pidal, Marqués de Villaviciosa, wearing rope-soled sandals, and Gregorio Pérez, a legendary hunter from Caín, who was barefoot, reached the summit via the north-east face. A Munich climber, Gustav Schulze, covered the same route solo two years later. The west face, featuring a stomach-turning 500-m drop, was not conquered until 1962.

A large mountain refuge, the **Refugio de la Vega de Urriellu**, stands near the foot of El Naranjo. Climbers and hikers approach it either via Fuente Dé and the cable car (see above), or from the village of Sotres, or from Bulnes. In Bulnes a plaque commemorates Luis (El Cuco) Martínez, who 'lived and died in art and beauty'. He was the first to die on the Naranjo, in 1928, but not the last.

PICOS DE EUROPA

The name of this limestone range is believed to have been coined by Spanish fishermen. Far out to sea, the first – and last – sight they had of their homeland and the continent was of the sharp 'peaks of Europe'.

The Picos are split into three massifs, west, central, and east, and penetrated by the narrow gorges of the rivers Sella, Cares, Duje, and Deva. While the valleys are lush and leafy, the heights, covering about 35 by 15 km, present a lunar landscape of barren, tortured rock, almost bare of vegetation.

It is easy to get lost in the Picos because of the complexity of the terrain, a labyrinth of precipices, razor-edged ridges, and unexpected ravines. Deep gorges are known as *canals*, while creviced hollows are called *jous*. Rain and snow filter away very quickly, carving caverns and galleries, so that there are no running streams at high altitudes.

Walkers and climbers should be properly equipped, particularly as the weather can change abruptly as a front sweeps in from the Bay of Biscay. The most settled weather tends to be in September. Throughout the year, the

Picos are often mist-covered or bathed by the *orbayu* , a pleasant word for the gentle rain that makes Asturias so green. See also Walking in the Picos, page 214.

POTES ✕
Potes, reached from the coast by the spectacular Hermida Gorge through which runs the Deva River, is the main town of the fertile **Liébana Valley**. It is a pleasant little place with old balconied houses, though increasingly over-run with tourists. Nearby is the **Monasterio de Santo Toribio de Liébana**, where a piece of the 'true Cross' is preserved. The road from Potes towards Riaño offers some truly spectacular views.

SOTO DE SAJAMBRE
Soto is a picturesque little village high in the mountains on the western edge of the Picos. From its secluded valley you can see one of the most prominent peaks, the **Peña Santa de Castilla**, which rises 2,596 m. It is reached from Cangas via the dramatic gorge of the Sella River, the **Desfiladero de los Beyos**.

SOTRES
Reached by a narrow, winding road, Sotres, at over 1,000 m above sea-level is a lonely mountain village. Buy cheese here. From Sotres you can walk to the Naranjo de Bulnes (page 216) or down to the village of Bulnes (page 214), with magnificent views all the way.

Northern Spain

Covarrubias and Santo Domingo

280 km; map Michelin 442, 1:400,000

C aptivating medieval villages, such as Covarrubias, eye-catching castles and wild mountains rising to more than 2,000 m lie within easy reach of Burgos to the east and south-east. Locked away in its valley, the vast monastery of Santo Domingo is memorable for its feeling of timelessness, while impressive buildings in Lerma and Peñaranda de Duero bear witness to past military and political ambitions.

From Salas de los Infantes, east of Santo Domingo, a particularly attractive road, the C113, climbs up into the Sierra de la Demanda, snaking along the Najerilla valley. La Demanda, a mountainous area stretching into the Rioja region (see Local Explorations: 9) is popular with hikers and hunters. Count on at least two days to do the main sights.

1:1,000,000

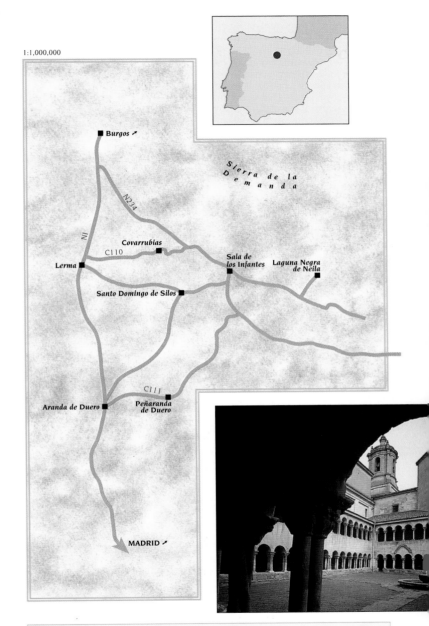

Burgos ↗

S i e r r a   d e   l a
D e m a n d a

N234

NI

C110

Covarrubias

Lerma

Sala de
los Infantes

Laguna Negra
de Neila

Santo Domingo de Silos

C111

Aranda de Duero

Peñaranda
de Duero

MADRID ↗

TRANSPORT

Between Burgos, Lerma and Aranda, you have no problem. Trains and buses are frequent. Away from the main route marked on the simplified map, you are down to one or two buses a day from Burgos and may find yourself having to walk between villages to pick up a connection. The Burgos-Santo Domingo bus leaves at 5.30 pm, 2 pm on Saturdays, no service Fridays or Sundays.

SIGHTS & PLACES OF INTEREST

ARANDA DE DUERO ✕
The market town of Aranda, once important for its strategic position and now a road and rail junction, does not excite the eye. However, it is worth a halt to sample the excellent Duero wines and the food: the town claims that its roast lamb and suckling pig are the best in Castile.

BURGOS
See *Spain Overall*: 2.

COVARRUBIAS 🛏
The drive along the Arlanza River valley to Covarrubias is beautiful, particularly in autumn when the poplars are changing colour. Just as pleasant is a stroll around Covarrubias, a delightful medieval walled village. Mighty beams and stone pillars abound. The 15thC **collegiate church** contains a notable Flemish triptych of the Adoration and 20 medieval tombs, including those of Fernán González and his wife. Fernán González was the first Count of Castile, a 10thC warlord who united much of

northern Spain and pushed the Moors south. A few kilometres east of Covarrubias are the ruins of the **Monasterio de San Pedro de Arlanza** where Fernán González was first buried.

LAGUNA NEGRA DE NEILA
A spectacular run through the Sierra de la Demanda brings you to the Black Lagoon, a glacier lake. Close by is the **Mirador San Francisco**, a look-out point with great views of the mountains, including **Campiña**, 2,049 m. Another black lagoon, the Laguna Negra de Urbión, lies to the east in Soria province (see Spain Overall: 5).

LERMA 🛏
In the early 17thC, the Duke of Lerma, as favourite of Philip III, virtually ruled Spain. He squandered cash while the country headed for ruin and the Moriscos (Moors converted to Christianity) were expelled from Spain. The scheming, fun-loving duke spent freely in his home town before final disgrace forced him into exile at Tordesillas. His grandiose ideas bequeathed Lerma, topping a rise on the Madrid highway, two large squares and some imposing buildings, including the huge **Palacio de los Duques**.

Sacked by the French in the Peninsular War, it is being restored. The adjacent **collegiate church of San Pedro** contains an impressive bronze statue of Lerma's uncle, Cristóbal de Rojas y Sandoval, Archbishop of Seville.

PEÑARANDA DE DUERO
A spectacular **castle** stands above the medieval, half-timbered village, including a picturesque porticoed square. The Renaissance **Miranda Palace** has a fine patio, a grand staircase, and rooms with coffered ceilings. Peñaranda also boasts a 15thC **pillory**.

SANTO DOMINGO DE SILOS 🛏 ✕
One of my most haunting memories of Castile is that of vespers in the plain, white stone **Monasterio de Santo Domingo de Silos**. Twenty-four black-robed Benedictine monks raised their voices in Gregorian chant: a sound unchanged down the centuries in this tranquil valley. At the end of the service, they filed down the central aisle and into the monastery, their echoing voices gradually fading away.

Founded more than 1,000 years ago by Fernán González, the monastery was sacked by the Moors and rebuilt by Domingo, a monk who arrived from Navarre. His tomb can be seen in the north gallery of the magnificent 12thC two-tier cloister. Several different sculp-

• *Santo Domingo de Silos.*

RECOMMENDED RESTAURANTS

ARANDA DE DUERO
Mesón de la Villa, PP; *Rodriguez Valcárcel, 3; tel. 947 50 10 25; credit cards* AE, DC, MC, V; *closed* Mon *last two weeks* Oct.

If you are going to eat lamb in a place that boasts its lamb is the best in Castile, why not do so in the best restaurant in town? Ask to see the vaulted, subterranean *bodega* where a vast selection of Rioja and Duero wines are stored.

SANTO DOMINGO DE SILOS
Santo Domingo, PP; *tel.* 947 38 07 27; *credit cards* V.

The reasonably-priced restaurant, which is particularly busy on weekends, is downstairs, below the bar and *hostal*. My advice: go for the *cabrito asado* (roast kid), but avoid the enticingly-named *tarta de monjas* (nuns' tart), unless you like sickly, creamy sponge.

---

tors worked on the Romanesque cloister, in a corner of which rises a lofty cypress tree. Twin columns support the arches and the capital's adornments are amazingly varied, including monstrous birds, harpies, lions, and fantasy creatures, while the corner pilasters bear low reliefs depicting religious scenes.

Priceless medical volumes and a copper still are stored in the pharmacy, whose walls are lined with antique flasks and jars of Talavera pottery. These contain potions and herbs, with which the monks used to treat the sick, apparently with miraculous results.

Recordings of the monks' Gregorian chant have been a huge success, one album shooting to the top of the Spanish charts. Records are on sale at the monastery, which is closed on Tuesdays; on holidays it opens only in the afternoon. You can hear the Gregorian chant daily at 7 pm and 9.30 pm. To stay at the monastery, call 947 38 07 68. The price is low, but only males are allowed and the 22 rooms are usually booked some weeks ahead.

Five kilometres east of Santo Domingo, a railed walkway threads its way through the spectacular **Yecla Gorge**, only a few metres wide in places, with a torrent rushing below. Not for the claustrophobic or feeble-footed.

<u>North-Western Spain</u>

The Galician Coast –
Costa do Morte and Rías Baixas

426 km; map Michelin 441

Battered by the restless Atlantic, the Galician coastline is a series of rocky inlets, spray-flecked headlands, and sandy coves. Fingers of blue water push into rugged indentations below green pastures and heavily wooded slopes. These narrow sheltered bays are known as *rías*.

The wildest part of the coast is the stretch north of Cabo Finisterre (Fisterra in local usage). Parts of it really do feel like the end of the world, where the land runs out and the threshing waves of the Atlantic take over. Not for nothing is it termed the Costa do Morte (Coast of Death): countless ships have sunk off this coast or been skewered on the rocks. There are few facilities on the windy coast west of A Coruña to Finisterre, the roads are tortuous, and the sea is chilly, even in summer. Inland, you find a rain-washed mixture of moorland, farmland and woodland.

Further south, geography and climate are less extreme. There are sandy beaches, pine woods and time-worn granite settlements. These are the Rías Baixas (the lower *rías*), which are highly popular in summer. Fortunately, the high-rise blight that has afflicted the Mediterranean coast is largely absent.

The coastal route as shown on the map makes a terrific drive, but of course, as with every local exploration in this guide, you don't have to follow the route: just use the gazetteer entries as a guide to what's worth seeing and doing in the area. Many of the places mentioned are natural side-trips from Pontevedra and Santiago on Spain Overall: 3. The Coast of Death is reached from the C552 between A Coruña and Carballo, branching north on the LC414 to Malpica.

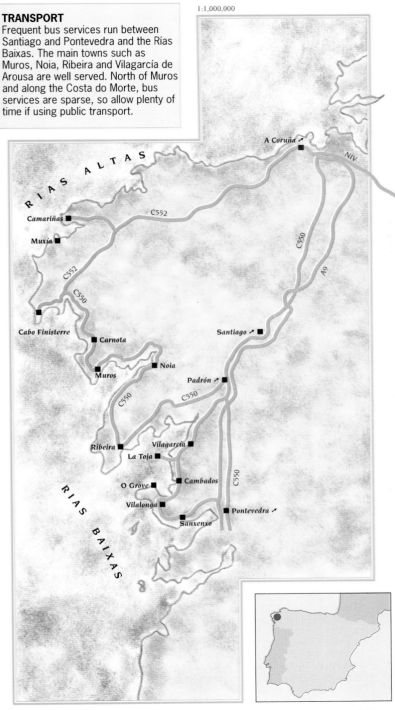

TRANSPORT

Frequent bus services run between Santiago and Pontevedra and the Rías Baixas. The main towns such as Muros, Noia, Ribeira and Vilagarcía de Arousa are well served. North of Muros and along the Costa do Morte, bus services are sparse, so allow plenty of time if using public transport.

1:1,000,000

A Coruña

NIV

RIAS ALTAS

Camariñas

Muxía

C552

C550

A9

Cabo Finisterre

C552

C550

Carnota

Noia

Muros

Santiago

Padrón

C550

C550

Ribeira

La Toja

Vilagarcía

O Grove

Cambados

Vilalonga

C550

Sanxenxo

Pontevedra

RIAS BAIXAS

223

SIGHTS & PLACES OF INTEREST

CAMARINAS
Tucked into a corner of its *ria* on the Costa do Morte, opposite Muxia, Camariñas is an important fishing port but is also famed for its lacework. Busily creating intricate patterns, the *palilleiras* (lace makers) sit outside the shops or their houses, painted in a variety of colours. Visit the nearby lighthouse on Cabo Vilán for magnificent views along the wild coast.

CAMBADOS ⌇
There is nothing so becomes Camba-

dos as the entering of it, via the splendid medieval Plaza de Fefiñanes. Traffic cuts diagonally across the stone-paved square which is so vast that you can get lost half way across. The plaza's most impressive building is the balconied palace, proudly emblazoned with a coat of arms, from whose *bodega* you can buy the local Albariño wine – a fresh, clean, fruity white, the perfect accompaniment to seafood.

In the 1980s production of this wine expanded dramatically and new *bodegas* used the latest technology to improve quality. It has, however, become rather over-priced. You will find it on sale all along this coast as you pass carefully tended rows of vines supported by granite pillars.

Cambados has a fishing port facing the Ría de Arousa, a tree-lined promenade; and there are some pleasant old streets lined with noble stone houses.

CARNOTA

This village's claim to your attention, apart from offering a majestic sweep of beach, is its **hórreo**. Just off the highway, in a paddock near the church and cemetery, there it stands, a veritable monster of a grain store, 35 m long and said to be the largest in Galicia.

CORCUBION

See Recommended Restaurants.

FISTERRA (FINISTERRE)

An old fort by a sandy beach, fishing boats, and a huddle of houses... that more or less sums up the village of Fisterra. At the Casa Gallega on the main square I tucked into a thick rich stew helped by some glasses of Ribeiro wine. I needed sustenance after visiting the torm-tossed headland just down the road, where the Finisterre lighthouse stands vigil above the waves on its buttress of rock. The best view is from the **Monte do Facho**, to which a track winds up just behind the lighthouse. But drifting smoke got in the way on my last visit – I was thunderstruck to discover that even this spot had fallen victim to an old Spanish custom, that of dumping garbage over any convenient hillside.

People made pilgrimages to 'the end of the world' long before Christianity; indeed the place was the centre of a sun-worshipping cult. A researcher into Galician legends told me that somewhere among the broom on the wild headland is a stone shrine with supernatural qualities. Infertile women visited the shrine – and may still do. Couples wanting a child have made love on the stones.

By the way, Cape Finisterre is not, despite its name, Spain's westernmost point. The real end of the earth is Cabo Touriñan, a little to the north.

GROVE, O (EL GROVE) ⌫

In summer thousands of families descend on O Grove, on a peninsula just opposite Cambados, to take advantage of the adjacent beaches and the Atlantic breezes. A bridge leads to **La Toja**, a pine-dotted island where one of Spain's most luxurious hotels and a casino are located. It has the somewhat sedate, even soporific, air of a spa, where you can either recharge your batteries or become bored out of your mind.

RECOMMENDED RESTAURANTS

CARNOTA A Revolta, P; *O Pindo; tel. 981 76 48 64; closed Mon and Sept.*

There is not much choice in this area near Finisterre, although you can rarely go wrong ordering seafood. This is a pleasant restaurant where you can try traditional local dishes.

NOIA Ceboleiro, P-PP; *Rua Galicia, 15; tel. 981 82 44 97; credit cards AE, DC, MC, V; closed Christmas to mid-Jan.*

Galician seafood at reasonable prices.

VILAGARCIA DE AROUSA Chocolate, PP-PPP; *Vilaxoán (Villajuán); tel. 986 50 11 99; credit cards AE, DC, MC, V; closed Sun, mid-Dec to mid-Jan.*

This restaurant, outside Vilagarcía on the Cambados road, is famous for the flamboyant style of its owner Manolo Cores, aided by his wife Josefina. Its walls record visits by a legion of international celebrities and it is often crowded. The shellfish, fish stews, and mighty steaks are first-rate and there is an interesting selection of wines.

El Lagar, P-PP; *Pazo Sobrán, Vilaxoán (Villajuán); tel. 986 50 09 09; credit cards AE, V; closed Sun and holiday eves.*

On the Cambados road, just outside Vilagarcía. Dine here simply for the atmosphere. The fortress-like building, guarded by two square towers and two very large dogs, is one of Galicia's oldest *pazos* (pazo: palace or mansion), at least 500 years old. A previous owner was an ambassador to Tamerlane's court. The present proprietors are two characterful sisters, Rachel and Ana, who serve wholesome regional food.

• *The grain store at Carnota - see page 225.*

of *percebes* (barnacles), which attach themselves to rocks at the waterline. Suspended by ropes, the harvesters lever the things off the rocks and pop them into baskets. *Percebes*, little black stumpy things which remind me of miniature elephant legs, are regarded as delicacies and fetch high prices.

NOIA ⇔ ✕

Alfonso, the architect of the 14thC bridge over which you pass on entering from Muros, is said to be buried under a cross on the bridge. This pleasant old town at the mouth of the Tambre river was once known as 'the key to Galicia' because of its busy port. These days it is has a new nickname, 'the widow of the sea', because only when the tide is really high does water reach its quays. There are some stately old mansions and two churches worth visiting: **San Martín**, with its sculpted rose window, and **Santa María a Nova**, where you can enjoy a few morbid moments contemplating an unusual collection of tombstones. Each is engraved with the symbols of a trade, although it is also thought that the symbols have cabalistic or astrological associations. Close to the sea at Porto do Son, midway between Noia and Ribeira on the C550, is the **Castro de Baroña**, the remains of a Celtic settlement.

PADRON

See *Spain Overall: 3*.

MUROS

Muros spreads picturesque arms around its fishing harbour. Pillars support the old houses, threaded with narrow alleys and dominated by the Gothic **parish church**. Incidentally, the women from this area of Galicia have a reputation for outstanding beauty.

MUXIA

On the rocks near this fishing village stands Santa María de la Barca, the scene every year of a pilgrimage by fisherfolk. Nearby is a large, **balancing boulder**, whose movements were said to indicate future events when interpreted by experts. Sadly, the latest information is that the Pedra de Abalar has broken and no longer rocks.

Fishing is perilous enough in these waters, but even riskier is the collecting

RIBEIRA

This fishing and canning centre on the north shore of the Ría de Arousa has no outstanding sights, but there are several points of interest in the vicinity. A short distance away on the **Corrubedo beach** are some of the biggest dunes to be found in Galicia. For one of the best panoramic views on the coast, travel the 8 km north-west from Ribeira to Puebla del Caramiñal and then 6 km inland to the **Mirador de la Curota**, nearly 500 m above sea level. There is a monument here to Valle Inclán, who wrote many of his novels and plays at a nearby *pazo* (mansion).

SANXENXO

This town on the north shore of the Ría de Pontevedra is a resort whose population swells from 15,000 to more than

70,000 in summer. The **Lanzada beach**, a vast arc of sand, lies on the road to O Grove. On the last Sunday in August a **fiesta** rooted in ancient fertility rites takes place at a shrine by the beach. Driving towards Combarro and Pontevedra, you have beautiful views of the *ría*, dotted with rafts, beneath which mussels grow suspended on lines.

VILAGARCIA DE AROUSA ×

This is a popular summer resort, with facilities for sailing and other water sports. Boats cruise the Arousa estuary and you can visit the beaches on the delightful **island of Arousa**.

Recently, the town has acquired increased prosperity and a new name, Vilagarcía de la Coca. Smuggling has always been important along this coast. Tobacco used to be the most profitable contraband, but in the 1980s the close connections between Gallegos and

• *Rowing boats at Muros - see page 226.*

South America helped create a new source of fast money. Cocaine began arriving by the hundreds of kilos and Galicia became the funnel through which most of Europe's cocaine supplies arrived. The Arousa estuary became notorious: speedboats capable of 50 knots or more appeared in the ports; humble mechanics and fishermen acquired portable telephones, expensive cars and gaudily-decorated houses. Civil Guards suspected of collusion with the 'contrabandistas' were abruptly posted elsewhere. Vilagarcía is regarded as the capital of this shady business, although you won't find many locals eager to discuss the subject.

VILALONGA

See Recommended Hotels, page 224.

North-Western Spain

Vigo Estuary, Atlantic Coast and Miño Valley

335 km; map Michelin 441

Wild horses are a notable attraction of this part of Galicia: they inhabit the hills rising inland behind the Vigo Estuary and the Atlantic coast. The yearly round-ups are spectacular events, held between May and August. Another attraction is the vineyard country of the Miño Valley. Strabo, the Greek geographer, wrote that the Miño was navigable for some 150 kilometres and the Romans panned for gold here, but today the slow-moving waters carry few craft, and eels and lamprey are the most valuable harvest. Driving up this misty valley is a pleasant experience, with vines supported on stilts climbing the hillsides and shifting views of Portgual.

From Ourense, capital of one of Spain's least-known provinces, you can explore the wild country to the east. From Monforte you can return to Santiago on the C533 and the N525, or continue northwards via Lugo to join Spain Overall: 3 at Betanzos.

If exploring this area by car, allow at least two days, especially if you intend following the marked circuit. If you're using local transport, allow at least three.

1:1,000,000

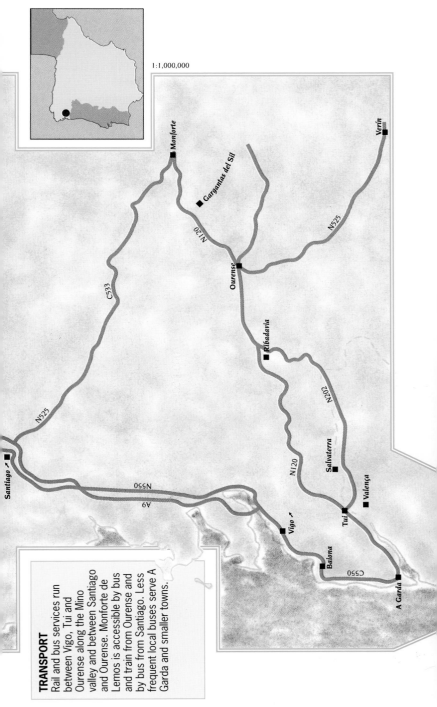

TRANSPORT

Rail and bus services run between Vigo, Tui and Ourense along the Miño valley and between Santiago and Ourense. Monforte de Lemos is accessible by bus and train from Ourense and by bus from Santiago. Less frequent local buses serve A Garda and smaller towns.

SIGHTS & PLACES OF INTEREST

BAIONA 🛏

In a little square on the sea front, a stone monument recalls that in March 1493 one of Columbus's three ships, the *Pinta*, commanded by Martín Alonso Pinzón, returned to this port from its historic voyage to the New World. Baiona's inhabitants were thus the first to learn of the 'discovery' of North America. The small town has indeed had an adventurous past thanks to its exposed position at the southern edge of the Ría de Vigo, where treasure galleons from the New World, pirates and other invaders often made landfall. Monte Real, the wooded promontory guarding Baiona, is surrounded by medieval walls. It is a pleasant walk around the walls (small admission charge), within which is the castle converted into a parador. The Romans were here, Al Mansur took the fortress in 997, and in the 15thC Don Pedro de Sotomayor occupied the place in the name of the Portuguese king. There are splendid views over the mouth of the estuary and towards the **Islas Cíes**, three rocky, salt and wind-burnished islands where there are large colonies of seabirds. Ferries run to the islands from Baiona and Vigo in the summer months.

GARDA, A (LA GUARDIA) 🛏

It is a barren lonely, windswept coastline between Baiona and A Garda. More often than not, rain draws a veil over it all, including the former Cistercian monastery of **Monasterio de Santa María la Real**, which you will sight near the sea outside the village of Oya.

The small port of A Garda, famed for its lobsters, sits at the extreme southwestern corner of Galicia, close to the mouth of the Miño River and Portugal.

Take the road which coils up the 340-m **Monte Santa Tecla**. On the right, among the trees, you will come across the remains of a Celtic settlement. Two replicas of the circular stone, thatched huts have been made;

• *The Celtic settlement near A Garda.*

looking at them, you may reflect that the Celts were a hardy bunch to have survived at all in this climate.

These Bronze Age inhabitants ate considerable quantities of mussels, barnacles and other shellfish to judge by the remains on display at the museum on top of the mountain. Stones bearing swastikas carved in different forms, Roman columns, and a small idol, with hands crossed over its stomach, are among the finds displayed. The idol may have been pressed against sick people in an ancient healing ritual. From the top of Santa Tecla you can gaze out to sea and into Portugal, or so I am assured, when rain and mists are not present. A café and a hotel offer shelter.

GARGANTAS DEL SIL

An excellent new road, the N120, runs along the Miño valley north-west from Ourense to the junction of the Sil River. Red-tiled granite houses are pinned to the slopes, surrounded by vineyards. Just before entering Lugo province, you turn right along a narrow road by the Sil. It twists up to a viewing point. (The river cuts through a narrow gorge where climbers like to test their skill.)

• *Vineyards of the Miño Valley.*

On the granite heights above, wild moorland extends into the distance. Continue on the road as it doubles back above the gorge and look for a turning down the hillside to the **Monasterio de San Esteban de Ribas de Sil**. Its history, in as lost and lonely a spot as one can imagine, dates back possibly 1,400 years. Mingling Romanesque and 16thC Gothic, the building has three cloisters of vast proportions, which are slowly being restored.

MONFORTE DE LEMOS

On the approach to Monforte from Ourense, the N120 switch-backs spectacularly upwards above the dammed Miño River, passing slopes which in spring are aflame with broom. The road flattens out as you run across the verdant plateau around Monforte, an ancient town with a castle crowning a hill above it. The chapel of the huge Instituto, or **Colegio de la Compañia**, once a Jesuit convent, has a magnificent reredos by Francisco de Moure. Two early works by El Greco, and paintings ascribed to Andrea del Sarto, are also on view.

═══════════════════════
RECOMMENDED HOTELS
═══════════════════════

BAIONA
**Parador Conde de Gondomar,
PPP**; *Ctra de Baiona; tel.* 986 35 50 00.

A lofty Gothic lobby, huge chandeliers, a stone staircase built for grand entrances, wide galleries, panelled and beamed public rooms, magnificent views, and all on a spot of historic importance. The restaurant serves local specialities, including lobster, but if you find the prices too steep there are a number of reasonable seafood restaurants in town.

GARDA,
A Convento de San Benito, P-PP; *Plaza de San Benito; tel.* 986 61 11 66.

This 24-room hotel near the port was converted from a convent in 1990. More than 30 nuns once lived in the Benedictine monastery founded in 1561. The character of the old building, including the cloister and elegant stonework, has been retained and the rooms are attractively furnished, with television and heating.

OURENSE
Gran Hotel San Martín, PPP; *Curros Enriquez,* 1; *tel.* 988 37 18 11.

Ourense's best-appointed hotel, spacious, and rated four stars. At least by staying here you are spared the sight of the exterior: it occupies the tallest and ugliest building in town.

VERIN
Parador de Monterey, PP; *Verín; tel.* 988 41 00 75.

Located on a hill next to a 13thC castle, with outstanding views, this is a useful halt on the N525, 72 km south-east of Ourense and a short distance from northern Portugal. The parador, whose restaurant specializes in Galician dishes, is outside the pleasant old town of Verín, known for its wine and bottled mineral water.

OURENSE ⇆ ✕
They've done their best to ruin Ourense, throwing up soulless blocks everywhere. Even so, the **old quarter**, with its arcaded streets and ageless stone walls, still has charm. That is where you will find the teeming *tapa* bars, medieval buildings (some on the point of collapse), and splendid squares such as the **Plazuela de la Magdalena**, with its cross depicting a weeping Mary Magdalene.

Blocked in by the structures around it, the cathedral dates from the 12thC. Its most striking feature is the **Pórtico del Paraiso**, which imitates the entrance of the same name in Santiago's cathedral; the sculpted figures here, however, retain the colours painted on in the Middle Ages. John of Gaunt assuredly attended services here during his brief reign as King of Castile in 1386.

A walk down Santo Domingo Street brings you to the San Lazaro park, where the former **Monasterio de San Francisco** has a remarkable cloister with 62 arches supported by slender double columns. Ask for permission to enter.

The city grew up around the **hot springs of Las Burgas**, and there they still are, spouting water, 300 litres a minute, at a temperature of 67°C. Rich in minerals, the water is said to have medicinal properties and you will see people dabbing it on parts of their anatomy while others arrive to fill containers.

Just around the corner from the Plaza Mayor at Avenida Pontevedra, 5, is the **Café Victoria**, one of those establishments left over from a more leisurely era. There are newspapers to read, marble-topped tables, and time to savour your coffee and brandy. The international fashion designer Adolfo ('wrinkles are beautiful') Dominguez, was born in Ourense and opened his first shop in the city.

An ancient bridge spans the Miño at Ourense. Although claimed to be Roman, the handsome **Puente Viejo** has been rebuilt on at least two occasions.

RIBADAVIA
This town hops and jumps down the banks of the Miño at its junction with the Avia rivers. The old Jewish quarter

and the impressive remains of the castle of the Condes de Ribadavía are worth seeing. Ribadavía is the centre of the wine-growing district of Ribeiro and a museum on Santiago Street gives plenty of information about this refreshing white. A **wine fiesta** is held at the end of April and large quantities are also consumed at the **annual fiestas** which take place in the second week of September.

SANTIAGO
See *Spain Overall: 3.*

TUI ×
Perched on a hill facing Portugal across the Miño River, Tui (Tuy in Castilian) has a solid, aloof air, emphasized by the fortress-like appearance of its cathedral. According to legend, the town was founded by Diomedes, a hero from The Iliad who found peace here from his spiteful wife. She had been converted into an adulteress by Venus, seeking revenge after she was wounded by Diomedes at Troy.

Tui has, in fact, been a settlement since ancient times and the name could have derived from the Greek Tyde. It was an episcopal seat under the Romans and the Visigoth King Witiza established his court here. During the Middle Ages it changed hands several times as Castile and Portugal battled for supremacy.

There is a bourgeois confidence about the town, which has prospered from trade with Portugal. From the narrow streets of the old quarter rises the **cathedral**, consecrated in 1232. It is a mixture of austere Romanesque and Gothic embellishments. The choirstall carvings relate the life of San Telmo, patron of Tui. There are two unusual portrayals of the Virgin Mary, one on a portico column showing her pregnant, another on the tympanum depicting the birth of Christ. Beside the cathedral is the San Telmo Chapel, a piece of Portuguese Baroque.

Besides the old **iron bridge**, built by Eiffel, the French engineer, a new road bridge now leaps across the Miño to the picturesque Portuguese frontier town of **Valença**. This is worth a brief excursion. The old walls have been preserved, from which you have excellent views along the Miño Valley. Within the ramparts are a number of restaurants

and shops catering to tourist traffic, particularly weekend visitors from Spain. A vaulted hall in the walls houses the **Restaurante Monumental**, which offers plentiful portions of traditional Portuguese dishes at fair prices.

From Valença you can follow the Miño eastwards on the Portuguese side via the N101 or return to Spain and take the narrow PO400 as it weaves its way along the green valley. Occasionally ferries crank across the river. A new bridge is to leap the waters at **Salvaterra de Miño**, an old fortified town which once belonged to Portugal and around which flourish the Condado wines.

One of Spain's most curious fiestas, that of **Santa Marta de Ribarteme**, takes place on July 29, near the village of As Neves, just east of Salvaterra. People who have made a vow to the saint are carried in a procession of open coffins.

VERIN ⋈
See *Recommended Hotels, page 232.*

VIGO
See *Spain Overall: 3.*

Northern Spain

Salamanca Province:
Ciudad Rodrigo and La Alberca

320 *km; map Michelin* 441, 1:400,000

Travel south of Salamanca to the fringes of Extremadura and you may well feel that you have entered a time warp. Mountain villages with cobbled streets and half-timbered houses look as though they have hardly changed since the Middle Ages, except for the ever-present television aerials. In the Sierra de la Peña de Francia, which rises to more than 1,700 m, you will find Alpine meadows and thick forests, granite peaks and wild boar. The name originated with the arrival here in the 11th century of settlers from France. Because it has always been away from the mainstream, the area has preserved many of its old customs as well as the traditional architecture. The richness of local folklore is most brilliantly in evidence during the fiestas in La Alberca.

The western part of Salamanca province, towards the Portuguese border, is little visited by tourists. At first you travel across a monotonous plain, the land of the *charros*, countryfolk with a distinctive style of dress now only seen on festive occasions. Pigs graze under forests of holm oaks and fighting bulls are reared. The plain gives way to rolling hills around the pleasant town of Ciudad Rodrigo, a strategic stronghold in the past. The Duke of Wellington took it from the French after a siege in 1812; he was made a Grandee of Spain with the title of Duque de Ciudad Rodrigo.

The direct route to Ciudad Rodrigo from Salamanca is via the N620. From there the C515 will take you to La Alberca and then through the sierras to Béjar. The trip can be done in a day, but you will better appreciate the atmosphere by staying a night in La Alberca and exploring the area south of it, the wild, under-developed region known as Las Hurdes.

TRANSPORT

Regular bus and train services run between Salamanca and Ciudad Rodrigo and between Salamanca and Béjar. There is a daily bus between Salamanca and La Alberca. Bus connections are few in the area around La Alberca.

1:1,000,000

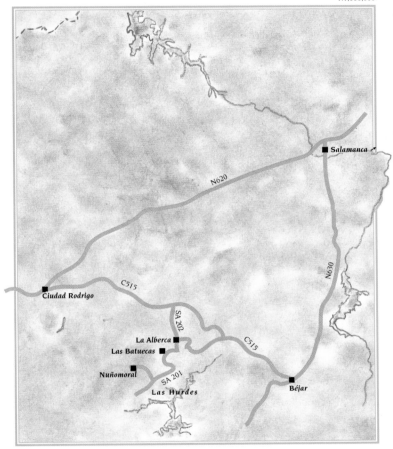

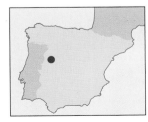

SIGHTS & PLACES OF INTEREST

ALBERCA, LA ⌂

Without a doubt, La Alberca is one of Spain's prettiest villages, a gem of medieval architecture that has miraculously survived from the Middle Ages and is now protected as a national monument. But a monument with plenty of life in it, for the villagers carry on their rural ways as ever, except that donkeys are disappearing and souvenir shops have sprung up on the edge of town. If possible, steer clear of weekends and other holiday periods.

The village lies in the **Sierra de la Peña de Francia**, among forests of chestnut and oak. Crooked houses jostle for space, their balconies almost meeting overhead in some alleys. The walls are of granite blocks wedged between solid beams, sometimes covered with adobe and whitewashed. Over doorways you may find such ancient inscriptions as 'Conceived without sin' or the insignia of the Inquisition. La Alberca's inhabitants are thought to have Moorish, Jewish, and French blood in their veins, a blend which possibly accounts for the exotic grandeur of the women's fiesta costumes. Richly embroidered velvet and silk in vivid colours are set off by antique jewellery and necklaces reaching to the knees. The best time to see this finery is during the August celebration of the patron saint, **Nuestra Señora de la Asunción**, when the village elders in white stockings, velvet breeches and silver-buttoned blue velvet waistcoats assemble in the plaza. As crowds pack the arcades and balconies on August 15, offerings are made to the Virgin, followed by traditional dances. On August 16, **La Loa**, a morality play, is enacted before the 17thC church. A flame-breathing dragon with seven heads, representing the seven capital sins, meets his doom at the hands of the Archangel San Miguel.

Try the snacks at the half dozen bars around the plaza, although the restaurant of **Las Batuecas** (see Recommended Hotels, left) is the best choice for a full meal. Cured ham and first-rate honey are two local specialities on sale. There are many pleasant walks in the surrounding hills and you can visit picturesque villages nearby such as **El Cabaco** and **Miranda del Castañar**. For splendid views, follow a tortuous road which climbs the highest peak, the Peña de Francia (1,723 m), 15 km from La Alberca. A Dominican monastery stands on the summit, with refreshments available in summer.

BATUECAS, LAS
The road from La Alberca climbs over the Portillo Pass, 1,240 m, from where you can enjoy spectacular views south towards the region of Las Hurdes. Then it zig-zags down into the verdant valley of Las Batuecas, forests of oak, chestnut, and pine rising on all sides. Prehis-

DETOUR – **CANDELARIO**
This pretty mountain village, a pleasant 4-km excursion from Béjar, is full of flowers, wooden balconies and steep streets. It is famed for the unusual hair-style adopted by the women and for its sausages and other pork products.

toric wall paintings are to be found in the Batuecas valley. A side-road leads to the Carmelite **Monasterio de Las Batuecas**. One of the first tasks of the inmates when the monastery was founded in 1599 was to exorcize the evil spirits which apparently abounded in the area.

A small community of monks live a hermit-like existence here and only men can enter. Film director Luis Buñuel stayed on the premises when he was making his film *Land Without Bread*, but it is doubtful if film-makers would get a welcome now. When I visited, a sign on the locked monastery door warned: 'This is not a place of tourism nor entertainment. It is a place of prayer and penitence.' The sign may be gone by the time you get there, but the message has not changed.

BÉJAR

Béjar is strategically situated to explore the neighbouring *sierras* of la Peña de Francia and of Candelario. In the past, as the remains of its walls indicates, it was strategically situated from a military viewpoint too. The town, known for its textiles, has several Romanesque and Gothic churches of interest. The 16thC castle, the **Palacio de los Duques de Béjar**, has a beautiful façade and a Renaissance patio.

CIUDAD RODRIGO ⌖

Tourism Office, Casa de Cultura, Plaza Conde. British cannon balls have left their marks on Ciudad Rodrigo's cathedral, testifying to a turbulent past. You can wander the 2,200 m of sturdy **ramparts** built 700 years ago and reinforced in 1710. They guard the well-preserved old quarter, which has numerous mansions decorated with coats of arms. Many date from the golden age in the 15th and 16thC when local boys such as Francisco Montejo won fame and fortune, in his case by

the conquest of Yucatán and Cozumel. Overlooking the River Agueda is the square tower of the 14thC *alcázar*, a fortress now converted into a parador. The river is spanned by a **bridge** built by the Romans, who had a settlement here. After the Reconquest from the Moors, Rodrigo González repopulated the town and it is believed that it acquired its name from him.

In the Peninsular War (known in Spain as the War of Independence) the French ousted the Spanish garrison in 1810 and were ejected two years later by the Duke of Wellington's soldiers, who blasted a hole in the walls to enter and then set about an orgy of looting.

Among the more outstanding buildings are the **Casa de los Aguilas** (House of Eagles), a Gothic mansion now the **Post Office**, and the **Palacio de los Castros**, with a Plateresque façade. In the **cathedral** (Romanesque-Gothic), note the choir stalls carved by Rodrigo Alemán and the apse, the work of Gil de Hontañón. A statue of Saint Francis of Assisi above the stalls is said to be the oldest in existence. The lengthy main square is graced by the 16thC **Ayuntamiento** (Town Hall) with a fine *loggia*, and a palace known as **Casa de Los Cueto**. The square is very lively on the first and third Tuesday of every month when farmers are in town to attend a large cattle market.

RECOMMENDED RESTAURANTS

It is not easy to recommend restaurants in this area: none stands out. Three of the better ones are located in the Recommended Hotels, page 236.

You will find tasty snacks available in village bars. In the Sierra de la Peña de Francia, the sausages and cured ham are excellent and the local wine, vino del Soto, a hearty red, will soon make you forget about sophisticated dining, about everything, in fact.

• *Village square, La Alberca – see page 236.*

One of the bars they crowd into is the authentically old **El Sanatorio**. At the rear is a restaurant (Formica-topped tables) where you can have a cheap *menu del día*. That will give you time to inspect the photographs taken during the annual **Carnival** in February, including shots of the *encierros*. These are bull-runs, on the same lines as those held in Pamplona but not as famous (Hemingway having unaccountably not written about them). Local youths show their daring by running along the streets before the horns of the animals which are to perform in the daily bull-fights.

HURDES, LAS

This remote mountain wilderness lies in Cáceres province, near the border with Salamanca province and the Portuguese frontier. Access was difficult until recently and Las Hurdes – its people locked into narrow valleys by gaunt ribs of granite – still remains impenetrable in some ways.

You can reach the area from La Alberca, Ciudad Rodrigo, or Plasencia. From Ciudad Rodrigo, head south-east to Serradilla del Llano through open,

rolling cattle country. Chestnut trees line the roadside as you climb higher than 1,000 m to cross the wild Sierra de la Canchera. Wolves and wild boar roam this bleak range, rising to more than 1,592 m and standing on the threshold of Extremadura. Once over the pass, the road descends towards **Nuñomoral**, the principal community in this part of Las Hurdes. From there a road winds up the Hurdano Valley. Lichened rocks jut through slate and sparse soil on valley sides, where vines and olive, almond and fig trees somehow find a grip. In the valley bottom, potatoes and maize grow in pocket-handkerchief plots laboriously created by the farmers.

An old man in the humble village of Fragosa told me, after showing me his operation scars: 'The land is no good here. When it gets hot, the soil dries out, and when it rains the soil is washed away away. A man needs flesh and bone to survive, but here we only have bone.' Lean and short-statured like most of the older folk, he could have stepped straight out of *Land Without Bread*, the film made by Luís Buñuel in the 1930s which exposed the primitive conditions in Las Hurdes. It did not make Buñuel popular because it showed a negative image of Spain.

The villages are traditionally composed of low slate-roofed houses, the same brown colour as the surrounding rocks so that they merge into the landscape. But new brick houses are replacing them, and roads, schools, and medical facilities have finally arrived.

According to one theory, the inhabitants are descendants of the Moors who took refuge from Christian persecution centuries ago. Because of their isolation, the people follow customs that have disappeared elsewhere and can be suspicious of strangers, although in conversation they reveal a refreshing simplicity. But they are hyper-sensitive about being photographed. Do not take pictures without asking permission first. There are a few spartan inns where you can stay.

NUÑOMORAL

See Hurdes, Las, left.

• *Opposite: Village in Las Hurdes (Cáceres).*

Around Madrid

Map Michelin 444. 1:400,000

Madrid sits plum in the middle of Spain, surrounded by the strange and varied landscape of Castile, famed for its harsh terrain and endless vistas, its great castles and its cultured and beautiful cities. To the north and east of the capital a chain of mountains, part of the Cordillera Central, rears up from the *meseta*. To the south stretches flat and featureless La Mancha, Quixote country. You can sample all of these in this section.

Madrileños love their city with a fierce pride; they also love to leave it, especially at weekends and in August. Even a short drive away there are many lures: historic towns and great royal palaces built as country retreats, mountain scenery with skiing and walking, and pretty villages to whose restaurants the city dwellers flock for noisy family gatherings, especially on a Sunday.

This Local Exploration confines itself to places of interest which are in close proximity to Madrid and are usually tackled in day trips from the capital, which is why no distance is given. However, a night spent in each place, especially Toledo, is highly recommended. Some of the sights around Madrid are covered by other routes in the book and are cross-referenced accordingly.

1:1,500,000

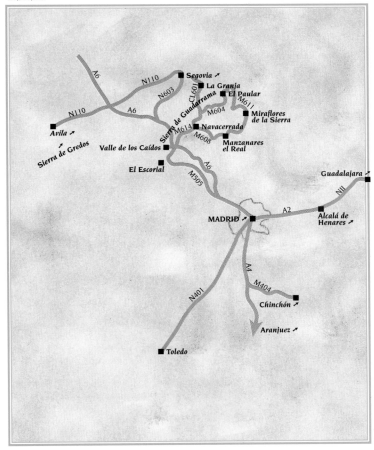

TRANSPORT
Most of the places of interest mentioned in this section are easily accessible by public transport, either RENFE main line trains or by bus. See individual entries for details, which usually assume you will start from Madrid.

SIGHTS & PLACES OF INTEREST

ALCALA DE HENARES
See Spain Overall: 7.

ARANJUEZ
See Spain Overall: 13.

AVILA
See Spain Overall: 4.

CHINCHON
See Spain Overall: 14.

EL ESCORIAL ⇋ ✕
Frequent trains from Madrid's Atocha or Chamartín railway stations to San Lorenzo de El Escorial; bus transfer from there to the town and monastery. Buses from Herranz line on Paseo Moret near Moncloa metro direct to San Lorenzo de El Escorial. Tourism Office: Floridablanca, 10.

You could either visit El Escorial as part of a trip round the Sierra de Guadarrama (see page 243), or as a day trip from Madrid. Many people combine it with El Valle de los Caídos (see page 249). If you have a car, go first to the viewpoint, called **Silla de Felipe II**, where the king sat and watched the building, over a mere 21 years, of his deadly serious *folie de grandeur*. (To reach the viewpoint, leave El Escorial on the Avila road and turn left at the sign for the prestigious golf club, Herrería-Golf).

The first sight of the **Real Monasterio de San Lorenzo de El Escorial** itself, begun in 1563 by Juan Bautista de Toledo and completed after his death by Juan de Herrera, is likely to make your heart sink, especially on a broiling summer's day with thousands of others for company (try to avoid weekends). So vast that you can see it from a passenger jet, forbidding, unrelentingly severe, it looks more like a granite prison than a palace and it is hard to imagine that what lies within is not gloomy, but surprisingly airy. Only sunset softens its lines and it's worth staying the night in the little town when monastery and avenues are pleasantly floodlit and the crowds have all gone home.

Just as the Sun King epitomizes Versailles, so El Escorial *is* Philip II of Spain, and you need to know something of the man to understand his monument. His father, the Habsburg Charles I of Spain who was also Holy Roman Emperor as Charles V, had abdicated in his favour and retired to the seclusion of Yuste (see page 152); in his will he commanded his son to build a royal pantheon. When the king's troops won a decisive battle at St Quentin against the French on St Lawrence's day, Philip decided to build a combined monastery, palace and pantheon as awe-inspiring as his country was great and to dedicate it to that saint. Begun in 1453 by Juan Bautista de Toledo, it was completed after his death by Juan de Herrera. The architects' style well reflected the king's character: autocratic, austere, driven, and deeply religious. And yet despite his best intentions, his reign was far from successful: a long saga of expensive wars, expensive building and expensive mistakes – most notably that of sending the Spanish Armada to England. When he died in 1598 Spain was much poorer and no longer a great sea power; its decline had begun. You will visit the simple room where he expired, its principal asset being that he could watch the celebration of Mass in the adjoining basilica as he lay in bed suffering from the gangrene (a complication of gout) that would kill him.

Once you have negotiated the complicated ticket system, you will find yourself in the grip of an obligatory official tour, at least through the most noteworthy parts of the complex. Enough, therefore, to mention the highlights: the extraordinary **Pantéon de los Reyes**, which contains the bodies of almost every king since Charles V, and the bizarre **Pantéon de los Infantes**; Philip's quarters in the **Palacio de los Austrias** (the Habsburg part of the royal apartments which contrast so strikingly with the sumptuous **Palacio de los Borbones**); the **Sala de Batallas**, with frescoes vividly depicting Spanish victories; and the magnificent **Biblioteca**, equipped by Philip with over 10,000 books and full of important manuscripts. There is a great deal more – depending on how strong you are.

GREDOS, SIERRA DE
See Spain Overall: 12.

GUADALAJARA

See Spain Overall: 7

GUADARRAMA, SIERRA DE

Trains to Cercedilla (en route for Segovia) from Madrid's Atocha station. Buses to Manzanares el Real from Hermanos de Julia Colmenarejo line, Mateo Inurria, 11; metro Plaza de Castillo.

The steep-sided, snow-capped mountains north of Madrid are a popular weekend destination for fume-choked city dwellers. If you are driving, the area is best explored by doing a circuit from Navacerrada down to La Pedriza and Manzanares el Real, then up to Miraflores and El Paular and back to Navacerrada via the high pass of Puerto de Navacerrada. The following lists the places of interest along the way:

Navacerrada The main resort for the ski area. Nearby, on the railway line but not the main road, is Cercedilla, an alpine-style village popular for summer walking.

La Pedriza An area on the southern slopes of the Sierra designated a National Park, with lovely scenery. Perfect for walking (serious climbing at the top) or a picnic. Clothed in white cistus in spring.

Castillo de Manzanares el Real A classic square-plan castle which bristles with turrets and battlements, although its history, as a fortress-palace, has been entirely peaceful.

Miraflores de la Sierra A pleasant mountain village whose shops and restaurants cater for its sophisticated weekend visitors. A five-hour hike from here leads through the mountains to El Paular.

El Paular Set in the pretty Valle del Lozoya, the **Monasterio de El Paular** was founded by King Juan I as Spain's first Carthusian community and is still inhabited by a handful of Benedictine monks. The church has a lovely Gothic retable (decorative screen behind the altar). Attached to the monastery, somewhat incongruously given the monks' adherence to a life of simplicity, is a smart hotel, prices pitched high, (**Santa María de El Paular, PPP**; *tel.* 91 869 10 11).

Puerto de Navacerrada Ski station set on a bald mountain pass at 1,860 m.

LA GRANJA DE SAN IDELFONSO ⌘

Buses from Segovia. On summer evenings between 6 and 7 pm the wonderful fountains at the **Palacio Real de La Granja** are switched on. This is the best time to visit the frothy summer palace of the first Bourbon king, Charles IV. It was in fact his Italian widow, who, much influenced by Versailles, created the building's Rococo flourishes and the formal gardens. The palace, gutted by fire in 1918, has little to detain you, save the vast chandeliers from the town's illustrious glassworks and a collection of tapestries. The gardens, however, are a delight, and the Late Baroque fountains, each different, make a real spectacle.

The little town, with its grid-plan streets, was laid out at the same time as the palace.

LOS CAIDOS, VALLE DE

Buses from San Lorenzo de El Escorial; also from Madrid: Herranz line on Paseo Moret near Moncloa metro. If you drive towards Segovia from Madrid you cannot fail to notice the vast (150-m high) stone cross, visible on a hillside from miles around. A religious symbol, certainly, but this one seems coldly menacing, and if you visit you will find out why.

El Valle de los Caídos (Valley of the Fallen) is Franco's chilling memorial to the dead of the Civil War. Though supposedly meant to commemorate both sides, it was defeated Republican prisoners who were forced to erect the cross and carve a basilica out of the hillside in the 1950s. This immensely long, echoing, creepy yet impressive tunnel must be one of the world's most unpleasant ecclesiastical buildings, though the flocks of jolly tourists lighten the mood. The tombs of both Franco and Primo de Rivera, the Falangist founder, are within, near the altar. A funicular railway takes you to the cross.

MADRID

See pages 170-192.

SEGOVIA

See: Local Explorations: 8.

TOLEDO ⇌ ✕

Frequent trains from Madrid's Atocha station and buses from Estación Sur des Autobus. Taxis available at Toledo bus/train station. Motorists should park outside the walls. Tourism Office: by the roundabout outside Puerta de Bisegra.

Toledo is richly rewarding, but it is beseiged by tour groups who disappear at the end of the day, so a night's stay here is strongly advised. It can also be very hot and dusty during the summer. The first sight of old Toledo is a stirring one, despite the modern town sprawled out below the encircling city walls, pierced by great gates. As you approach, the Montes de Toledo rear up from the flat Castilian plain to provide a brooding back-drop to the huddle of brown roofs, the soaring cathedral spire and the bulky outline of the Alcázar. (The best panorama can be had from across the gorge of the River Tajo [Tagus], which curves round the hill on which Toledo stands, at the Parador Conde de Orgaz or the belvedere nearby.)

In 1561 Philip II transferred the capital of united Spain to Madrid, and there ended centuries of glory for Toledo (although it has remained the Primate See of Spain). Ever since, the city has lived for its past. Colonized by the Romans, it became a capital for the Visigoths and then an important frontier city for the Moors. When Alfonso VI recaptured it in 1085 with the help of El Cid, the city's reputation as a place of culture and learning where Muslims, Christians and Jews lived in harmony did not diminish, and this sense of oneness is still tangible in the buildings and monuments which remain. At the end of its reign, Toledo was endowed with beauty from another quarter when it became the city of El Greco, who moved here about 1577 after failing to get work on Philip II's Escorial.

The only realistic way of seeing Toledo is to walk, stopping for frequent bouts of refreshment. I have devised two routes which cover the principle sights and which each take a morning or an afternoon. If you have a choice, I would suggest doing the Judería walk in the afternoon (when you might catch the sunset from the garden along Reyes Católicos on your return), and

---

RECOMMENDED HOTELS

LA GRANJA DE SAN IDELFONSO
Roma, P-PP; *Guardas, 2; tel. 921 47 02 78; closed Nov to mid-Dec.*

Simple but pleasant *hostal* right by the palace gates; decent restaurant.

SAN LORENZO DE EL ESCORIAL
Parilla Principe, PP; *Floridablanca, 6; tel. 91 890 16 11.*

Fairly serious restaurant downstairs; 14 simple but comfortable and reasonably priced rooms upstairs, perfectly adequate for an overnight stay.

TOLEDO
Cardenal, PP; *Paseo Recaredo, 24; tel. 925 22 49 00.*

Highly recommended for a night's stay in Toledo, providing value for money and peaceful accommodation in the 16thC one-time residence of Cardinal Lorenzana. Bedrooms are cool and white-painted with attractive wooden furniture; bathrooms have tiled floors and deep baths. Every-

where there are patios and pretty corners, as well as a terrace garden and well-regarded restaurant (see Recommended Restaurants). The *hostal* is well placed for my Toledo walks (see above), set just inside the city walls between Puerta de Bisagra and Puerta del Cambrón.

Parador Conde de Orgaz, PPP; *Paseo de los Cigarrales; tel. 925 22 18 50.*

Cigarrales are country houses, typically with an orchard, found in Toledo province, and this famous modern parador lies amongst them across the River Tagus from the city. Inconvenient for sightseeing, its position does however afford a wonderful panorama of the city from its terrace and from those rooms that have balconies. The parador has a swimming-pool and is carefully furnished in Toledan style. Worth having a drink or a meal here even if you don't stay the night.

Juderia Walk

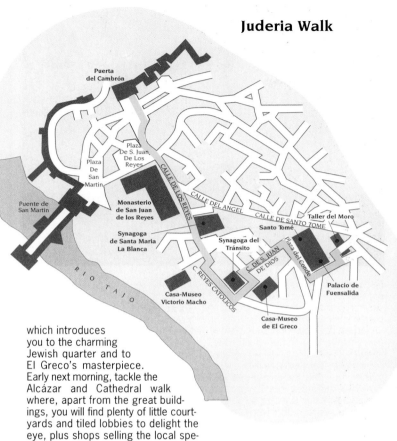

Puerta del Cambrón

Plaza De S. Juan. De Los Reyes

Plaza De San Martín

Puente de San Martín

Monasterio de San Juan de los Reyes

CALLE DE LOS REYES

CALLE DEL ANGEL

CALLE DE SANTO TOMÉ

Taller del Moro

Santo Tomé

Synagoga de Santa María La Blanca

Synagoga del Tránsito

C. DE S. JUAN DE DIOS

Plaza del Conde

RIO TAJO

C. REYES CATOLICOS

Casa-Museo Victorio Macho

Casa-Museo de El Greco

Palacio de Fuensalida

which introduces you to the charming Jewish quarter and to El Greco's masterpiece. Early next morning, tackle the Alcázar and Cathedral walk where, apart from the great buildings, you will find plenty of little courtyards and tiled lobbies to delight the eye, plus shops selling the local specialities of marzipan, damascene, swords and ceramics. Don't expect the carefree spirit of so many Spanish cities here: rather, it is a treasure box which soberly guards its jewels. By and large the sights open at 10 or 10.30 am, close for lunch, reopen around 3.30 pm and close again between 6 and 7 pm. Some (Alcázar, El Tránsito, Casa-Museo El Greco) close on a Monday.

Judería Walk

Start Puerta del Cambrón. To find it, walk along the walls anti-clockwise from Puerta de Bisagra, the main entrance where most tourists pour in. Ahead is the lovely late Gothic façade of the **Monasterio de San Juan de los Reyes**, founded by Ferdinand and Isabel and designed by Juan Gras. The chains you see were those of Christ-

ian prisoners released after the Reconquest of Granada.

In summer, entering the airy Isabelline (late Gothic) interior, covered with heraldic motifs (notice the F and Y monogram and their coat of arms, a yolk and seven arrows) is as refreshing as a cool dip. The cloisters are beautiful, with lacework carving, Mudéjar ceiling and jokey gargoyles added in the 1880s during restoration. A very laidback looking skeleton reclines over the entrance.

Walk ahead, and on the left a wooden doorway gives on to the courtyard of **Synagoga de Santa María La Blanca**. When tolerance of the Jewish community gave way in the 15thC, all the synagogues save this and El Tránsito were destroyed. Both a highlight of Mudéjar architecture (note the fusion: Muslim architecture for a Jewish

245

• *Toledan ware.*

place of worship) and of Toledo, its interior is a delicate, frozen forest of horseshoe arches decorated with a frieze of filigree stucco work.

Reyes Católicos runs past shaded gardens overlooking the countryside, dotted with cypress trees. At the start of the gardens, by the ice cream kiosk, look to your left for **Synagoga del Tránsito**, the other remaining synagogue, built a century later by Samuel Levi, treasurer to Pedro I (The Cruel) of Castile who later had him executed. It is splendid, with a beautiful *artesonado* (carved wooden) ceiling and upper walls covered with inscriptions as at the Alhambra, although these are in Hebrew. The upper gallery, shielded by wooden lattice-work, was for women. A small but compelling **Museo Sefardí** (Sephardic Museum) adjoins the synagogue.

You could dispense with the **Casa-Museo Victorio Macho** (home of the early 20thC sculptor), signposted off Reyes Católicos, and instead go up Tránsito to **Casa-Museo de El Greco**, beseiged by tourists and recently enlarged and improved (with a second phase of work in progress). Though charming, this is a mock-up of what the artist's home in Toledo (he lived there for 33 years, until his death) might have looked like. From here it makes sense to go straight to El Greco's most famous painting, *The Burial of the* *Count of Orgaz* which is housed in its own chapel adjoining the church of **Santo Tomé**.

To get there, walk up Calle San Juan de Dios to Plaza del Conde. In season, herds of people stand and gaze, often waiting in queues to do so. Notice that the plaque beneath the painting acts as a sarcophagus, as if St Stephen and St Augustine were about to lower the Count's body into it. Above this earthly scene, witnessed by a line of local nobility, the Count's soul is carried aloft by an angel. The eye sweeps upwards past a celestial assembly who point the way towards the distant figure of Christ on his heavenly throne. This is Mannerist painting at its most thrilling, yet though the colours and the foreshortened composition are electrifying, the business of burying Count Orgaz seems more like an aristocratic ritual than a spiritual release.

The lovely building to the right of the chapel is the **Palacio de Fuensalida**, now local government headquarters. The wife of Charles V, Queen Isabel, died here aged 36. Around the corner in Calle Taller del Moro is the entrance to **Taller del Moro** (Moor's workshop) which was once part of a Mudéjar mansion and, later, a workshop for craftsmen employed on the cathedral. It displays some of the things they made.

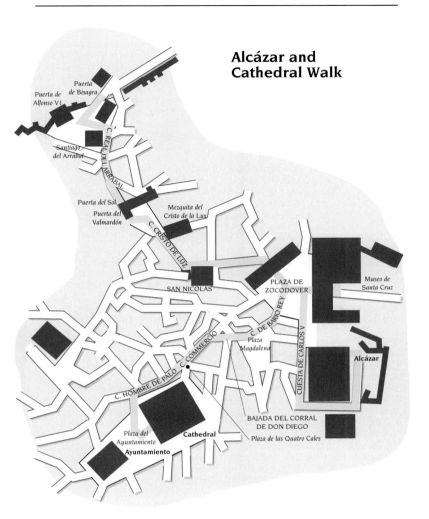

Alcázar and Cathedral Walk

For a nearby restaurant try **Placido**, Calle Santo Tomé 4, with tables outside under the trees or in a shady interior courtyard.

Alcázar and Cathedral Walk
Start Puerta de Bisagra, the city's main gate, which bears the coat of arms of Charles V. Nearby is the original 9thC gate through which Alfonso VI and El Cid entered the city in triumph. Walk straight ahead, leaving the Mudéjar church of **Santiago del Arrabal** to your right. Just after the Bar Arrabal, take the Calle Cristo de la Luz uphill to the battlemented **Puerta del Sol** and a view of the Toledan landscape with the River Tagus snaking through it. Bear right under the **Puerta del Valmardón** (a vestige of the town's Visigoth walls) to see the minute **Mezquita del Cristo de la Luz**. Built on the site of a Visigoth church, this is Toledo's, if not Spain's, oldest Moorish monument: the arched and vaulted nave dates from 922. (No set opening hours; find the caretaker there or in the house opposite. He will also show you to the top of the Puerta del Sol.)

Continue uphill along Cristo de la Luz. At the top, glance right along a street of protruding bay windows, and at Plaza San Nicolas, go straight ahead, noticing the splendid **Casa de**

Los López de Toledo on your left. These are the quiet back streets where you will leave the other visitors behind, but now turn right into **Plaza Zocódover**, rebuilt after the ravages of the Civil War, and still Toledo's meeting place and site of a Tuesday market. Here you can pause in one of the many cafés (be warned, prices are high).

Facing the arcaded building with the clock, the Alcázar lies to the right along Cuesta de Carlos V, while the highly recommended **Museo de Santa Cruz**, with a marvellously crusty Plateresque façade, lies through the central arch. Open all day, and often delightfully quiet, this former Renaissance hospital is a cool haven, filled with beautiful, simple furniture and other diverse objects that catch the eye (or not) as you wander round. One that does will be the blue-and-gold banner flown by Don Juan of Austria at the Battle of Lepanto; another the collection of El Greco's, particularly his *Assumption*, painted three months before his death, and a touching *Madonna Penitente*, another perhaps the painted wood *Ecce Homo* and *Mater Dolorosa* amongst the religious statuary. The exit is via a charming double-arched cloister where a small archeological exhibition can be found. Notice too the splendid staircase by Covarrubias.

Since Roman times, some sort of fortress has always stood on the site of the **Alcázar**. Its past is a catalogue of destruction and rebuilding, culminating in 1936 when it was occupied by Nationalist rebels and besieged by Republicans. The siege lasted for two months until Franco sent forces to relieve them. The building is now a reconstruction of its appearance when Charles V converted it from fortress to royal residence. The architects were first Covarrubias and then Juan de Herrera, of Escorial fame, who designed the typically severe south front. Inside, the vast building is part military garrison, part museum of weaponry, part unpleasant homage to the siege and the Franco regime (it was rebuilt by Franco after the Civil War as a monument to Nationalist bravery). In the office of the Nationalist leader Colonel Moscardó, preserved as it was, the story of how he offered to sacrifice his son is extremely cloying and highly suspect: it recalls the almost identical story of Guzmán el Bueno at Tarifa in 1294.

Retrace to Plaza Zocódover and take the little Calle de Bario Rey past some delicious food smells to Plaza Magdalena (you can eat quite cheaply at **Bar Ludena**). Facing the square arch, take the right hand exit, the Bajada del Corral de Don Diego. At the crossroads, turn left along Commercio, the smart shopping area of Toledo. At Plaza de las Quatro Calles, ignore the side entrance to the cathedral which lies straight ahead but may disorientate you and does not sell tickets to the private chapels, and instead walk diagonally across down Hombre de Palo. Bear left into Plaza Ayuntamiento with its elegant **Ayuntamiento** (Town Hall) by the son of El Greco, and head for the main cathedral entrance in front of the cloisters (tickets to the choir, sacristy and so on are sold at the souvenir stand).

Impressive from afar, the Gothic **cathedral**, begun in 1226 and finished in 1493, is too encroached on by neighbouring buildings to be appreciated close-up. This has the effect of making the wealth of craftsmanship and art inside even more overwhelming. First inspect the 15thC *coro* (choir) which in the Spanish way sits slap in the middle of the nave and is admired for its intricately carved stalls (those to the south depict the Reconquest of Granada).

Facing the choir, the magnificent retable (decorative screen) of the high altar in the Capilla Mayor (sanctuary) drips with gilded and polychromed larchwood; behind this the famous Baroque extravagance known as the **Transparente**. Built by Narcisco Tomé and sons in the mid-18thC in order to cast a stream of light (best at midday) over the high altar, it is an outrageous gold, white and marbled confection which has to be seen to be believed. White cherubs crowd round a golden sunburst and sweep up to the figure of Christ who stands under a painted ceiling which in turn sweeps across to the skylight where yet more angels appear to hold the chain of a great lamp. Observing this, we feel pretty remote from the delicacies of Mudéjar Toledo. Close to the lamp, do you see a tattered red object hanging over a plaque on the floor? It is Cardinal Moreno's hat and you will notice others, in varying states of decay, dotted about. Cardinals of Toledo Cathedral have the right to be buried wherever they wish, and the hats denote the chosen spot.

Now follow the double ambulatory, peering into its chapels. Nearby is the **Sala Capitular** (Chapter House) with a wonderful painted Mudéjar *artesonado* ceiling and good frescoes by Juan de Borgoña. On the other side, the **Sacristía**; here the almost stifling riches of the cathedral are left behind for a dignified gallery of paintings, dominated by El Greco's *Espolio* in which Christ's robe is about to be stripped from him.

In other quiet rooms, ecclesiatical garments and other objects are displayed, and further on, in the former **treasurer's house**, are more works of art. Also of interest are the **Capilla Mozárabe** in the cathedral's southwest corner, where the ancient Mozarabic liturgy, dating from the Visigoths, is still celebrated, and the **Tesoro** (Treasury), just by the public entrance and guarded by a massive door, which contains a huge and elaborate silver monstrance. It was made in the 15thC to carry the host during the **Corpus Christi procession**, which it still does on June 20 each year.

Two possible lunch spots near the cathedral: **Aurelio**, No. 8 Plaza Ayuntamiento with a *tapa* bar upstairs and cosy restaurant downstairs; and round the corner in Pozo Amargo, **Casa Paco**, a local bar with spotless, simple comidor at the back. *Gazpacho, paella*, wine for next to nothing.

Link Walk
The two walks described above end close to one another. If you have finished one walk and want to reach the start of the next, simply drop downhill to the north-east or north-west through a network of silent streets, past unadorned little plazas, convents and churches. Half the fun is getting lost in this hardly changed and highly atmospheric part of town. The Colegio de Doncellas and Pintor Malías Moreno will lead you to San Juan de los Reyos at the start of the Judería Walk, and the Alfonso X El Sabio and Carmelitas will lead you to the Mezquita del Cristo de la Luz on the Alcázar and Cathedral Walk. *En route* you may come across the **Museo Visigótico** in the frescoed Mudéjar **church of San Román**, the **Convento de San Clemente** with a doorway by Covarrubias (who was also responsible for the door to the treasury in the cathedral), and the **Casa de Mesa** at no. 11, Esteban Illán which has a superb *artesonado* ceiling. If you care to walk a little to the north of San Román, you will find the **Convento de Santo Domingo el Antiguo**, where El Greco was buried and whose altarpiece was his first major commission in Toledo.

RECOMMENDED RESTAURANTS

SAN LORENZO DE EL ESCORIAL
La Cueva, P-PP; *San Antón 4; tel. 91 890 15 16; closed Mon.*

El Escorial is a favourite weekend lunch spot when the restaurants are jammed. A favourite amongst those with terraces is **Charolés, PP** (*Floridablanca*, 24; *tel.* 91 890 59 75). In the evening, however, it is fun to go to La Cueva, a little-changed Castilian inn with a warren of rooms set on three floors around a galleried and painted entrance hall. Full meals in the restaurant or *tapas* in the bar area.

MIRAFLORES DE LA SIERRA
Las LLaves, PP; *Calvo Sotelo, 4; tel. 91 844 40 57; credit cards AE, DC, MC, V;* *closed mid-Sept to mid-Oct.*

Try the local fat white beans, *judiones de la Granja*; or *cocido*, the stew of chick peas, meat and vegetables whose broth is first served as a soup. Booked solid at weekends.

TOLEDO
Cardenal, PP-PPP; *Paseo Recaredo, 24; tel. 925 22 49 00; credit cards* AE, DC, MC, V.

Highly-rated restaurant adjoining the hotel (see Recommended Hotels), although in my experience the food was no more than average except for the excellent *entremeses*. Service is smooth and polished in the airy first floor dining room.

Lunch spots near the cathedral are mentioned in Toledo Walks, above.

Central Spain

Segovia and Province

143 km; map Michelin 442, 1:400,000

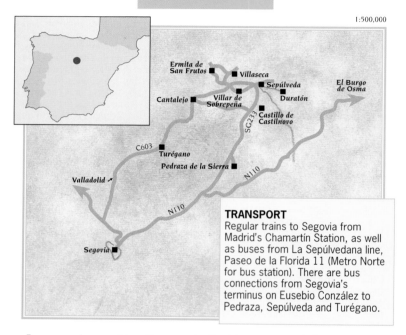

1:500,000

TRANSPORT
Regular trains to Segovia from Madrid's Chamartín Station, as well as buses from La Sepúlvedana line, Paseo de la Florida 11 (Metro Norte for bus station). There are bus connections from Segovia's terminus on Eusebio Conzález to Pedraza, Sepúlveda and Turégano.

Anyone who considers the *meseta,* Spain's vast central plateau, unworthy of close exploration is missing a trick. North of Madrid, beyond the mountain range (Sierra de Guadarrama) which cuts diagonally across the plain, the landscape, though relieved by low, tree-covered hills and dramatic gorges, is mostly flat, harsh and impoverished. Huge tracts are given over to wheat and to herb-scented grass for sheep grazing.

Such terrain may sound unpromising, yet an excursion there yields lasting memories. Prominent amongst them will be the beautiful honey-coloured Romanesque churches, each with a distinctive portico peculiar to the province and known as Segovian Romanesque; the storks' nests perched on every tower, spire or stack in sight; the castles; and the great feasts of Castilian roast lamb, the much vaunted regional speciality, cooked to perfection in the many *hornos de asar* (roasting ovens) which vie for your attention as you pass by.

Segovia itself is a marvellous sight as you approach from Turégano, the cathedral and Alcázar coming into ever sharper focus, and it makes a perfect base from which to explore.

SIGHTS & PLACES OF INTEREST

ERMITA DE SAN FRUTOS
To visit the Romanesque chapel of San Frutos, park in the hamlet of Villaseca, where the 5 km track begins. It is worth the walk. Set in dramatic isolation above a loop in the dammed Duratón River, the chapel, with its typical portico and fine carvings between the corbels, was administered by Benedictines from 1076 until 1836, but was a site of worship even before their arrival.

PEDRAZA DE LA SIERRA ⇌ ✕
Compared to the crumbling villages that are typical of this region, Pedraza comes as a surprise: it is an immaculate, pretty medieval village, a careful combination of preservation and restoration. Its massive encircling walls are pierced by just one entrance, the **Puerta de la Villa**. The irregularly shaped **Plaza Mayor** has upper storey balconies supported by an assortment of stone pillars, and the narrow streets are lined by fine, honey-coloured houses.

Pedraza's **castle** guards the village from a rocky promontory. Its tower was restored and lived in by the painter Zuloaga and now houses a small museum to his memory.

SEGOVIA ⇌ ✕
Tourism Office, Plaza Mayor (also called Plaza de Franco). One of the most seductive small cities in Spain, Segovia deserves a lingering visit rather than a hurried day trip from Madrid.

It is graced by three famous monuments: Spain's last-built Gothic **cathedral**; the fairytale but fake **Alcázar**; and the **Roman Aqueduct**, in use until just a few years ago (you will see it as you arrive, striding across Plaza Azoguejo. From there, drivers should follow signs for *centro historico* and make for Plaza Mayor).

In addition, Segovia possesses a shower of lovely Romanesque churches and peaceful streets and squares lined by elegant honey-coloured houses. There is a welcome sense of space and an easy-going atmosphere, encapsulated by the gentle evening *paseo*.

To take in the main sights, and at the same time enjoy the backwaters, I suggest two leisurely strolls, each starting from **Plaza Mayor**:

Cathedral and Alcázar
Begin at the **cathedral** just off Plaza Mayor. It was begun as late as 1525, at the start of the city's decline. No excessive ornamentation here: austerity, *à la Escorial*, was the prevailing theme. The harmonious building was designed by the leading exponent of this style, Juan Gil de Hontañon and carried out by his son Rodrigo; both are buried within. The stepped, semi-circular east end is a fine sight, with its buttresses, balustrades and pinnacles. The interior has a cold, uncluttered elegance, though a major irritation is the late 15thC choir, imprisoned in a ghastly marble block dating from 1784. The 15thC cloisters, by Juan Gras, belonged to the old cathedral and were rebuilt on this site stone by stone.

Leave the cathedral and proceed down Marqués del Arco towards Plaza Merced and the rounded contours and golden hues of 12thC **San Andrés**. Continuing, the road leads past intriguing little side passages and ends at the flowery plaza in front of the **Alcázar**. Jutting out like a great ship over the bald surrounding countryside, the building has all the accoutrements of a storybook medieval castle. If a sense of unreality pervades, that is because it is indeed a sham. While doing duty as a military school in the 19thC it was burned down. What you see now is mainly the charming fantasy of its anonymous recreators (although the keep is original) who imagined what it might have been like during its period as one of the great royal residences of Spain. The interior, being mainly post-fire fake, can happily be skipped.

As you leave the Alcázar, you can see below, on your left, across the Eresma, the little **church of Vera Cruz** with the 17thC **Convento de las Carmelitas Descalzas** close by. Vera Cruz was built in 1208 for the Order of the Knights Templar; typically, it is 12-sided, with an inner chamber at its centre for the Templars' secret rites. Walk or drive here if you can (by one of the two northern city gates, then turn left downhill). From the bell tower there are views of the city and the Sierra de Guadarrama. Also in the valley of the Eresma is the lovely **Monasterio de El Parral** and the **Convento de Santa Cruz**.

From the plaza, take the Calle Velarde (signpost for Oficina de Turismo). At the end of the street (in front of a pink building) turn left down Puzuelo and, with the delicate, Italianate tower of **San Esteban** ahead, carry straight on to reach this atypical Segovian Romanesque church with its portico facing on to Plaza Esteban. Leave the plaza by the street to the left of the severe grey stone **Palacio Episcopal**. Turn right and then left into Trinidad to see the pretty **church of La Trinidad** with a restored interior, dark, simple and calm.

San Millán and Roman Aqueduct

Now for the western end of the old town and a couple of sights outside the walls. From Plaza Mayor, take the Isabel La Católica and shopping street Juan Bravo. This passes Plaza San Martín with the Romanesque **church of San Martín** and the **Torre de Lozoya**, which proclaimed the power of the family for whom it was built in the 14thC. Where Juan Bravo curves to the left and becomes Cervantes, notice on the left the 15thC **Casa de los Picos**, the *picos* being the diamond-shaped stone points which cover the façade. Across the road is the **Palacio de los Condes de Alpuente**, covered with the type of plasterwork known as *esgrafiado*, much copied in this region.

At the start of Cervantes, take the flight of steps down to the right. You are now leaving the historic old town and entering the new. Walk down Arturo Merino and then turn left by La Cocina de San Millán into San Millán. Cross the open area to Felix Gila and walk round the back of the wall, then thread round to the left and up the hill where you will see the **church of San Millán** on your right, its simple beauty emphasized by the unattractive modern buildings nearby. This is a superb, though early, example of Segovian Romanesque. Turn left on to the main Calle Fernández Ladreda with a fine view of the **Roman Aqueduct** before you. Built in the 1stC AD, it is a typically brilliant piece of Roman engineering, 728 m long, and here, 28 m high.

SEPULVEDA ✕

A delightful place in which to while away a few hours, especially if lunch is included (the town styles itself *Capital Mundial del Cordero Asado*). Sepúlveda is distinguished by its crop of Romanesque churches and by its past as a centre of power and influence. A natural fortress,

DETOUR – **DURATON**
This Segovian Romanesque church is hard to beat for its isolated setting, its lovely atrium and terrific stork's nest set at a rakish angle.

built on a bluff above the wild and deep Duratón Gorge it was buffeted back and forth between Moors and Christians.

Of the 15 parish churches that existed in the Middle Ages, just a handful remain, all examples of Sepúlvedan Romanesque, which was a precursor of the more refined Segovian Romanesque. In Plaza Mayor, facing the remains of the old castle, take the street to the right and walk away from the town until you reach the little church of **Nuestra Señora de la Peña** on a promontory overlooking the gorge. It dates from the early 12thC and has an unusually elaborate tympanum over the entrance. Retrace, and cross Plaza Mayor to see the charmingly simple **San Bartolomé**.

The 1,000-year-old church of **El Salvador** can be found by taking the left-hand road out of the plaza (facing the castle), and at the corner, turning right (by restaurant Hernanz) and, through an arch in the old wall, ascending a flight of steps. The church stands at the town's highest point and is the oldest Segovian Romanesque church still standing.

TUREGANO

On a dead straight road, the pink-hued **castle** of Turégano stands in a sea of wheat, with the Sierra de Guadarrama as a back-drop. The bell tower inside the mainly 15thC castle is a Baroque addition to the lovely Romanesque **church of San Miguel** which it enfolds. The town has a galleried Plaza Mayor.

VALLADOLID

See Spain Overall: 2.

DETOUR – **CASTILLO DE CASTILNOVO**
In a pleasant grove just off the road between Pedraza and Sepúlveda, on the C112 (signposted Cerezo de Abajo) stands the Mudéjar castle of Castilnovo. Once a military stronghold, it now looks very domesticated, complete with swimming-pool.

RECOMMENDED HOTELS

PEDRAZA DE LA SIERRA

Molino de Rio Viejo, PP; *Collado Hermoso (10 km SW on the N110); tel. 921 40 30 63.*

Phone in advance – closed when there are no prior bookings. Tiny converted mill, very simple, but furnished with flair. There are six bedrooms and a communal dining table where basic country fare is served. Riding can be arranged.

Posada de Don Mariano, PPP; *Mayor, 14; tel. 921 50 98 86.*

When things are quiet you can choose which bedroom you prefer – attic ones are the most charming, but all are attractive and individually decorated with the sophisticated *madrileño* in mind. Prices are only just in our 'expensive' catagory. Family run; avoid the chi-chi restaurant.

SEGOVIA

Parador Nacional de Segovia, PPP; *Carreterade Valladolid; tel. 921 44 37 37.*
One of the up-market paradors, modern and light, with indoor and outdoor pools and a well-regarded restaurant. The views are exceptional, though staying outside atmospheric Segovia (2 km) is a disadvantage.

Las Sirenas, PP; *Juan Bravo, 30; tel.* 921 46 26 63.

Old town stalwart, with well-equipped (TV, air-conditioning) if dull rooms, and a matronly air.

A more expensive alternative in the area is **Los Linajes, PPP** (*tel.* 921 46 04 75) which has a lovely position stepping down the hillside beside the city wall, but a soulless modern interior.

RECOMMENDED RESTAURANTS

PEDRAZA DE LA SIERRA

Hostería Pintor Zuloaga, PPP; *Matadero, 1; tel. 921 50 98 35; credit cards* AE, DC, MC, V.

Well known for its serious Castilian cooking, this is a grand little restaurant, part of the Parador group, with prices to match. The setting is a charming señorial house decorated in traditional Castilian style. There are several smart restaurants to choose from in Pedraza, though often they are shut on weekday evenings out of season.

Also well spoken of is **El Yantar de Pedraza** (*tel.* 921 50 41 07) with balconies overlooking Plaza Mayor.

SEGOVIA

Méson José María, P-PPP; *Lecea, 11; tel.* 921 46 60 17; *credit cards* AE, DC, MC, V.

Popular and animated, with swift service and very good food: a Segovian institution, in fact. If you don't want to indulge in a full meal, you can enjoy the atmosphere by staying in the bar, which has the luxury of several tables, and eating your *tapas* or *raciónes* in comfort while the locals stand and chat. Beyond is the large, brightly decorated dining room, equally well patronized by merry families tucking into the Segovian speciality of roast suckling pig.

The best known restaurant in town is **Mesón de Cándido** (*Plaza Azoguejo, 5; tel.* 921 42 59 11), run since 1931 by Señor Cándido and now his son, its walls plastered with the faces of the famous who have eaten there.

SEPULVEDA

Figón de Zute El Mayor (Tinín), PP; *Tetuán, 6; tel.* 921 54 01 65; *open lunch only, closed Tues.*

The room is plain, the menu even more so – *cordero asado* so tender that it is parted from the bone with a spoon; a salad, a jug of wine, followed by *tarta ponche* (delicious local cake), *carne de membrillo* (quince jelly served with *manchego* cheese) and a wicked yellow liqueur called El Afilador. The eponymous Tinín officiates with gusto. He will bustle you out to see the roaring furnace in which your hunk of lamb is cooking, and he will proudly tell you that King Juan Carlos has been his guest.

Another recommended restaurant in Sepúlveda specializing in *cordero asado* is **Hernanz, PP-PPP** (*Conde de Sepúlveda, 4; tel.* 921 54 03 78).

The Rioja Wine Region: Haro and Santo Domingo de la Calzada

200 km; map Michelin 442, 1:400,000

Rioja is a household word, thanks to the quality of its wine, but there are other attractions in this small region wedged between the Basque provinces and Castile. The *riojanos* determined they were not going to be swallowed up by these larger neighbours when Spain was divided into autonomous units in the early 1980s and La Rioja too was granted autonomy, with Logroño as its capital. The eastern part of the region is covered in Spain Overall: 5. In this section you can discover areas west and south-west of Logroño, the lush wine country and the mountainous zone respectively.

South of the Ebro rise the heights of the Sierra de la Demanda, a glorious wilderness area of chasms, forests and stone hamlets. But at La Rioja's heart lies the Ebro Valley, particularly delightful to visit in autumn when a golden glow spreads over the rolling landscape of the vineyards and the air is heavy with the odour of fermenting grapes. Hundreds of wineries, many of which welcome visitors, are located in or near the towns and villages dotted along the valley, such as Fuenmayor, Cenicero, Elciego, and Haro.

The fertile soil produces first-class fruit and vegetables, while from the sierra come excellent lamb, beef, and game – so you can eat well. Specialities include stuffed peppers (sweet red peppers pop up in many dishes), lamb chops grilled over vine shoots, and stew of quail and beans. When you eat *tapas* in a village bar, you can be assured that the regular wine will be of a certain quality, something not guaranteed in other parts of Spain.

Rioja is rich in historical associations, with fine examples of Romanesque and Gothic architecture. The Romans built roads and soldiers of the rival kingdoms of Navarra and Castile marched through. Thousands of pilgrims came too, for the Ebro Valley was a main route on the Camino de Santiago (Pilgrim's Way to Santiago).

TRANSPORT

Buses run several times a day between Logroño, Nájera and Santo Domingo. Haro is well served since it is on the Logroño-Vitoria highway and on the main rail line between Logroño and Miranda de Ebro. One or two buses a day stop at San Millán de la Cogolla and the smaller towns.

1:600,000

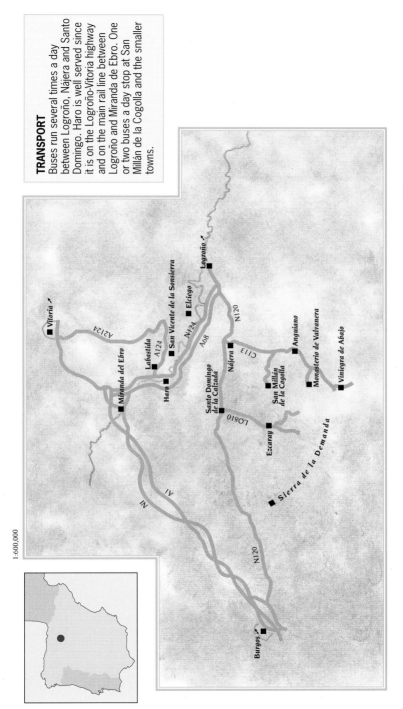

SIGHTS & PLACES OF INTEREST

ANGUIANO
The stiltmen of Anguiano have become famous for their acrobatic gyrations on July 22, the day of Magdalena (St Mary Magdalene). Verses are recited to the saint, asking for favours and an abundant harvest. Dancers on stilts accompany the image in procession and after Mass rush madly down steps and career along cobbled streets to the plaza.

Carry on south-west from Anguiano up the Najerilla Valley, take a right turn on the LO803 and you reach the **Monasterio de Santa María de Valvanera.** Here, among the mountains, Rioja's patron saint is enshrined. The Benedictine monks make a liqueur flavoured with herbs. There is a two-star *hostal*, (P; *tel.* 941 37 70 44).

BURGOS
See Spain Overall: 2.

DEMANDA, SIERRA DE LA
Extending from La Rioja into Burgos province (see also Spain Overall: 2), the Sierra de la Demanda rises more than 2,000 m. Largely uninhabited and forested with beech, birch and pine, it is excellent hiking country and popular with trout fishermen. Adjoining is the Sierra de Cameros, hunting country, with boar and deer.

ELCIEGO
See page 254.

EZCARAY ×
A useful centre for exploring the Sierra de la Demanda (above). The village has some noble mansions with coats of arms and the 14thC **church of Santa María,** a national monument. In snow-free months you can enjoy a beautiful mountain excursion starting from Ezcaray (enquire about road conditions): you follow the surfaced road to the Valdezcaray ski resort, at 1,550 m, then loop through wild country, returning to Ezcaray via the Oja valley.

HARO ⇥ ×
As capital of the Rioja Alta wine district, Haro is a small but prosperous town with some noble mansions. The **church of Santo Tomás** has a notable Plateresque façade carved by Vigarni and the **Ayuntamiento** (Town Hall) is a neo-classical attention-grabber created by Villanueva, who designed Madrid's Prado Museum.

Important *bodegas* here include Berceo, Martínez Lacuesta, Muga, and Federico Paternina. Visits can be

---

RECOMMENDED HOTELS

HARO
Los Agustinos, PPP; *San Agustín, 2*; *tel.* 941 31 13 08.

This distinguished building housed a convent, founded in 1373, and later a school, hospital and jail – on the cloister columns you can see writing made by the prisoners. Now it has been beautifully restored and converted into a four-star hotel.

NAJERA
Hispano, P; *Duques de Nájera, s/n*; *tel.* 941 36 36 15.

A two-star *hostal* in a quiet area.

SANTO DOMINGO DE LA CALZADA
Parador Santo Domingo, PPP; *tel.* 941 34 03 00.

A 14thC pilgrim refuge, recently expanded and refurbished, just opposite the cathedral, featuring luxuries the pilgrims could not have dreamed of, including a gourmet restaurant, a gymnasium and sauna.

Monasterio de la Anunciación, Hospedería del Cister, P; *tel.* 941 34 08 60.

Genuinely monastic. Doors closed at 11 pm.

VINIEGRA DE ABAJO
Goyo, P; *Ctra de Lerma, km 99*; *tel.* 941 37 80 07.

An old inn, with an echoing modern hotel extension, in a lonely spot in the Sierra de la Demanda. A favourite stop for sportsmen: hunting trophies adorn the walls. The restaurant, with a large fireplace, offers solid home cooking at budget prices. Try *Alubias rojas con chorizo* (red beans with sausage), a very filling stew.

RECOMMENDED RESTAURANTS

EZCARAY
Echaurren, PP; Héroes del Alcázar, 2; *tel.* 941 35 40 47; *credit cards* AE, DC, MC, V; *closed Sun eve in winter*, Nov.

A highly-rated, family-run restaurant with some unusual dishes, such as stuffed leg of lamb. In the same building is the comfortable Echaurren hotel, Book at weekends and during the ski-ing season.

HARO
Las Cigüeñas, PP; Plaza de la Paz; *tel.* 941 31 01 22; *credit cards* AE, DC, MC, V; *closed Wed eve*.

This spacious third-floor restaurant has no-frills decoration, apart from a mighty display of Rioja wines, but the food and wine is exceptional value for money, and service is speedy. Recommended: the *Cordero asado* (roast lamb).

SANTO DOMINGO DE LA CALZADA
El Rincón de Emilio, PP; Bonifacio Gil, 7; *tel.* 941 34 09 90; *credit cards* MC, V; *closed Tues eve*, Feb.

Regional cooking at reasonable prices.

---

arranged by calling in advance. The prestigious CVNE (pronounced 'coon-ay') company matures its wine in 25,000 barrels. You can see the cob-webbed cellars where, on the occasion of the *bodega's* centenary, a selection of its best wines was locked away for 100 years, not to be opened until 2079.

An alcoholic battle occurs on September 8, when pilgrims to a local shrine bombard one another with wine. A certain amount is drunk too.

LABASTIDA
This town in Alava province prospered until, at the turn of the century, *phylloxera* destroyed the vines and forced half the population to leave. Many palatial houses remain, including those of the **Paternina** and the **Garizábal** families on the main street. The **church of Asunción** is the scene every Christmas of a Nativity celebration, with shepherds and traditional songs and dances. On the edge of town, you can visit the **Ermita del Cristo**, a Romanesque tower with Renaissance additions containing a venerated 13thC image of Christ.

LOGROÑO
See *Spain Overall*: 5.

NAJERA ⬦
For a time this small town was the seat of the kings of Navarra. Later the Castilian monarch Ferdinand III, The Saint, was crowned here. The chief point of interest is the **Monasterio de Santa María la Real** (admission charge, closed Monday), bulking large between the river and a red sandstone bluff. It is built on the spot where a ruler of Navarra found an image of the Virgin. More than 30 members of the royal families of Navarra, Castile and León are buried in the monastery, which has a Gothic cloister distinguished by lace-like stonework.

SAN MILLAN DE LA COGOLLA
This tranquil and beautiful valley, sheltering two monasteries, has a special significance in Spanish history, thanks to the scribblings of an unknown monk (or student) in the 11thC. He was reading a Latin manuscript and for his own, or others' enlightenment, wrote in the margin translations of certain phrases. These annotations, known as the *Glosas Emilianenses*, are considered the first examples of written Castilian; other annotations on the manuscript are the first writings in Basque. Not until the early 20thC did a scholar draw attention to their significance.

Suso is the higher monastery. Its little church, which displays Visigothic and Arab influences, shelters the tombs of the Siete Infantes de Lara, seven nobles whose murder is chronicled in a medieval epic poem. **Yuso**, the lower monastery founded in the 11thC, was rebuilt in the 16th and 17thC. Only a dozen monks now reside in the immense, echoing building (closed Monday), which has a fine Gothic cloister and a Renaissance church with a magnificent gilded reredos (decorative screen behind altar). In the first-floor museum is a collection of ivory bas-reliefs depicting the life of San Millán, the 6thC hermit who led the first religious community here, and priceless

Rioja wine flows from more than 2,000 *bodegas* (wineries), not all of which are in the region named La Rioja. The producing area is split into three sections, Rioja Alavesa in the province of Alava, Rioja Alta, mostly in La Rioja region but with a few *bodegas* in Burgos province, and Rioja Baja, in the north-east of Rioja but including some wineries in Navarra province.

The micro-climate is regarded as ideal for production of quality wine, aided by methods similar to those of Bordeaux. Up to 30 per cent of the 1.3 million hectolitres of wine produced annually is exported.

Traditionally, Rioja wines have an oaky or 'vanilla' bouquet and flavour, the result of storing in oak barrels, but the modern trend is to reduce the maturing time in barrels. The most highly-regarded recent vintages are those of 1978, 1981, 1982 (outstanding), 1987 and 1991.

Quality controls are strictly maintained by the regulatory body, the Consejo Regulador de la Denominación de Origen. The labelling tells you how long the wine has been matured. *Crianza* indicates red wine at least two years old, of which one at least was in barrels. *Reserva* must pass at least one year in the barrel and two years in bottle. Wine marked *Gran reserva* must have matured at least two years in barrel and three in bottle. White wine regulations provide for much shorter maturing times.

illuminated manuscripts and codices (manuscript books). Ask to see the volumes on sacred music: 60 or more sheep were killed to provide parchment for each book, the whole collection requiring the skins of 2,600 animals.

During the 13thC the priest Gonzalo de Berceo wrote the first known Castilian poem while at Yuso.

SAN VICENTE DE LA SONSIERRA

With its hill-top **castle** and 16thC **church**, San Vicente makes a pretty picture. Not so pretty is the Holy Week procession spectacle of penitents scourging themselves, a medieval throw-back.

SANTO DOMINGO DE LA CALZADA 🚪 ✕

Santo Domingo was an 11thC holy man who dedicated his life to helping the pilgrims *en route* to Santiago de Compostela. He effectively founded the town, building a road (*calzada*), an inn, a hospital, now a parador, and a bridge across the Oja River (the region's name, incidentally, comes from the Río Oja, a tributary of the mighty Ebro).

Today's footsore pilgrims stay at an old hospice with a 40-bed dormitory. In the guestbook somebody has noted 'Hier was het goed' ('This was a good place'); while a British visitor groaned: 'How much water is there in a blister?'

Within the Gothic cathedral, which contains Santo Domingo's tomb, you may be surprised by the crowing of a cock. One is always kept there with a hen in a lofty coop in memory of a miracle. An innkeeper's lustful daughter vengefully accused a young pilgrim from Cologne of theft after he – to quote one version – refused 'to medyll with her carnally'. He was hanged, but visiting the scaffold his parents heard him say 'Santo Domingo has saved me'. They rushed to ask the magistrate to cut him down. The worthy scoffed that their son was as alive as the roast chicken he was about to eat, at which two chickens sprang up and began crowing. The youth was reprieved.

Between May 10 and 15, colourful processions take place in homage to **Santo Domingo**. Young maids, in virginal white, walk through town bearing on their heads baskets containing 'the saint's bread'.

VALVANERA, MONASTERIO DE
See Anguiano, page 256.

VINIEGRA DE ABAJO 🚪
See Recommended Hotels, page 256.

VITORIA
See Spain Overall: 5,

• *Opposite: Across the vineyards of Rioja to San Vicente de la Sonsierra.*

<u>North-Eastern Spain</u>

Valleys of the Pyrenees: Ordesa Park and Vall d'Aran

Map Michelin 443, 1:400,000

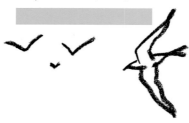

Once you could meet few people besides smugglers, shepherds and frontier patrols on the limestone heights of this middle section of the Pyrenees, where the range reaches its highest with peaks over 3,000 m. Then came the Spanish Civil War, when thousands of Republican supporters trekked over the passes to seek refuge in France. In the Second World War, escaped Allied prisoners of war were spirited across to find safety in neutral Spain. Later they were followed by Spanish guerrillas, who sneaked through the mountains to launch a doomed anti-Franco campaign.

Today hikers, climbers, skiers, bird-watchers, rafters and other outdoor enthusiasts roam this majestic barrier between France and Spain. Only a handful of brown bears hold out in the Pyreneen fastnesses, but deer, ibex, boar, otter, capercaillie, lammergeier, vultures and eagles haunt the crags and hushed verdant valleys. Old pilgrim routes and remote villages, each with its weathered Romanesque church, await exploration.

It is self-defeating to rush your discovery of the Pyrenees. Slow down, and you'll better appreciate the rhythms of village life and the delights of mountain excursions. The roads are not built for fast travel, so if you have limited time, concentrate on a small area. It is difficult to give any realistic distance because so many valleys are involved. To see them all would meaning driving around 1,000 km since in many cases you have to go up the valleys and back down them again.

If you want more detail than is given on Michelin map 442 (scale 1:400,000), Firestone produce two maps of the Pyrenees at the scale of 1:200,000. Walkers and climbers will be interested in the series of guides produced by Editorial Alpina, with maps at a scale of 1:25,000 and 1:40,000; and in the sheet maps published by the Servicio Geográfico del Ejercito and the Instituto Geográfico Nacional at 1:25,000 and 1:50,000.

TRANSPORT

Few rail lines penetrate the Pyrenees, but there is a one-a-day service between Jaca and Canfranc. From Jaca, Huesca and Lleida bus services reach out to the valleys, although you may have to make time-consuming changes at such points as Ainsa, Barbastro and Sabiñanigo. As there are only one or two buses a day to most villages, count on an overnight stop once you step off. The Vall d'Aran is most easily accessible by a daily bus from Lleida, via Pont de Suert. Another arrives from Barcelona via Pobla de Segur, a long and somewhat tedious journey – though the scenery is splendid.

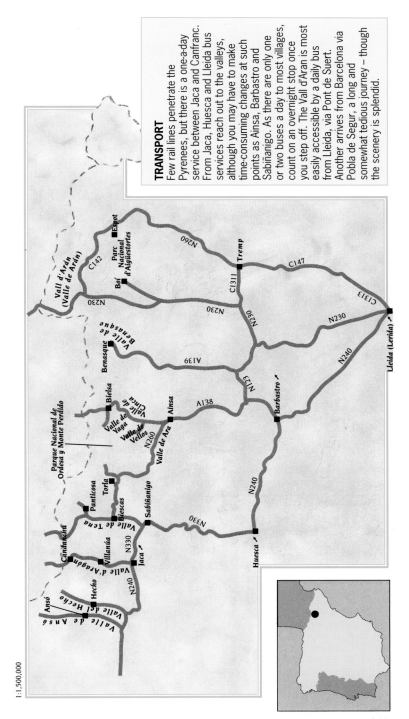

1:1,500,000

SIGHTS & PLACES OF INTEREST

AINSA ✕

With only a few more than 1,000 inhabitants, Ainsa is the capital of a mountainous zone known as the Sobrarbe, where many villages have been abandoned. Its medieval quarter, with an arcaded main square, stands on a promontory above the Ara and Cinca rivers, while new development has taken place at its foot.

The **Vellos, Yaga and Cinca valleys** north of Ainsa offer challenges for climbers, walkers and fans of canyoning, which apparently consists of hurling oneself down waterfalls and precipices in an inflatable craft.

Bielsa (on the A138, 34 km N of Ainsa) was burned down during the Civil

• *Pyrenees.*

War, but rebuilt in traditional style. It is popular with French trippers and is a useful base for exploring the mountains. There is a museum of local costumes and tools in the handsome town hall. The beautiful **Pineta Valley**, a favourite with campers, leads west to the Ordesa y Monte Perdido National Park.

One of the remoter villages, **Plan**, 19 km E of Bielsa, achieved international fame of a sort during the 1980s when its desperate bachelors advertised for brides. A grand fiesta was organized for the women who responded, also attended by an army of reporters and television cameramen. Several marriages resulted.

AIGUESTORTES I ESTANY DE SANT MAURICI, (PARC NACIONAL DE AIGUESTORTES) 🛏️

Access to the 10,000-hectare park, just south of the Vall d'Aran, is via Espot, off the C147, 157 km N of Lleida, and via Boí, off the N230, 144 km N of Lleida. Scores of glacier-carved lakes, hanging valleys and spectacular *cirques* are features of Aigüestortes ('twisted waters' in Catalan). Peaks over 2,500 m attract climbers and there are numerous well-marked paths; the park has four mountain refuges and campsites and you will find small hotels in the surrounding villages. Hydro-electric installations, permitted before the park was created, have done some damage to the natural beauty. The number of vehicles allowed in the park is limited, but four-wheel-drive taxis can be rented to get you there. Information from Boí, tel. 973 69 61 89, and Espot, tel. 973 62 40 36.

ANSO

On the HU202, 52 km NE of Jaca. Ansó has typical Pyrenean stone houses with wooden balconies. Its valley and that of neighbouring Hecho are characterized by green pastures, rushing torrents and thick woods beneath harsh limestone peaks. An annual summer art symposium is held at **Hecho** (on the HU210, 44 km north-west of Jaca), which has an open-air museum of modern sculpture. Up the Hecho Valley is the 9thC **Monasterio de Siresa** and further along a narrow gorge dubbed the **Boca del Infierno** (Hell's Mouth).

ARAN, VALL D' (ARAN, VALLE DE)

🛏️ ✕ *Tourism Office, Sarriulera, 8, Viella; tel. 973 64 01 10.* Isolated from Spain until recently, the beautiful Arán Valley blends Catalan customs, French cuisine and *aranés* hospitality. Many of the 6,000 inhabitants speak French as well as their own language, a mixture of Catalan and Gascon with some Basque words. Below lofty peaks, waterfalls cascade down wooded slopes to the green pastures of the valley, through which flows the Garona River into France, allowing easier access from that country than from Spain.

More than 30 stone-built villages dot the valley, each with its Romanesque church. Arán is great for fishing, hiking, and skiing. It snows an average of 56 days a year and **Baqueira Beret** is

• *Skiing at Baqueira Beret in the Vall d'Aran.*

Spain's most prestigious ski resort, a favourite with King Juan Carlos, who democratically queues at the lifts.

If all this sounds too good to be true, it is. Arán has grown trendy and expensive and it gets crowded with French and Spanish visitors. Apartment blocks and supermarkets have intruded and **Viella**, the main town, has lost some of its sleepy charm. The only access from Spain used to be the Bonaigua Pass, blocked by snowfalls for up to eight months of the year. But in 1948 a 5-km tunnel opened linking Arán with Lleida via the N230 and heavy traffic now thunders through the valley.

But the scenery is magnificent. And the food is good too. You will find some of the best food at village houses: try quail grilled on open fireplaces and cream cheese with honey.

BARBASTRO
See Spain Overall: 6.

BENASQUE
On the A139, 150 km NE of Huesca. Picturesque Benasque, a summer and winter resort, offers outdoor activities from paragliding to hunting. The ski resort of **Cerler** lies 400 m above the town. Among the ancient mansions is the **Palacio de los Condes de Ribagorza** and the **church of San Marcial** dating from the 13thC.

From Benasque climbers can scale **Aneto**, at 3,408 m the highest peak in the Pyrenees, and Maladeta, 3,308 m, usually starting from the Renclusa refuge, near Benasque. To do this you need climbing experience and you must carry ice equipment as the route traverses the Aneto glacier.

You can hike into France from Benasque by an old smugglers' route, used during the Civil War by fleeing Republicans.

BIELSA ⇌
See Ainsa, page 262.

BIESCAS ✕
See Recommended Restaurants, page 265.

MOUNTAIN VALLEYS IN HUESCA PROVINCE
For information on this series of valleys cutting south through the mountains, look under other headings as follows: (travelling east to west) the Ansó and Hecho valleys, see Ansó; Aragón, see Candanchú; Tena, see Panticosa; Ara, see Torla; Vellos, Yaga and Cinca, see Ainsa; Benasque, see Benasque.

CANDANCHU
On the N330, 33 km N of Jaca. This is a major downhill and cross-country skiing resort in the Aragón valley, below the 1,600-m **Somport Pass**. Roncesvalles, also in this valley (see Spain Overall: 6) is a main entry point for Santiago pilgrims. A tunnel 5,850 m long is being cut beneath the pass to link Spain and France.

HECHO ✕
See Ansó, page 263.

HUESCA
See Spain Overall: 6.

JACA
See Spain Overall: 6.

RECOMMENDED HOTELS

AIGÜESTORTES NATIONAL PARK
Casa Escudé, P; *Boí (Lleida province), off the N230, 50 km S of Viella; tel. 973 69 60 17.*

Low-priced accommodation in a village house with cooking facilities, part of Catalunya's rural tourism scheme.

ARAN, VALL D'
Deth País, P-PP; *Salardú; tel. 973 64 58 36.* Excellent value in a small, comfortable two-star hotel.

Parador Don Gaspar de Portolá, PPP; *Ctra Baqueira, s/n, Artiés; tel. 973 64 08 01.*

Built in traditional Arán style with comfortable rooms and fine views. The name comes from the explorer of California and founder of the San

Diego mission, born in the adjoining 17thC structure.

BIELSA
Parador Monte Perdido, PP; *Valle de Pineta; tel. 974 50 10 11.*

A four-storey stone building in the magnificent surroundings of the Ordesa National Park.

TORLA
Bujaruelo, P; *Ctra Ordesa; tel. 974 48 61 74.*

Small one-star hotel with home cooking.

VILLANUA
Faus Hütte, PP; *on the N330, 15 km N of Jaca, Ctra de Francia, km 658; tel. 974 37 81 36.*

A cosy Alpine-style hotel, only ten rooms, in the Aragón valley just outside Villanúa, with beautiful views.

LLEIDA (LERIDA)
See Spain Overall: 7.

ORDESA Y MONTE PERDIDO, PARQUE NACIONAL DE
Access via Biescas, 150 km NW of Lleida. An information office opens in summer. There is glorious walking through the pine, beech and fir forests of the Ordesa canyon in this 15,600-hectare park in the Aragonese Pyrenees, dominated by the 3,355-m Monte Perdido.

A seven-hour hike to the Soaso Circle takes you past a series of waterfalls, including the spectacular **Cola de Caballo** (horse's tail). Only local shepherds knew about the valley until a French alpinist explored it in the early 20thC.

Sole survivors of the Pyrenean sub-species of mountain goat are to be found here as well as griffon vultures, otters, and the increasingly rare lammergeier, or bearded vulture, a bird of prey with a mighty wing span that extracts marrow from bones by dropping them on to rocks. The Ordesa Park has 171 species of birds, 32 mammals, eight reptiles and five amphibia.

Directly north of Ordesa (in France) is the magnificent natural amphitheatre, the **Cirque de Gavarnie.** Seeing it involves a strenuous walk and climb, or a lengthy detour by road.

PANTICOSA
Off the C136, 80 km N of Huesca. A side road off the Tena Valley leads north-east to the village of Panticosa, trying hard to be a ski resort, and onwards through a narrow chasm, the **Garganta del Escalar**, to the **Balneario de Panticosa**. There are ambitious plans to refurbish this spa, where the Emperor Tiberius is said to have tried the health-giving waters. The setting, below the beetling brows of the mountains, is somewhat claustrophobic.

Parts of the Tena Valley have been flooded to create hydro-electric power. Nearing Sallent (off the C136, 54 km north-east of Jaca), you see the rooftops and church tower of an inundated village. There are some fine walks into the mountains from this village, which can become crowded in summer. Nearby is **El Formigal**, a modern ski resort, beyond which the road curls into France via the Col de Portalet.

TORLA 🛏
Approached up the Ara Valley, this is a typical Pyrenean village of slate-roofed, stone houses, which becomes thronged due to the proximity of the Ordesa National Park. It has bars, restaurants and accommodation.

VIELLA
See Vall d'Aran, page 263.

VILLANUA 🛏
See Recommended Hotels, 264.

RECOMMENDED RESTAURANTS

AINSA
Bodegas del Sobrarbe, PP; *Plaza Mayor, 2; tel. 974 50 02 37; credit cards MC, V; closed Nov 1 to Easter week.*

In the cellar of a medieval house. Speciality: roast lamb.

ARAN, VALL D'
Casa Irene, PPP; *Mayor, 4, Artiés; tel. 973 64 09 00; closed Mon in winter, May, Nov.*

Irene's restaurant is *the* place to eat at in the Vall d'Aran and a favourite of the Spanish royal family. Irene is the meticulous host while her son prepares the many courses, often French-influenced, from a gourmet menu.

Campaneta, PP; *San Pedro, 16, Escuñau; tel. 973 64 15 20; credit cards V.*

Hearty home cooking in a typical village house.

BIESCAS
Casa Ruba, PP; *(on the N260, 29 km NE of Jaca) Esperanza, 18; tel. 974 48 50 01; credit cards AE, V; closed Oct, Nov.*

A restaurant serving traditional local dishes, also a long-established hotel (**P**).

HECHO
Gaby-Casa Blasquico, PP; *tel. 974 37 50 07; credit cards V; closed Sept.*

Excellent game dishes and home-made desserts.

<u>North-Eastern Spain</u>

Catalunya Region: Costa Brava and Interior

300 km; map Michelin 443, 1:400,000

C atalunya embraces both the sparkling waters of the Mediterranean and the snow-capped heights of the Pyrenees. The region's north-eastern corner, covered in this section, includes the Costa Brava, the fertile pastures and historic towns of the interior and the mountain zone. You can snorkel, raft through canyons, fish for trout, explore 1,000-year-old monasteries, sample the best of sea and mountain food, and visit Andorra, a feudal relic.

If you are based at a Costa Brava resort, use this local exploration to make interesting excursions into the interior. If you are following the N11 highway for the red (fast) route described in Spain Overall: 8, you can dip in and out. It takes at least a day to drive the tortuous coast road. To see the whole area, count on four to five days.

TRANSPORT

Trains run between Barcelona, Girona, Figueres, and Portbou at the French frontier. Another line runs from Barcelona to Puigcerda, near the frontier, via Vic and Ripoll. Two buses a day run from Barcelona to La Seu d'Urgell and Andorra. Bus services reach out from Figueres and Girona to the coastal towns. From June to September, you can enjoy a splendid coastal cruise. A boat runs daily between Calella (Barcelona province), Blanes, Lloret, Tossa, Sant Feliú, Platja d'Aro and Palamós.

1:2,000,000

SIGHTS & PLACES OF INTEREST

ANDORRA ⌦ ✕

Tourism Office, Carrer Dr. Villanova, Andorra La Vella; tel. 376 8202 14. The tiny (464 square km), mountainous principality of Andorra welcomes skiers, shoppers and tax-dodgers. It has no army, no political parties and levies no taxes. Now, the bad news. It is being dragged into the 20thC. In 1993 a democratic constitution was adopted, Oscar Ribas became the first prime minister, and the medieval mini-nation joined the United Nations. Although not in the EC, Andorra is having to adjust to the depressing pressure for uniformity throughout Europe.

Its independence dates from 1278 when the Counts of Foix and the Bishops of Urgell resolved a long and bloody territorial argument by making Andorra a jointly owned principality. Andorra pays an annual tribute called *la questia*: one year a sum of money goes to the president of France, the next year cash, 12 chickens, 24 cheeses and six hams to the Spanish bishop.

Since the 1950s Andorra has changed sharply, from a feudal bucolic paradise, inhabited by shepherds and smugglers, into a thriving commercial centre and a tax haven. Large amounts of cash are stashed in Andorra's banks, so discreet that they make Swiss banks look loose-tongued. The population has swelled to 61,000, but only 14,000 are native Andorrans; the rest are mainly Spanish (30,000), French and Portuguese.

The principality's main valley has been desecrated by ugly modern buildings, totally out of character with the traditional architecture of granite and timber. On the road in from Spain, vast hypermarkets sell duty-free goods and bargain-priced petrol (customs checks can cause lengthy traffic queues at the Spanish frontier, especially at weekends). Twelve million visitors a year pour in and the capital, **Andorra la Vella**, is polluted by traffic and gaudy signs. Luxury goods cram the stores: both pesetas and francs are accepted. Serene amid the frenetic consumerism stands the **Casa de la Vall**, the 16thC stone building where parliament meets. Escape the dire commercialism by heading for the hills. There you will find Alpine meadows, sparkling lakes, scores of peaks over 2,500 m high and aged Romanesque churches. **Ordino** is one relatively unspoiled village, 7 km north of the capital *en route* to **Arcalis**, one of five ski stations in the principality. From Ondino a road over the heights offers beautiful views on the way to Canillo. From there, the N22 wiggles up the **Puerto d'Envalira**, at 2,407 m the highest pass in the Pyrenees, before plunging down into France.

BARCELONA

See pages 193-200.

BERGA

A colourful fiesta – **La Patum** – is held here on the Sunday after Corpus Christi to commemorate the town's liberation from the Moors and its transfer in 1393 from Aragónese to Catalonian rule. Fire-breathing dragons, angels, devils and giants take part.

> ### COSTA BRAVA – REPUTATION, AND REALITY
>
> Until the late 1950s the Costa Brava (which means wild or rugged coast) was the ideal place to get away from it all. Unfortunately, it lay exposed to the army of cement mixers which announced the arrival of mass tourism. Many violations later, the coast is saddled, unfairly, with a downmarket image. Thoughtless development has blighted once-delightful fishing villages, but much charm remains.
>
> Stretching 200 km between the least developed section near the French border and Blanes, 62 km north-east of Barcelona, the Costa Brava has sandy beaches, intimate coves, rocky headlands, Roman ruins, and 2,500 hours of sunshine a year.
>
> You can choose from trendy, exclusive, cheap or cheerful accommodation. It can be difficult to find a room in high season. By October the crowds have gone, which is pleasant, but many hotels and restaurants then shut for the winter, turning resorts into ghost towns. See individual entries for further details.

BLANES

Tourism Office, Plaza Catalunya; tel. 972 33 03 48. A fishing port/resort with a 1-km beach. There is a ruined 10thC **castle**; some **jardineres botánicos** (4,000 plants) on Paseo Carlos Faust; and a **Jardín Tropical** at Cala Santa Cristina with 7,000 species.

CADAQUES

Tourism Office, Cotxe, 2; tel. 972 25 83 15. Poor communications and no decent beach have helped preserve picturesque Cadaqués as, perhaps, the pleasantest spot on the coast. It is arty, trendy and pricey, but has a delightful relaxed atmosphere as you stroll the waterfront past the fishing boats. Good swimming and snorkelling can be enjoyed off rocks in adjacent bays.

Hostal Marina (**PP**; *tel. 972 25 81 99*)**,** in the centre, is one of the few reasonably priced places to stay.

Salvador Dalí's rambling house at nearby **Port Lligat** is due to be turned into a museum, but won't be quite the same without the maestro himself. After camping on the beach one night, I cheekily knocked on the door and was soon being treated to pink champagne while Dalí rattled away in three languages, in none of which he made sense.

CARDONA ⛨

See Recommended Hotels.

FIGUERES (FIGUERAS)

See Spain Overall: 8.

GIRONA (GERONA)

See Spain Overall: 8.

LLORET DE MAR

Tourism Office, Plaça de la Vila; tel. 972 36 47 35. Mass tourism has converted Lloret into a kiss-me-quick resort, popular with British youths out to prove their virility by drinking themselves under the table. Falling or diving off hotel balconies is a popular diversion.

If you yearn for Dutch pancakes, German beer, torrents of *sangría,* pizza, chips and high-decibel entertainment, you will love Lloret.

NURIA

See Ripoll, page 270.

RECOMMENDED HOTELS

Turisverd, Plaça de Sant Josep Oriol 4, 08002 Barcelona, publishes an annual list of budget rural accommodation.

ANDORRA

Cerqueda, PP; *4 km S of Andorra la Vella at Santa Coloma; tel. 376 82 02 35.*

Just outside Andorra la Vella. Peaceful, with swimming-pool.

CARDONA

Parador Duques de Cardona, PP; *on the C1410, 100 km NW of Barcelona, Castillo de Cardona; tel. 93 869 12 75.*

Medieval splendours in an 11thC castle, crowning a hill near a mountain of salt.

PALAFRUGELL

Aigua Blava, PP; (*10 km E of Palafrugell), Playa de Fornells, Aigua Blava; tel. 972 62 20 58; closed mid Nov-mid Feb.*

Splendid sea views in a renowned four-star hotel, surrounded by gardens. Family-owned. Tennis and swimming-pool.

S'AGARO

Hostal de La Gavina, PPP; (*off the C255, 2 km NE of Sant Feliu), Plaça Rosaleda; tel. 972 32 11 00; closed end Oct to Easter Week.*

One of Spain's top luxury hotels, furnished with antiques and set amid gardens and pines. Its expensive elegance attracts celebrities: Charlie Chaplin and Ava Gardner were guests. Recommended restaurant (**PPP;** *credit cards* AE, DC, MC, V), with romantic summer dining by the pool.

SEU D'URGELL, LA

Grandia, PP; *Passeig Joan Brudieu, 24; tel. 972 35 03 00.*

A charming old hotel with a comfortable modern wing.

TOSSA DE MAR

Casa Zügel, PP; *Avda de sa Palma, 10; tel. 972 34 02 92; closed Oct-Easter.*

Cheerful, correct accommodation, German-run.

PALAFRUGELL ✉

An old market town not totally swamped by visitors, with beautiful coves nearby between Calella and Tamariu.

RIPOLL

Tourism Office, Plaça Abat Oliva; tel. 972 70 23 51. Modern Ripoll is a grey industrial town in a mountain valley, but it has one outstanding sight: the heavily restored 11thC **church of Sant María Monastery,** founded in 880 by Wilfred The Shaggy, who is regarded as the founder of the Catalan nation. It was later an important centre of learning, and remains a remarkable example of early Catalan Romanesque. Note the massive pillars and barrel vaulting. The church's grandiose 12thC façade, regarded as a landmark in European art, is something of a let-down: now glassed in, it is badly weathered and damaged. With sharp eyesight and some imagination, you can make out sculptures depicting Christ in majesty and Biblical stories. There is a small charge to view the two-storey cloister, with 252 columns, and the museum.

Next door is a **Folklore Museum.** Climb 70 steps to view old iron forges and details of firearms manufacture, for which Ripoll was once famous. A wall plaque outside placed by the American Society for Metals informs: 'The Catalan Forge employed an original process now known as the "Catalan process" for making iron and steel from the 10thC until recent times.'

North of Ripoll (14 km on the N152) is Ribes de Freser, from where you can take a breath-taking ride on the **Cremallera,** a rack railway that climbs through magnificent mountain scenery to **Núria,** where there is a large religious sanctuary.

ROSES (ROSAS) ✕

Tourism Office, Avda Rhoda; tel. 972 25 73 31. Roses, with a vast sandy beach, has grown into a major tourist resort. The Greeks established the settlement of Rhode here in the 9thC BC. On the other side of the wide bay, near the small resort of L'Escala, the extensive ruins of **Empúries (Ampurias)** stand on a slope overlooking the sea. This was the important Greek and, later, Roman port of Emporion, where Scipio's army landed in 218 BC during the

Second Punic War. A forum, villas and amphitheatre have been discovered. The **museum** contains reproductions of the most valuable finds, which have been removed to Barcelona and Girona.

S'AGARO ✉

See Recommended Hotels, page 269.

SANT FELIU DE GUIXOLS ✕

Tourism Office, Plaça Monestir, 54; tel. 972 82 00 51. This pleasant resort grew up around the ruins of an 11thC Benedictine monastery. Pavement cafés and restaurants line the front.

SANT PERE DE RODES, MONASTERIO DE

Located 4 km from El Port de la Selva, 20 km E of Figueres. Brooding on scrub-covered heights, up a vertiginous road from the fishing and pleasure port of El Port de la Selva, Sant Pere would make a fine lair for Vlad The Impaler. The huge, fortress-like, Benedictine monastery was founded in the 9thC at a spot where St Peter's head was supposedly hidden to save it from the barbarians. Sant Pere exerted great power before being abandoned and sacked in the 19thC.

SEU D'URGELL, LA (SEO DE URGEL) ✉ ✕

Entry point for Andorra, La Seu is an historic town in magnificent surroundings in the Segre river valley. Balconies almost touch overhead in the narrow arcaded streets near the **cathedral** which is 12thC Romanesque with Lombard influence.

The **Diocesan Museum** has some notable religious art.

Important for its dairy produce, Seu is also a tourist centre. It got a promotional boost by hosting the 1992 Olympic Wildwater Canoe Slalom. At **Segre Park,** constructed for the occasion, beginners and experts can enjoy canoeing, rafting, hydrospeed, and roller skating (tel. 973 36 00 92).

Nearby is a network of cross-country ski trails and to the south-west is the **Parque Naturel de Cadí-Moixeró,** 41,000 hectares of deep valleys, rock walls and peaks.

For further rafting and canoeing possibilities, take the N260 to **Sort,** 53 km west, where there is a watersports centre in the spectacular Noguera Pallaresa River valley.

SORT
See Seu d'Urgell, La, page 270.

TOSSA DE MAR
Tourism Office, Terminal de Autobuses, tel. 972 34 01 08. Marc Chagall called Tossa a 'blue paradise' when he painted it back in 1933 and, despite the tourist invasion, it remains one of the coast's more attractive towns.

Medieval walls and round towers encircle the Vila Vella (old town) with its cobbled streets and white houses. The **Museo Municipal** exhibits paintings by Chagall and many other artists who visited, also archeological finds. A Roman villa has been excavated in the town.

Tossa has several pleasant beaches. Traverse the corkscrew coastal road to **Sant Feliu** (see page 270) for striking views of an azure sea and tawny cliffs.

VIC
An industrial town on a wide plain, Vic is famous for its sausages. Many monuments testify to its cultural prominence in the past. Only the crypt survives from the original Romanesque **cathedral of Sant Pere**, built in 1038. The present neo-classical building, constructed in the 18thC, is adorned with dramatic religious murals by a noted Catalan painter, José María Sert. He had to

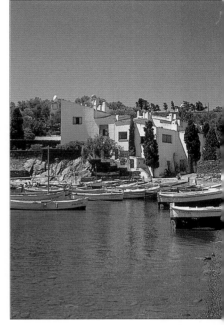

• *Salvador Dalí's house at Port Lligat, near Cadaqués - see page 269.*

paint them twice: the first set were destroyed in a Civil War fire. The **Museo Municipal** next door on Plaça Bisbe Oliva, contains an outstanding collection of medieval Catalan art.

RECOMMENDED RESTAURANTS

ANDORRA
Borda Estevet, PP; *Ctra Comella, 2, Andorra La Vella; tel. 376 86 40 26; credit cards AE, MC, V.*

A typical stone house converted into a restaurant serving Spanish and Andorra dishes.

ROSES
El Bulli, PPP; *(6 km from Roses), Cala Montjoi; tel. 972 15 07 17; credit cards AE, DC, MC, V; closed Mon, Tues (except summer), Oct 15-Mar 15.*

The yachting fraternity drop in at this very expensive restaurant, magnificently located in gardens by the sea, rated among Spain's best. Try the *menú degustación* (sample menu)

for a variety of innovative dishes.

SANT FELIU DE GUIXOLS
Los Panolles, PP; *(5 km NE of Sant Feliu), Ctra Gerona, km 27, Santa Cristina de Aro; tel. 972 83 70 11; credit cards AE, DC, MC, V; closed Wed, Jan.*

Catalan and national dishes are served with careful attention to detail in this 17thC farmhouse.

SEU D'URGELL, LA
El Castell, PPP; *Ctra Puigcerdá, km 129; tel. 973 35 15 74; credit cards AE, DC, MC, V; closed Jan 15-Feb 15.*

Superbly situated below a castle, with views of the Sierra del Cadí, this restaurant in a stylish four-star hotel offers quality regional and international dishes. Try the lobster in a peppers and tomato sauce.

<u>South-Eastern Spain</u>

Costa Blanca Interior:
Alcoy and Játiva

165 km; map Michelin 445

H ere is an exploration of the mountainous interior backdrop to Alicante and the Costa Blanca. If you're driving through the region, it doubles as a 'green' alternative to the coastal route between Valencia and Alicante, described in detail in Spain Overall: 9. If you're staying in the area, it adds an interesting dimension to the more obvious pleasures of the coast.

The N340 looks like the direct route between Valencia and Alicante, but it is much slower driving, with endless twists and turns. There is some magnificent scenery.

You can extend your exploration by making a detour west from Alcoy on the C3313 to the ancient towns of Villena and Almansa, both dominated by medieval fortresses. They are described in Spain Overall: 14.

1:1,000,000

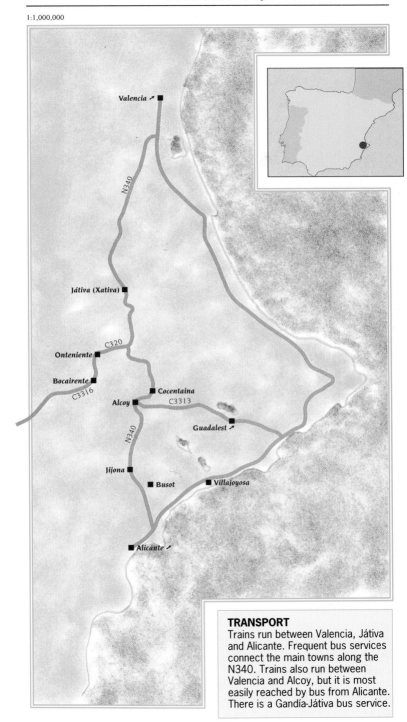

TRANSPORT

Trains run between Valencia, Játiva and Alicante. Frequent bus services connect the main towns along the N340. Trains also run between Valencia and Alcoy, but it is most easily reached by bus from Alicante. There is a Gandía-Játiva bus service.

SIGHTS & PLACES OF INTEREST

ALCOY 🛏

Tourism Office Puente San Jorge, 1; tel. 96 533 09 00 (only open during fiestas). Alcoy may not be the most beautiful of towns but it is strikingly situated among mountains (Moncabrer, at 1,352 m, is the highest point hereabouts). The town's various neighbourhoods are linked by 14 bridges spanning three rivers.

A plentiful water supply has contributed to Alcoy's growth as an industrial centre (paper, textiles, toys). Inspired by the Paris Commune, textile workers staged an unsuccessful revolt here in 1873 and in the Civil War the town was an anarchist enclave.

The most exciting event these days is the annual re-enactment of a battle

• *Fiesta of Moors and Christians, Alicante province - see page 112.*

between Moors and Christians in 1227 when Sant Jordi (St George) came to the aid of the *Cristianos*. Some 400 million pesetas are spent on the fiesta, April 22 to 24, when more than 6,000 people, in splendid apparel and attended by 30 bands, parade through the streets. At the cacophonous climax several tons of gunpowder go up in smoke as the rival armies let off their blunderbusses. Scores of other towns have *Moros v Cristianos* fiestas, but Alcoy's is one of the largest and most exuberant. Costumes worn in the battles can be seen in the **Museo de Fiestas del Casal de Sant Jordi**.

If you have your own transport there is a picturesque drive through wild mountains to the sea via the Callosa road, the C3313. Call in on the walled village of Penáguila, climb over the 966 m-high Confrides Pass, and continue past the rock fortress of Guadalest, described in Spain Overall: 9.

ALICANTE
See Spain Overall: 9.

BOCAIRENTE
An unusual community, slotted into terraces below a rock crowned by a church. There are many caves in the district, which were apparently carved

out by the Iberians for burial chambers. Bocairente holds a folk dance festival at the end of August or start of September.

COCENTAINA ⇌ ×

The small industrial town is worth a halt to visit the richly-decorated, 15thC **Palacio de los Duques de Medinaceli** and to view the carvings and reredos in the **Convento de las Clarisas**.

GUADALEST

See *Alcoy, page* 274, *and Spain Overall:* 9.

JATIVA (XATIVA) ×

Tourism Office Alameda San Jaime, 35; *tel.* 96 227 33 46. Two future popes, a son of Hannibal, and a noted painter are among the sons of this walled town set among hills covered with vines and orchards. Under the Visigoths, there was an episcopal see here and the Moors established one of Europe's first paper-manufacturing industries here in the 12thC. Decline set in with the expulsion of the Moors and a low point came when Játiva joined the resistance to the accession of Philip V. English troops defended the town, but it was sacked and renamed San Felipe, the old name not being restored until the 19thC. You can trek up to the crenellated castle walls to enjoy the view. Hamilce, wife of Hannibal, is said to have given birth to a boy here.

Calixtus III and Alexander VI, members of the Borgia family, were also born in Játiva. The artist José Ribera, born here in 1591, went to Italy where his artistic talent was recognized as considerably larger than his stature – he was dubbed Lo Spagnoletto (The Little Spaniard). Játiva has a Plaza del Españoleto and the **Museo Municipal** has some of Ribera's pictures. There is also a portrait of Philip V, deliberately hung upside down: they have long memories in Játiva.

In the old town's main street there are several fine mansions and the **collegiate church,** dating from 1596 and fire-damaged in the Civil War, has a tomb of one of the Borgias.

JIJONA

Jijona lies below the Puerto de la Carrasqueta, a 1,042 m-high pass from which there are superb panoramic views; if you're driving, you won't enjoy them since the road hairpins dramatically. Jijona has the usual castle and Gothic church but it owes its fame to the manufacture of *turrón* (nougat). It is delicious stuff, made from ground almonds and honey, but guaranteed to wrench out anybody's fillings (belated revenge of the Moors?), eaten by the ton all over Spain at Christmas. Jijona's **El Lobo factory** has a museum where you can see how nougat is made and sample it. They don't only eat nougat in Jijona: a local speciality is *giraboix* (cod with garlic-mayonnaise sauce).

A turning off the Alicante road near Jijona leads to the **Cueva de Canalobre** in the stark Cabeco d'Or mountains, near the village of Busot. Well-lit walkways lead through vast caverns filled with giant stalagmites and stalactites.

ONTENIENTE

Once of considerable importance, the town has the remains of old walls and the **church of Santa Maria Church**, with a Plateresque portal.

VALENCIA

See *Spain Overall:* 8.

RECOMMENDED RESTAURANTS

Possibilities are limited. Generally you have to take your chance with the local *tapa* bars, but the following are worth trying:

COCENTAINA

L'Escaleta, PP-PPP; Avda País Valencía, 119-*bajo; tel.* 96 559 21 00; *credit cards* AE, DC, MC, V; *closed* Sun eve, Mon, Holy Week, *last two weeks of* Aug.

Unusually located down some steps in a cellar, this establishment offers Basque cooking, with such specialities as *Hojaldre de codorniz deshuesada* (deboned quail in puff pastry).

JATIVA

Casa La Abuela, PP; *Reina,* 17; *tel.* 96 227 05 25; *credit cards* AE, MC, V; *closed* Sun, *second half* Jul.

Noted for its Valencia dishes.

South-Eastern Spain

Sierra Nevada and the Alpujarras

230 km; map Michelin 446

S now-fed streams, fertile valleys, and angry crags make the Alpujarras region, on the steep southern slopes of the Sierra Nevada, well worth visiting. Until recently, it was one of Spain's most isolated and primitive areas. The distinctive Berber-style architecture of the villages is inherited from the Moors, who took refuge here after Ferdinand and Isabella conquered the Kingdom of Granada.

The great bulk of the Sierra Nevada, part of the Penibetic system, runs parallel to the coast for 80 km. Although the summits do not form spectacular pinnacles as in the Alps, the range has imposing vistas and the unique mix of high altitude and Mediterranean climate creates an amazing diversity of life. Wild goats, hawks and eagles patrol the glaciated slopes, 40 plants are found only in this Nature Park, and wild flowers abound. In winter skiers head for the rapidly developing resort area at Pradollano. Snow lingers on the peaks until late summer.

Several refuges exist to shelter walkers and climbers. A popular three-day hike takes in the 14 peaks over 3,000 m, one of which Mulhacén, at 3,482 m, is the highest point on mainland Spain. But nobody should attempt it unless properly equipped and ready for some tough scrambles.

Alpujarras food is hearty rural fare. Try the *plato alpujarreño*, which includes pork, ham and blood sausage, accompanied by potent, pink Vino de la Contraviesa served in earthenware jugs.

Most people come here before or after seeing Granada. From Granada, follow the N323 south, turning left on the C333 towards Lanjarón. Near Orgiva, you can join the tortuous GR421 which visits many of the villages slotted into the mountainside, typical of the Alpujarras region. The most detailed map of the area is that produced by the Federación Española de Montañismo and the Instituto Geográfico Nacional on a scale of 1:50,000.

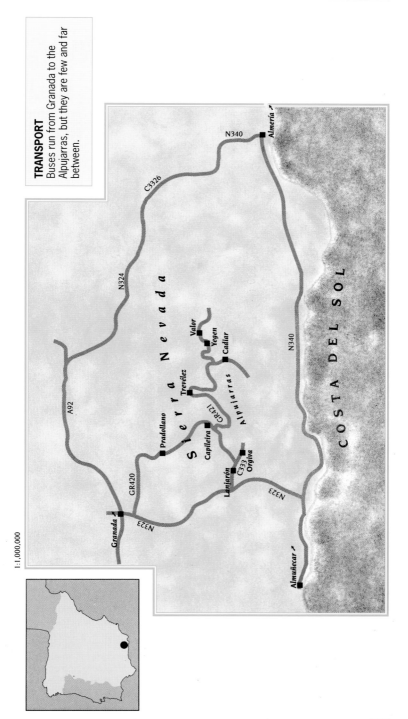

TRANSPORT
Buses run from Granada to the Alpujarras, but they are few and far between.

1:1,000,000

SIGHTS & PLACES OF INTEREST

ALMERIA
See *Spain Overall*: 10.

ALMUÑECAR
See *Spain Overall*: 10.

CADIAR
When the persecuted Moriscos (Muslim converts to Christianity) crowned a king under an olive tree here in 1568, it sparked off a bloody war with the Christians. On market days farmers trek in to the village from the hills to trade mules and donkeys. A **wine festival** is held in October.

GRANADA
See *Spain Overall*: 10.

GRANADA TO CAPILEIRA
The highest road in Europe runs over the top of the Sierra Nevada, but it is only passable from July onwards when the snow has receded sufficiently on the heights (check with the Civil Guard, *tel.* 958 48 03 51). The drive is not particularly difficult because there are no really steep gradients.

From Granada you take GR420 along the Genil Valley, with its orchards and

poplar trees. As this climbs it crosses a track once used by the *neveros*, muleteers carrying loads of snow and ice to the city.

Conifer plantations dot the approaches to **Pradollano**, 2,100 m up and the centre of the **Solynieve ski area**, scene of the 1995 World Skiing Championships. The Philistines who nuked the Mediterranean coast have been at work here too. However, the complex looks tolerable when blanketed with snow. The wide, treeless slopes are ideal for the less experienced skier, the season lasting from December to early May.

Beyond Pradollano, the road makes wide sweeps to climb to the **Veleta Peak** passing a radio telescope across the valley to the right. After the Veleta (3,398 m), the route is unsurfaced, passing several lakes and slate-grey crags. A rocky side-track runs up towards **Mulhacén**; walk the last few hundred metres to the summit.

The track meanders over moorland before curving down through pinewoods to **Capileira** (see Poqueira Valley, below), 25 km from the Veleta, with magnificent views of the Poqueira Valley.

LANJARON
Lanjarón water is on sale all over Spain. Thousands of the old and infirm arrive during summer months to take therapeutic baths and to drink the water, which is said to be good for everything from arthritis to lumbago. The gracious old town has that rather melancholy atmosphere common to spas.

ORGIVA
A main administrative centre, Orgiva achieves something close to a bustle on market days. The twin-towered, 16thC Renaissance **church** is the most impressive structure. A number of foreigners have settled in the vicinity.

POQUEIRA, VALLE DE
Three villages shelter in this well-watered cleft. The beauty of the valley and the charm of Capileira, Bubión, and Pampaneira attract many visitors, particularly from Granada at weekends when it can be difficult to find accommodation or a seat at a restaurant table. There are facilities for horse-trekking.

• *Just for the day - a Moorish leader in Valor.*

Corkscrew streets and flat-roofed dwellings are typical of the Alpujarras. The houses, unique in Spain, have stone walls and roofs of beams with slate laid across them. Over this is spread earth and a layer of slate rubble.

Capileira, at 1,436 m the highest of the villages, is most popular with visitors. A museum exhibits typical artefacts of the region. Beyond Capileira, the road curls upwards over moorland to cross the sierra to Granada (see Granada to Capileira, page 278).

PRADOLLANO

See Granada to Capileira, page 278.

TREVELEZ

At 1,500 m, Trevélez claims to be Spain's highest village. It is split into three *barrios* (quarters). The most picturesque are the middle and upper ones. Modern construction mars the lower section, where you find most of the bars and *hostals* and where thousands of hams hang in large sheds.

Mountain-cured ham is a speciality of the region and particularly of Trevélez.

VALOR

Every September more than 50 villagers of Valor re-enact a battle between Moors and Christians. The play is based on a 17thC document in the town hall archives. Although the Christians always win, to a cacophony of discharging shotguns, the Moors enjoy abundant support. Around here the King of the Moriscos, Aben Humeya, waged his desperate war against Christian troops and a musical group and a disco bear his name.

YEGEN

A plaque marks the house where the English writer Gerald Brenan lived during his stay in this sleepy village in the 1920s, as related in his classic *South from Granada*. He brought with him 2,000 books and rented a house for 120 pesetas a year.

South-Western Spain

Ronda and its Sierra

240 km; map Michelin 446, 1:400,000

S ome of Spain's wildest and most majestic scenery lies in the interior of Cádiz and Málaga provinces. It is a region of fierce mountains and lush valleys, specked with whitewashed towns and villages perched on pinnacles or crouching in clefts.

You will hear people talking about 'the white towns' as if there were a special group of such towns. This is a somewhat misleading concept, coined by the tourist industry (and many a guidebook): there are few dwellings in Andalucía which are not whitewashed. Some 'white towns' are much visited by coach parties from the coast; two of the most popular, Ronda and Grazalema, are featured in this section. (Another famous 'white town', Arcos de la Frontera, features in Local Explorations: 15.)

Smugglers, runaways, bandits and rebels have traditionally taken refuge in these mountains – the last anti-Franco guerrilla surrendered here in 1976 after hiding out for 27 years.

Ideal for walkers, climbers, horse-trekkers, and naturalists, the region includes two Nature Parks, the Sierra de Grazalema and, further west, Los Alcornocales, a 170,000-hectare area of mighty cork oaks, sheltering vultures and imperial eagles.

The C339, a modern highway running from San Pedro on the coast to Jerez via Ronda, gives the easiest access.

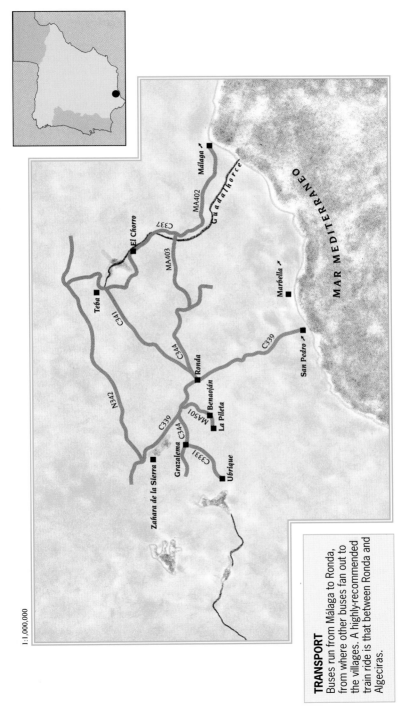

1:1,000,000

TRANSPORT

Buses run from Málaga to Ronda, from where other buses fan out to the villages. A highly-recommended train ride is that between Ronda and Algeciras.

SIGHTS & PLACES OF INTEREST

BENAOJAN ⌑

A little south of this village, in a secluded valley, is **La Pileta cave**. In the maze of dark galleries and caverns are impressive stalactites and stalagmites and also relics of prehistoric man, including pottery and wall paintings. José Bullón, a farmer looking for bat dung, came across the cave in 1905. There are tours of the cave on the hour from 9 am until 1 pm, and from 4 to 6.

RECOMMENDED HOTELS

BENAOJAN
Molino del Santo, PP; *tel.* 95 216 71 51. An English couple converted this old water-mill into a relaxing hideaway complete with willow-shaded pool. You awake to the sound of the rushing millstream, which remains the constant (and indeed soothing) background music to your stay. Excellent walking from the door; mountain bikes available.

Benaoján is accesible by train from Ronda or via the MA501.

GRAZALEMA
Villa Turística, PP; *Ctra de Ronda*; *tel.* 95 613 21 36.

One of Andalucía's government-financed chain of village-style developments. Choose between hotel rooms and self-contained chalets with one or two bedrooms.

RONDA
Reina Victoria, PPP; *Jerez, 25; tel.* 95 287 12 40.

It has known better days, but it remains a stately old hotel splendidly situated on a cliff top.

Royal, P; *Virgen de la Paz, 42; tel.* 95 287 11 41.

Hostal near the bull ring.

ZAHARA DE LA SIERRA
Marqués de Zahara, P; *San Juan, 3; tel.* 956 13 72 61.

Comfortable, centrally located *hostal*.

GARGANTA DEL CHORRO
Take the MA402 out of Málaga towards Cártama and Pizarra to reach this spectacular gorge. You pass lush citrus orchards in the Guadalhorce River valley before arriving at the hill-top town of Alora, at which point a narrowing road winds north to El Chorro.

The river flows through the Garganta, a narrow chasm with 200 m-high walls, and the main railway line threads along its side in a series of tunnels. A catwalk pinned to the rock face runs through the gorge, but is in a dangerously bad state of repair. On a flat-topped mountain near the gorge, the rebel Moorish leader Omar Ben Hafsun reportedly located his capital, Bobastro, 1,000 years ago.

Continuing northwards, you reach the three **Guadalhorce lakes**, surrounded by pine forests and offering boating and fishing, as well as being a pleasant picnic spot.

GRAZALEMA ⌑

'Fastened like a marten's nest to the face of a mountain', as one writer described it, Grazalema has long been known for its quality hand-woven woollen products. The tradition is carried on at the Nuestra Señora del Carmen factory. You can see the weavers at work Monday to Thursday. The Carmen shop is also open Friday, Saturday and Sunday (closed August).

Located at the foot of high mountains, Grazalema is reputed to be the wettest spot in Spain. It stands in the 51,000-hectare Sierra de Grazalema Natural Park, where you can glimpse wild goats, deer and eagles. The *pinsapo*, the lofty Spanish fir unique to this part of Europe, grows in the area. There is a specimen in the main square: probably your best chance of seeing one. The village itself is a quintessential 'white town', and appears immaculately well-kept. Worth a lingering stop, perhaps with lunch in one of the simple restaurants.

MALAGA
See Spain Overall: 10.

MARBELLA
See Spain Overall: 11.

RONDA ⌑ ✕
Tourism Office, Plaza de España, 1; tel. 95 287 12 72. If you come by car, park by the bull-ring, or in nearby Plaza de

España: both are close to the Puente Nuevo (new bridge). Start your explorations from either.

Set in an amphitheatre of mountains, the old town of Ronda was once the capital of a Moorish fiefdom and retains an independent character. The older part of town, known as La Ciudad, is separated from the 'modern' section, El Mercadillo, by a mighty rift in the rock. Three bridges span the gorge, one built by the Arabs, the 17thC Puente Viejo, and the one used by traffic today, the Puente Nuevo.

When the architect was inspecting the new bridge in 1793, his hat blew off. He tried to grab it and fell to his death. At the start of the Civil War, right-wingers were hurled into the chasm, an incident Hemingway made use of in his book *For Whom the Bell Tolls*.

Ronda is hailed as the cradle of modern bullfighting, thanks to the Romero family who 200 years ago established the sober Ronda style, fought on foot rather than on horseback. The exploits of Pedro Romero, who killed 5,600 bulls, are immortalized in Goya's paintings and every September a *corrida goyesca* is held, in which the participants wear 18thC costumes. The beautifully-proportioned *plaza de toros*, one of Spain's oldest bull-rings, is owned by retired matador Antonio Ordóñez, a steadfast friend of Hemingway. The ashes of Orson Welles were, in accordance with his wishes, scattered on Ordóñez's land near Ronda.

Having seen the bull-ring and contemplated the abyss below the bridge, it is delightful to wander in La Ciudad, with its peaceful streets, patios, courtyards and Renaissance portals, and steps leading down to the river. Sights of interest include the **Baños Arabes** (Arab Baths), the **Colegiata de Santa María la Mayor**, a church built on the orders of Ferdinand the Catholic, and the **Casa de Mondragón**, thought to be the palace of the Moorish kings.

The ruins of a Roman town, known as **Ronda La Vieja**, with a theatre, can be seen on a hilltop a short distance from Ronda. Take the C339 towards Arcos and turn right after 12 km at a sign pointing to Acinipo.

SAN PEDRO
See Spain Overall: 11.

TEBA
Straddling a rocky outcrop, Teba is accessible from Antequera or by heading north-west from the Garganta del Chorro, skirting the Guadalhorce lakes. In the Plaza de España stands an unusual monument, a handsome block of white granite from Scotland. It commemorates the heroism of Sir James Douglas, killed in battle here on August 25, 1330.

Known as the Black Douglas, Sir James accepted a death-bed request by King Robert the Bruce of Scotland to take his heart to the Holy Land. *En route*, he joined Castilian forces fighting the Moors. While laying siege to Teba, he was surrounded and slain.

UBRIQUE
Buried in the mountains, Ubrique appears isolated, but its leather products grace high fashion shops across Europe. Dozens of small workshops turn out wallets and handbags.

ZAHARA DE LA SIERRA 🛏
The tranquillity of this village belies its melodramatic appearance. A castle caps the crag thrusting above the huddle of white houses.

An attack on Zahara in 1481 by the Moorish king of Granada, Muley Hacen, so angered the Castilians that it contributed to the final defeat of Granada.

RECOMMENDED RESTAURANTS

RONDA
Don Miguel, PP; *Villanueva, 4; tel.* 95 287 10 90; *credit cards* AE, DC, MC, V; *closed* Sun *in summer,* Jan 15-31.

In a dramatic setting beside the Puente Nuevo, with terraces overlooking the gorge. The restaurant serves the local speciality, *pierna de cordera lechal* (young lamb).

Pedro Romero, PP; *Virgen de la Paz,* 18; *tel.* 95 287 11 10; *credit cards* AE, DC, MC, V.

Right by the bull-ring and decorated with taurine mementos. If you don't like crowds, eat downstairs: the groups go upstairs. Try *conejo a la rondeña* (rabbit Ronda-style).

Jerez and Sanlúcar

130 *km; map* Michelin 446, 1:400,000

E very stereotyped image of southern Spain comes to life in this corner of Cádiz province, truly a land of wine, bulls, and flamenco. Vines
sheath the area of rolling country known as the Sherry Triangle, with the
towns of Jerez de la Frontera, El Puerto de Santa María and Sanlúcar de
Barrameda at its corners. A tour of these towns and a leisurely sampling
of their products at the *bodegas* (wineries) is as enjoyable a way to pass
a day – or a month – as I can imagine.

The grapes which make sherry – known as Palomino and Pedro
Ximénez – thrive on the area's chalky white *albariza* soil, which absorbs
water efficiently, later compacting into a hard crust under the summer
sun, retaining essential moisture. Sherry matures in the *solera* system,
whereby wine is transferred down from cask to cask, blending with older
vintages until reaching the bottom deck where it is drawn off for bot-
tling.

Britain is intimately linked with the sherry industry. It has long been
the biggest sherry importer, followed by the Netherlands, and English and
Irish have intermarried with the local sherry families. The addiction goes
back at least to Shakespeare's time when he gave Falstaff the line in
Henry IV: 'If I had a thousand sons, the first human principle I would teach
them should be, to forswear thin potations and to addict themselves to
sack' (the old English name for sherry).

One famous *bodega* was founded by William Garvey, from Ireland,
whose ship ran aground in Cádiz harbour. Rescued by a Spanish captain, he stayed at his house, fell in love with his daughter, and you can
guess the rest.

TRANSPORT
Trains run between Jerez and El Puerto de Santa María and there are regular bus services between the three major towns of the sherry region, Jerez, El Puerto, and Sanlúcar. In summer, pleasure craft run between Sanlúcar and Seville along the Guadalquivir River.

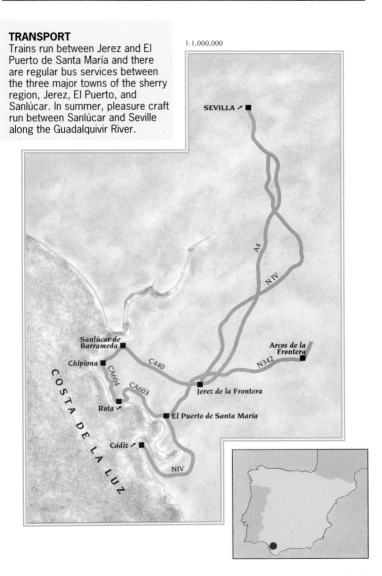

Another sherry empire, that of Domecq, extends to North and South America. It was started by a French aristocrat, Pierre Domecq, who arrived in Spain in 1730. So complex is the dynasty that it takes a 200-page book to set out all the family ramifications. The Domecqs typify the country squire life-style of the sherry barons, who like to boast: 'We are famous for three things, fine wine, fine horses, and fine women – in that order, of course.'

Today, however, more and more the *bodegas* are controlled by shrewd accountants hired by multi-national owners.

SIGHTS & PLACES OF INTEREST

ARCOS DE LA FRONTERA 🛏

Balancing on the edge of the Guadalete River gorge, Arcos is one of Andalucía's most eye-catching 'White Towns'. (See also Local Explorations: 14.) If you are good at threading needles, you will enjoy driving up the the ever-narrower and steeper medieval streets leading to the *plaza* at the top of the town. On one side is the parador, on the other a well-preserved **castle**, still inhabited by the English-born Marquesa de Tamarón. You peer over a hawk-patrolled cliff face to view the river below. On the

• T*he church at* La Cartuja de Jerez - *see page* 288.

SHERRY AND SPANISH BRANDY

There are three basic types of sherry: *fino* (dry); *amontillado* (darker with a nutty flavour); and *oloroso* (medium dry with a fuller body). The best *amontillados* may be more than 50 years old. The Jerez area also produces large quantities of brandy, which is more popular in Spain than sherry.

• *Anyone for sherry?*

fourth side, dominating all, is the Gothic-Mudéjar **church of Santa María.** Climb the tower for stunning views of town and rolling countryside.

'De la Frontera' refers to the fact that Arcos was a frontier post during the wars with the Moors, who were finally ousted 600 years ago by Alfonso the Wise of Castile. Legend has it that a Moorish king had to leave his favourite, Nanafassi, in the castle to go to war. When he failed to return, she died of a broken heart and her spirit turned into a large black bird. Local mothers used to – may still – frighten their children with: 'Eat up your *churros* or Nanafassi will get you.'

Arcos seems to belong to another age, especially during the elaborate **Holy Week processions**. On Easter Sunday a fighting bull is released in the streets. Americans from the Rota naval base have been among those tempted to dance before its horns, sometimes ending up in hospital.

CADIZ

See Spain Overall: 11.

CHIPIONA

Chipiona is crowded with Spanish families in summer thanks to its fine beach. Along the coast towards Rota (site of a massive Spanish-U.S. naval base) are more pleasant beaches, but the coast needs a clean-up, which may come as big tourism projects gain momentum.

JEREZ DE LA FRONTERA 🛏 ✕

Tourism Office, Alameda Cristina, 7; tel. 956 33 11 50. Around one million oak barrels are stashed away in the *bodegas* (wineries) of Jerez, the sherry capital. You can visit the *bodegas* on most weekday mornings (but most close in August); some charge for the privilege. Guides usually speak English, reflecting the industry's close connections with England – see page 284. The city itself (population 176,000) is pleasant but hardly exciting. The **Pedro Domecq** and **González Byass** *bodegas* are a step away from the **Alcázar**, a 12thC fortress where the Caliph of Seville once lived, and the Baroque and Renaissance **collegiate church of San Salvador**, whose tower is an unusual mix of Gothic and Moorish influences.

Jerez has a number of impressive mansions and palaces. These include: the **Casa del Cabildo** with a Plateresque façade; **Ponce de León**, with a Renaissance patio; and that of the **Marqués de Bertematí**, with a Baroque façade.

The **Palacio de Atalaya** on Cervantes Street houses the **Museo de**

Relojes, which displays a mind-boggling collection of clocks (closed Sun).

Definitely not to be missed is the **Real Escuela Andaluza de Arte Ecuestre**. This is located in the grounds of another palace, on the Avenida Duque de Abrantes, and features superbly trained steeds, the so-called 'dancing horses'. Training sessions are open to the public on weekday mornings and at Thursday noon you can see the full show.

The Spanish-Andalucían horse is highly-coveted for its spirit, strength, and temperament. Many a king, from Henry VIII to Louis XIV, rode one, and

Napoleon's favourite battle horse was of this breed – the skeleton of his animal is preserved in the Natural History Museum in Paris. The famed Vienna riding school was founded with studs and mares from Spain. Spanish-Andalucíans helped conquer America: they were the mounts of *conquistadores* such as Cortes and Pizarro. Those that were released, or escaped, bred the mustangs of North America.

Just out of Jerez is the former **Monasterio de la Cartuja de Jerez** where, on the banks of the Guadalete River, some of the finest examples of Andalucían horses were bred in the Middle Ages by Carthusian monks. Founded in 1477, the building was for long derelict, but has been restored. The Baroque **façade** is outstanding.

Flamenco enthusiasts should visit the **Fundación Andaluza de Flamenco**, housed in an 18thC palace on Plaza San Juan (open mornings).

To visit a fighting bull ranch or farms where horses are reared, enquire at the Tourism Office. Jerez comes vibrantly alive during the **Horse Fair** (early May).

PUERTO DE SANTA MARIA, EL
🛏 ✕

Tourism Office, Guadalete s/n, tel. 956 54 24 13. As well as several large wineries, the Puerto is famed for its fresh seafood. The best place to sample this is at a riverside café on the Ribera del Río. You pick out what you want from the vast selection on display. The prawns, crabs, squid and so on are weighed into paper bags, which you take to a table where a waiter serves drinks.

Early risers who want to see an impressive sight should visit the modern fishing quay across the Guadalete River, where the catches are auctioned every morning.

A Greek prince is credited with founding the town, which under the Romans was named Portus Gaditanus. Columbus's ship the *Santa María*, named in honour of the port, was constructed in local shipyards. A golden age ensued with so many Indianos (rich returned migrants) settling and building large houses that El Puerto was called 'the city of a hundred palaces'.

The **Castillo de San Marcos** (open Saturday mornings) was a watch-tower built on the site of a mosque, later a church and a dwelling, and has figured in several novels.

Visits can be made, by prior arrangement, to **Terry** and **Osborne**, two large winemakers with headquarters in El Puerto. The Osborne company was founded in 1772 by Thomas Osborne, from Devon, England. One of his sons built the nobly-proportioned bull-ring, inaugurated in 1880. This is one of the strongholds of bullfighting and *aficionados* will point out the plaque at the entrance, quoting the matador Joselito 'El Gallo': 'He who has not seen the bulls in El Puerto does not know what a day's bullfighting is.'

Bulls loom large in Osborne history. Members of the family breed fighting bulls and, as you travel through the countryside, you cannot fail to notice the huge silhouettes of the Osborne bull that have become part of the Spanish landscape. Among the Osborne archives are letters from the Czars, from Windsor Castle, and from the Belgian court ordering casks of wine.

Just outside the town, the **Puerto Sherry** tourist development with a colossal marina has taken shape. The **Bahía de Cádiz Casino** is on the highway to Jerez (open 5 pm to 5 am, passport must be shown, entry fee).

ROTA
See Chipiona, page 287.

SANLUCAR DE BARRAMEDA ⌫ ✕
Tourism Office, Calzada del Ejército, s/n; tel. 956 36 61 10. Sanlúcar was the launch-pad for some of Spain's great navigators – Columbus sailed from here on his third voyage in 1498. It has spruced itself up lately and retains some fine medieval buildings. You can visit local *bodegas* whose pride is *manzanilla*, a dry sherry with an almost salty flavour, attributed to the sea breezes.

The church of **Santa María de la O** has a striking Mudéjar portal. The **Palacio de la Duquesa de Medina Sidonia** is also worth noting. One of her ancestors commanded the ill-fated Armada which sailed against England 400 years ago. A ferry service carries visitors across the Guadalquivir to the **Parque Nacional de Coto Doñana** (see Local Explorations: 16). A particularly stirring sight occurs every year at the end of May or start of June, when thousands of pilgrims make the trek to the sanctuary in the marshes of El Rocío. Horses, tractors and other vehicles are ferried across the river. In the last week of August horse races are held on the beach.

SANLUCAR DE BARRAMEDA ⌫
See Recommended Hotels, page 288

SEVILLA
See page 201.

RECOMMENDED RESTAURANTS

JEREZ DE LA FRONTERA
La Mesa Redonda (PP); *Manuel de la Quintana, 3; tel. 956 34 48 35; credit cards AE, MC, V; closed, Sun, holidays, Aug.*

An intimate, family-run restaurant with excellent dishes. Try the *perdiz a la jerezana* (partridge, Jerez style).

Tendido 6 (PP); *Circo, 10; credit cards AE, DC, MC, V; closed Sun.*

Decorated in rustic style, this is an appropriate place to try bull's tail: the restaurant is next to the Jerez bull-ring.

PUERTO DE SANTA MARIA, EL
Las Bóvedas, PPP; *Larga, 27; tel. 956 54 04 40; credit cards AE, DC, MC, V.*

Top-class French-influenced cuisine served in a vaulted dining room in a former convent.

La Goleta, PP; *Ctra Rota km 0.75; tel. 956 85 42 32; credit cards AE, DC, MC, V; closed Mon, early Nov.*

A popular restaurant in a house outside town, specializing in fresh seafood.

SANLUCAR DE BARRAMEDA
Bigote PP; *Bajo de Guía, s/n; tel. 956 36 26 96; credit cards AE, MC, V; closed Sun.*

You can hardly go wrong at the restaurants along the Guadalquivir waterfront, all specializing in seafood. This is one of the most popular. Particularly recommended: *langostinos* (prawns) or *pijotas* (whiting).

Southern Spain

Huelva and the Doñana National Park

Round trip to Portuguese border up to 380 km if based in Seville; map Michelin 446 1:400,000

The province of Huelva, tucked away between Seville and the Portuguese border, is surprisingly little known, considering its varied history and attractive scenery. The legendary Kingdom of Tartessus is believed to have existed somewhere along its coast and precious metals were mined here by Phoenicians and Romans. Columbus's dream of voyaging westwards to discover a new route to Asia might never have been realized if it had not been for assistance from Huelva friars – see page 295. His 1492 voyage to North America began here, from the port of Palos de la Frontera.

Huelva's coastline, with its long tracts of sandy beach, shares with Cádiz the title of Costa de la Luz (Coast of Light): it enjoys intense, clear light for much of the year. At the mouth of the Guadalquivir lies the Doñana National Park, embracing a vast stretch of dunes, pine forest and marshland known as Las Marismas, with a wealth of birdlife, from flamingos to booted eagles. Here also is the sanctuary of the Virgen del Rocío, object of one of Spain's biggest pilgrimages.

Huelva has little industry and large areas of nature reserves. Strawberries and citrus fruits flourish in the mild climate near the coast; more than 90 per cent of the country's strawberries are grown here, making Spain the world's biggest strawberry exporter. Much of the interior is covered with pine and eucalyptus forests.

You can take in the Doñana Park and the principal Columbus sites in one day. If you have more time, extend your explorations to the Portuguese border. To appreciate the best of Huelva, try to see Riotinto and Aracena, too.

TRANSPORT

Trains connect Huelva, the provincial capital, with Seville. A line meanders north from Huelva through the Sierra de Aracena to Extremadura, but its services are none too frequent. Buses link Huelva with the principal centres of the province. The four-lane Autopista del Quinto Centenario has cut driving time between Seville and Huelva to less than an hour.

There are also daily bus services between Seville and Aracena. Access from the Portuguese Algarve coast has been speeded by the opening of a new frontier bridge across the Guadiana River.

1:1,250,000

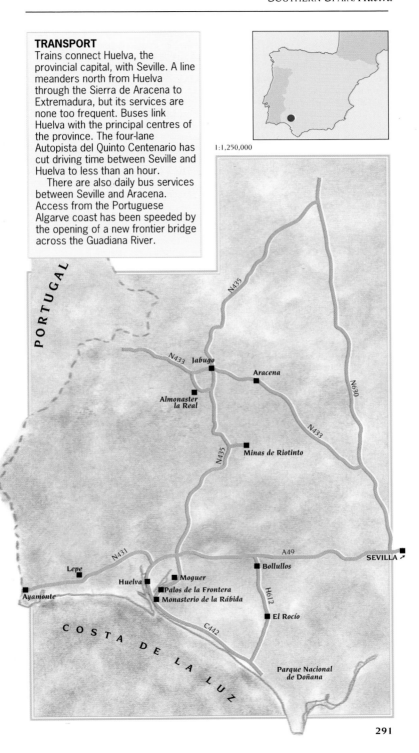

SIGHTS & PLACES OF INTEREST

ALMONASTER LA REAL
Climb the hill above the sleepy village to the remains of a Moorish fortress. Next to a bull-ring is what appears to be a church but is actually a 1,000-year-old mosque. Penetrate the gloomy interior and you will find that it is split into four naves by 17 arches. The mosque, a national monument, incorporates structures built by Romans and Visigoths.

ARACENA ⊭
Aracena sits among rolling wooded hills which are a happy hunting ground for mushroom connoisseurs and acorn-gobbling pigs. Above the town stands the 13thC **church of the Knights Templar**, with its Mudéjar tower. An imposing Renaissance façade graces the **church of Asunción**, which seems to be abandoned. In fact, part of the church is in use, but the massive edifice was only partly-restored when money ran out.

Tourists flock to visit the **Gruta de las Maravillas** (the Cave of Marvels). A guide conducts groups around chambers from the floors and ceilings of which ooze petrified castles, cascades, and other naturally-created fantasies.

Near the cave is **Casas**, a restaurant specializing in ham and pork dishes (**PP**; *tel.* 959 12 82 12; *credit cards* AE, V; *lunch only*). Or try **La Serrana, PP**; *tel.* 959 11 16 13; *credit cards* MC, V.)

Aracena is a useful base from which to explore the surrounding **Sierra de Aracena**, a region of rounded hills. They are clothed with apple and cherry orchards, chestnut, walnut, and oak forests. Every sleepy village seems to have a medieval fortress crumbling in the background. For a fine view, visit **Arias Montano**, a hill at Alájar, 11 km to the east, named after a celebrated humanist who lived there. A sanctuary on the hill attracts many pilgrims, including newly-weds who donate their wedding-dresses to the Virgen de los Angeles. There is an annual *romería* to the sanctuary on September 6.

ARACENA ⊭
See *Recommended Hotels, page 293*

AYAMONTE ⊭
Ayamonte, once a scruffy, somnolent border town living off fishing and smuggling, has acquired new life, thanks to improved communications. In the past, when Spain and Portugal resolutely turned their backs on one another, it was necessary to queue for a ferry across the Guadiana to Vila Real de Santo António and the Algarve coast of Portugal; now a handsome new bridge allows you to cross the river in minutes. The nearby **Isla Canela**, a flat expanse of marsh and sand, has pleasant beaches and is being developed as a tourist resort, although ecologists have been protesting.

BOLLULLOS, PAR DEL CONDADO
Bodegas line the main street, where you can snack on shellfish while trying *mosto*, new wine straight from the barrel. Condado wines are similar to those of Jerez, but have never achieved the same fame and prestige. It is quite likely that the first wine drunk in the New World by Columbus and his men came from here. Recently, light white wines have been developed and these are well worth trying.

A local bar and restaurant, **El Reñiero**, on Cruz de Montefina, 6, has a cockpit at the rear where on Sunday afternoons from January to July *peleas de gallos* (cock fights) are held. Those of queasy stomach should keep away.

DOÑANA, PARQUE NACIONAL DE
The delta of the Guadalquivir is commonly known as the Coto Doñana, *coto* meaning hunting reserve. Originally, it was just that: terrain used for hunting by kings and nobles. Doña Ana, a duchess of Medina Sidonia, gave her name to the area when she built a palace here – it still stands. The story goes that an 18thC duchess of Alba, dallying there with Goya, posed for his famous picture *La Maja Desnuda* (*The Naked Woman*). The present Duchess is not amused by such fables. And indeed the tale seems unlikely – the mosquitoes of Doñana are ferocious.

Today, the park is one of Europe's key wetlands, with the added interest of being on the bird migration route between Europe and Africa.

Within the park, **Las Marismas**, a wilderness of dunes and marshes near the mouth of the Guadalquivir, is an especially important sanctuary for endangered species such as the imperial eagle and the lynx, a breeding ground for tens of thousands of water fowl and a resting place for migrating birds. It also harbours flamingos, red deer, vultures, rare gulls, wild cattle, even stray camels.

Ecologists have been battling to protect the National Park (of 50,000 hectares, with 26,000 hectares on its periphery also protected), from a variety of dangers, including pollution from chemicals used on farmland, drainage and tourist developments. It is hard to forgive or to forget the monstrous Matalascañas development which has mushroomed right next to the park. As this Guide went to press there were reports of drainage to important areas resulting in loss of birds.

You can only visit the park on a four-hour conducted tour by four-wheel-drive, leaving from El Acebuche reception centre on the Almone-Matalascañas road (except Monday). Reserve places in advance by calling 959 43 04 32. Information on walks around the park outskirts is also available from La Rocina centre (959 42 34 07). Most waterfowl are to be seen in the winter months, but then much of the park is inaccessible. By March, spoonbills are building their nests in the cork oaks and large numbers of birds migrating between Europe and Africa appear.

HUELVA 🚪 ✕

Tourism Office, Avda Alemania, 1; *tel.* 959 25 74 03. Entering Huelva from the east along the N442, at the junction of the Odiel and Río Tinto rivers, you will see a 40 m-high **monument** dedicated to Christopher Columbus. Carved by Gertrude Vanderbilt Whitney, it was donated in 1929 by the United States. Unfortunately, the approach is somewhat marred by the petro-chemical plants and refineries nearby.

The Phoenicians called their colony here Onuba, hence the name *onubenses* for Huelva residents, although locals are also nicknamed *choqueros* because of their addiction to *chocos* (cuttlefish). In the 19thC, when British owners acquired the Rio Tinto mining company, they shipped its copper, gold and silver out through the port. In many ways the British managers treated the locals as they would have any colonized people, improving social conditions but abstaining from 'mixing with the natives'. They introduced their sports (Huelva's soccer, golf, and tennis clubs were the first in Spain) and left behind a curiously English suburb called Barrio Reina Victoria.

Another curiosity (there is not much to excite interest here) is the grave in the city cemetery of **The Man Who Never Was**. It contains a body found floating off the coast during the Second World War. Apparently that of a British officer who had died in a plane crash,

---

RECOMMENDED HOTELS

ARACENA
Finca Buen Vino, PPP; *Los Marines* (7 *km* W *of Aracena, off* N433); *tel.* 959 12 40 34.

A three-storey pink mansion among wooded hills offers the atmosphere of an English country house. Excellent meals. Clients are mostly British. Reservations essential.

Sierra de Aracena, PP; *Gran Vía*, 21; *tel.* 959 12 60 19.

Comfortable two-star hotel in centre.

AYAMONTE
Ríu Canela, PPP; *Paseo Gavilanes, Isla Canela*; *tel.* 959 47 71 24; *closed Nov-Mar.*

This large four-star hotel, facing the sea, is newly built in palatial Alhambra style, complete with marble floors, fountains, and tiled roofs. A variety of sports. Popular with German groups.

HUELVA
Tartessos, PPP; *Avda Martín Alonso Pinzón*, 13; *tel* 959 28 27 11.

Modern hotel in the city centre. It contains the El Estero restaurant, rather cold atmosphere but with interesting dishes.

MAZAGON
Parador Cristóbal Colón, PPP; *Ctra. Matalascañas, km* 24; *tel.* 959 63 73 00.

Set in pinewoods. Lawns sweep down to the pool and to cliffs overlooking a long beach. An ideal spot from where to explore Columbus territory and the Coto Doñana.

it carried secret documents. The documents were returned to Britain, but not before German agents had taken a good look at them. In fact, the body was a plant and the British had carefully prepared the information to mislead the Germans – successfully, it was later – claimed about the North African landings.

For excellent *tapas* of ham and grilled pork, try **Los Encinares**, at 20 Avenida Alonso Pinzón, not far from the Tourist Office. Barrels, woodwork, and pottery give it a friendly, traditional air.

JABUGO
Once notorious for its smugglers, this hamlet is now famous for its *pata negra* hams and sausages. The hams, from free-range Iberian pigs reared on acorns, are first packed in salt for ten days, then washed and hung to cure for a year or more in dry, fresh air. Experts say that in authentic hams from naturally-reared pigs the meat is marbled with yellow (not white) fat. Sliced thinly, the ham will melt in the mouth.

You can buy a variety of pork products from the best-known local producer, the Cooperativa Sánchez Romero-Carvajal. In the surrounding villages of the sierra there are scores of other ham-curers, who are sure their product is as good or better.

LEPE
Large plantations of oranges, strawberries and asparagus, employing the latest irrigation systems, have made this town prosperous. But Spanish jokes about the locals, the *leperos*, along the same lines as Dutch jokes about the Belgians, and so on, are still common. Perhaps the most famous *lepero* was Rodrigo de Triana, a lookout on the Columbus voyage. As Columbus's journal for October 12, 1492, recalls: 'And because the caravel *Pinta* was faster and was going ahead of the Admiral, it found land and made the signals the Admiral had ordered. This land was seen first by a sailor called Rodrigo de Triana.'

MAZAGON ⇔ ✕
See *Restaurants, page 295.*

MINAS DE RIOTINTO
Copper, silver and gold have been mined here since Roman times. One

open-cast mine is 660 m deep. Train buffs will be interested in the **museum**, opened in 1993 in a bid to attract tourists as the mining industry sank into decline.

MOGUER ✕
Moguer is a pleasant whitewashed town with two principal points of interest. One is the Gothic-Mudéjar **Convento de Santa Clara**, where Columbus made an all-night vigil to give thanks for safe return from his voyage. The convent museum is open to visitors, except Sunday and Monday afternoons. Juan Ramón Jiménez, the Nobel Prize-winning poet, was born in Moguer in 1881, but spent his later years in political exile, dying in Puerto Rico. The house where he spent his youth, at number 10 on a street named after him, is open as a **museum**. Many of his possessions, including 4,000 books, are displayed. Plaques around town quote from his works; the most popular one, *Platero and I*, a children's book, has been translated into 50 languages.

PALOS DE LA FRONTERA
Palos, which played a key role in Columbus's voyage to the New World, is a sleepy place, surrounded by fields of fat strawberries. In the Gothic-Mudéjar church of San Jorge, a royal decree was read out ordering that three caravels built in Palos should be delivered to Columbus.

Below the church you will find **La Fontanilla**, a low structure of Mudéjar brick. This is the well – now dry – where his crews filled their ships' casks before starting their epic voyage on August 3, 1492. Straggling trees grow in a park created between the well and the Tinto River. The quay from which the *Discoverer* sailed rotted away long ago and ships can no longer navigate the river. The Pinzón brothers, local boys who sailed with Columbus, are Palos heroes and there is a statue to Martín Alonso Pinzón, who helped recruit the ships' crews. The **Casa Pinzón** lies on the main street, Calle Colón. Ask for the key at the **Ayuntamiento** (town hall).

RABIDA, MONASTERIO DE LA
Standing among orange and palm trees on the banks of the Río Tinto, this whitewashed monastery – refurbished for the 1992 celebrations – surely looks lit-

tle different from when Columbus came this way four centuries ago. His grand project – to discover the New World – having been initially rejected by Queen Isabel, he was a gaunt, threadbare figure when he stayed here in 1491. Legend has it that he told the friars: 'I am called Cristóbal Colón. I am a sea captain from Genoa, and I must beg my bread because kings will not accept the empires that I offer them.'

One of the Franciscan monks shows visitors around. A chapel contains a battered alabaster Virgin and Child, to which Columbus and his men knelt before and after their voyage. In one of the cells Columbus held long talks with the Prior, Juan Pérez, and a monk named Antonio de Marchena, a cosmographer of repute: talks that would change the course of history. They introduced him to Martín Alonso Pinzón, a respected local sea-captain who would play a key part in the great voyage. Juan Pérez, formerly Queen Isabel's confessor, wrote a letter which so moved her that she recalled Columbus to court. She reconsidered her earlier decision, and the great adventure was about to begin.

Alongside the monastery is the small **Hostería de la Rábida**, a three-star hotel (**PP**, *tel.* 959 35 03 12). Below, by the river, are three **replicas of Columbus's ships**, the *Niña*, the *Pinto*, and the *Santa María*, which form part of a permanent exhibition. Note how small the vessels were. Nearby is an auditorium where events associated with the Hispano-American University of La Rábida are held. A paved walk runs from La Rábida to Palos de la Frontera.

By the river stands a **statue of a winged man**, erected by Argentina in tribute to a pioneer flight to Buenos Aires in 1926. General Franco's brother Ramón was one of the four fliers.

ROCIO, EL

For most of the year this is a ghost town among the marshes. But at Pentecost it is the scene of one of Spain's most amazing spectacles, in which it is hard to distinguish between Christianity and paganism.

Up to a million visitors cram the dusty avenues to pay tribute to the **Virgen del Rocío**, also known as La Blanca Paloma (The White Dove) and La Reina de las Marismas (Queen of the Marshes). Eighty or so *hermandades* (religious brotherhoods) journey for days to reach the sanctuary, travelling on horseback, on foot and in four-wheel-drives. Each brotherhood escorts a *simpecado*, a portrait of the Virgin, carried in a flower-decked cart drawn by oxen. Some cross the Guadalquivir at Sanlúcar de Barrameda and trek through the Doñana National Park, leaving a sad trail of garbage.

Piety and hedonist excess mingle during the festival: wine flows freely and the whirl of flamenco-dancing never stops. In the early hours of the Sunday morning, excitement reaches a climax as the Virgin is carried from her vast white temple by young men of the Almonte religious brotherhood, who fight to defend 'their' Virgin. The Almonte boys know it is theirs because of the legend. This relates that in the 13thC an Almonte shepherd found a beautifully-carved image of the Virgin in a hollow tree. He started carrying her to Almonte, but stopped for a nap. When he awoke, the Virgin had miraculously flown back to the tree. The present sanctuary stands on that spot.

RECOMMENDED RESTAURANTS

HUELVA

Las Candelas, PP; *Ctra Punta Umbria, Aljaraque crossroads; tel.* 959 31 83 01; *credit cards* AE, MC, V; *closed Sun.*

Fresh seafood is the speciality of this restaurant on the site of an old inn.

MAZAGON

Albaida, PP; *Ctra Huelva-Matalascañas, km.* 18; *tel.* 959 37 60 29; *cards* AE, DC, MC, V; *closed Sun evening.*

The decoration is not exactly cosy, but a Galician chef produces some excellent seafood dishes and tasty desserts. Located in a modern, three-star hotel of the same name.

MOGUER

La Parrala, P; *Plaza Monjas*, 22; *tel.* 959 37 04 52.

Home-spun fare at reasonable prices. Just across from the convent. La Parrala was a passionate café singer in local mining areas.

North-Eastern Andalucía:
Jaén Province, Ubeda and Cazorla

250 km; map Michelin 446, 1:400,000

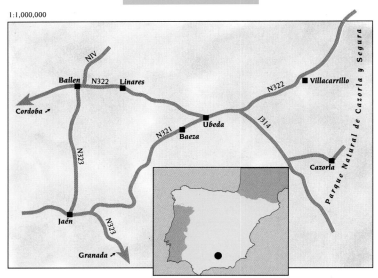

1:1,000,000

Two historic cities crammed with architectural treasures and Spain's largest Nature Park await your discovery in Andalucía's north-eastern corner, just off the main Madrid-Seville highway.

Jaén province long enjoyed strategic importance and played a vital part in the wars between Christians and Moors. When Ferdinand III marched through, ousting the Moors from Baeza in 1227 and from Ubeda in 1234, some of his knights stayed, constructing noble mansions. Later bursts of prosperity brought both Baeza and Ubeda an astonishing wealth of Renaissance buildings.

East of those two towns is the Cazorla and Segura Park, a great place for camping and walking among limestone peaks, trout streams, meadows and pine forests.

Jaén province floats on olive oil, producing more than 220,000 tons of the green-golden liquid every year. Where there are not craggy mountains, the trees stretch endlessly over plains and rolling hills. Olives are picked in December and January, crushed and filtered. Virgin olive oil is the most esteemed, for its flavour and because, unlike 'pure' olive oil, it is not treated with chemicals or heat.

As Baeza and Ubeda are close together, you can easily visit the two in a day. To appreciate Cazorla Park, allow at least two days.

TRANSPORT

Trains are few and far between, but buses link Jaén, Baeza and Ubeda regularly, with once- or twice-daily services to smaller towns. To reach Cazorla Park, your own transport is needed.

SIGHTS & PLACES OF INTEREST

BAEZA 🛏×

Tourism Office, Plaza del Pópulo s/n; tel. 953 74 04 44. This agreeable town was the first in Andalucía to be snatched from the Moors and the first Mass of the Reconquest was celebrated from a balcony of the Plateresque mansion which houses the Tourism Office. The **Puerta Jaén Gate**, built to commemorate a visit by Emperor Charles V, is in one corner of the plaza. In the centre is a fountain and a female **Iberian-Roman statue**, said to be Hannibal's wife.

Close by is the Plaza de la Constitución, the heart of town, with the Arab tower **Los Aliatares** at the northern end. Thread your way along cobbled streets to reach the Renaissance-Baroque building, on San Felipe Neri, which housed a **university** for three centuries from 1542. Close by is the Gothic grandeur of the **Jabalquinto Palace**, with a fine Renaissance patio. A few steps on stands Baeza's **cathedral**, reconstructed in the 16thC to the designs of Andrés de Vandelvira (see also Jaén and Ubeda). He is credited with making the Renaissance style more monumental, with less superficial adornment, than it was previously. The Sagrario Chapel has a grille made by the Jaén master, Bartolomé. If you insert a coin before one niche, a shield slides back to reveal the towering silver monstrance carried in procession at Corpus Christi. Priceless old volumes are in the cathedral archives.

Opposite Baeza's **Ayuntamiento** (Town Hall), breathing Plateresque self-importance, is the **Casa Antonio Machado,** where the poet lived when he taught French here in the early 20thC. On the same street are a couple of reasonable *tapa* bars.

CAZORLA 🛏

Nature Park Office, Martínez Falero, 11 *(open mornings); tel.* 953 72 01 25. This attractive little town on the edge of the mountains is a useful base from which to explore the nature park nearby.

RECOMMENDED HOTELS

BAEZA
Baeza, PP; *Concepción,* 3; *tel.* 953 74 81 30.

A comfortable, modern hotel in the town centre.

Juanito, P; *Avda Arca del Agua, s/n; tel.* 953 74 00 40. Modern comforts at a reasonable price.

CAZORLA
Villa Turística, PP; *Ladera de San Isicio; tel.* 953 71 01 00.

A village complex built in traditional style, with fireplace, terrace and cooking facilities.

CAZORLA AND SEGURA PARK
Noguera de la Sierpe, PP; *tel.* 953 71 30 21.

A former farm and hunting lodge has been transformed into a hotel in the heart of the park. Riding, fishing, hiking.

Parador El Adelantado, PP; *Sierra de Cazorla; tel.* 953 72 70 75.

Tranquillity; views of woods and mountains. The restaurant serves game dishes in season.

JAÉN
Parador Castillo de Santa Catalina, PPP; *tel.* 953 23 00 00.

Modern comfort in a Moorish castle, with beautiful views of Jaén and the surrounding mountains. Acceptable restaurant, regional dishes.

UBEDA
Parador Condestable Dávalos, PP; *Plaza Vázquez de Molina,* 1; *tel.* 953 75 03 45.

A 16thC palace ideally situated near the main monuments.

Enquire about guided tours at the Tourism Office.

(You will find bars serving good *tapas* if you wander along the main street [pedestrians only in the evening] to the Plaza de la Corredera.) Continuing downhill through tortuous streets, you reach a square with the ruins of the **church of Santa María** at one end. Near it is the Cueva de San Pedro, pleasant for snacks and meat grilled on the open fire; in winter they slide a brazier of glowing embers under your table for warmth.

(The **Museum of Popular Art and Customs** [open mornings] is in the Castillo de la Yedra, one of two castles guarding the town.)

CAZORLA Y SEGURA, PARQUE NATURAL DE ✍

This is Spain's largest Nature Park, covering 214,000 hectares of Jaén province. Within it you can see *muflón* (wild sheep), ibex, eagles and fallow and red deer. One of my most vivid memories is hearing stags bellowing their challenges from the depths of the woods on a September evening. A rare violet, the *Viola cazorlensis*, lives in shady crevices and two species of daffodil are also endemic. Spring is the ideal time to visit; avoid Easter Week and July and August.

From Cazorla take the road past La

Iruela's spectacular **castle** and continue over a 1,290-m pass. After passing the Empalme del Valle junction, you cross the Guadalquivir River, turning right up a road through beautiful surroundings (on an unsurfaced track) to reach **La Cañada de las Fuentes**, source of the Guadalquivir.

Return to the Empalme to take the Carretera del Tranco north along the Guadalquivir Valley to the **Centro de Interpretación**, at Torre de Vinagre, where you can learn about the flora and fauna and hiking trails. When General Franco came to hunt, he stayed at the solid stone building next door and the whole valley was sealed off from outsiders.

A particularly attractive walk begins not far from the information centre. Cross the river to reach the *piscifactoria* (trout farm). Near there a track runs up the Borosa Valley. At one point a walkway passes through a narrow gorge over the torrent. To view wildlife the easy way, visit the **Parque Cinegético**, where before 10 am and after 6 pm fodder is provided near a viewing point. (Soon deer, *muflón* and other creatures appear out of the undergrowth.)

JAEN ✍×

Tourism Office, Arquitecto Berges, 1; *tel.* 953 22 27 37. Jaén, 570 m above sea-level, often seems closer in character to Castile than to the rest of Andalucía. The most striking aspect of the modern provincial capital (population 110,000) is the hill-top Arab **Castillo de Santa Catalina**, built by the creator of Granada's Alhambra. Some old streets remain in the upper town, but even the locals say, with a certain complacency, that theirs is a dull city.

The Romans mined silver in the area, while the Moors made it the capital of a small kingdom. An earthquake knocked it about in 1712 and the French sacked it in 1808.

Andrés de Vandelvira planned the Renaissance **cathedral**, not completed until 1802. The twin towers, the carved choir-stalls, the sacristy, and the museum treasures are the most noteworthy features, apart, that is, from the **Relic of the Santo Rostro**, a veil said to have been used by St Veronica to wipe Christ's face. It is on view to the public after Mass on Fridays.

RECOMMENDED RESTAURANTS

BAEZA
Palacio Andrés de Vandelvira, PP-PPP; *San Francisco*, 14; *tel.* 953 74 81 62; *credit cards* DC, MC, V; *closed Sun eve*.

The former San Francisco Convent has been converted into a restaurant with a vast, glassed-in cloister. Dishes combine sophistication with local products.

JAEN
Casa Vicente, PP; *Maestra*, 8; 953 23 28 16; *credit cards* MC, V; *closed Sun in June, July, Aug, Sun eve winter*.

Located in a welcoming old house, this popular restaurant is a good place to try *Cordero mozárabe* (lamb Arab-style).

Step into 400-year-old San Andrés Chapel to see the beautiful **gilded iron screen** created by the Jaén master craftsman Bartolomé in the 16thC. It shields **La Purísima Chapel**, a Plateresque masterpiece.

Near San Andrés is the **Palacio de Villardompardo**, which has Arab baths, rated the most important of those surviving in Spain. Entry is free but you must show some form of identification.

Also of interest is the **Museo Provincial**, Paseo Estación, with Iberian, Greek and Roman relics.

(You will find *tapa* bars in the narrow streets near the cathedral and along the pedestrian street of Calle Nueva.)

LINARES

Guitar maestro Segovia was born here. Manolete was gored to death here. World chess championships are held here. But it is an ugly town with dying industries.

UBEDA 🛏

Tourism Office, Plaza de los Caidos; tel. 953 75 08 97. Ubeda is a hymn to Renaissance architecture. It is also an interesting place to browse for pottery and *esparto* ware. The town, on a hill above endless olive groves, was once an important stopover for travellers. In Spanish the expression 'irse por los cerros de Ubeda' (to go via the Ubeda hills) means to stray from the point.

Modern construction on the outskirts and the dark narrow streets of the old quarter contrasts strongly with the glorious structures of the 16thC. Head for the Plaza de Vázquez Molina to see the most remarkable collection.

Next to the parador, itself a splendid mansion, is the **church of El Salvador**, created as the family pantheon of Francisco de los Cobos, whose patronage and that of his second cousin Juan Vázquez de la Molina were responsible for Ubeda's flowering. Cobos was the greedy and ambitious secretary to Emperor Charles V and Vázquez was secretary to Philip II.

El Salvador, one of the gems of Spanish Renaissance, was built by Andrés de Vandelvira from the plans of Diego de Siloé. A sculpture by Berruguete crowns the altarpiece and the sacristy has dazzling ornamentation.

Another of Vandelvira's works is the

• *Castle at Segura in the Cazorla y Segura Nature Park.*

beautifully proportioned **Palacio de las Cadenas**, now the Town Hall. Opposite Las Cadenas is the **church of Santa María**, the Gothic cloister of which stands on the site of a mosque's patio. The church has fine ironwork by the *maestro* Bartolomé.

A short distance north, on Plaza Primero de Mayo, stands the **church of San Pablo**, a mixture of Gothic and Isabeline styles. Vandelvira had a hand in its design, but perhaps his most impressive work is the imposing **Santiago Hospital**, with a patio embellished by 20 marble columns from Genoa and a grand staircase with magnificent vaulting. The hospital lies near the entrance to the town from the west.

INDEX